# The Shape of Things

## Still Life in Britain

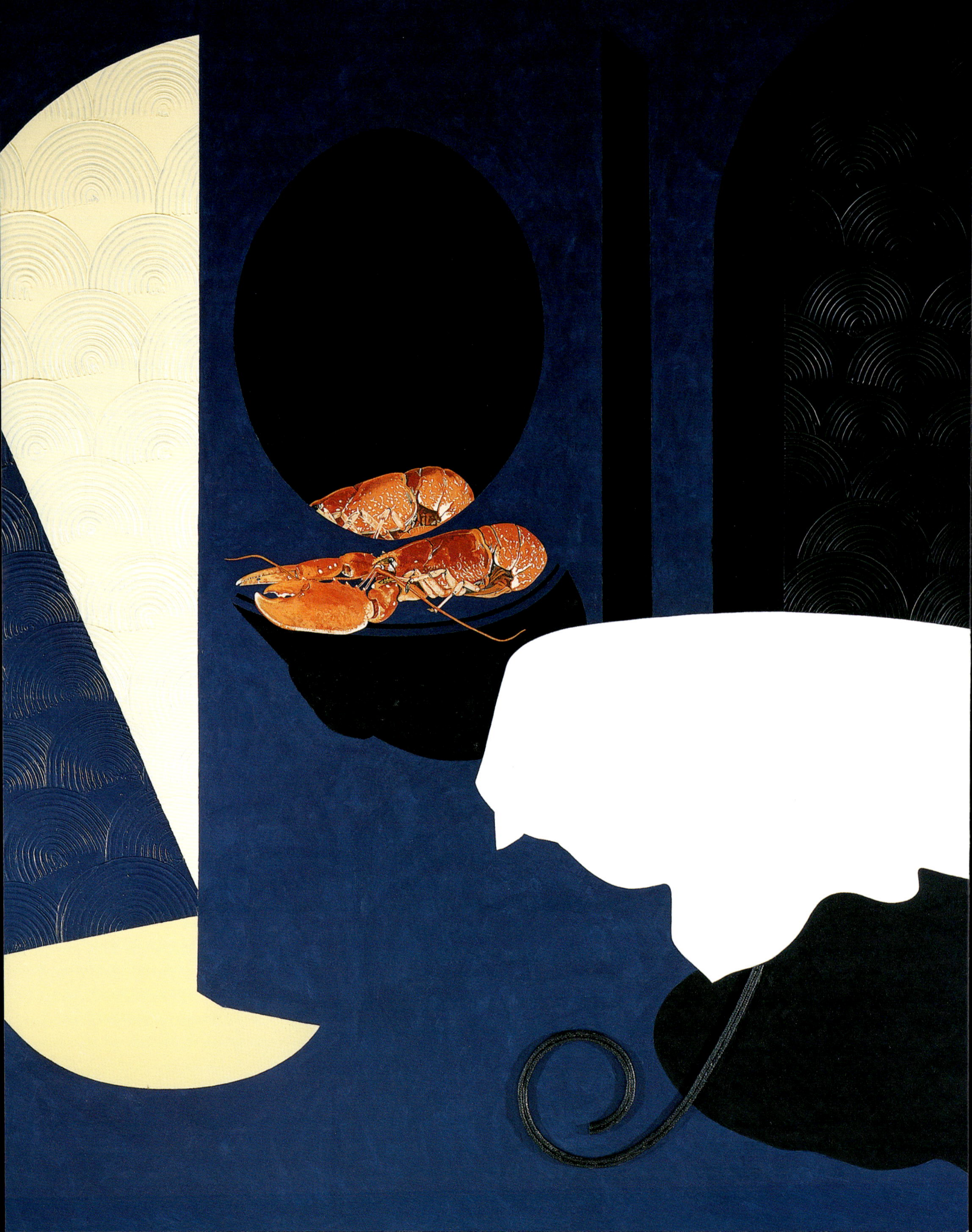

# The Shape of Things

## Still Life in Britain


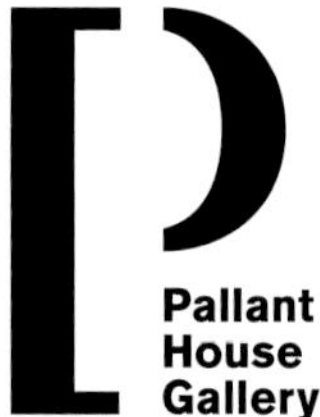


Distributed by
Yale University Press

*The Shape of Things: Still Life in Britain*
Pallant House Gallery, 11 May to 20 October 2024

Pallant House Gallery
8–9 North Pallant
Chichester
West Sussex PO19 1TJ
United Kingdom
+44(0) 1243 774557
www.pallant.org.uk

British cataloguing in Publication Data
A catalogue record for this book is available from the British Library

ISBN: 978-1-869827-68-7
Library of Congress Control Number: 2024935049



Publishing manager: Harriet Olsen
Copy-editor: Susannah Worth
Designer: Adrian Hunt
Set in Meno and Akzidenz Grotesk
Printed in the UK by Gomer Press Ltd

Distributed for Pallant House Gallery by Yale University Press
New Haven and London

Headline Exhibition Sponsor

SOFAS & STUFF

Exhibition Sponsor

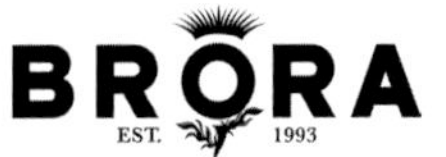


With thanks to

**The Shape of Things Supporters Circle**

Cover (detail of fig. 71):
Edward Wadsworth (1889–1949)
*Bright Intervals*, 1928

p. 2 (detail of fig. 17)
Patrick Caulfield (1936–2005)
*Reserved Table*, 2000

pp. 174–5 (detail of fig. 124):
Peter Blake (b.1932)
*Love*, 2007

# Contents

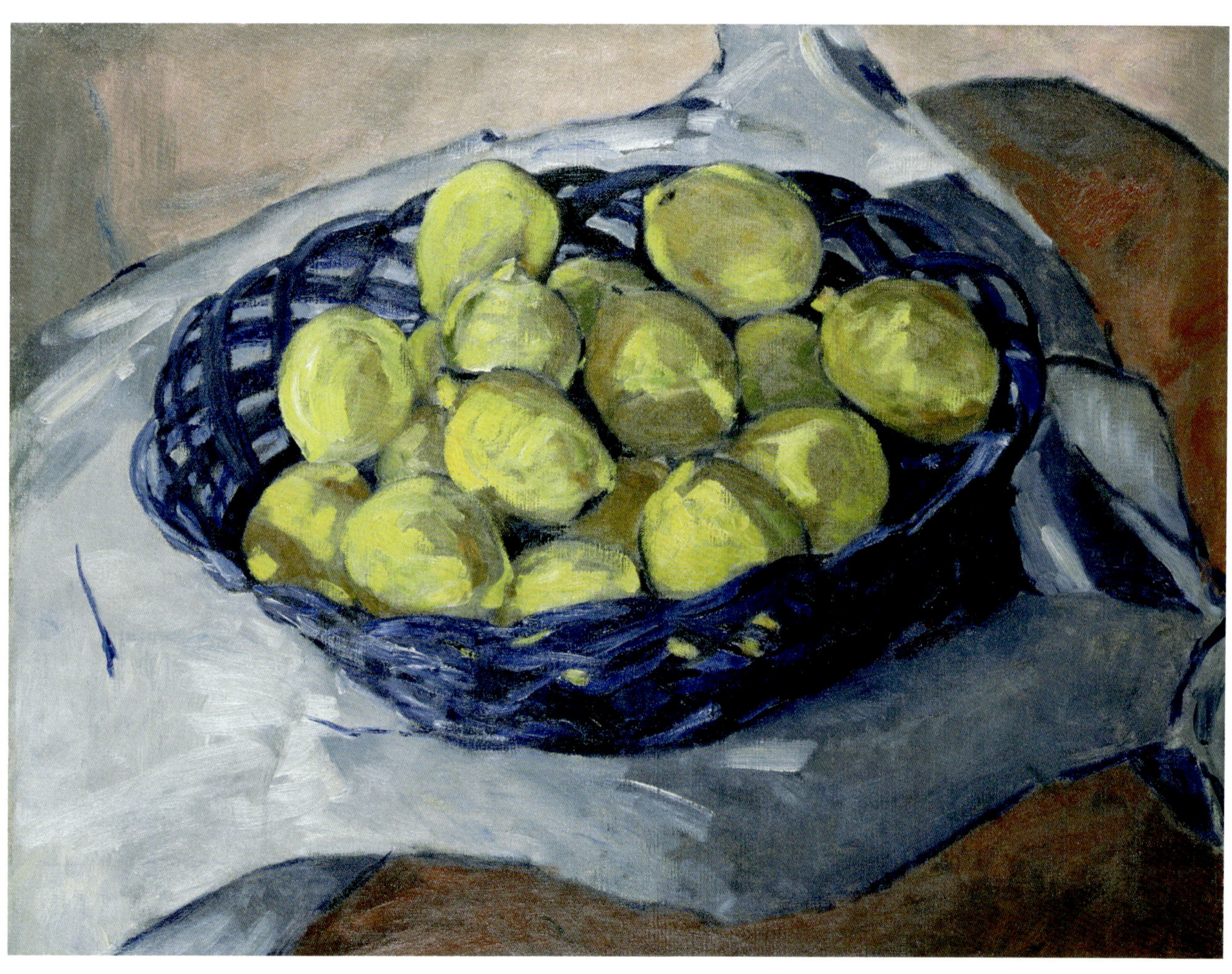

Fig. 1
Christopher Wood (1901–1930)
*Lemons in a Blue Basket*, 1922
Oil on canvas, 44 x 62 cm
Pallant House Gallery, Chichester (Hussey Bequest, Chichester District Council 1985)

# Foreword

SIMON MARTIN

In May 1922, in a letter to his mother from Sicily, the painter Christopher Wood described his rendition of some lemons:

> The tablecloth is all ruffled, wrinkled, and troubled with dark shadows and ups and downs which to me suggest the world that these lemons live in, everything that is going on around them. I expect that you think all this is madness, but I have thought a good deal about still life and I think it is a means of expressing one's thoughts in a delicate manner which everyone else can't quite understand.[1]

*Lemons in a Blue Basket* (fig. 1) is one of numerous still-life paintings in Pallant House Gallery's notable collection of Modern British art. As Wood's words suggest, his painting of lemons not only reveals the beauty that can be discovered in an ordinary and inanimate subject, if only we took the time to appreciate it, but also how it can be expressive of deeper concerns and thoughts. Still life has historically been viewed as a 'minor genre' but in the modern era it has provided a framework in which artists have explored formal, conceptual and emotive concerns.

Rather than through depictions of great battles, classical gods and goddesses, religious miracles, voluptuous nudes or grand portraits, it is often through inanimate quotidian objects that artists most powerfully and succinctly conveyed metaphors for the great human themes that affect us all: life and death, love and loss, stillness and contemplation. The metaphysical qualities of symbolic objects in historic still life have, over time, given way to an appreciation of the extraordinary in the ordinary which was harnessed by the Surrealists, and a recognition that simple objects can provide a vehicle for experimentation, even for ostensibly abstract artists, and a means to address wider concerns in art and society.

There is a surprising paucity of books on the subject of still life, with the notable exception of Charles Sterling's 1954 study *Still Life Painting from Antiquity to the Present Time.* On visiting the magisterial exhibition *Les Choses: Une Histoire de La Nature Morte* (Things: A History of Still Life) at the Musée du Louvre in Paris (17 October 2022 – 9 January 2023), a vast survey with over 400 exhibits (many of which were in Sterling's book), which swept visitors through the history of art from Roman mosaics to Dutch and Flemish 17th-century flower paintings, the French Impressionists and onward to contemporary art, I was struck that only five of the artists were British, and two of those were a partnership. Perhaps there were no notable examples, or still life has just not been part of our tradition? But the more I thought about the genre in relation to British art, the more examples I discovered; after all there is no shortage of the genre in either public or private collections in the UK. It turns out that a great many Modern British and contemporary artists have created still lifes. Yet, with the notable exception of a 1989 Arts Council Collection touring exhibition of 33 works, entitled *It's a Still Life*, there have been relatively few significant exhibitions dedicated to the subject of the still life in 20th- or 21st- century Britain. *The Shape of Things* is thus an attempt to address that omission, exploring how the genre has been used by modern and contemporary artists in the UK, with a historical prelude to set the *mise en scène* featuring examples of symbolic 17th- and 18th- century flower and *vanitas* paintings that have become such a point of reference for more recent artists.

Whilst in its origins, still life was not a native British tradition, but a foreign import from the continent, it is a tradition that has been adopted and embraced by artists working in this country. As an artform, still life, its subjects and its artists, encapsulate the flow of ideas, individuals and objects across national boundaries through trade and migration. It can be seen as a manifestation of Britain's status as a former maritime power, and the long legacy of empire. From Simon Verelst and Edwaert (later anglicised Edward) Collier, who arrived from the Netherlands in the late 17th century, to Mary Moser, the child of Swiss immigrants in the 18th century and Walter Sickert, the German-born son of a Danish father and English mother in the 19th century who moved between France and Britain in the early 20th century, many pre-eminent artists associated with the genre were immigrants or the children of immigrants. The list grows even longer in the 20th and 21st centuries: Lucian Freud (born in Germany), Anwar Jalal Shemza (born in Shimla to Kashmiri parents, before moving to Pakistan and Britain), Jann Haworth (born in the USA), Lee Miller (born in the USA) and Eduardo Paolozzi (born in Scotland to Italian parents).

Fig. 2
Duncan Grant (1885–1978)
*Still Life with Black Coffee Pot*, 1949
Oil on canvas, 58 x 38 cm
Pallant House Gallery, Chichester (Acquired with support from Art Fund, Arts Council England / V&A Purchase Grant Fund, Cate and Nash Olson, and legacies from Margaret Treacher Brown and Lady Heath, 2024)

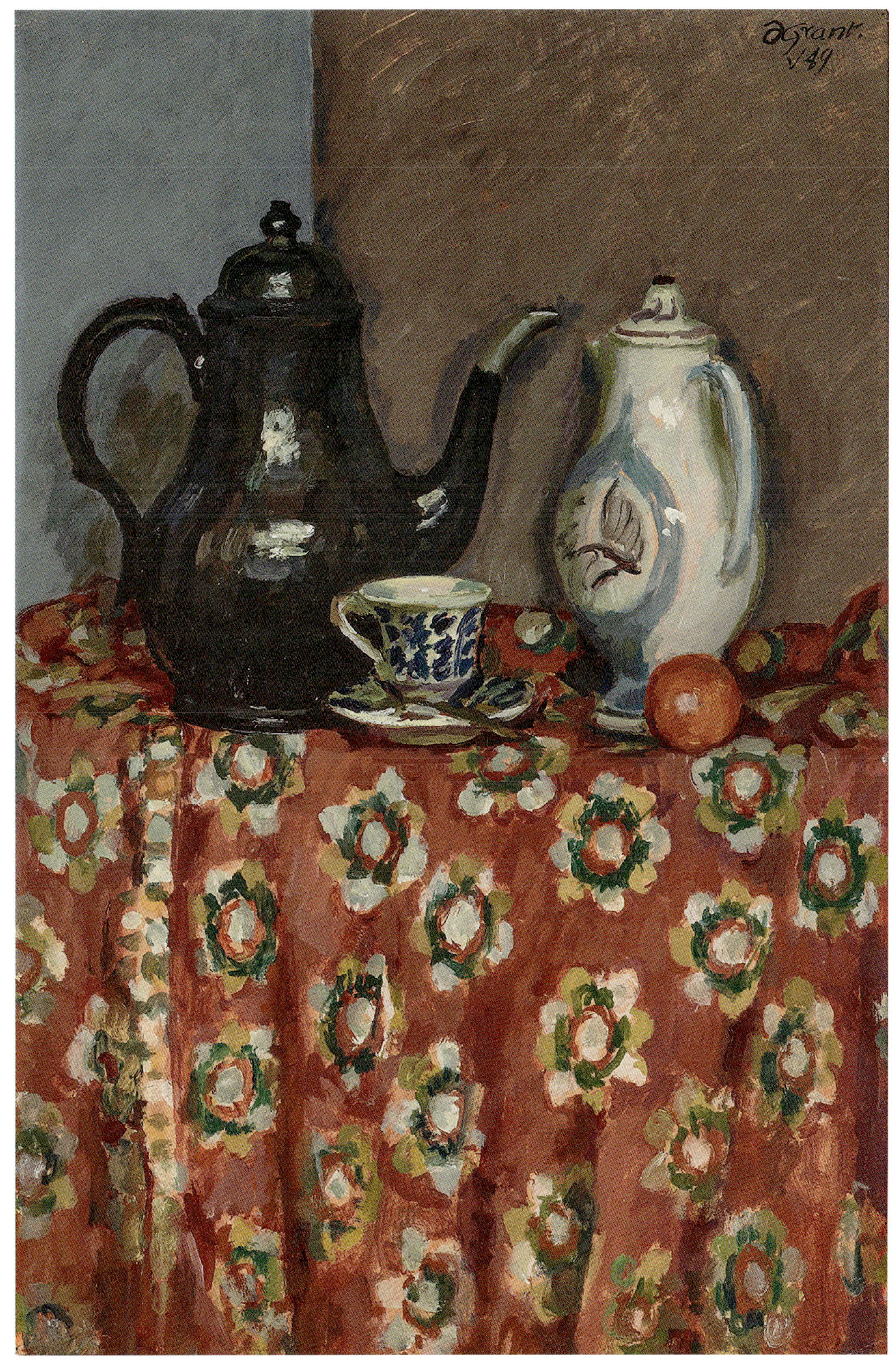

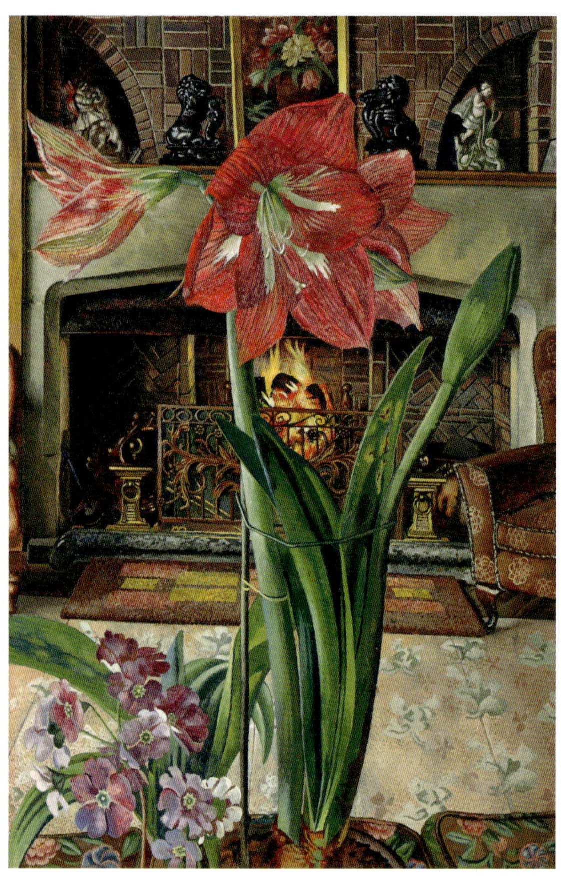

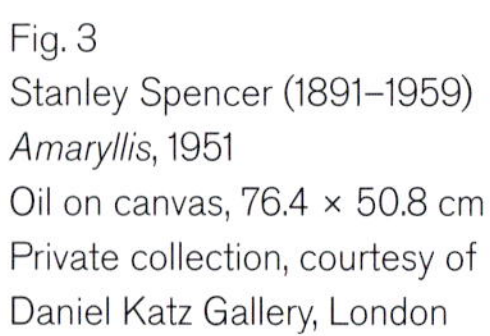

Fig. 3
Stanley Spencer (1891–1959)
*Amaryllis*, 1951
Oil on canvas, 76.4 × 50.8 cm
Private collection, courtesy of
Daniel Katz Gallery, London

Fig. 4
Mary Fedden (1915–2012)
*Still Life with Artichoke*, 1972
Oil on canvas, 66.4 × 76.5 cm
Pallant House Gallery, Chichester
(Percy Brown Bequest, 1996)

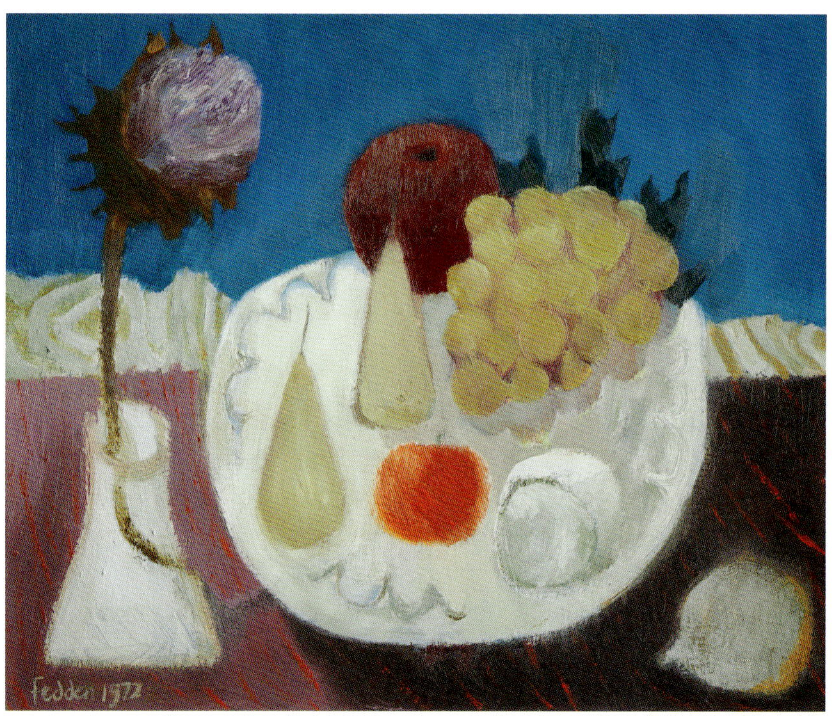

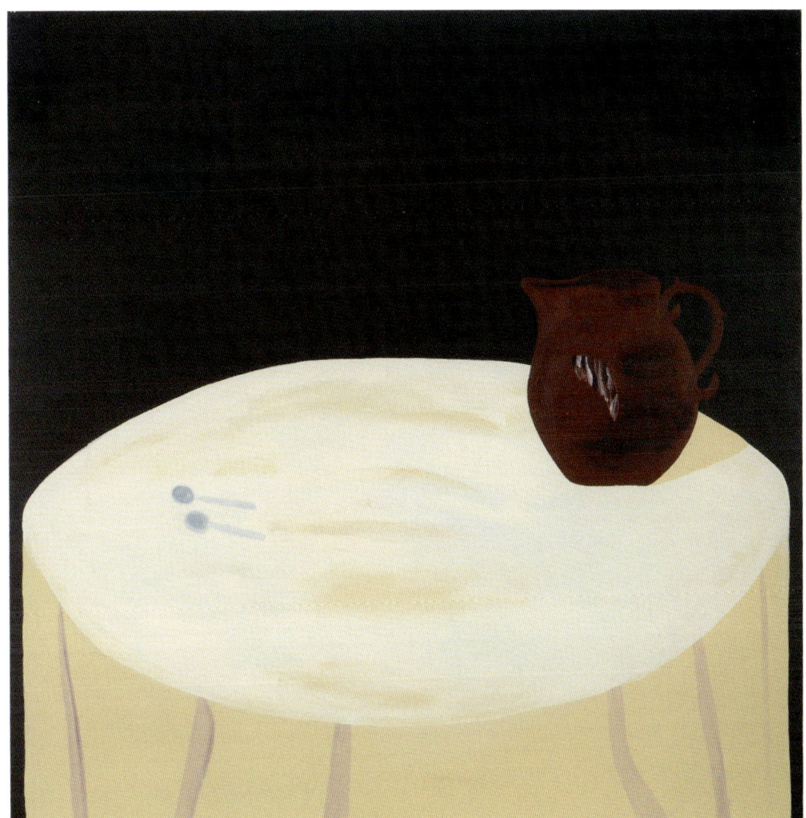

Fig. 5
Lubaina Himid (b.1954)
*Jug and Two Spoons*, 1989
Acrylic on canvas, 182.8 × 182.8 cm
Courtesy of the Artist and Hollybush

The more recent generations of artists in the exhibition include Hurvin Anderson (born in Britain to Jamaican parents), Gordon Cheung (born in Britain to Chinese parents), Ori Gerscht (born in Israel), Mona Hatoum (born in Beirut to Palestinian parents), Lubaina Himid (born in Zanzibar), Lisa Milroy (born in Canada), Jorge Orta (born in Argentina), Mohammed Sami (born in Iraq), Mike Silva (born in Sweden to a Sinhalese father and English mother), Wolfgang Tillmans (born in Germany), Bouke de Vries (born in the Netherlands) and Edmund de Waal, whose complex family history is the subject of a novel. The focus on things, as opposed to landscape, for example, is perhaps understandable.

One of the strongest themes in the exhibition is how modern and contemporary artists have reinterpreted the history of art. It is process of endless renewal: looking back in order to look forward; using devices from the past to comment on the present. The present exhibition features a new painting by Clare Woods entitled *Motionless* (fig. 10) which is based on a mid-19th-century Staffordshire mochaware jug with banded decoration. It had been owned by both William Nicholson and his son Ben Nicholson, who painted both realist and abstract renditions of it, which were featured alongside the jug itself in the Pallant House Gallery exhibition and accompanying book *Ben Nicholson: From the Studio* in 2022. It is heartening

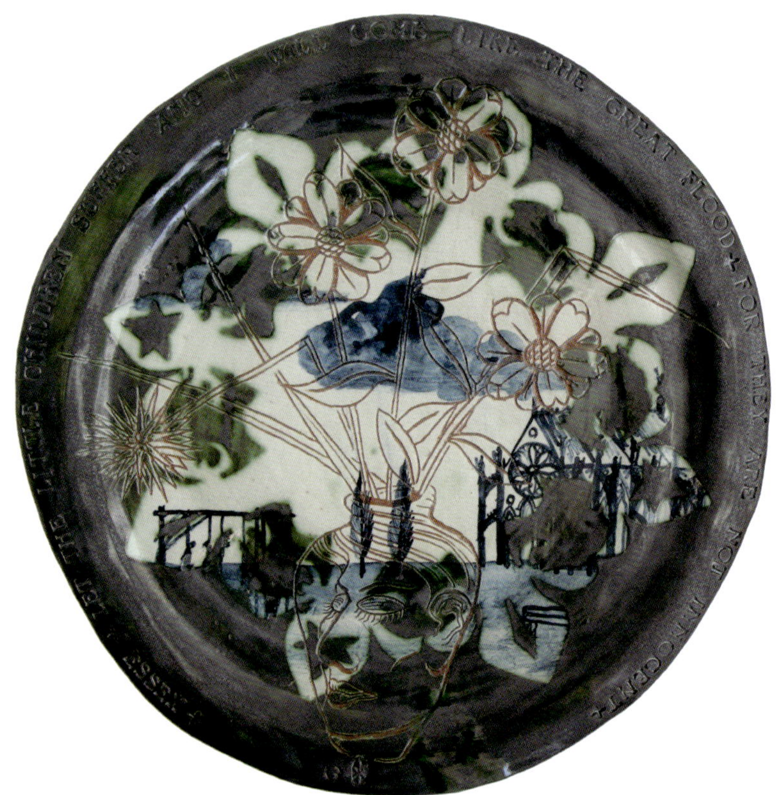

Fig. 6
Grayson Perry (b.1960)
*Let the little children suffer*, c.1986
Ceramic plate, 29.2 cm diameter
Private collection, courtesy
England & Co

to see our exhibition programme so directly inspiring artists in this way, and one hopes that this exhibition might have a similar effect. Still life is currently having what might be described as a 'moment' – with numerous contemporary artists producing bodies of work that engage with the genre as a way of addressing contemporary concerns. In 2023, Woods selected and hung a room of hundreds of still lifes in the Royal Academy Summer Exhibition and in spring 2024, she has a solo exhibition of new still-life collages entitled *Soft Knock* at the Cristea Roberts Gallery, London whilst Poppy Jones's exhibition *Solid Objects* at Herald St, London, and Mat Collishaw's exhibition *Petrichor* at the Royal Botanic Gardens Kew feature innovative riffs on early flower paintings.

Although I conceived the broad structure of an exhibition that tells a history of modern and contemporary British art through still life, with a historical and contemporary prelude, followed by a chrono-thematic series of sections exploring different moments and tendencies, much of the credit for its realisation must go to our Chief Curator Melanie Vandenbrouck and our Assistant Curators Lydia Miller and Miriam O'Connor Perks. They took my structure and first ideas and improved them, researching and finding examples that, although not always the same, were often more intriguing. Melanie arrived at the Gallery in August 2023 and with the support of Lydia and Miriam set about realising the lists of suggested

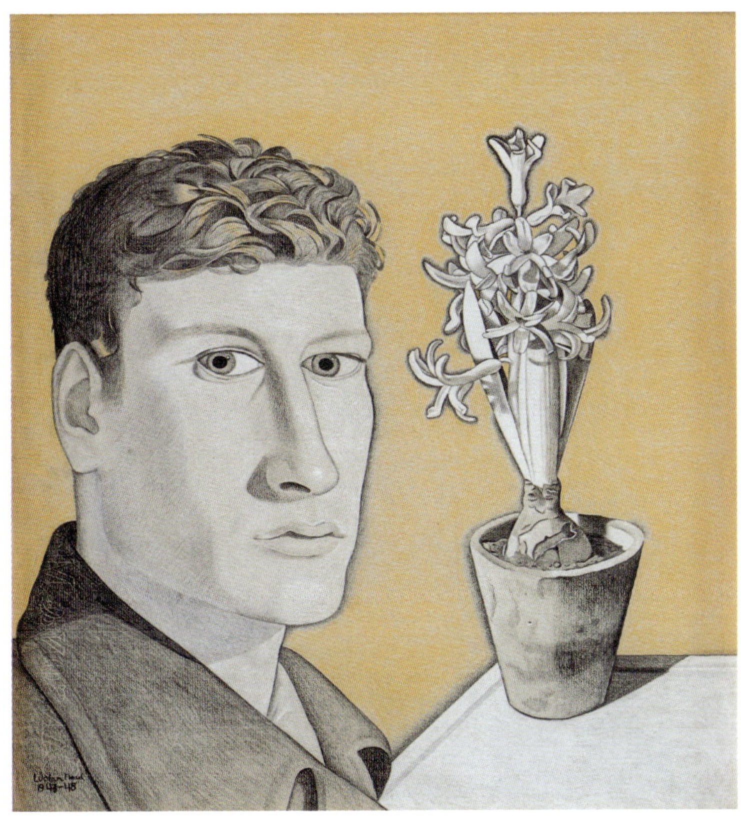

Fig. 7
Lucian Freud (1922–2011)
*Self-portrait with Hyacinth in Pot*, 1947–48
Black, white and yellow crayon on paper
Pallant House Gallery, Chichester (Wilson Gift through Art Fund, 2006)

works and artists that I had given them, with tremendous dedication and rigour, supported by our Registrar Eleanor Chant, our Head of Collections Sarah Norris and Art Technician Nick Benham.

There have been many discussions about what is, and what is not, a still life. Inevitably the boundaries are often blurred. As Ben Nicholson was to observe in 1957: 'My "still life" paintings are closely identified with landscape, more closely than are my landscapes which perhaps relate more to "still life".'[2] One of the most significant works in the Gallery's collection is Lucian Freud's iconic *Self-Portrait with Hyacinth in Pot* (fig. 7), in which portraiture and still life are held in an uneasy balance, but ultimately limited space has meant this work was not included in the exhibition. Almost every artist will have, at some point, created a still life. When we held the exhibition *Sussex Landscape: Chalk, Wood and Water* (12 November – 23 April 2023), I received numerous letters and emails from friends and relations of artists asking why their loved one had not been included as they too had lived and worked in the county. In a similar way, everyone will have their own version of an exhibition about still life in Britain. This exhibition makes no claim to be comprehensive; no exhibition can. But it should, hopefully, set out a broad framework for understanding the importance of still life to art in Britain.

There are over 100 artists in this exhibition, working in a variety of media: painting, drawing, sculpture, textiles, photography, printmaking, ceramics and installation. We are hugely grateful to all the living artists in the exhibition, 40 in all, and their galleries, and to the estates of those no longer alive, for their enthusiastic support for the exhibition and for providing copyright consent for press, education and this book. In addition to several recently created works in the exhibition, such as Wolfgang Tillmans's 2020 photograph *Hampstead still life* (fig.136) that captures the atmosphere of the Covid-19 pandemic, Mike Silva's luminous painting *Window Light* (fig.137), Poppy Jones's *Water Glass & Thistle* (fig.148) and Toby Ziegler's *Purple Prose* (fig. 24), several new works have been created especially, each markedly different in character and intent. Caroline Walker has painted the autobiographical *My Bottles and Pumps* (fig.135) featuring her baby-feeding apparatus in a drying rack; Glenn Brown has painted

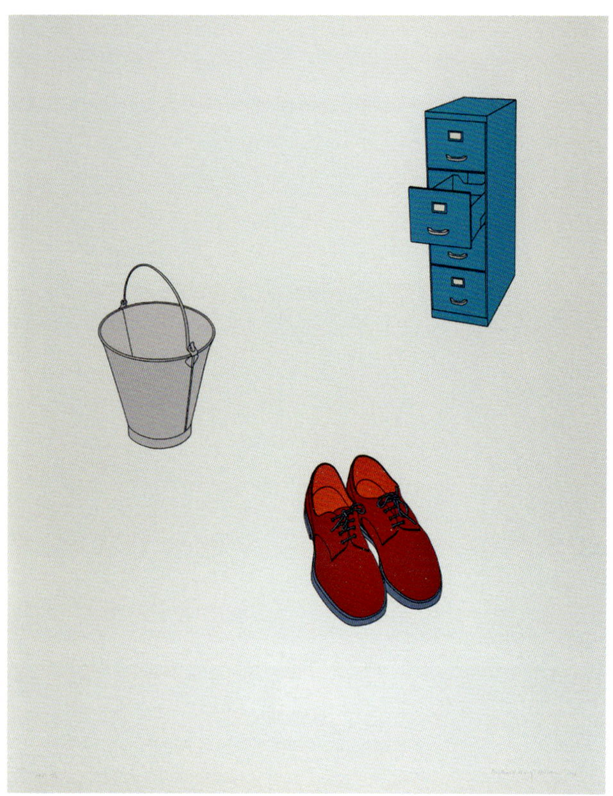

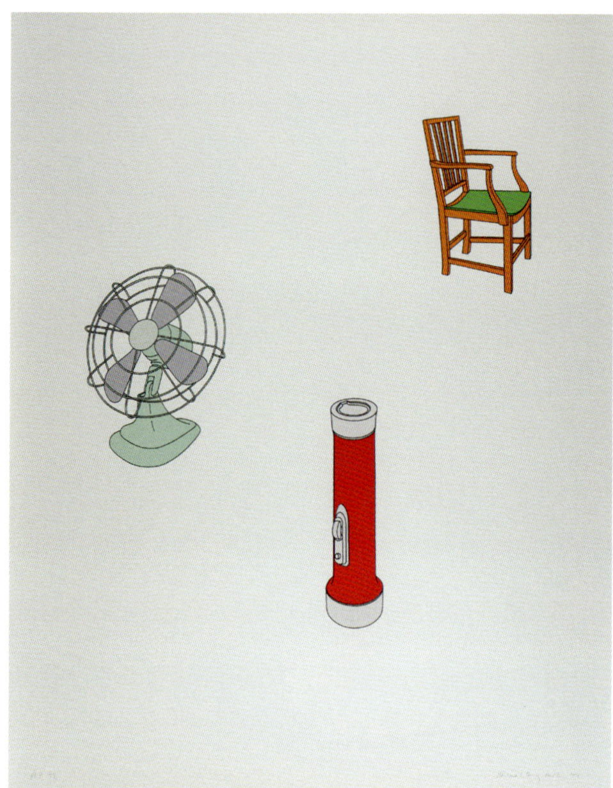

Fig. 8
Michael Craig-Martin (b.1941)
*Distant Relations*, 1996
Screenprint on paper, 96.5 × 76.3 cm
Pallant House Gallery, Chichester
(Presented by Cristea Roberts Gallery 2021)

Fig. 9
Michael Craig-Martin (b.1941)
*Close Relations*, 1996
Screenprint on paper, 96.5 × 76.3 cm
Pallant House Gallery, Chichester
(Presented by Cristea Roberts Gallery, 2021)

*Saint Bimbo* (fig.25), a reimagining of a Baroque turnip; and Lindsey Mendick has created two monumental ceramic vessels crawling with skulls, crustaceans and other motifs from still life (fig.29). To accompany the exhibition, Phoebe Cummings is creating a site-specific installation of clay plant-forms in the Gallery's Queen Anne townhouse. In advance of the exhibition, we have been able to acquire the Duncan Grant *Still Life with Black Coffee Pot* (fig.2) with support from Art Fund, the Arts Council England V&A Purchase Grant Fund, Cate and Nash Olson and bequests from Margaret Brown and Lady Heath, and we hope it may be possible to acquire other works to create a permanent legacy for the exhibition.

Alongside the exhibition, we are presenting *Significant Objects: The Things that Matter,* a display featuring artworks made by members of Pallant House Gallery's Community Programme, which provides adults with a range of support needs with meaningful, long-term opportunities to be creative. There will also be creative programmes for schools, families and adults inspired by the exhibition.

In addition to the artists, an exhibition of this scope and ambition is dependent on a huge number of individuals – mentioned individually in the Acknowledgements unless they chose to remain anonymous. We thank all the museums and public collections and their staff who have facilitated loans, the private collectors, and the auction houses and commercial

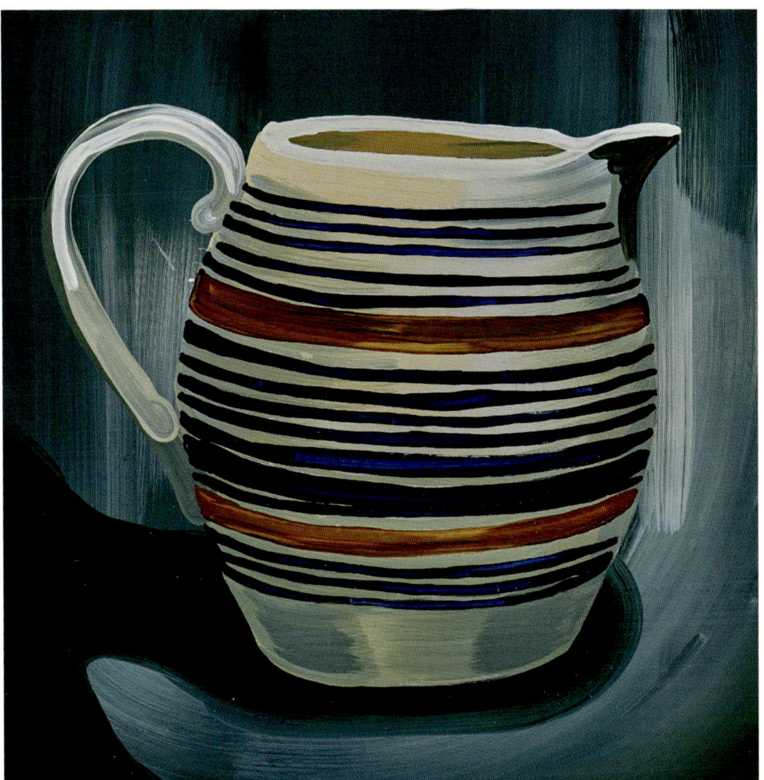

Fig. 10
Clare Woods (b.1972)
*Motionless*, 2022
Oil on aluminium, 50 × 50 cm
Courtesy the artist and Cristea Roberts Gallery, London

galleries who have assisted in locating works. We are also grateful to the Arts Council England Government Indemnity Scheme, which enables us to borrow such valuable works.

This exhibition could not have been realised without the generous support of the Headline Sponsor *Sofas and Stuff*, a British company with its head office in West Sussex that produces bespoke handmade sofas; the Sponsor *Brora*, a brand known for its clothing and luxury Scottish cashmere; the Official Paint Sponsor *Little Greene*; and Sparkling Wine Sponsor *Wiston Estate*, which is also based in West Sussex. We are grateful to each of these and to the members of *The Shape of Things Supporters Circle* (who are individually listed in the Acknowledgements), to Chichester District Council, and the Friends, Patrons, Supporters of Pallant House Gallery.

I am grateful to my fellow authors for their contributions to this book: Michael Bird, Phoebe Cummings, Lydia Miller, Chloe Nahum, Miriam O'Connor Perks, Emma Sharples and Melanie Vandenbrouck; and the designer Adrian Hunt, copy-editor Susannah Worth, Indexer Rob Gibson, our Head of Publishing Harriet Olsen and Mark Eastment and his colleagues at Yale University Press. Finally, I extend my sincere gratitude to all my colleagues at Pallant House Gallery who go the extra mile to realise ambitious exhibitions of a consistently high quality, and to our dedicated Trustees and Volunteers.

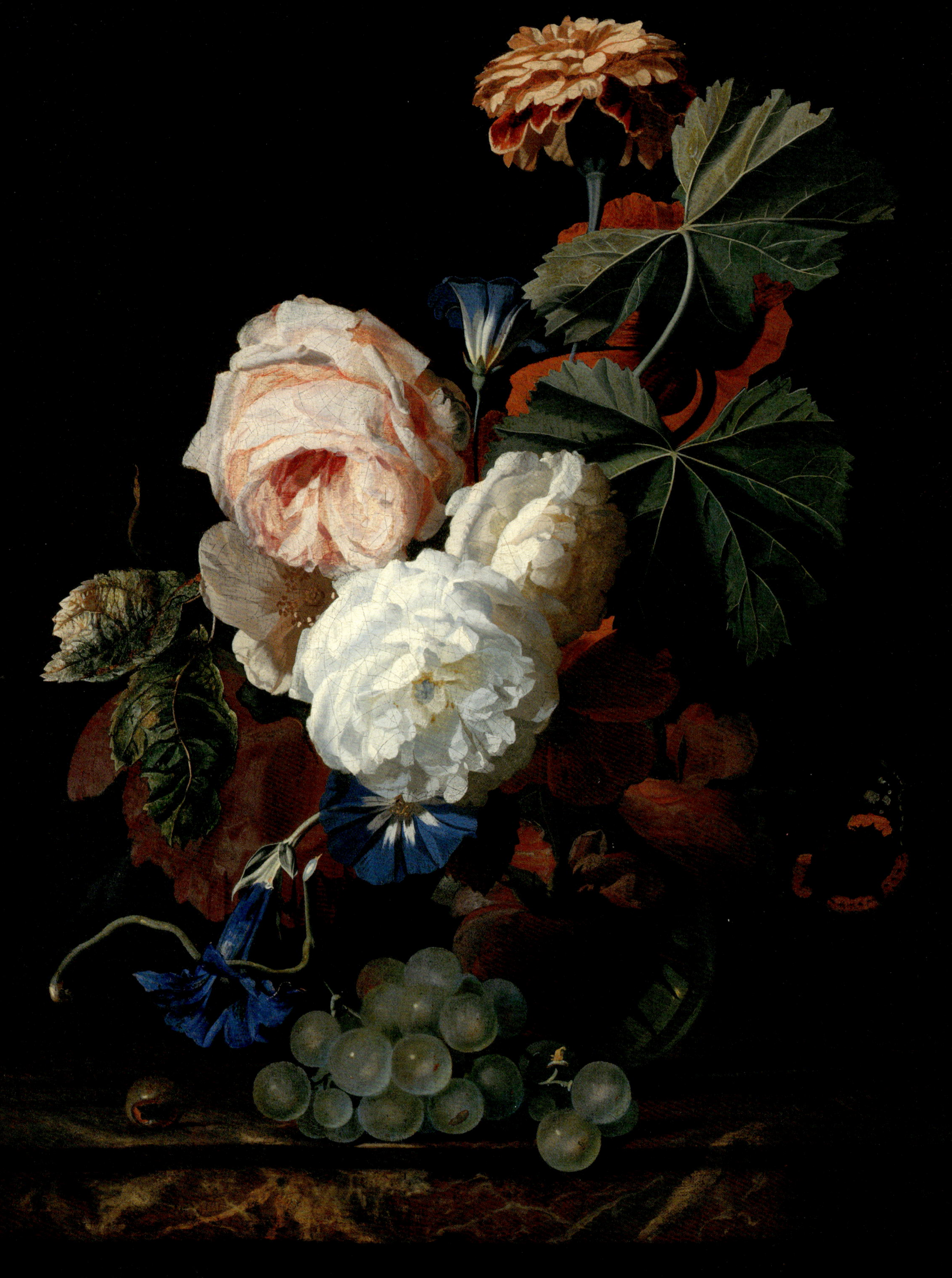

# 1 History Repeating: Still Life Between Past and Present

SIMON MARTIN

In 1669, the English diarist Samuel Pepys visited the still-life painter Simon Pietersz Verelst (1644–c.1721) at his studio near St James's Market, London:

> A Dutchman newly come over, one Everelst [sic] ... did show us a little flower-pott of his doing, the finest thing that ever I think I saw in my life – the drops of Dew hanging on the leaves, so as I was forced again and again to put my finger to it to feel whether my eyes were deceived or no. He doth ask £70 for it; I had the vanity to bid him £20 – but a better picture I never saw in my whole life, and it is worth going twenty miles to see.[1]

At this time, Pepys was Chief Secretary to the Admiralty. Verelst had arrived in England in the aftermath of the Second Anglo-Dutch War, which was concluded by the signing of the Treaty of Breda between the two warring nations, and a Triple Alliance between the Dutch Republic, England and Sweden in 1668. Somehow, despite first appearances, still life has never been divorced from trade, politics, religion and metaphysical concerns. Verelst was one of the first artists to introduce the continental genre of still life to the British Isles; prior to his arrival there was no native tradition to speak of. Although its roots can be traced as far back as ancient Greece and Rome, with Pliny's account in his *Natural History* of Zeuxis (5th century BCE) painting grapes 'so true to nature' that birds came to peck at them,[2] and it featured as incidental and decorative elements within Renaissance altarpieces serving to ground the image and assure viewers of the veracity of the miracles depicted, it was really in the Netherlands and Flanders in the early 17th century that still life emerged as an independent

Fig. 11
Simon Verelst (1644–1721)
*Roses, morning glory and a carnation on a marble ledge with some grapes*, n.d
Oil on canvas, 45.7 × 35.6 cm
Private collection

form of art admired by an affluent and cultivated audience. Prior to 1650 there was no term to describe the genre: artists would refer to 'flower, fruit and fish pieces' or 'bouquets and breakfast pieces'. The art historian Charles Stirling explained the semantics of this:

> In the Dutch jargon of the 17th century, *leven* (life or nature) simply meant 'model' or 'living model'; *still*, of course, meant 'motionless'. *Still-leven*, then in contradistinction to the painting of figures or animals, was the painting of things incapable of moving.[3]

Simon Pietersz Verelst was born in The Hague, the son of the Dutch Golden Age painter Pieter Harmensz Verelst (c.1618–c.1678). In his paintings he adopted a distinctive format of colourful, floral arrangements painted against a dark background, rendered with extraordinary finish and exactness.[4] His highly refined 'bouquets' were typical of Dutch still life in that they were decorative and a display of virtuosity, yet they were also laden with symbolic meaning, often related to Christian belief in the promise of an afterlife. While *Roses, morning glory and a carnation on a marble ledge with some grapes* (fig. 11) can be understood as conveying the bounty of God's creation, it also functions as a meditation on the transience of life. Beauty is fragile; it fades and decays. The rose petals are on the cusp of wilting, their leaves already blighted by the sun. A grape has fallen, or been plucked, from the bunch, bruised and already starting to decay. But beyond the general moral message, each element carries further meaning. Roses were symbolic of love and of the Virgin Mary. The blue and white morning glory (*Ipomoea aquatica*) could be considered to signify humility before God, while carnations represented resurrection and eternal life, just as the red admiral butterfly (*Vanessa atalanta*) fluttering alongside was also a metaphor for life, death and resurrection.[5]

With such paintings, Verelst was to become the most acclaimed flower painter in England. So fashionable was he that at least six of his paintings entered the Royal Collection. The painter Gérard de Lairesse (1640–1711) wrote in 1707:

> The writer holds up Verelst as the most celebrated flower painter there ever was. Verelst topped everything in astonishment for those who knew him at his peak. Indeed, if there was an illustrious flower painter, it was he.[6]

However, according to George Vertue, an 18th-century writer on English artists, such was his success that Verelst 'grew very proud and conceited' and he took to calling himself 'God of Flowers' and 'King of Painting' before experiencing a mental breakdown, which resulted in his incarceration in an asylum.[7]

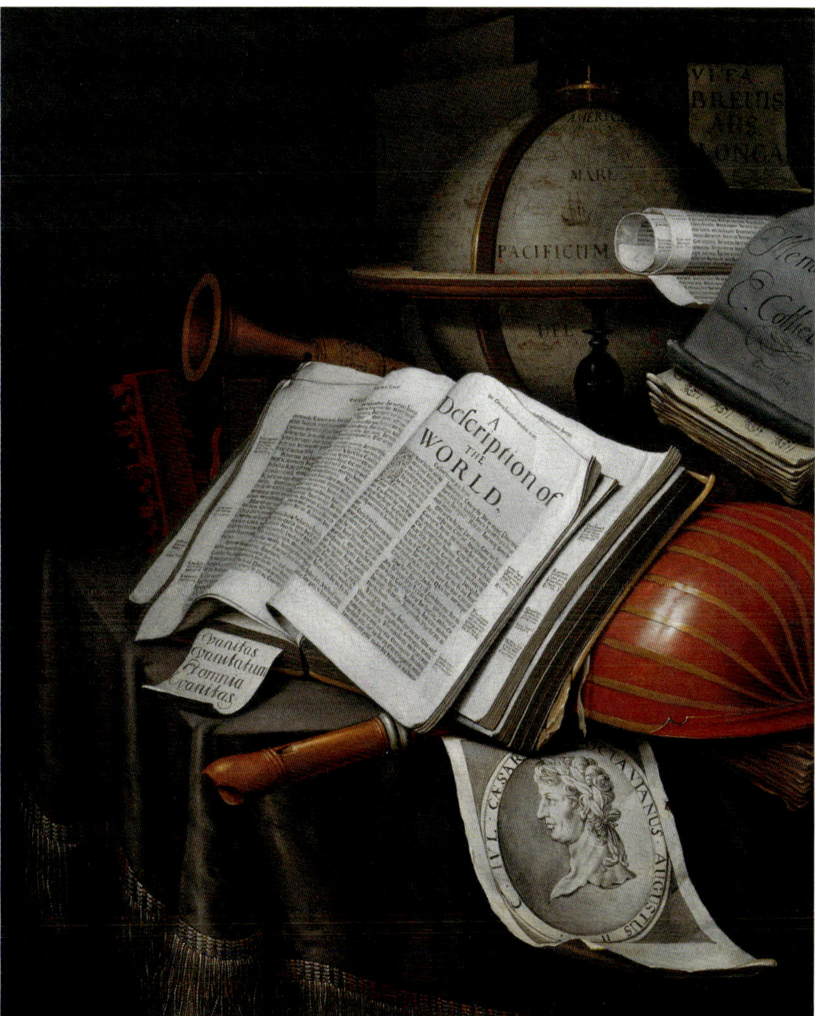


Fig. 12
Edwaert Collier (c.1640–c.1707)
*Vanitas Still Life*, 1694
Oil on canvas, 75.3 × 62.9 cm
National Maritime Museum, Greenwich, London; purchased with the assistance of the Society for Nautical Research Macpherson Fund

Twenty-five years after Verelst had first arrived in England, he was followed in 1693 by another Dutch still-life artist, Edward Collier (1642–1708, also known as Edwaert or Evert Colyer).[8] It is perhaps worth noting that following the Glorious Revolution in 1688 which led to the overthrow of King James II, England was jointly ruled by the Dutch-born King William III (Prince of Orange in the Netherlands, and the grandson of King Charles II) and his English wife and first-cousin Queen Mary, which further deepened Anglo-Dutch sensibilities and the taste for all things Dutch. Collier had trained in Harlem, later working in Leiden and Amsterdam before his move to England. He became known for his *trompe l'œil* as well as *vanitas* pictures, a form of emblematic still life that represented worldly goods alongside symbols of mortality. These pictures take their name from the second verse of the book of Ecclesiastes in the Old Testament of the Bible: '*Vanitas vanitatum, dixit Ecclesiastes; Vanitas vanitatum, et omnia vanitas*' (translated in the King James Bible as: 'Vanity of vanities says the Preacher; Vanity of vanities, all is vanity').

Collier even incorporated the Latin words '*Vanitas Vanitatum Omnia Vanitas*' as an inscription in the foreground of his *Vanitas Still Life* (fig. 12), which is believed to have been painted the year after his arrival in England. The painting includes visual suggestions of the fleeting nature of time to remind the viewer of their mortality and the futility of worldly possessions and earthly pleasures and pursuits, which do not preclude us from the inevitability of death. To emphasise this point, Collier inscribed in the top right-hand corner '*Vita Brevis Ars Longa*' (which translates as 'life is short, art is long'). Books, a globe and musical instruments are instantly recognisable symbols for learning, science, history, literature and artistry, but also serve to remind the viewer that knowledge and intellect are impermanent. The musical instruments – a recorder, lute and what appears to be a shawm (a precursor to the oboe) – illustrate the idea of music as a transient art form, associated with earthly pleasure: the lute was understood to represent marital love or erotic lust, while the recorder had phallic connotations. On the globe can be seen the words 'AMERICA', 'MARE' and 'PACIFICUM' – a reminder that while globes could function as shorthand for science, geography and scholarship, they were also emblems of power and empire, and a reminder to us today that the maritime nations of England and the Netherlands derived wealth from trade and slavery. The engraved portrait of Caesar Augustus further invites comparison between the Roman Empire and England and the Netherlands. However, ultimately, a *vanitas* painting served to assert that all earthly power is doomed to disappear, just like the Roman Empire (and, indeed, latterly the Dutch and British Empires).

Fig. 13
George Smith (c.1714–1776)
*Still Life with Joint of Beef on a Pewter Dish*, c.1750–60
Oil on canvas, 61 × 73.7 cm
Chichester City Council

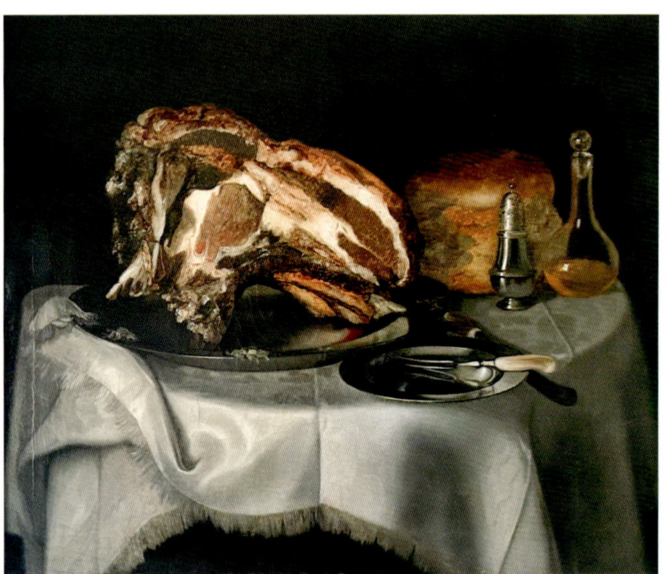

Conscious of the market for Dutch art, in the mid-18th century the three 'Smith Brothers of Chichester' began to paint still lifes and, as such, they were perhaps the first native-born English artists to specialise in the genre. The sons of a Chichester cooper (a barrel-maker), their careers were largely made in London. Under the patronage of the Duke of Richmond, the eldest son William (1707–1764) had been placed to train with a portrait painter in St Martin's Lane in London.[9] His brother George (1714–1776) joined him to train in the capital but would regularly return to Chichester to paint with their younger brother John (c.1717–1764). Just as they painted landscapes of the South Downs as if seen through the eyes of Claude Lorrain (1600–1682), their still life style is based upon continental

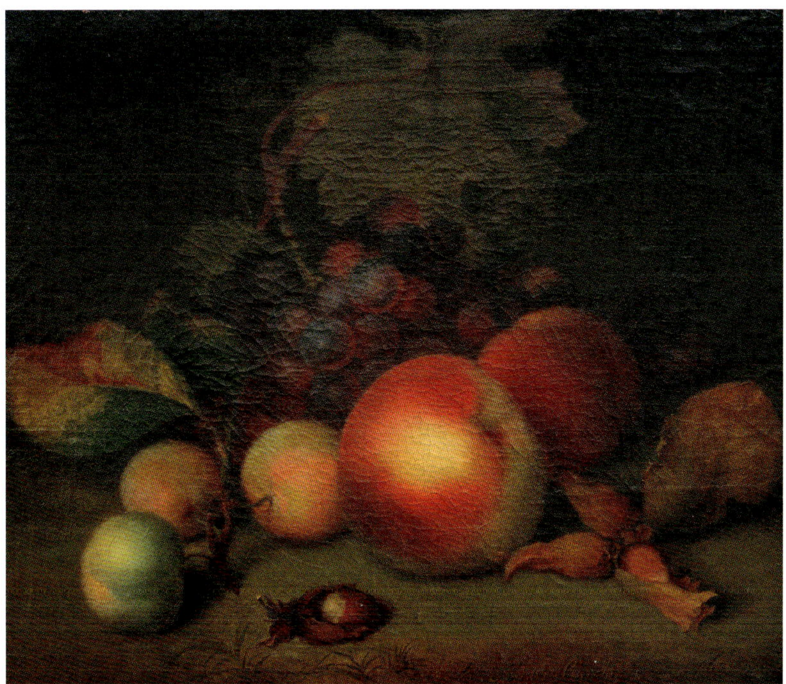

Fig. 14
William Smith (1707–1764)
*Still Life with Grapes, Peaches and Plums*, 1763
Oil on canvas, 30.2 x 36 cm
Pallant House Gallery, Chichester
(Bequest of Mrs Pat Roth, 2016)

prototypes. While William Smith (1707–1764) painted modest groups of seasonal fruits such as *Still Life of Peaches, Plums and Cobnuts* (1757, private collection) and *Still Life with Grapes, Peaches and Plums* (fig. 14), his brother George produced more emphatic still-life compositions based on simple country meals with pewter, glassware and linen cloths that enabled a bravura rendition of different surface qualities in paint, such as *Still Life with Joint of Beef on a Pewter Dish* (fig. 13). The format of foodstuffs presented on a white tablecloth before an impenetrable black background follows the celebrated *'ontbijt'* (or 'breakfast pieces') of Dutch artists such as Pieter Claesz (c.1597–1660) and William Claesz Heda (1593/94–1680/82). George Smith's (c.1714–1776) presentation is rooted in everyday reality and far less sumptuous than the images of his Dutch predecessors.[10] Contemporary viewers would have recognised the dish as solidly English fare and no doubt associated it with the patriotic ballad 'The Roast Beef of Old England' which was written in 1731 by Henry Fielding for his play *The Grub-Street Opera*, and which increased in popularity in the 1740s when given a new setting by Richard Leveridge, after which it became customary for theatre audiences to sing it before and after a new play.

> When mighty Roast Beef was the Englishman's food,
> It ennobled our veins and enriched our blood.
> Our soldiers were brave and our courtiers were good
> Oh! the Roast Beef of old England,
> And old English Roast Beef![11]

During the 17th and 18th centuries, a rigid hierarchy of genres was established by the fine art academies in France and England. At the pinnacle was history painting (including religious, mythological and allegorical subjects), then portraiture, followed by genre scenes of everyday life, landscape painting, animal painting and, finally, in the lowest category, still life. Scale also came into play, with history paintings tending towards grandeur and still life comparatively diminutive in scale. In France, still life became known as '*nature morte*' (literally 'dead nature') from the mid-18th century onwards. The French theorist André Félibien had asserted in 1667:

> He who produces perfect landscapes is above another who only produces fruit, flowers or seashells. He who paints living animals is more estimable than those who only represent dead things without movement, and as man is the most perfect work of God on the earth, it is also certain that he who becomes an imitator of God in representing human figures, is much more excellent than all the others.[12]

The presence of objects of symbolic religious and philosophical significance in paintings thus served to elevate the composition above base nature.[13] In his third 'Discourse on Art', delivered to the students of the Royal Academy of Arts in 1770, its president Sir Joshua Reynolds stated:

> Even the painter of still life, whose highest ambition is to give a minute representation of every part of those low objects, which he sets before him, deserves praise in proportion to his attainment; because no part of this excellent art, so much the ornament of polished life, is destitute of value and use. These, however, are by no means the views to which the mind of the student ought to be PRIMARILY directed. By aiming at better things, if from particular inclination, or from the taste of the time and place he lives in, or from necessity, or from failure in the highest attempts, he is obliged to descend lower; he will bring into the lower sphere of art a grandeur of composition and character that will raise and ennoble his works far above their natural rank.[14]

Women artists were largely unable to paint history paintings because, in the interests of protecting their modesty, they were not allowed to study the nude model. Instead, they were encouraged to participate in the 'lower' forms of painting, such as portraiture, landscape and still life, which were considered more 'feminine' in the belief that they appealed to the eye rather than the mind. One of only two female founders of the Royal Academy, and its youngest founder member at just 24 years old, was Mary Moser (1744–1819), the daughter of the Swiss painter George Michael Moser (1706–1783) who had arrived in Britain in 1726. She specialised in vibrant

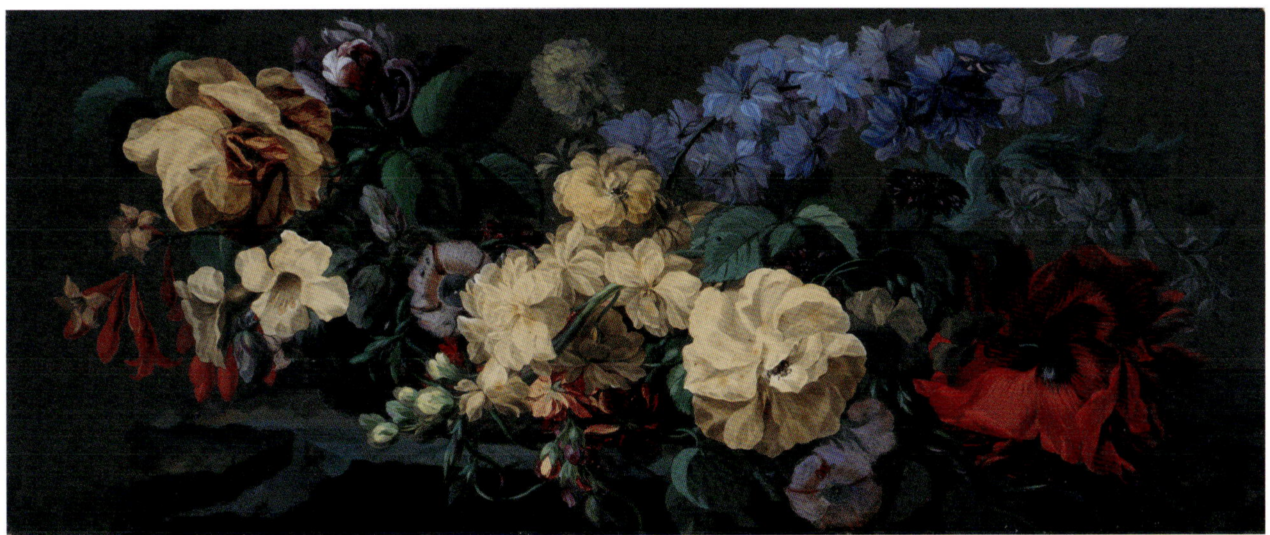

Fig. 15
Mary Moser (1744–1819)
*Summer Flowers on a Ledge*, 1768
Bodycolour on paper, 27.9 × 66 cm
The Courtauld, London (Samuel Courtauld Trust)

and luxuriant flower paintings, such as *Summer Flowers on a Ledge* (fig. 15), painted in the year of the foundation of the Royal Academy. According to Germaine Greer, Moser was not only 'the first significant British flower painter, she was also one of the best'.[15] She became the drawing mistress to Princess Elizabeth, daughter of King George III, and in the 1790s she was commissioned by Queen Charlotte to decorate a room at Frogmore House to create the illusion of an 'arbor open to the skies' composed of English flower arrangements. After her death in 1819, no further women were elected as full members of the Royal Academy until 1936.

During the 19th century, the lowly status of still life within the hierarchy of genres meant that in Britain it was largely the preserve of students and amateur artists, almost seen as a first technical exercise in copying, rather than something seeking to elevate the mind. In 1886, John Collier gave the following advice in his *Manual of Oil Painting:*

> In the case of a student who is able to make a fairly accurate – if somewhat bungling – drawing, the course of study I should recommend is this: he should begin by what is called 'still life', that is, he should carefully make an arrangement of some simple objects which are not liable to any change in appearance; it matters very little what they are as long as they conform to this rule, which, of course, excludes all living things. Perhaps china and pots and pans of all sorts make the best preliminary exercises, care being taken to avoid any elaborate patterns, or, indeed, anything in which the detail is small and intimate.[16]

It was only in the 20th century that the possibilities of still life as a vehicle for artistic experimentation began to be harnessed by modernist artists in the wake of Édouard Manet (1832–1883), Paul Cezanne (1839–1906) and the post-impressionist artists' explorations of form and colour, which had such an impact on the Bloomsbury Group, Camden Town Group and Scottish Colourists.[17] In the words of art historian Wendy Baron:

> It was not until the NEAC (New English Art Club) had challenged the tyrannical influence of the Royal Academy over the exhibition system that painters in Britain felt able to ignore the hierarchy of acceptable subjects, which led from history paintings, down through narratives with a moral dimension, to portraits, landscapes and genre scenes. Still-life was off the scale. Painters who wanted to represent inanimate objects generally did so by integrating still-life elements into genre or portrait elements.[18]

Even in 1929, when the Royal Academy held a major exhibition of Dutch Art 1450–1900 at Burlington House, only a couple of still-life paintings by Abraham van Beyeren (c.1620–1690) and Willem Kalf (1619–1693) were included out of 166 exhibits, mainly landscapes, portraits, seascapes and genre scenes. However, the formal qualities of Dutch still life remained a direct point of reference for British artists in the 20th century, most notably William Nicholson (1872–1949) whose exquisitely rendered paintings such as *The Silver Casket and Red Leather Box* (fig. 40) recalled the Dutch presentation of precious objects before a jet-black background. Nicholson's ability to convey lustrous reflections in glass or polished metal was peerless, and both of its time and yet somehow timeless. Similar dark backgrounds and arrangements were employed in a knowing manner to evoke past masters by numerous artists later in the 20th century, such as Gluck (1895–1978), Tristram Hillier (1905–1983), Keith Vaughan (1912–1977) and Michael Ayrton (1921–1975).

Fig. 16
Willem Kalf (1619–1693)
*Still Life with the Drinking Horn of the Saint Sebastian Archers' Guild, Lobster and Glasses*, c.1653
Oil on canvas, 86.4 × 102.2 cm
The National Gallery, London
(Bequeathed by R.S. Newall, 1978)

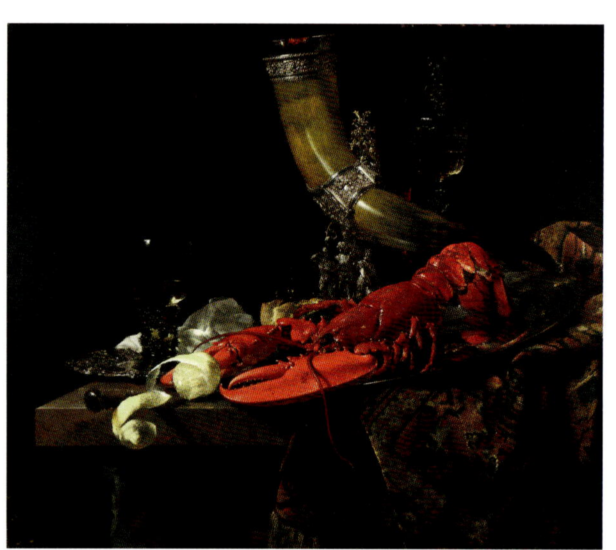

In more recent years, contemporary artists have re-engaged with the imagery and symbolism of 17th- and 18th-century still life. Although he came to be associated with the pop art generation in the 1960s, Patrick Caulfield (1936–2005) preferred, if anything, to see himself as a 'formal artist' and he avoided blatantly contemporary imagery. He was interested in 'the shock of the familiar', reinvigorating traditional genres from art history.[19] In the late 1990s, the National Gallery in London commissioned 24 artists from Europe and North America to produce work in response to their collection, resulting in the exhibition *Encounters: New Art from Old* in 2000, which its director Neil MacGregor described as an opportunity for 'great artists of our time to converse with the

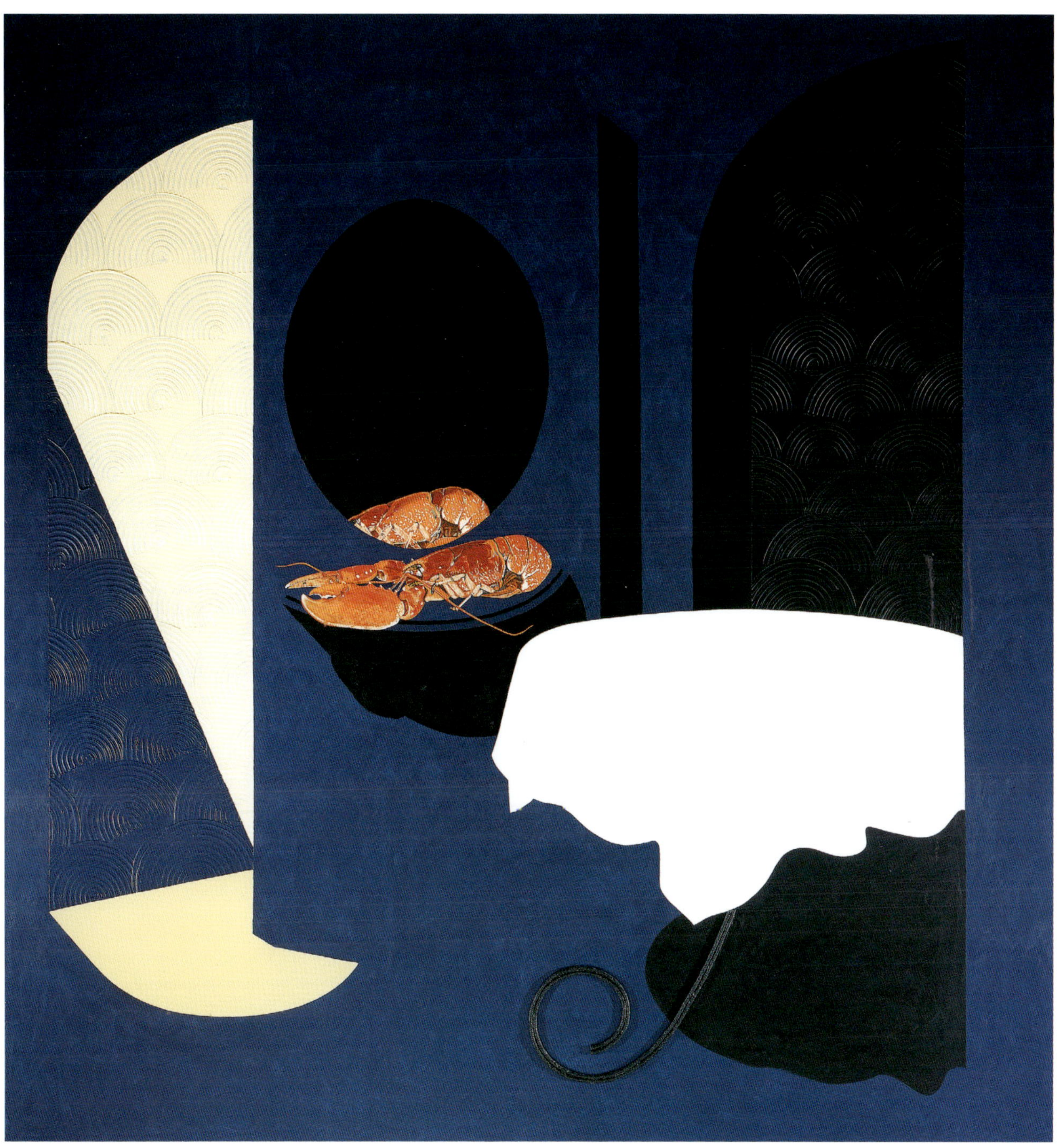

Fig. 17
Patrick Caulfield (1936–2005)
*Reserved Table,* 2000
Acrylic on canvas, 183 × 190 cm
Pallant House Gallery, Chichester
(Wilson Gift through Art Fund, 2006)

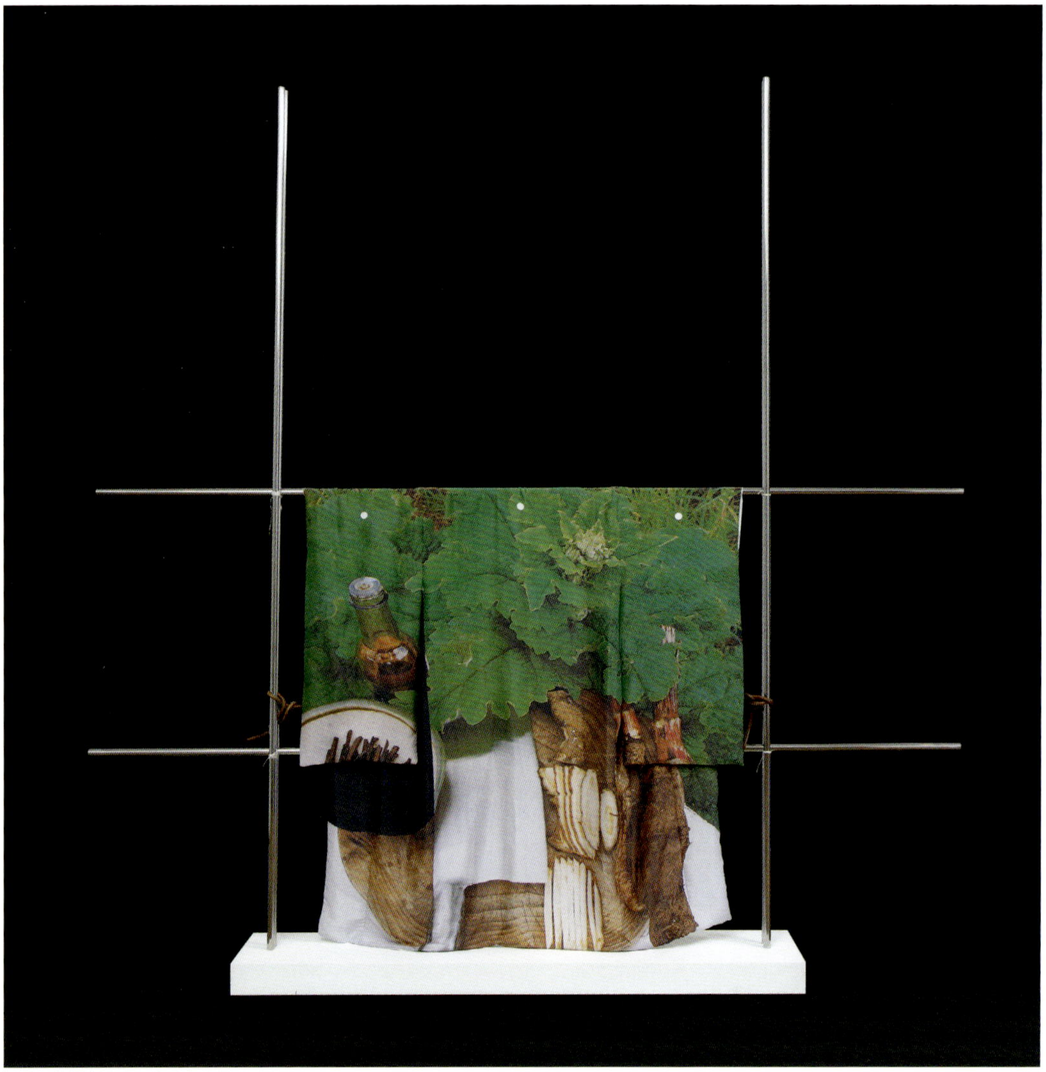

Fig. 18
Anthea Hamilton (b.1978)
*Wild Food*, 2012
Digital print on shantung dupion silk, silk viscose, leather, brushed steel, string, wood, 225 × 225 × 55 cm
Private collection, London

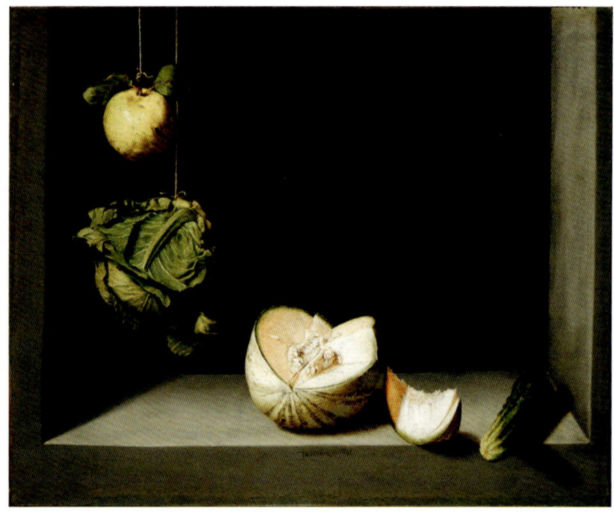

Fig. 19
Juan Sánchez Cotán (1560–1627)
*Quince, Cabbage, Melon and Cucumber*, c.1602
Oil on canvas, 67.8 cm × 88.7 cm
San Diego Museum of Art

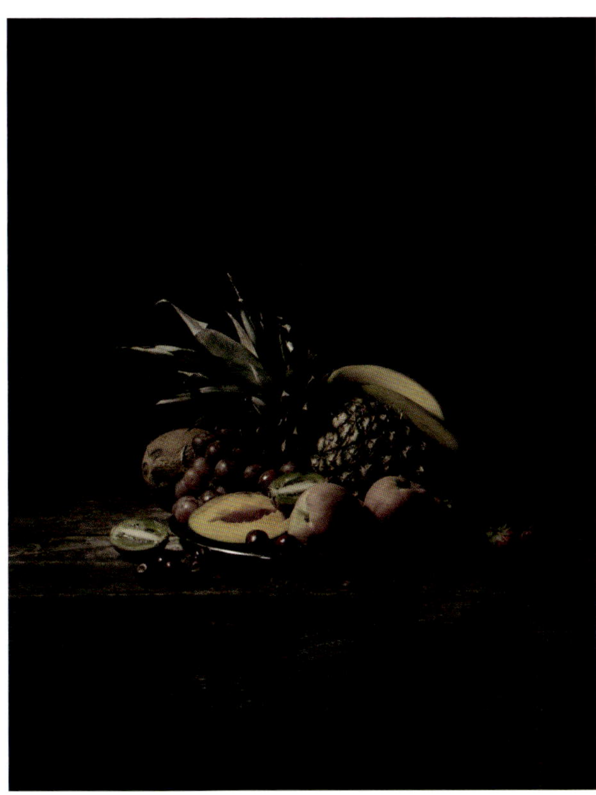

Fig. 20
Mat Collishaw (b.1966)
*Last Meal on Death Row, Texas (Louis Jones Junior)*, 2012
Digital transfer print on goatskin parchment, 66 × 55 cm
Mat Collishaw

greatest artists of all time'.[20] Caulfield's contribution to the exhibition, a depiction of a Spanish restaurant interior titled *Hemingway Never Ate Here* (1999, Tate) took as its central motif *A Cup of Water and a Rose on a Silver Plate* (c.1630) by the 17th-century Spanish painter Francisco de Zurbarán (1598–1664). At the same time, he painted *Reserved Table* (fig. 17) which quotes a sumptuous 'Pronkstilleven' or 'ostentatious still life' by Kalf entitled *Still Life with the Drinking Horn of the Saint Sebastian Archers' Guild, Lobster and Glasses* (fig. 16). The life-size painting presents a restaurant interior into which we are invited to take our seat, metaphorically, at the awaiting table with its crisp white tablecloth. The lobster on a pewter platter – a luxurious commodity in Kalf's painting – and its reflection are rendered in photorealist detail by Caulfield within an otherwise almost abstract composition, in which deep, raking shadows and sections of textured paint create an unsettling interplay between artifice and reality. Caulfield's decision to combine multiple visual languages within his paintings is rooted both in the way he viewed the world around him and how he recalled those experiences, as he has explained:

> I find that in treating different things in different ways, they become a point of focus. It's the idea that one doesn't encompass everything, and that your eye can look around and see things. I'm not sure whether it's your eye or whether it's that your memory remembers things in different ways. There seems no reason to treat everything evenly. It's more like a collaged memory of things. Some of the things are in sharp focus, and others, if you like, symbolise the object.[21]

In a different conceptual language, Anthea Hamilton (b.1978) has combined completely different cultural and visual languages drawn from the Spanish baroque painter Juan Sánchez Cotán (1560–1627), one of her favourite artists, with Japanese kimonos. Referencing Cotán's still-life paintings of fruit and vegetables and 'bodegones' (pantry items such as victuals, game and drink) in an austere style against black backgrounds, her installation *Wild Food* (fig. 18) features a kimono digitally printed with food images hung on a formal grid-like framework. Hamilton has said she uses the kimono as a logical composition aid, which is a method of tying together elements she wishes to explore in her artwork. The kimono references the body, and yet it is absent: it does not have its volume and is rendered in a two-dimensional way.

The sense of an absent seat at the dinner table, and the paintings of Kalf and his contemporaries, provided inspiration for a series of photographic works by Mat Collishaw (b.1966) in which he researched the last meals chosen by prisoners on death row (mainly in the USA) prior to their execution, and restaged them in the manner of 17th-century Dutch still-life paintings, with a digital transfer print on goatskin parchment. The artist has commented on how,

> many prisoners chose food that was either specific to their ethnicity or food that they would have enjoyed during childhood. The poignant choices they made, in this chillingly 'civilised' process, corresponded to the Vanitas tradition, a genre that reflects on man's futile accumulation of worldly goods and the transience of life. The photographs were framed in black heavily moulded frames typical of Dutch still life painting, so that they became surrogate portraits of the prisoners.[22]

*Last Meal on Death Row, Texas (Louis Jones Junior)* (fig. 20) presents the plate of exotic fruits that were requested by an African American former US soldier who was executed by lethal injection in 2003 for the brutal murder of Tracie MacBride in 1995. The series addresses the complex moral issue of the aestheticization of violence, and serves as a reminder that, in its understated qualities, still life is rarely about visual spectacle. In contrast, British-Israeli artist Ori Gersht (b.1967) has captured exactly that: the visual fragmentation of a previously motionless still life, in order to reference the fragility and fragmentation of the European Union. For the series, titled *New Orders*, Gersht physically recreated particular still-life paintings from different European countries: by Jean Siméon Chardin (1699–1779) from France, Zurbarán from Spain and Giorgio Morandi (1890–1964) from Italy. For *Evertime 05,* from the *New Orders* series (fig. 21) Gersht commissioned replicas of the distinctive white vessels and bottles that feature in Morandi's paintings, carefully arranging them to evoke his compositions before firing on the ceramics with an air rifle, while capturing the moment of fragmentation of the objects as they are destroyed with a high-resolution camera. In a similar way, Dutch-British artist Bouke de Vries (b.1960) creates 'exploded' artworks by fixing shattered ceramics as if in the moment of fracture. De Vries initially trained as a ceramics restorer, but instead of restoring broken historic domestic ceramics and hiding the evidence of their dramatic destruction, he deconstructs them. Drawing on the history of Dutch still life, such as the flower paintings produced in his hometown of Utrecht by the likes of Jan Davidsz de Heem (1606–1683/4), Willem van Aelst (1627–1683) and Jan van Huysum (1682–1749), among others, he incorporates motifs from these *vanitas* paintings, such as butterflies, which symbolise rebirth and reincarnation. *Vanitas (Still Life with Globular Teapot)* (fig. 22)

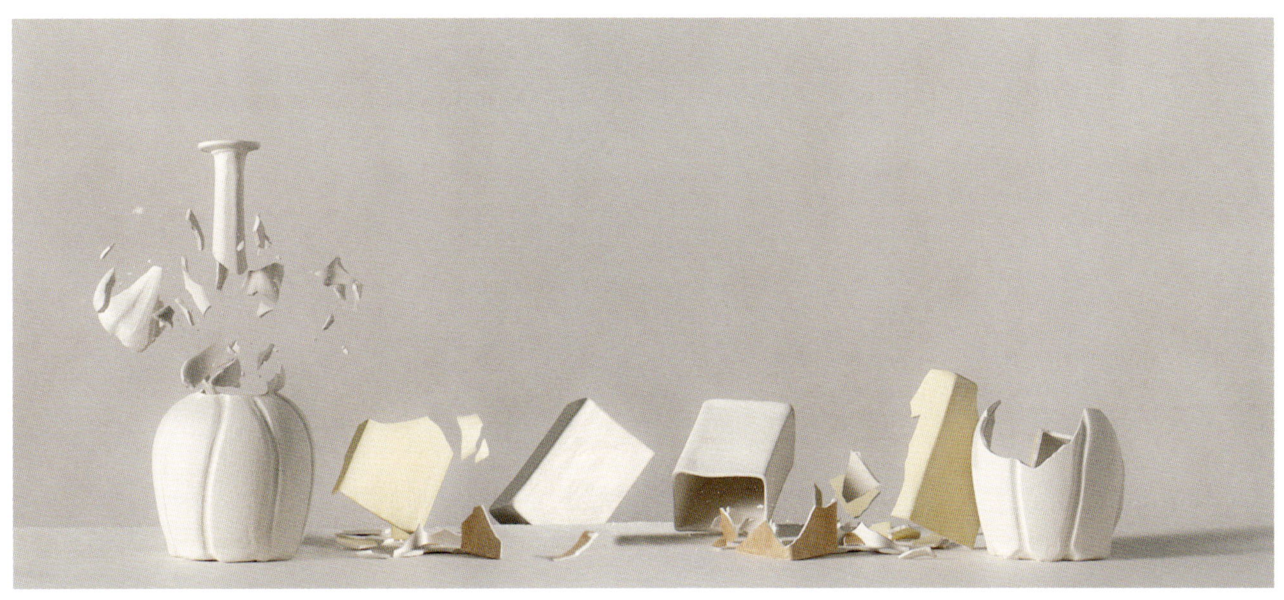

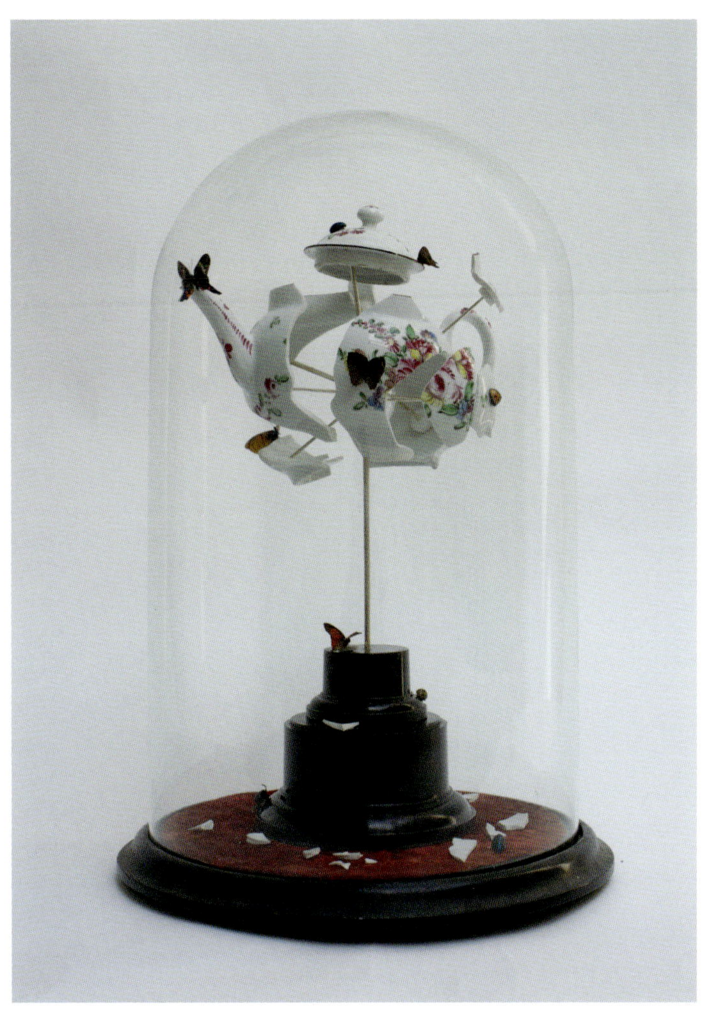

Fig. 21
Ori Gersht (b.1967)
*Evertime 05*, 2018
Archival ink on paper, 30 × 68 cm
Courtesy of Ori Gersht and
Michael Hoppen Gallery, London

Fig. 22
Bouke de Vries (b.1960)
*Vanitas (Still Life with Globular Teapot)*,
2009/c.1765
Fragmented Bow teapot, butterflies in glass
dome, 124 cm height x 12 cm diameter
Commissioned by Pallant House Gallery,
Chichester (2009) Geoffrey Freeman
Collection of Bow Porcelain (2002)

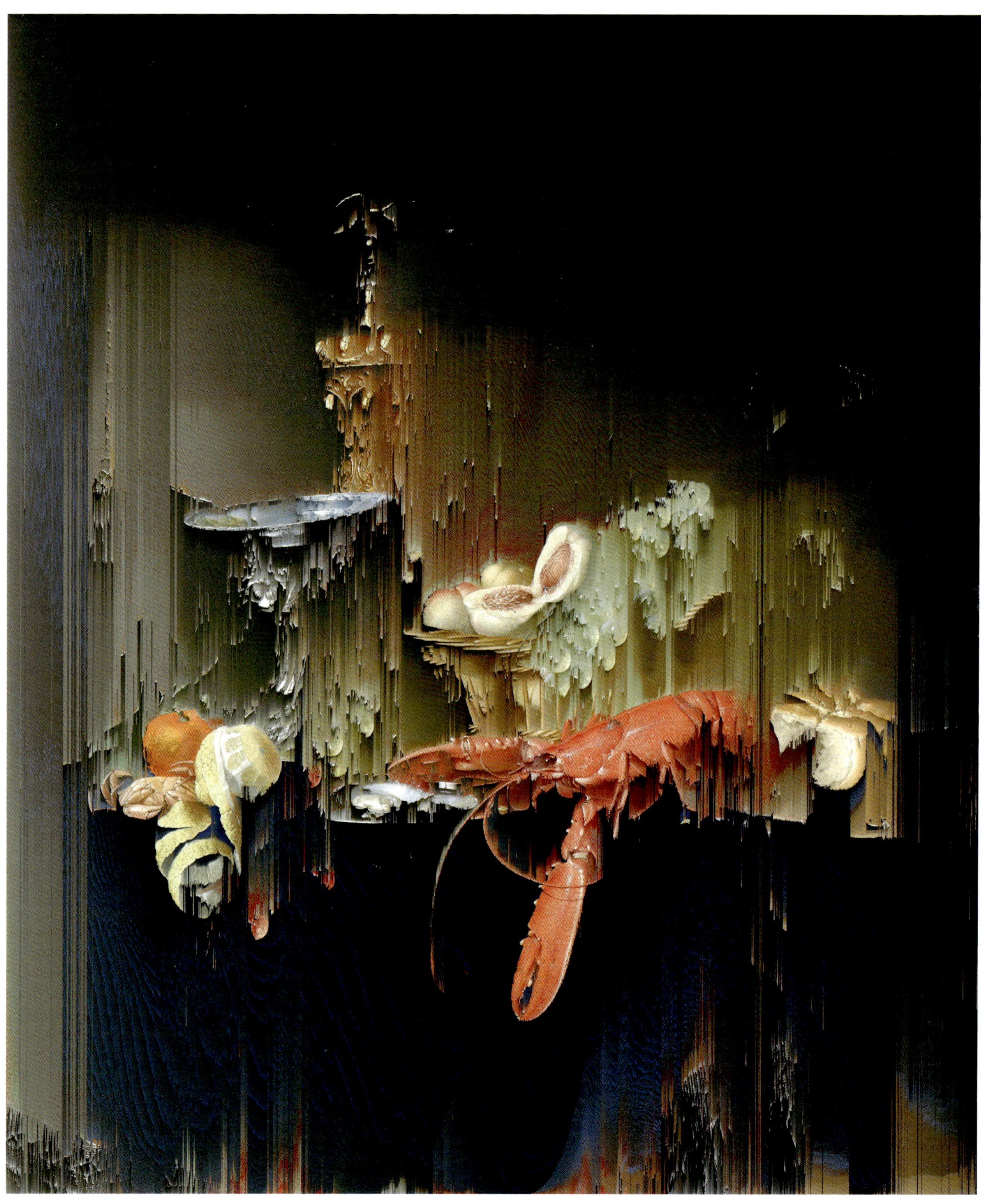

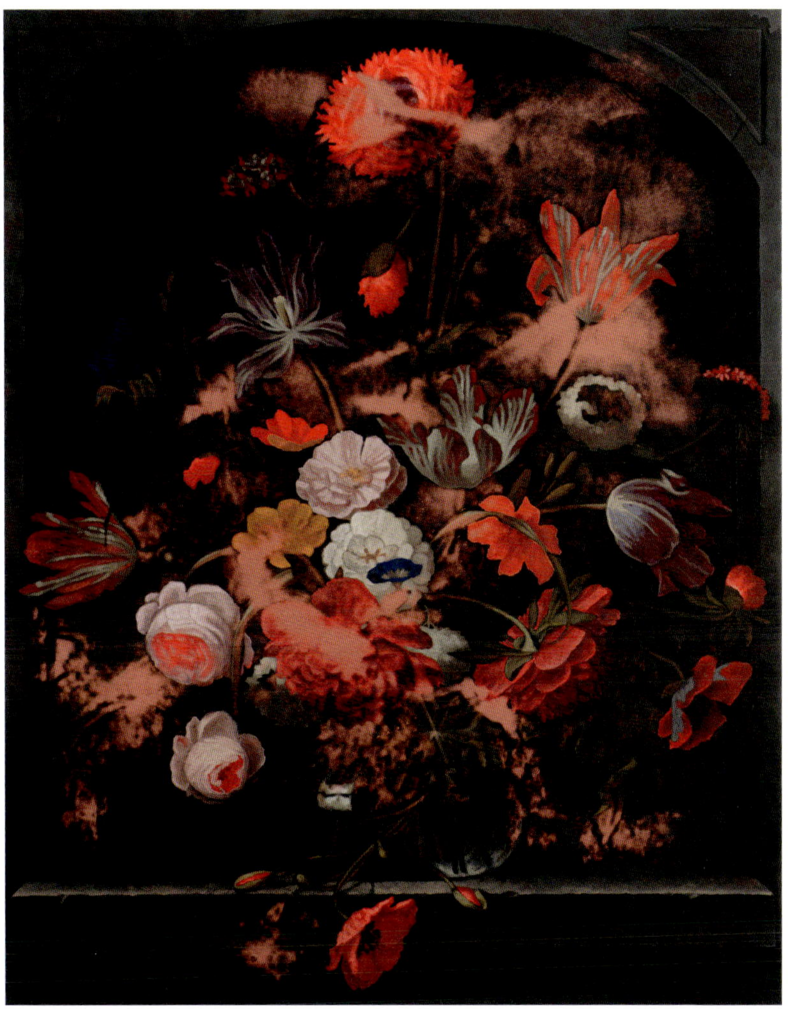

is a transformation of an 18th-century globular teapot, made at the Bow Factory in East London in around 1765, which produced soft-paste porcelain to rival the market in imported ceramics from China and Germany. Calling it the 'beauty of destruction', he re-assembled the pieces after the teapot was broken in an accident, to create a meditation on the fragility of existence and a reminder of mortality.

British-Chinese artist Gordon Cheung (b.1975) has adapted open-source images of Dutch Golden Age still-life paintings from the Rijksmuseum in Amsterdam as a mechanism to raise questions about global capitalism and the global exploitation of environmental resources for the development of certain nations. Using an open-source digital code created by artist Kim Asendorf (b.1981) that 'glitches' the image to create 4000 sequential images whereby the image is 'pixel sorted', Cheung is able to create the illusion that the painting is dissolving. He was inspired to look at Dutch still-life painting through an initial interest in 'Tulipomania', when Holland was the centre of what has been considered the first speculative economic bubble and a tulip bulb was traded at its peak for the equivalent price of a house. His *New Order* series, based on still-life paintings, refers to the English rock band of the same name, whose 1983 *Power, Corruption and Lies* album cover, designed by Peter Saville, featured an image of a still life in the National Gallery in London by French artist Henri Fantin-Latour (1836–1904). Cheung was struck by Saville's observation that the flowers 'suggested the means by which power, corruption and lies infiltrate our lives. They're seductive'.[23] His *Still Life with Golden Goblet (after Pieter de Ring, 1640–1660)* (fig. 23) takes as its starting point an opulent still life in the Rijksmuseum dating from c.1655–60 which features a sumptuous feast including crab, lobster, oysters, grapes, cherries and peeled citrus fruit and costly objects including a Chinese dish, a German 'Buckelpokal' lidded cup crowned with a phoenix and a flute glass. Cheung's manipulation of the visual reproduction almost makes it appear to be respiring, 'seemingly to

Fig. 23 (opposite)
Gordon Cheung (b.1975)
*Still Life with Golden Goblet (after Pieter de Ring, 1640–1660)*, 2017
Archival inkjet on 380gsm Hahnemühle Photo Rag paper, 103 × 88 cm
Courtesy the artist and Cristea Roberts Gallery, London

Fig. 24 (above)
Toby Ziegler (b.1972)
*Purple Prose*, 2023
Oil paint and gesso on aluminium, 100 × 80 cm
Courtesy of the artist

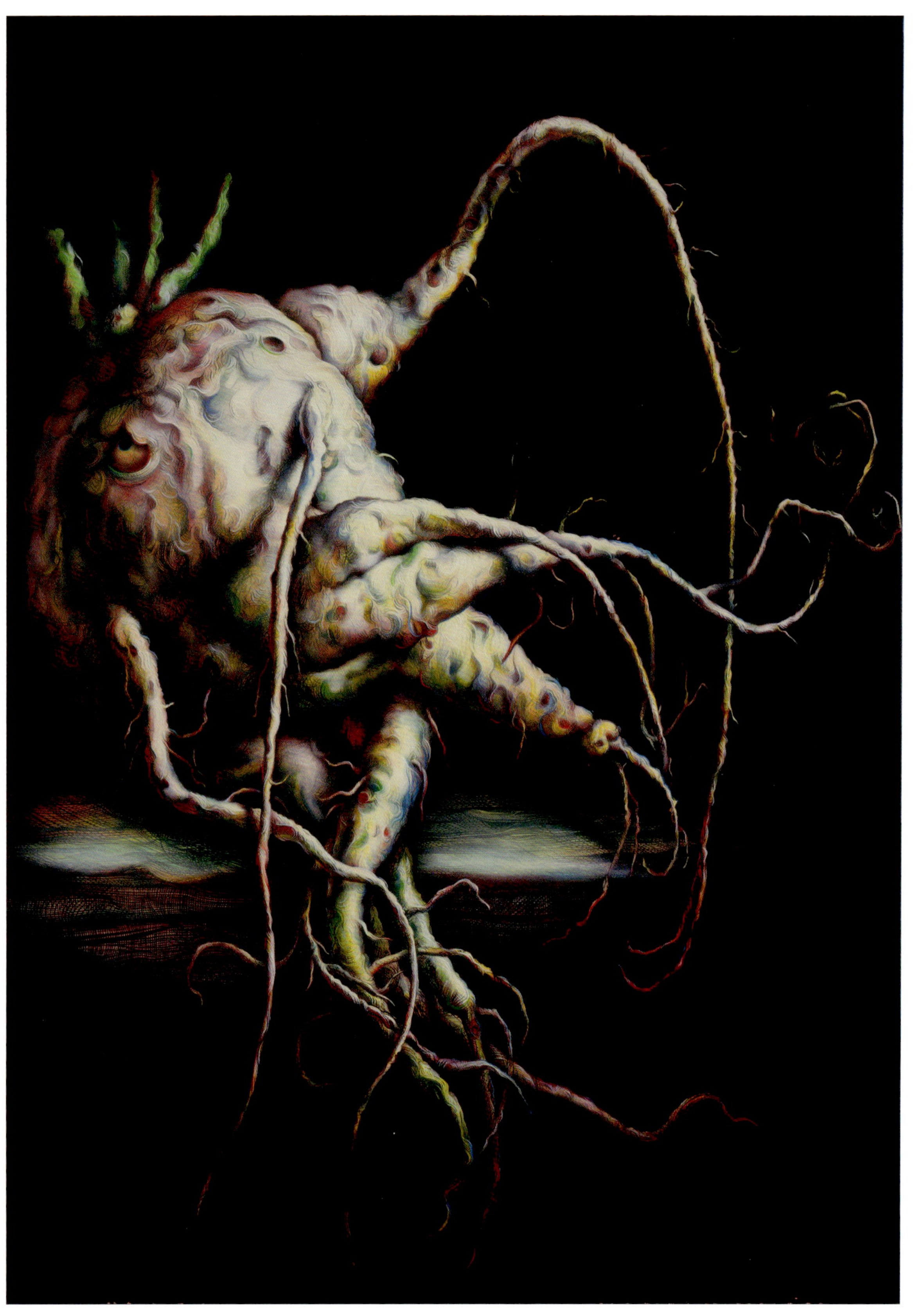

breathe in and exhale out of nature into the realm of digital abstraction'.[24] In a similar way, Toby Ziegler (b.1972) brings together traditional motifs from Dutch and Spanish still-life paintings and uses computer software to generate new forms and pictorial spaces, which often have idiosyncrasies and mistakes, which he painstakingly reproduces by hand. In works such as *Purple Prose* (fig. 24), Ziegler seeks to create a new image somewhere between the virtual and the actual, enjoying the physical act of decomposing and distorting the image. He has painted a figurative image on an aluminium panel followed by a very fast process of erosion carried out by an electric sander, which creates a non-figurative composition in parallel to the original. The artist has said:

> The choice of a historical *memento mori* as motif, and my approach to making the works, are totally interwoven. In the 17th-century Dutch still-lifes that these works reference, the flowers are loaded with insects, and drops of water hang off many of the leaves creating the illusion of a moment frozen in time. I chose to get rid of these elements as I want a less specific timeframe in my initial figurative image. In a lot of paintings that I love there are different speeds of mark making, that provoke different speeds of looking. Paintings also evoke different periods of duration. Some paintings seem to represent an instant, some make you conscious of time spent making them, and others seem to encapsulate an eternal statis. Sometime all three timeframes are folded into a single image.[25]

In a more analogue way, Glenn Brown (b.1966) transforms appropriated images from art history by changing their scale, colour and mood. As the point of departure for his painting *Saint Bimbo* (fig. 25) Brown has taken a section of a larger painting of a cauliflower and a turnip by the 17th-century Florentine painter Bartolomeo Bimbi (1648–1725, also known as Bartolomeo del Bimbo) who specialised in painting still lifes for the court of Cosimo III de' Medici (1642–1723).[26] Although Brown is an admirer of the Italian baroque, in the words of critic Michael Bracewell, he is 'less concerned with the art-historical status of those works he appropriates than with their ability to serve his purpose – namely his epic exploration of paint and painting'.[27] Bimbo's still life is only one of a number of reference points for Brown, who has said:

> I like the idea that by using multiple levels of appropriation my work resists specific placement within art history. The source subject matter may be 17th Century, but the colour is from Francisco Goya (1746–1828) entwined with Odilon Redon (1840–1916). The work is both drawing and painting. The work started out as a Baroque cross-hatched highly-detailed drawing in India ink, on top of which multiple

Fig. 25
Glenn Brown (b.1966)
*Saint Bimbo*, 2024
India ink and oil paint on panel,
112 × 80 cm
Collection of the artist

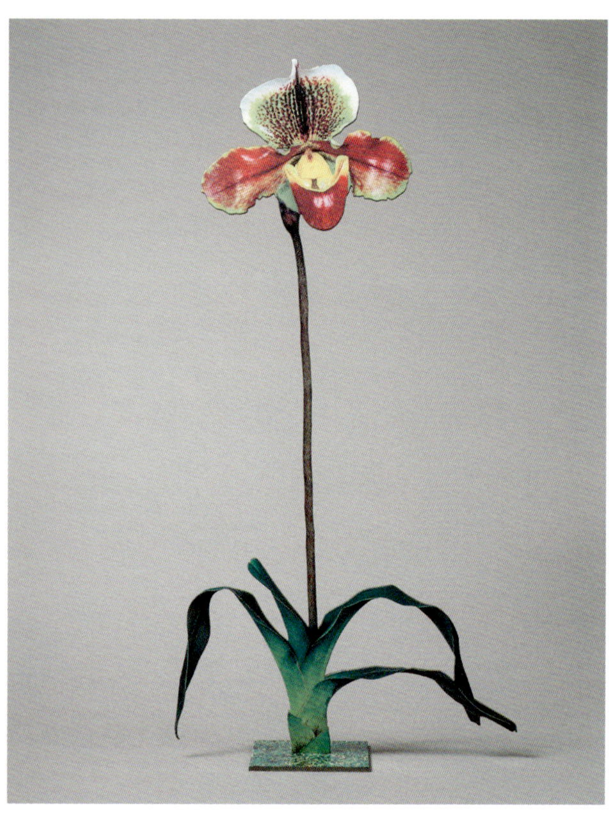

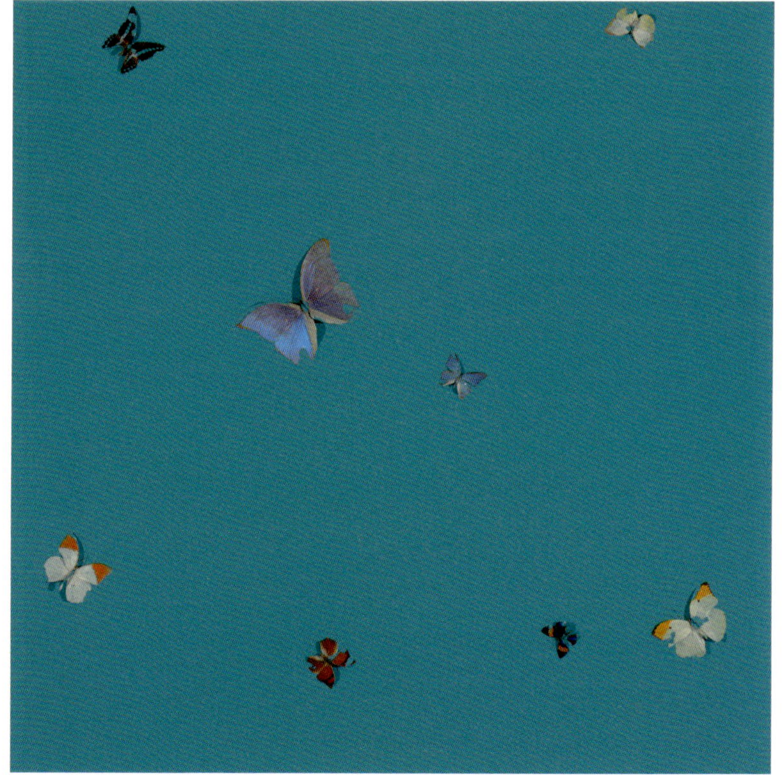

Fig. 26 (above)
Marc Quinn (b.1964)
*Orchid, The Overwhelming World of Desire (Paphiopedilum Winston Churchill Hybrid)*, 2002
Photographic image on steel, 57 cm
Pallant House Gallery, Chichester
(Purchased with support from Art Fund and John Ayton MBE and John Booth 2019)

Fig. 27 (right)
Damien Hirst (b.1965)
*Bognor Blue*, 2008
Butterflies and household gloss paint on canvas, 91.4 × 91.4 cm
Pallant House Gallery, Chichester
(Accepted under the Cultural Gifts Scheme by HM Government from Frank Dunphy and allocated to Pallant House Gallery, 2018)

Fig. 28 (opposite)
Cornelia Parker (b.1956)
*Falling Façade*, 1991
Stretched silver trophies, easel and mirror, 171 × 112.5 × 94 cm
Courtesy of the artist & Frith Street Gallery, London

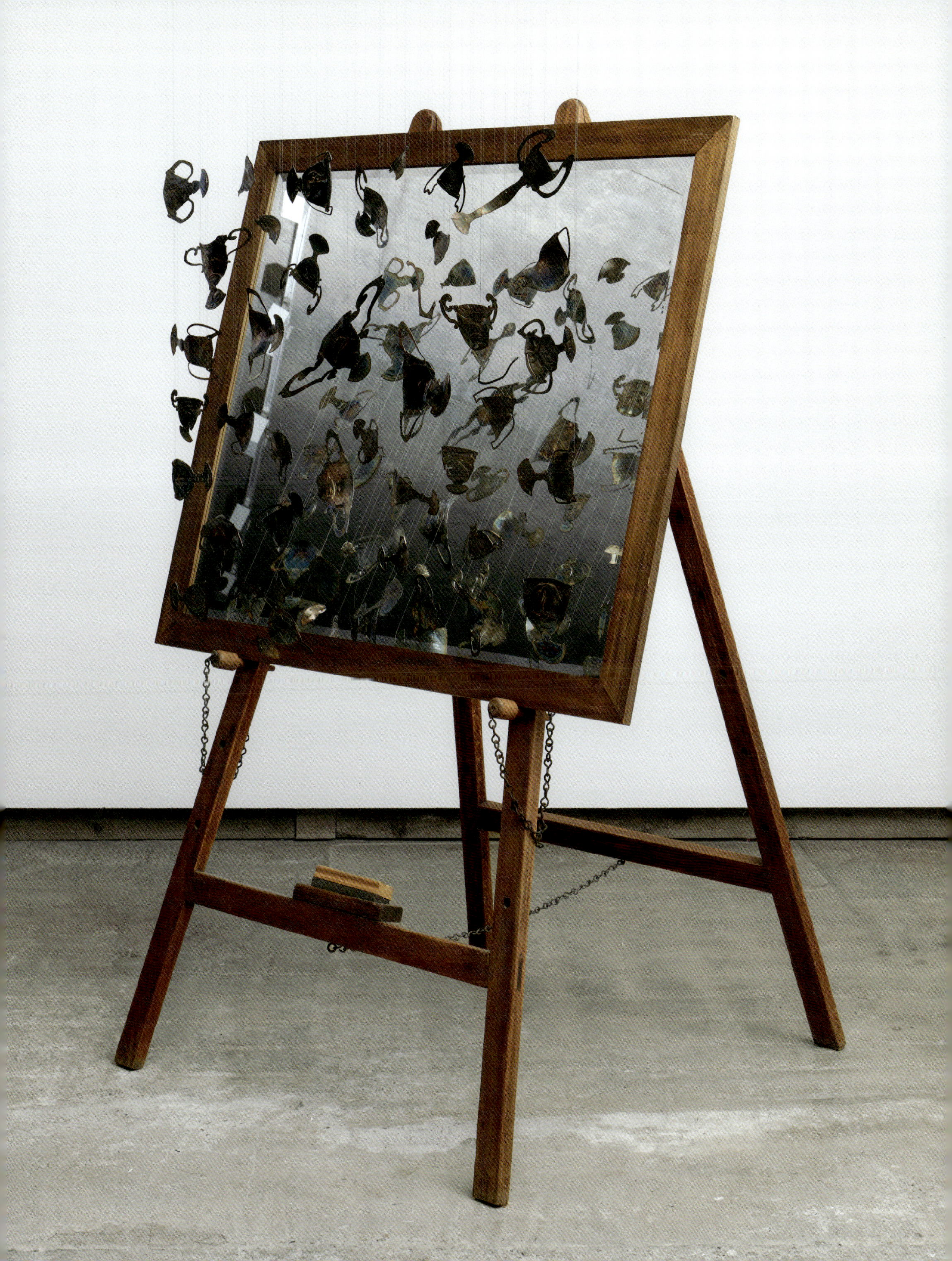

> fine glazes of oil paint build up to form volumes, adding shadows and light. The cross-hatching used for the initial India ink drawing refers to the etching techniques of Hendrick Goltzius (1558–1617), whilst the glazing techniques are from Lucas Cranach the Elder (1472–1553), amongst others.[28]

Brown has written of the importance of fluidity and transformation to all of his paintings: 'The anthropomorphic qualities of the turnip I focused on animates and brings it to life. In my Dr Frankenstein hand, I created a multiple-eyed Polichinelle masquerading as a vulgar vegetable. He is a comic, cross-limbed Humpty-Dumpty character precariously sitting on the edge of a table.'[29]

Like Pepys encountering the work of Verelst, viewers have expressed the desire to lick and touch the surfaces of Brown's paintings, for he renders the *trompe l'œil* illusion of expressive, painterly brushstrokes despite a uniformly flat surface.

The ceramic sculptures of Lindsey Mendick (b.1987) make no pretence of having any polite reserve, either with their surfaces or subject matter. Instead, references to *vanitas* paintings and *memento mori* burst out of the vessel: fish, skulls, flies and worms. Her exuberant pieces are replete with gothic humour: darkness combined with lightness of touch. While these may also include reminders of our mortality, it is as if Mendick is saying 'we're all going to die so we may as well enjoy ourselves first'.

During the past 350 years, the history of still life in Britain has been a history of the movement of artists and ideas: many of its protagonists have either moved to Britain from abroad, are the children of migrants, or have looked to inspiration from artists from overseas. But while it was once viewed as a 'lowly' form of art, over the past century it has been employed by many of Britain's leading artists. It is striking that, for a genre so concerned with the passing of time, it remains almost timeless today. The celebrated art historian E.H. Gombrich expressed this succinctly:

> The still life is compelled to challenge and at the same time perpetuate tradition. Without the elements of recognition and comparison, the discovery of the familiar in the unfamiliar, the genre would lose its meaning.[28]

Fig. 29
Lindsey Mendick (b.1987)
*That wriggled and jiggled and tickled inside her*, 2024 (work in progress)
*Still life with hermit crabs and tooth extraction*, 2024 (work in progress)
Glazed ceramic, 63 x 35cm, 68 x 54 cm
Courtesy of the artist and Carl Freedman Gallery, Margate

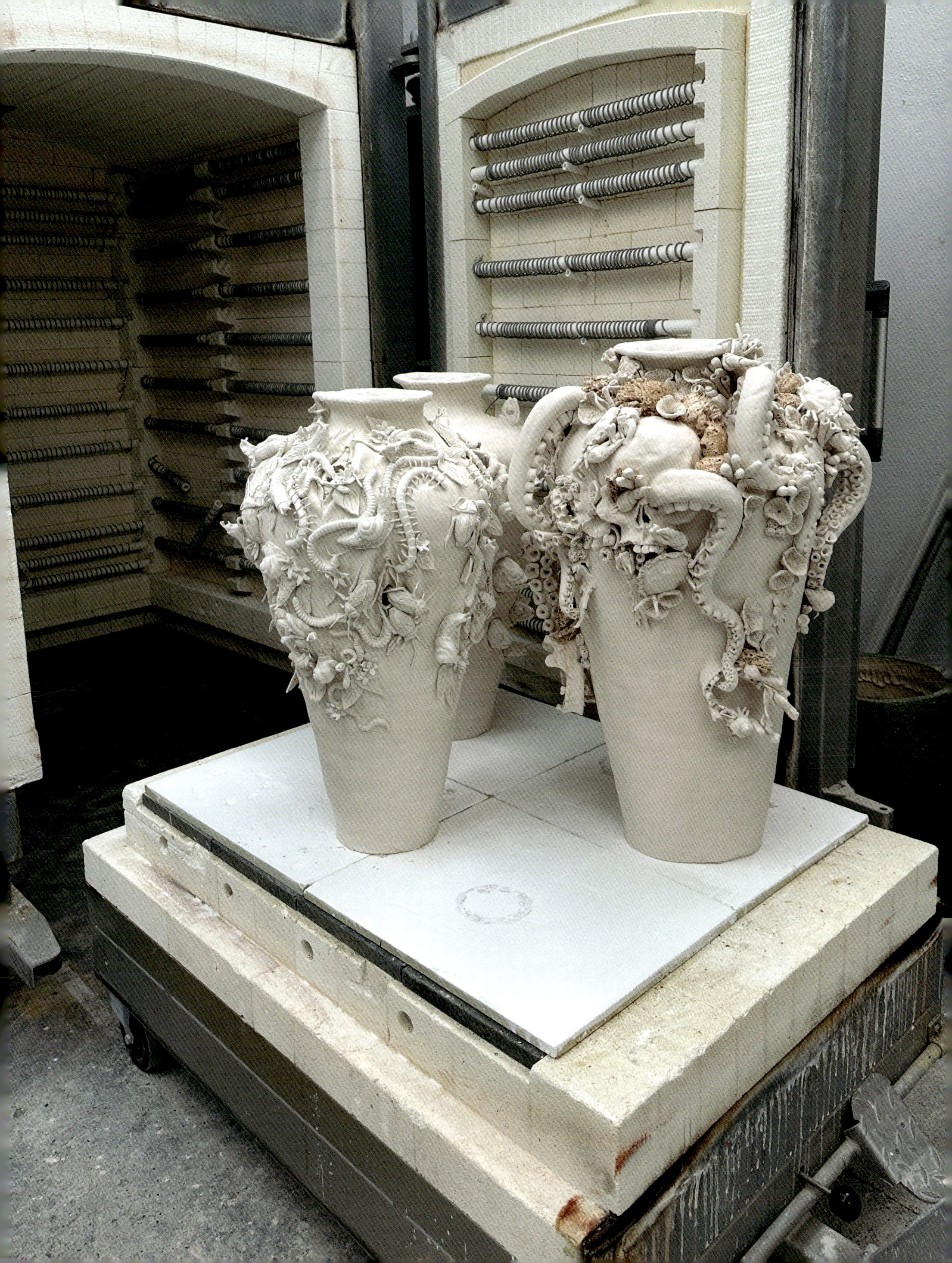

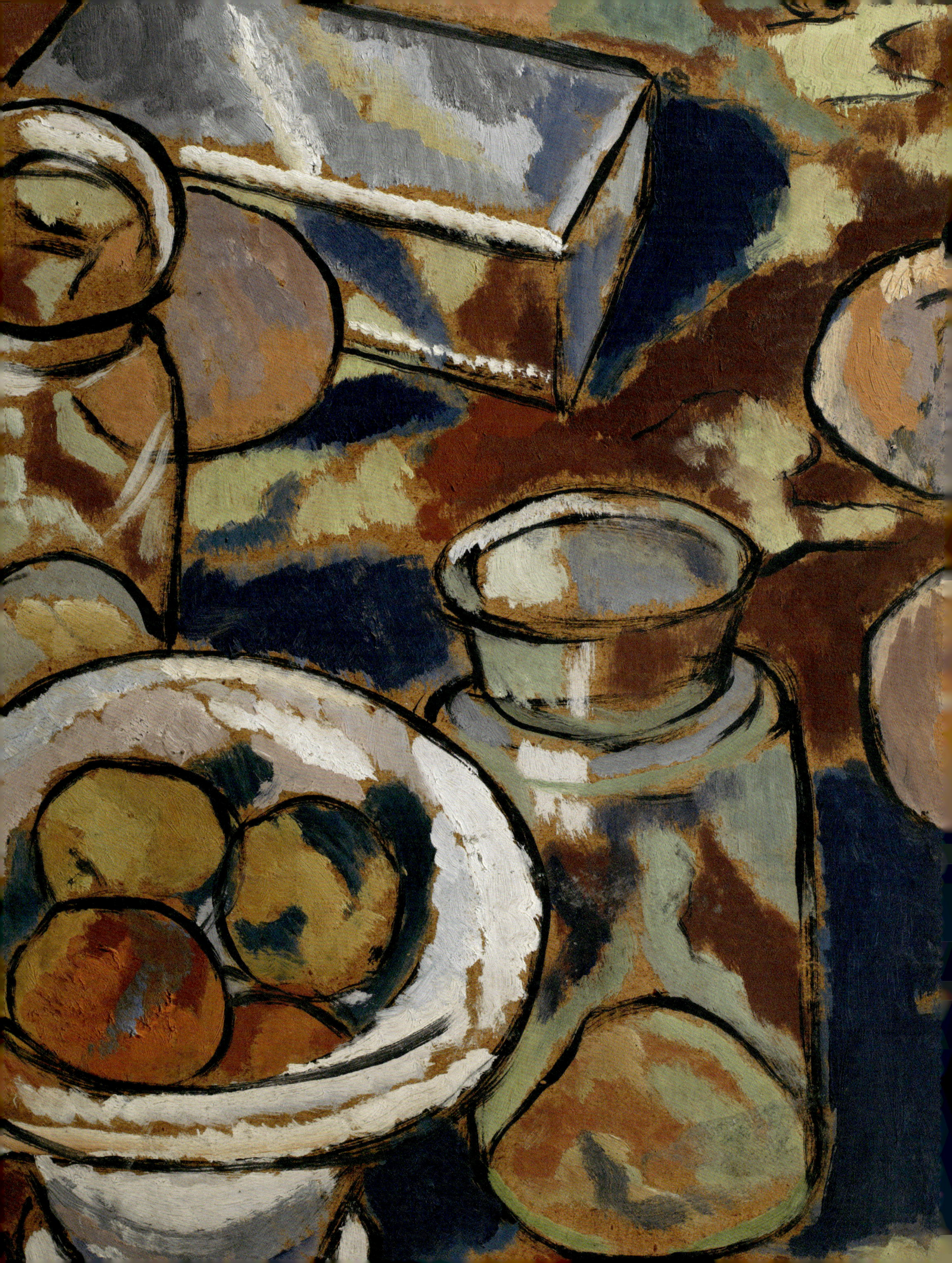

# 2 'Unbroken Quiet': How British Still Life was Stimulated by Post-Impressionism

LYDIA MILLER

In summer 1905, the artist Vanessa Bell (1879–1961) founded the Friday Club. The Club provided Bell's friends, family and acquaintances, several of whom were students at the Slade School of Fine Art and the Royal Academy Schools, with the opportunity to discuss creative ideas and support each other in their work. They also held regular lectures with guest speakers and organised exhibitions in rented rooms across London. Although art historian Richard Shone described the 'origins' of the Club as 'homely', with artists predominantly meeting at Bell's house in Gordon Square, the Friday Club helped set the wheels in motion for a new age of Modern British art – an age built on colour, significant form and post-impressionism.[1] This resulted in an exciting revival of still-life painting, a genre that was able to provide artists with the flexibility to experiment with modernism and that did not limit women artists in its accessibility.

At the turn of the 20th century still life was closely connected with the reception of French modernism in Britain. The Friday Club was a creative environment in which artists were able to nurture their interests in French modernism and where they were introduced to the painter and art critic Roger Fry (1866–1934) before his seminal post-impressionist exhibitions. Although the Friday Club metamorphosed into subsequent ventures by Bell and Fry, including the Omega Workshops, it was the forerunner to other breakaway groups, such as the Camden Town Group, which wanted to sever connections with exhibiting societies that were dismissive of modern European influences.

The Friday Club has often been misunderstood as exclusive to the Bloomsbury Group but its reach was much wider. Mark Gertler

Detail of fig. 36
Winifred Gill (1891–1981)
*Still Life with Glass Jar and Silver Box*, 1914

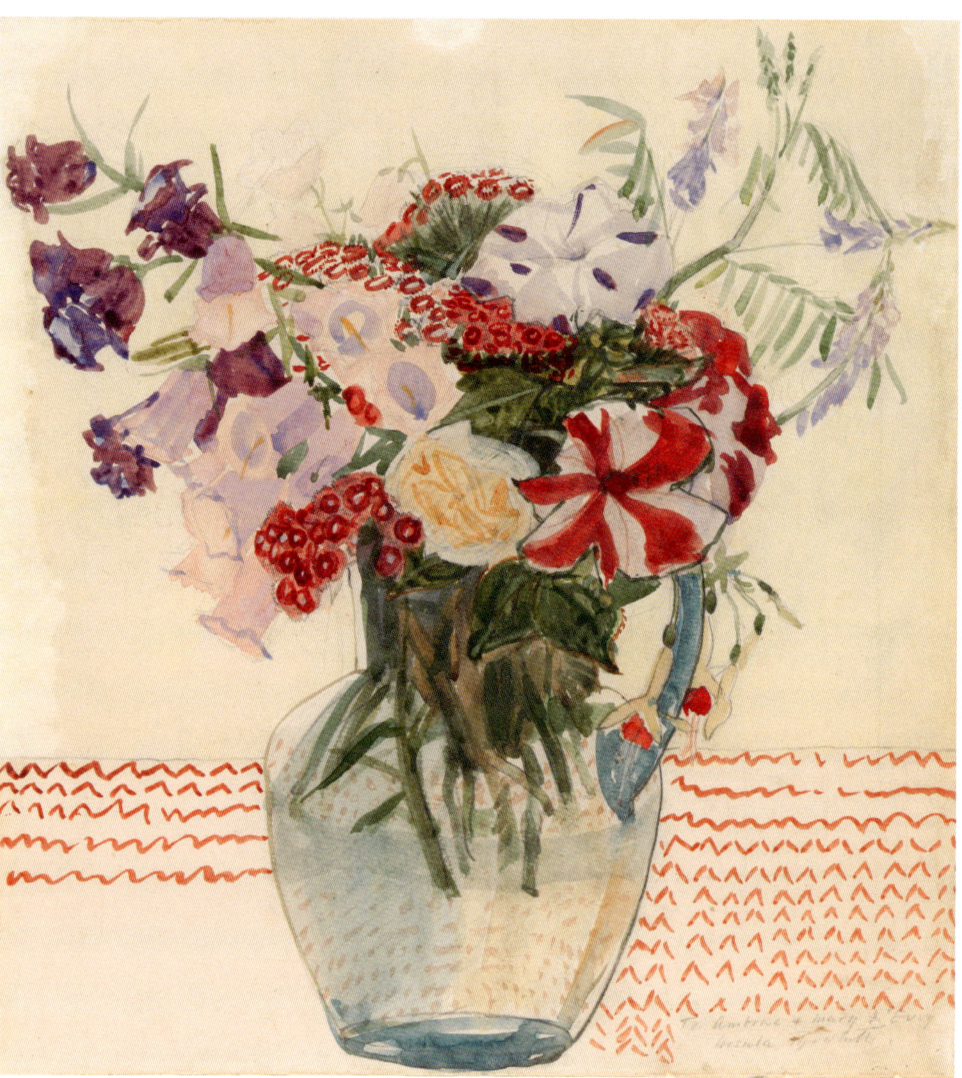

Fig. 30
Ursula Tyrwhitt (1872–1966)
*Flowers*, 1912
Watercolour on paper,
40.6 × 38.4 cm
Tate: presented by
Mrs Mary McEvoy 1935

(1891–1939), Nina Hamnett (1890–1956), Ursula Tyrwhitt (1872–1966) all exhibited with the Club but pursued individual painting styles influenced by European modernism. Tyrwhitt, who joined the Friday Club in its infancy, has often been overlooked as an artist, and yet her output as a flower painter and as part of a generation of Slade students described as part of a 'crisis of brilliance' by their tutor Henry Tonks is significant.[2]

*Flowers* (fig. 30), a vibrant watercolour by Tyrwhitt, depicts a glass jug brimming with flowers that are commonly found in an English garden, including petunias, Canterbury bells and fuchsia. In this painting, Tyrwhitt experimented with pattern, in the form of an incomplete tablecloth, and with distorted perspective through the water in the jug. Although this painting may look unfinished, it was gifted to her friends and fellow artists Ambrose (1877–1927) and Mary McEvoy (1870–1941) in 1912. The McEvoys, who had both been students at the Slade with Tyrwhitt, had married in January 1902 and this painting was likely given as a tenth wedding anniversary present. Like several artists of this period who will be explored in more detail in this essay, Tyrwhitt uses pattern playfully to give her vase perspective and bring a floral still-life composition into a new age of modernism.

Tyrwhitt would have likely seen Roger Fry lecture at the Friday Club in 1910, after which he became an exhibiting member. In the same year, Fry realised the first of two post-impressionist exhibitions at the Grafton Galleries in London (the second was in 1912), *Manet and the Post-Impressionists* – an exhibition that would change the reception of modern art in Britain. Paintings by Édouard Manet, Henri Matisse (1869–1954), Paul Gauguin (1848–1903), Vincent van Gogh (1853–1890) and Paul Cezanne, arguably the father of modern still life,[3] were exhibited together under a new movement coined 'post-impressionism' by Fry himself. This term described a group of modern European artists who intended to move away from the effects of natural light and colour as explored *en plein air* by the impressionists. Instead, they used colour and symbolism 'to express emotions which the objects themselves evoked; their attitude towards nature was far more independent, not to say rebellious'.[4]

Although post-impressionism was not a movement devoted to still life, the genre did play a major part. Cezanne – claimed by Fry to be the 'originator of the whole idea of Post-Impressionism' – painted nearly 200 still lifes during his career and raised the status of the genre in the 20th century.[5] However, by the time the term 'post-impressionism' was coined by Fry, Cezanne and many of his contemporaries were dead. Their work had been brought together and repackaged by Fry for a British audience – a decision that would have a lasting impact on several artists exposed to these exhibitions and their own exploration of still life.

*Manet and the Post-Impressionists* was poorly received. The work was said to resemble 'the decorative effect that might result from a child's miscellaneous handling of his first paint-box' and the artists themselves were described as 'mad'.[6] However, art historian and artist C.J. Holmes described the exhibition as 'stimulating', and said that 'art, like all other products of the active human mind, stagnates in surroundings of unbroken quiet'.[7] Post-impressionism had certainly cut through the silence and mundanity of British art which had been clinging to an age of Victorian interiors. Contemporary artists were undoubtedly influenced by Fry's exhibition which enabled many to see work by Manet, Matisse and Cezanne for the first time. However, other British artists were well aware of French modernism several years before Fry's exhibition from their travels and education in Europe.

John Duncan Fergusson, S.J. (Samuel John) Peploe, George Leslie Hunter (see fig.31) and Francis Campbell Boileau Cadell, known as the

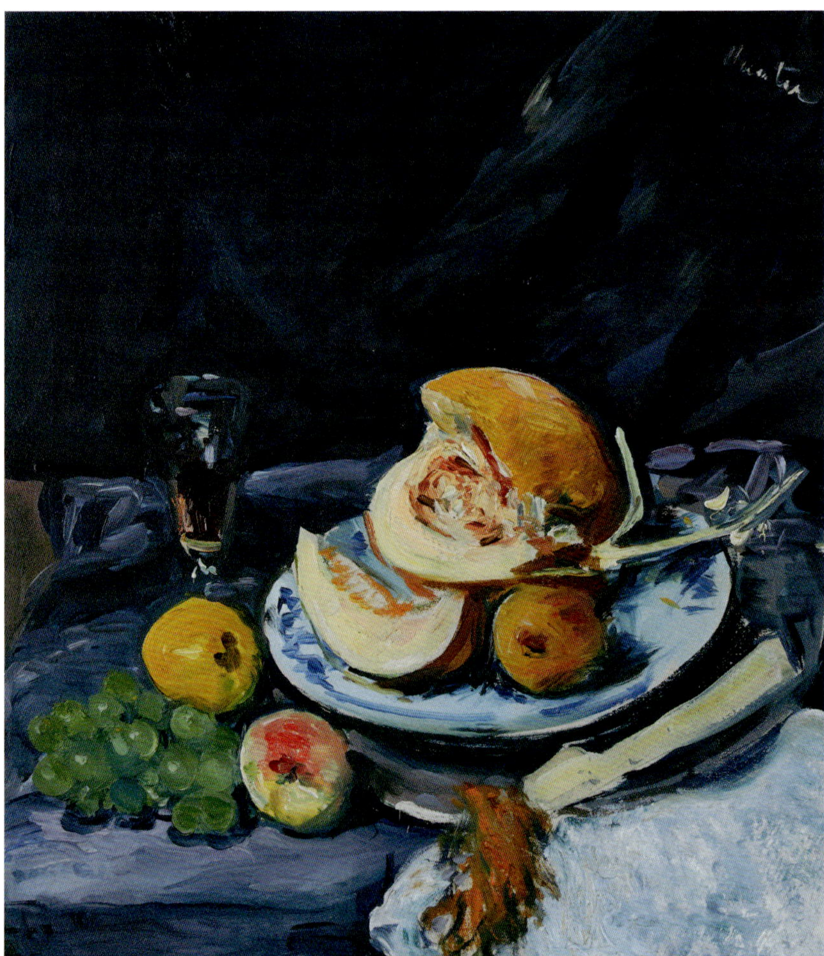

Fig. 31
George Leslie Hunter (1877–1931)
*Still Life with Cut Melon, Glass and Fan*, c.1919/20
Oil on canvas, 48.2 × 44.5 cm
Pallant House Gallery, Chichester (on loan from the Cross Family Collection, 2014)

Scottish Colourists, all spent time working and studying in France. They were influenced by impressionism, post-impressionism and fauvism, with Fergusson visiting Paris as early as the 1890s, at least ten years before the formation of the Friday Club and 15 years before Fry's first post-impressionist exhibition. French modernism had a significant effect on Fergusson's work and during his regular visits to Paris he

> wrote a long letter [to his friend S.J. Peploe] trying to explain modern painting. Something new had started and I was very much intrigued. But there was no language for it that made sense in Edinburgh or London – an expression like 'the logic of line' meant something in Paris that it couldn't mean in Edinburgh.[8]

Fergusson settled in Paris until 1913 when he moved to the south of France, following in the footsteps of his heroes Gauguin and Van Gogh. He was forced to return to Britain during the First World War but the

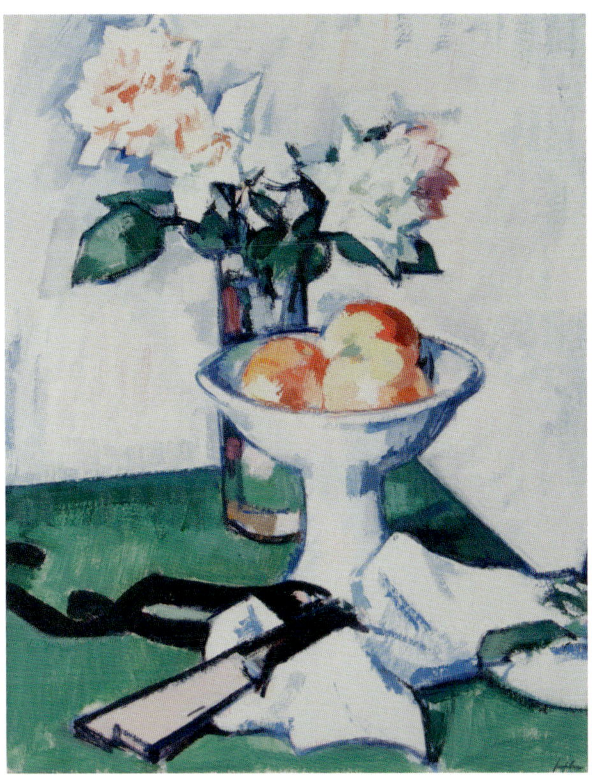

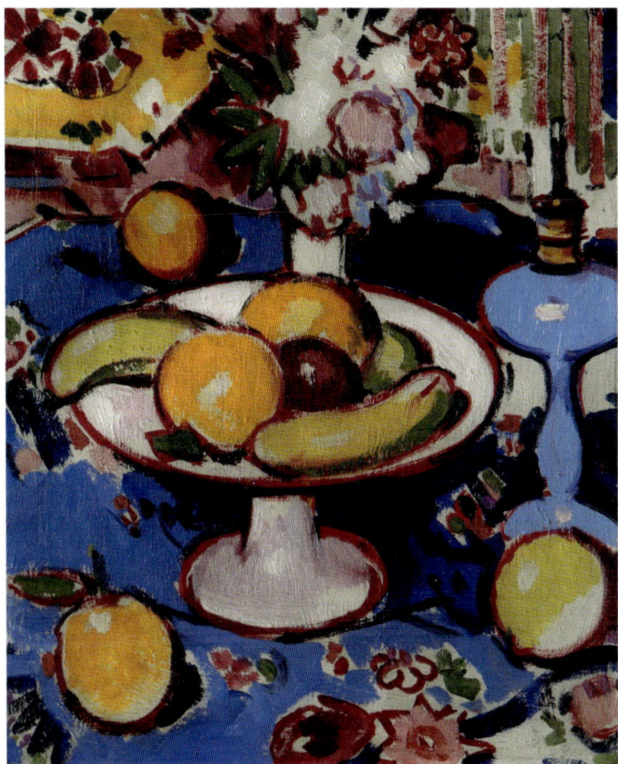

Fig. 32
S.J. Peploe (1871–1935)
*Still Life of Roses and a Bowl of Apples on a Green Tablecloth*, 1920s
Oil on canvas, 50.8 × 40.6 cm
Pallant House Gallery, Chichester
(on loan from a private collection, 2012)

Fig. 33
John Duncan Fergusson (1874–1961)
*The Blue Lamp*, 1920s
Oil on board, 45.5 × 40.3 cm
Rugby Art Gallery & Museum,
Rugby Borough Council

work he continued to create was still predominantly influenced by French modernism. His still-life paintings are not only characterised by his bold use of colour, but fruit and tableware are often outlined with prominent lines that make his compositions exceptionally stylised for the period. *The Blue Lamp* (fig. 33) is a subject the artist returned to on several occasions from around 1910. Fruit, flowers and a lamp, all placed on a decorative tablecloth, might seem like an innocent subject but Fergusson's still lifes often had strong sexual overtones: other examples of his blue lamp still lifes include a small pink box in the composition which is said to have contained Fergusson's condoms.[9]

Fergusson was close friends with Peploe and the pair would regularly work together on visits to Le Touquet, on the coast of northern France, before Peploe followed Fergusson to Paris in 1910. Peploe, originally a portrait painter, gave this up to pursue the perfect still life. Much as several of Fergusson's compositions featured the blue lamp, *Still Life of Roses and a Bowl of Apples on a Green Tablecloth* (fig. 32) is one of a number of compositions by Peploe that depict the same fan, bowl of fruit and roses, presented in different receptacles.

Just as the Scottish Colourists had been influenced by post-impressionism prior to Fry's first Grafton Galleries exhibition, several members of the Friday Club exhibited their own work inspired by the

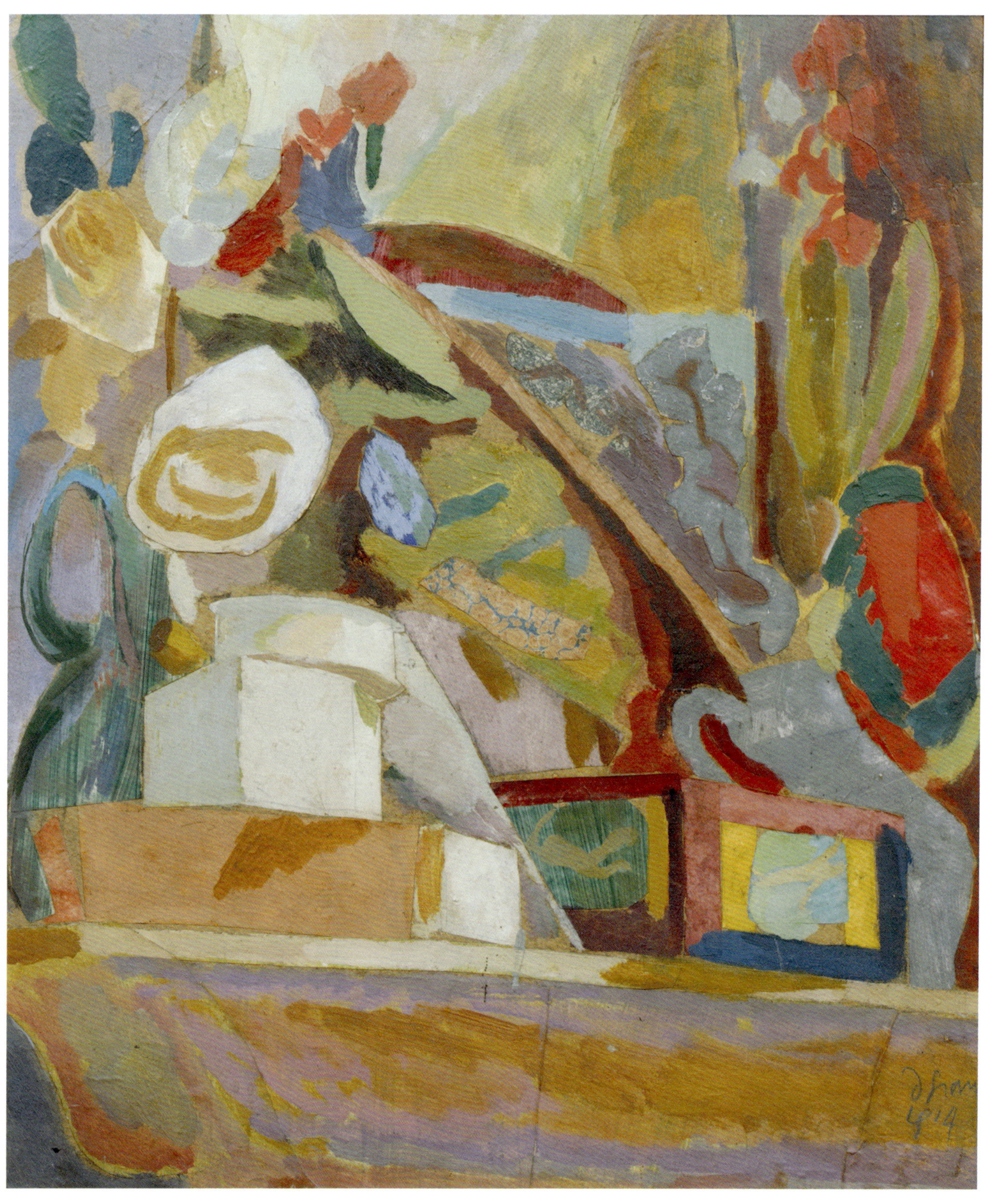

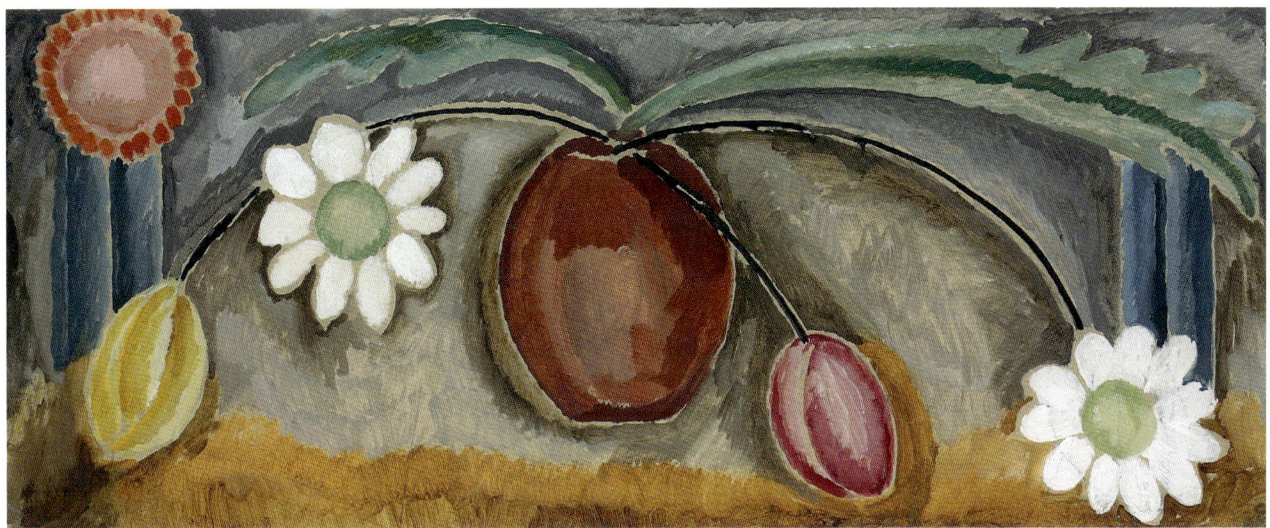

Fig. 34 (opposite)
Duncan Grant (1885–1978)
*The Mantelpiece*, 1914
Oil paint and paper on board, 45.7 × 39.4 cm
Tate: Purchased 1971

Fig. 35 (above)
Vanessa Bell (1879–1961)
*Design for Omega Bed-end: Vase of Flowers*, 1917
Oil on paper laid on board, 36.8 × 91.4 cm
Private collection, London

movement earlier in 1910, including *Lemon Gatherers* (1910, Tate) by Duncan Grant (1885–1978) which was shown alongside two still lifes by Vanessa Bell. A revival of still life as a genre was also incorporated into a new venture by Roger Fry, with Duncan Grant and Vanessa Bell as co-directors – the Omega Workshops. Founded in London in 1913, it aimed to provide a meeting place for English artists interested in post-impressionism, while also providing them with a livelihood. The Workshops had studios and a shop at 33 Fitzroy Square where artists designed fabrics, furniture and pottery, among other household items, which were for sale. They also staged exhibitions, including a display of still life in November 1916.[10]

Omega's intention to bridge fine art and decorative art meant that saleable objects often found their way into still life paintings by members. Roger Fry incorporated a paper flower and a black vase, both made in the Omega Workshops, in *Still Life with T'ang Horse* (fig. 38). In this work, he combines contemporary objects with historic Chinese objects, including a Han dynasty female statue and a sculptural horse from the Tang dynasty. Vanessa Bell and Duncan Grant both depicted the Workshop's signature paper flowers and a box by artist Frederick Etchells in *Still Life on Corner of a Mantelpiece* (1914, Tate) and *The Mantlepiece* (fig. 34), painted at Bell's home at 46 Gordon Square. The inclusion of decorative Omega objects enabled Grant and Bell to push the boundaries of Modern British still life with heightened colour and abstraction.

The same year that Grant and Bell completed their still lifes, Winifred Gill (1891–1981) painted *Still Life with Glass Jar and Silver Box* (fig. 36). This collection of objects and fruit uses a very different tonal palette to Bell's and Grant's, and unusually it is painted on the back of a laundry box top. For several years this work was thought to have been painted by Duncan

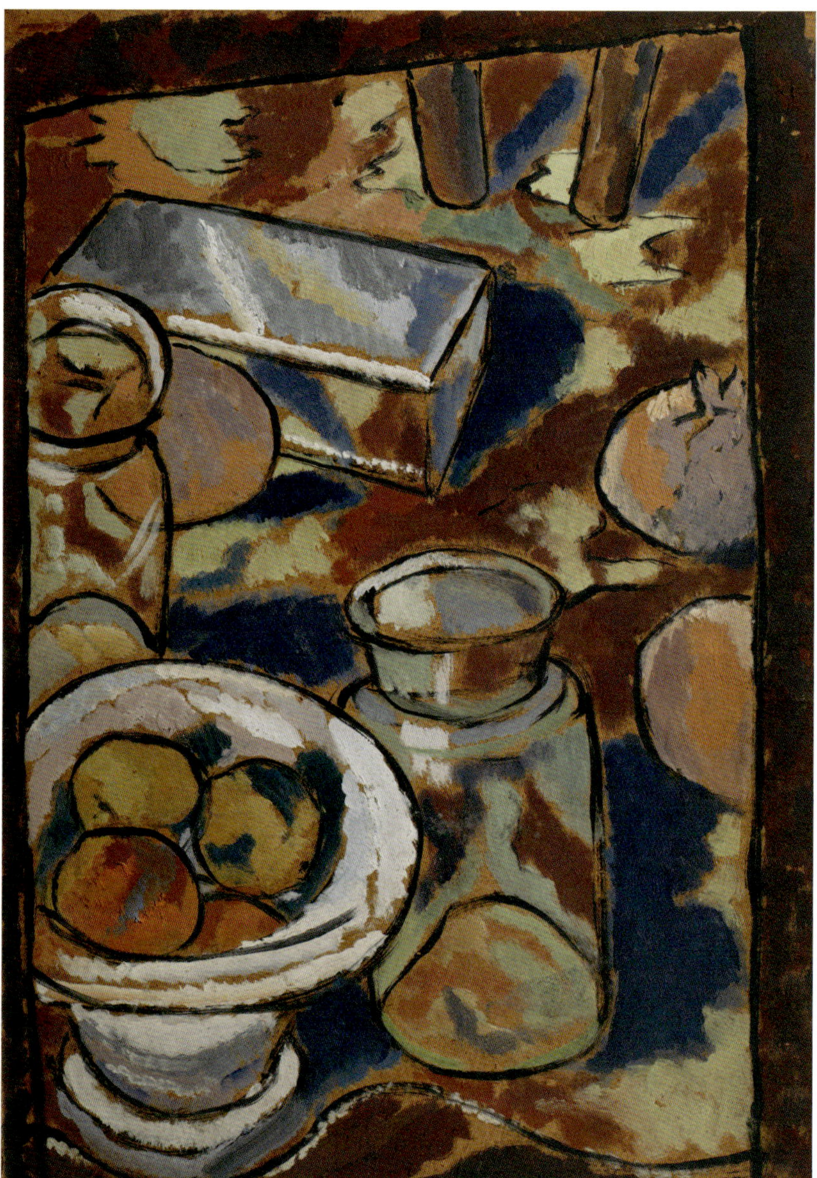

Fig. 36
Winifred Gill (1891–1981)
*Still Life with Glass Jar and Silver Box*, 1914
Oil on cardboard, 48 × 32.8 cm
The Courtauld, London (Samuel Courtauld Trust)

Grant. Stylistically their work is often similar and both artists worked at the Omega Workshops. Misattributions like this are not uncommon, with women artists often being overlooked and overshadowed by their male contemporaries. Like many women artists at the Omega Workshops, Gill was not involved in designing items for sale but was expected to translate existing designs onto articles. She did, however, create her own artwork in her spare time, while working three and a half days a week at Omega. Gill was a painter but also designed and built marionettes, similar to the wooden peg dolls explored by Mark Gertler in 1914 and again in 1926 in *The Dutch Doll* (fig. 37).

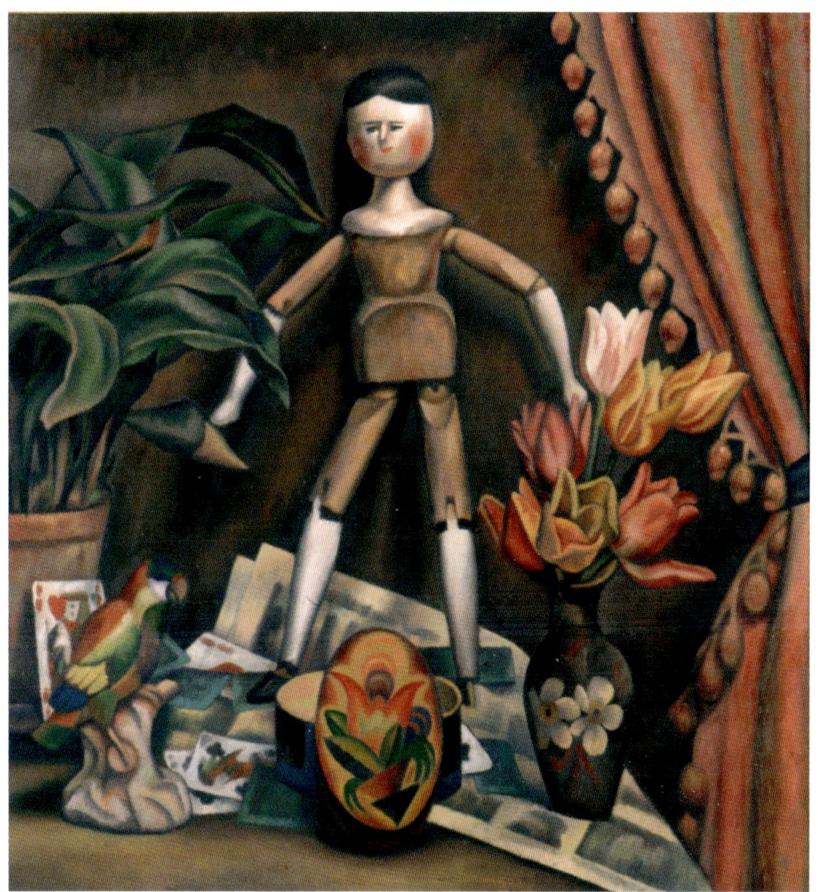

Fig. 37
Mark Gertler (1891–1939)
*The Dutch Doll*, 1926
Oil on canvas, 73.6 × 76.2 cm
Brighton & Hove Museums

Gill was instrumental in running the Omega Workshops and was made the business manager at the beginning of the First World War. Despite this dedication and her obvious capabilities, her artwork does not seem to have been valued by her contemporaries. Gill exhibited alongside Omega artists at the 1914 Grafton Group exhibition at the Alpine Club, an exhibiting society also organised by Fry. Although the Omega Workshops is often considered progressive in their inclusion of women, Gill was one of only three – with Bell and Nina Hamnett – represented in this exhibition out of 15 artists. She showed one work (undated and described only as *Interior*) which sold for only £5, the lowest price in the exhibition, while the majority of works by male artists were priced at least three times higher.[11]

Nina Hamnett began working for the Omega Workshops in 1913. She appears modelling fabric designs with Gill in one of the best-known photographs of the group.[12] With a strong interest in post-impressionism, inspired by both Fry's exhibitions at the Grafton Galleries and her own trips to Paris from 1912, Hamnett was drawn to Omega. She became known as an exceptional colourist and throughout the 1910s she produced a series of still life paintings.

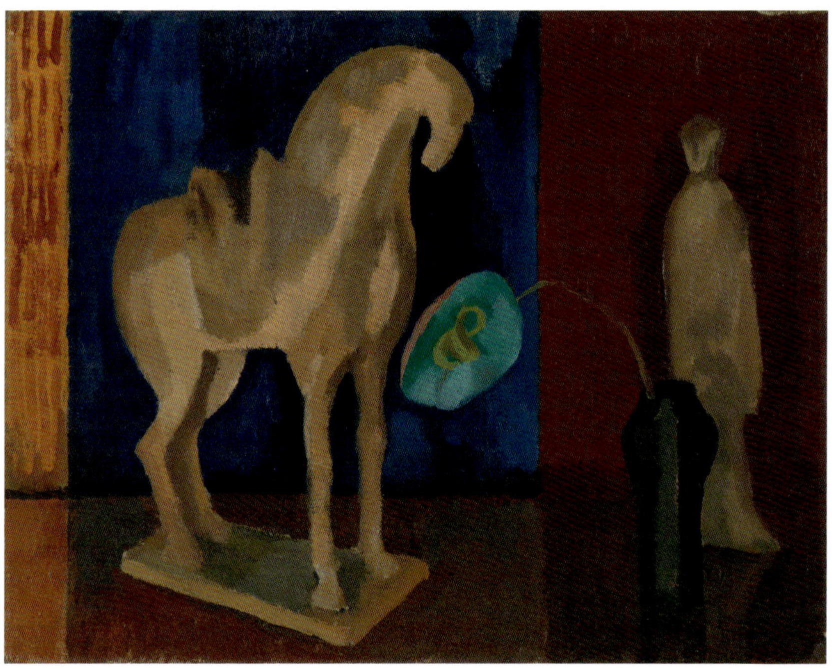

In 1918, a writer for *The Burlington Magazine* compared works by Bell and Hamnett which were on display at the Omega Workshops.

> Mrs Bell's *Paper Flowers* has the valuable qualities, especially of colour, peculiar to the rare work that may be classified as essentially feminine. Miss Hamnett is of a different type, with nerves less delicately sensitive and a robuster energy. Her paintings and drawings are vigorous and incisive.[13]

This author clearly regards Bell's paper flowers and their direct link to Omega craft as 'women's work', and yet neither Bell nor Hamnett are praised for their contributions to the exhibition in this review. Hamnett might have escaped the feminisation of her painting but to describe the artist as having 'nerves less delicately sensitive' trivialises her work by judging it through the lens of 'female hysteria'.

Hamnett's *Still Life (Blue Stove)* (fig. 39), which was probably painted a few years before 1918, shows a careful arrangement of objects at close range: a bottle and loaf of bread on a chequered tea towel and a yellow carton which could be a packet of cigarettes. The challenge in identifying some of these objects only enhances the appeal of this painting. The detail has been simplified, rendering these objects almost abstract. The background, presumably the edge of a wooden table, is made up of blocks of colour. The use of chequered fabric is comparable to work by French artists such as Pierre Bonnard (1867–1947) who, at the same time as

Fig. 38 (above)
Roger Fry (1866–1934)
*Still Life with T'ang horse*, c.1919–20
Oil on canvas, 35.6 × 45.7 cm
Tate: Presented by Mrs Pamela Diamand, the artist's daughter 1973

Fig. 39 (opposite)
Nina Hamnett (1890–1956)
*Still Life (Blue Stove)*, c.1915
Oil on canvas, 35 × 25 cm
Private collection

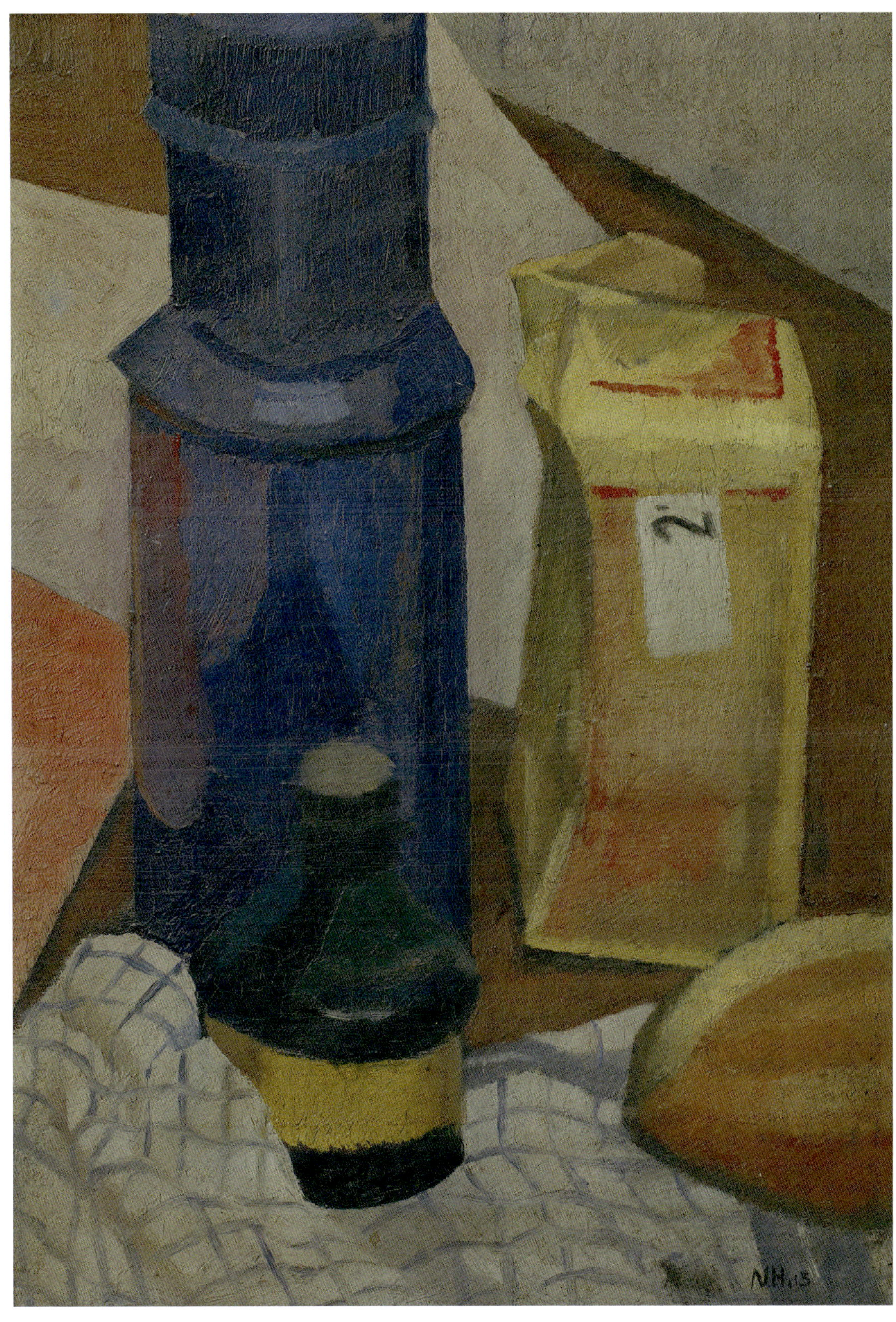

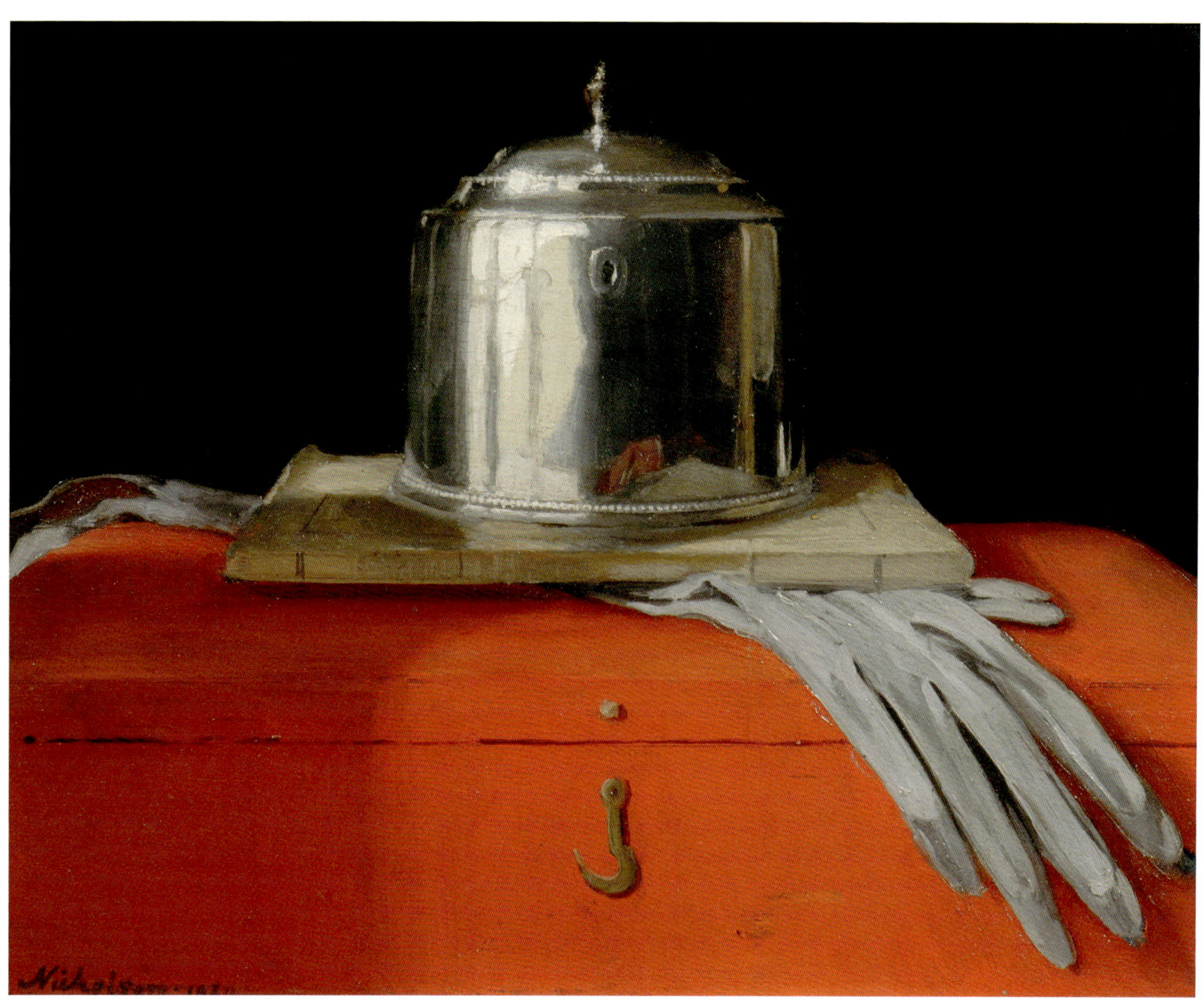

Fig. 40
William Nicholson (1872–1949)
*The Silver Casket and Red Leather Box*, 1920
Oil on panel, 33 × 40.5 cm
Private collection, courtesy
Hazlitt Holland-Hibbert, London

Hamnett, was using this fabric in his own still-life paintings such as *The Checkered Tablecloth* (1916, Metropolitan Museum of Art, New York).

Hamnett had studied at the London School of Art from 1907 until 1910 under William Nicholson, a celebrated portraitist who would become known for his realistic still-life paintings which were described as having 'a quiet poetic quality'.[14] In Hamnett's autobiography, *Laughing Torso*, she described Nicholson as 'an excellent teacher' of still life and he encouraged her to pursue her own approach to the subject.[15] Although Hamnett's still-life paintings draw on modern movements in a way that Nicholson does not, there are references to Nicholson's style in the meticulously painted reflection in the blue enamel of *Still Life (Blue Stove)*, as well as her use of a limited number of pigments.

In Patricia Reed's catalogue raisonné, she writes that 'we never simply *see* something in Nicholson; it is always being actively *described* to us' – a statement that is certainly the case in *The Silver Casket and Red Leather Box* (fig. 40).[16] In this work, Nicholson focuses the viewer's attention on the lock of the silver casket, just above centre. Here the artist plays with the 'paradoxes of containment and uncontainment'; the red box and the casket are both closed and yet the reflection on the silverware describes the room to the viewer, including a large floor-to-ceiling window.[17] The silverware in this still life is the same that Nicholson used in *The Silver Casket* (1916, private collection). The casket is by Hester Bateman (1708–1794), an 18th-century silversmith who became renowned for her flatware and ornamental silverware. Interestingly, the red leather box and the gloves in this painting have been altered since Nicholson first completed it. A black-and-white photograph, thought to have been taken just before the Goupil Gallery Salon exhibition at which it was displayed in 1920, shows a box decorated with diamond patterning and evidence of this pattern can be seen beneath the red paint. It is thought that Nicholson changed the colour of the box just before the exhibition for reasons unknown.

Unlike Nicholson, who often included expensive glassware and silverware in his still lifes, Hamnett focused on a range of increasingly simple domestic objects.[18] Like Walter Sickert (1872–1949), she excluded the reams of soft white linen cradling fruit that are often seen in French post-impressionist still lifes; instead, Hamnett and Sickert's tables are often bare wood and evoke farmhouse kitchens and bohemian pubs and bars in Fitzrovia rather than staged artists' studios. Sickert's still lifes often depict crockery and humble food items in pared-back compositions such as *Mushrooms* (fig. 42) which was painted around 1919–20. A preliminary sketch of *Mushrooms*, which was sold at auction in the late 1990s, shows Sickert's continuing development of this composition, with the glass in a different position from the finished painting.[19]

Hamnett's friendship with Sickert began in 1911 when she attended Saturday afternoon gatherings referred to as 'At Home' days at his studio

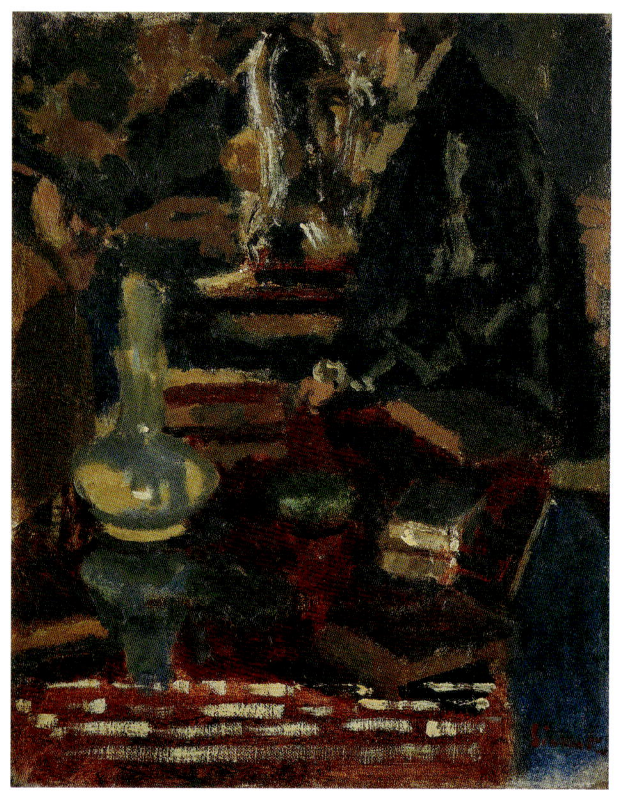

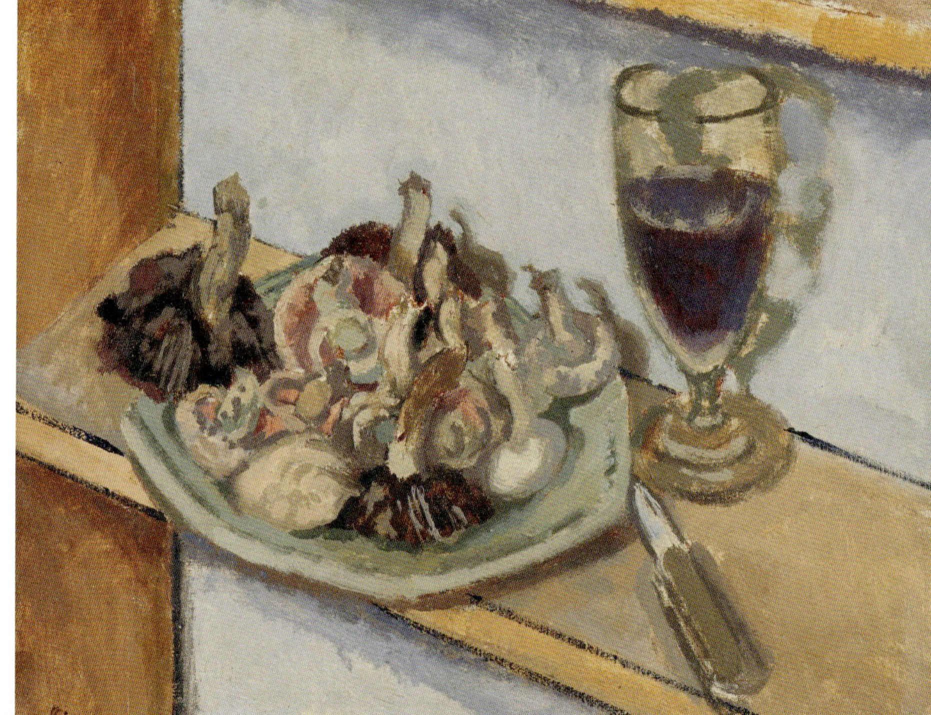

Fig. 41
Walter Sickert (1860–1942)
*Still Life on a Table*, c.1913
Oil on canvas, 41 × 33.5 cm
Pallant House Gallery, Chichester
(Kearley Bequest, through Art Fund, 1989)

Fig. 42
Walter Sickert (1860–1942)
*Mushrooms*, c.1919–20
Oil on canvas, 33 × 40.6 cm
Private collection

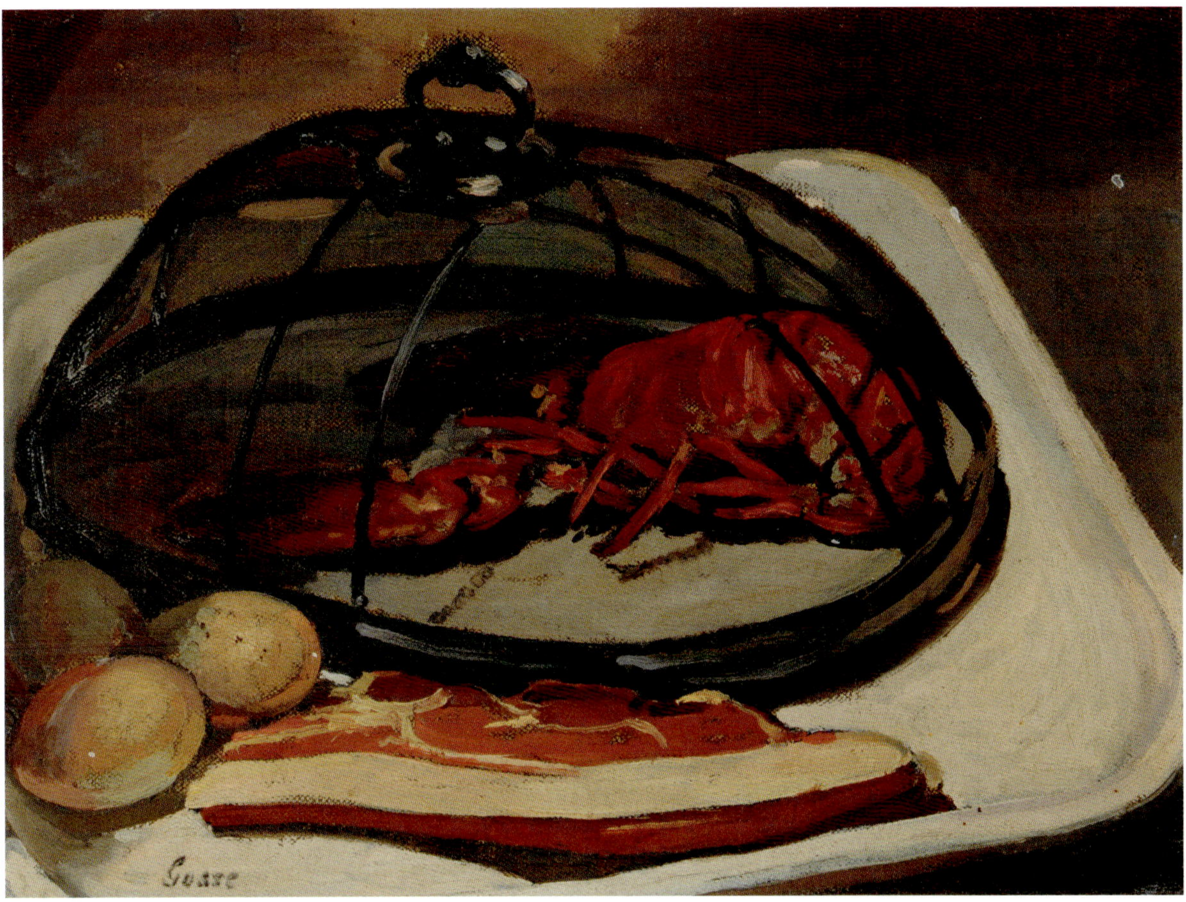


Fig. 43
Sylvia Gosse (1881–1968)
*Still Life with a Lobster*, c.1923
Oil on canvas, 26.7 × 35.6 cm
University of Hull Art Collection

in Fitzroy Street. For a period, Hamnett lived opposite Sickert and wrote in her autobiography that she painted artificial flowers in a white vase which Sickert had bought her and he began to invite her for breakfast.[20] Although Hamnett valued Sickert as a friend and certainly benefitted from his large network of artists and patrons, she did not appreciate Sickert trying to mentor her and often ignored his suggestions in order to develop her own style and technique.[21]

During the 1910s, Sickert had assumed the patriarchal role of a mentor for several artists including the Camden Town Group and the artist Sylvia Gosse (1881–1968). Following studies at St John's Wood School of Art and then the Royal Academy Schools until 1908, Gosse studied etching at Sickert's evening classes at the Westminster School of Art and then at his new art school on the Hampstead Road. After a year, Gosse took over the school's administration and finances, leading to it being renamed the Sickert and Gosse School of Painting and Etching.

Like Sickert and Hamnett, and no doubt reflecting his influence, Gosse's still lifes are often humble in subject. The simple white serving plate in *Still Life with a Lobster* (fig. 43) takes centre stage over lavish

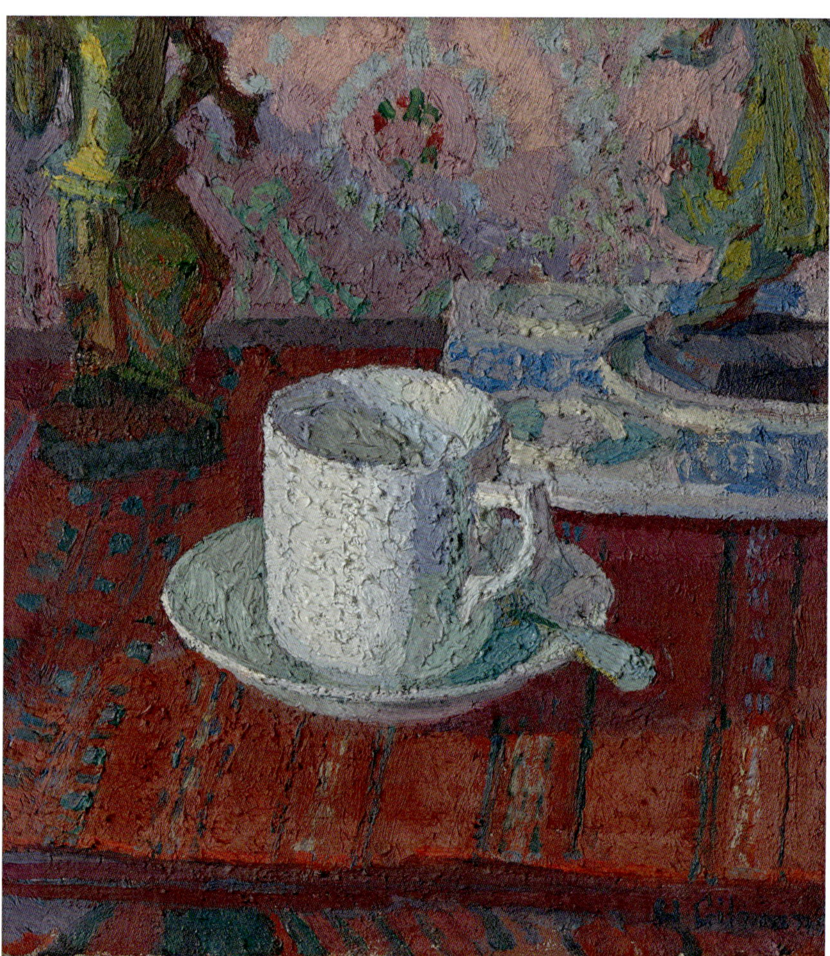

Fig. 44
Harold Gilman (1876–1919)
*The Cup and Saucer*, 1915
Oil on canvas, 29 × 27 cm
Private collection, courtesy of Offer Waterman, London

tableware. Her subjects – lobster, bacon and three potatoes – are an unusual choice for a woman artist of this period, yet her handling of the paint to create both modernism and realism in her work exceeds some of Sickert's most accomplished still lifes. The inclusion of a lobster in her painting recalls 17th-century Dutch still lifes by artists such as Willem Claesz Heda whose work she would have seen in the National Gallery in London; however, her close perspective of these objects and the tilted perspective of the plate reimagines the Dutch still life for a contemporary audience.

Following his 'At Home' gatherings, which were attended by both Hamnett and Gosse, Sickert formally established the Camden Town Group in 1911. Fry's poorly reviewed first post-impressionist exhibition had also prompted hostility from exhibiting societies such as the New English Art Club, which was making it increasingly difficult for artists interested in post-impressionism to exhibit. This led to several of Sickert's artist friends banding together to form their own group which would produce 'little pictures for little patrons'.[21] The Camden Town Group, which included

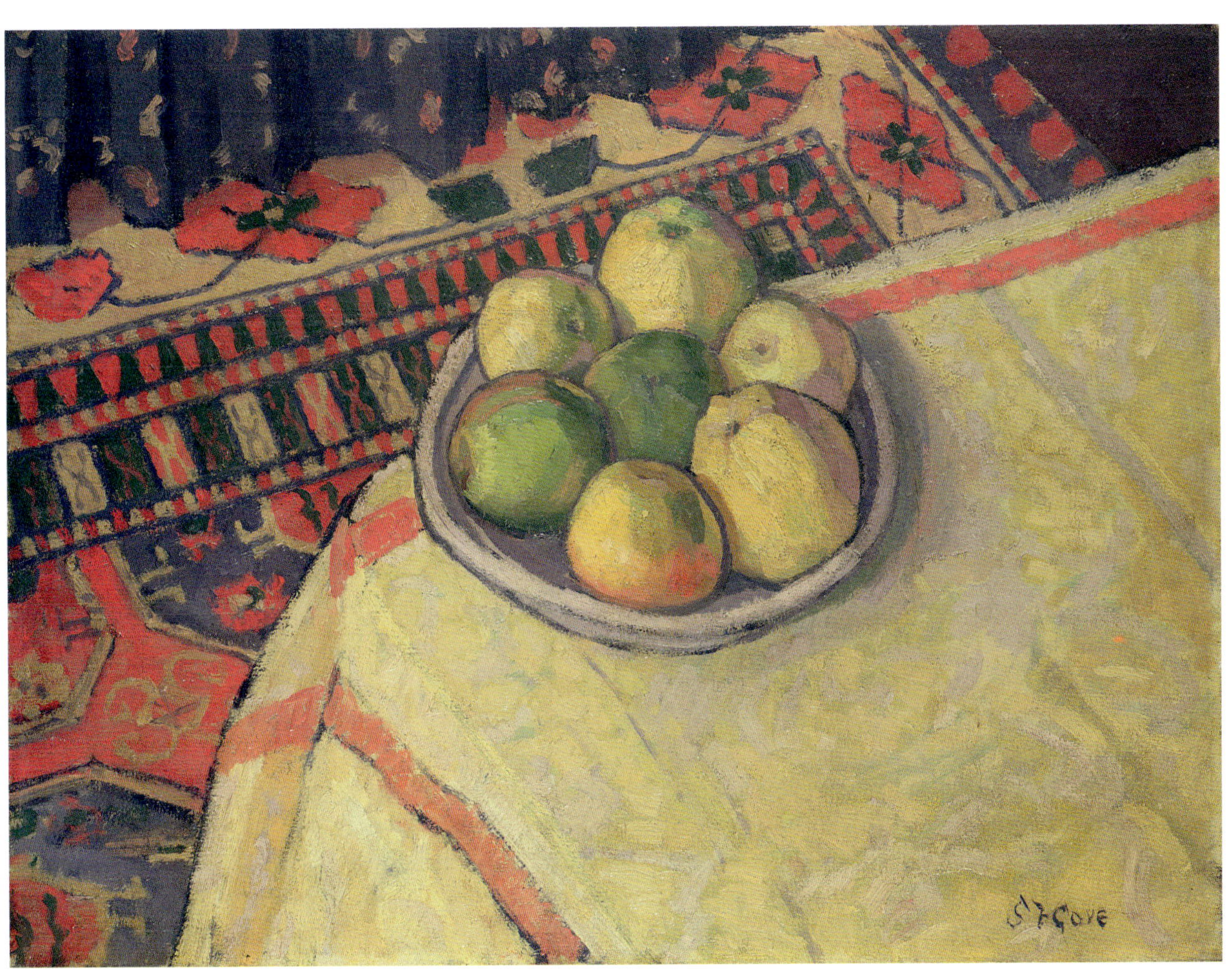

Fig. 45
Spencer Gore (1878–1914)
*Still Life with Apples*, 1912
Oil on canvas, 38.2 × 50.8 cm
Ferens Art Gallery: Hull Museums

Sickert, Charles Ginner (1878–1952), Robert Bevan (1865–1925), Spencer Gore (1878–1914) and Harold Gilman (1876–1919), insisted the group exclude women. Although Gosse and Hamnett are often associated with the Camden Town Group, and Gosse exhibited six works with the group in the *Exhibition of the Camden Town Group and Others* (1913–14, Brighton City Art Gallery), they were not members and their work has been marginalised and overlooked within the narrative of Modern British art history.

Through their portraits and urban landscapes, the Camden Town Group wanted their work to reflect the realities of modern life and, though perhaps not the obvious subject, still life allowed them to achieve this. Harold Gilman's painting *The Cup and Saucer* (fig. 44) shows simple white crockery surrounded by decorative surfaces of the patterned tablecloth and wallpaper, also seen in the background of his portrait of *Mrs Victor Sly* (1914–15, Hepworth Wakefield). Although the subject of this still life is relatively simple – it might even be interpreted as a portrait of a cup and saucer – Gilman chose to use a pointillist technique which not only gives the work an unusual texture, in contrast to the glossy finish applied by artists like Nicholson, but enabled Gilman to interpret French modernism in a new and exciting way.

Gilman was another artist who had been inspired by Fry's post-impressionist exhibitions but had also travelled to Europe to see work first-hand after leaving the Slade School of Fine Art in 1912. Among Gilman's friends was another former Slade student, Spencer Gore. Gore's *Still Life with Apples* (fig. 45) demonstrates a very different painting style to Gilman's with a matt, almost chalky texture, giving the work the quality of a pastel drawing at first glance. Yet his interpretation of French modernism has certainly been influenced by Cezanne's depictions of fruit, with unusual perspectives and flattened compositions. The use of shadows or *chiaroscuro* on the apples is the only direct perspectival reference point which cleverly draws the viewer's eye into the bowl.

The Camden Town Group did not last long and only exhibited their work between 1911 and 1914, when the organisation transitioned into the London Group and artists such as Matthew Smith (1879–1959), who had studied in Henri Matisse's atelier in 1911, joined their exhibitions. Although the Camden Town Group – including Gosse and Hamnett – were undoubtedly influenced by French modernism, each of these British artists found different methods and subjects within the genre of still life to create some of their most interesting work. The Camden Town Group, the Scottish Colourists, the Omega Workshops and Vanessa Bell's Friday Club, where it arguably all began, were all impacted by post-impressionism. However, it was the versatility of the genre of still life that allowed these artists to experiment with the movement and impact Modern British art for the first time.

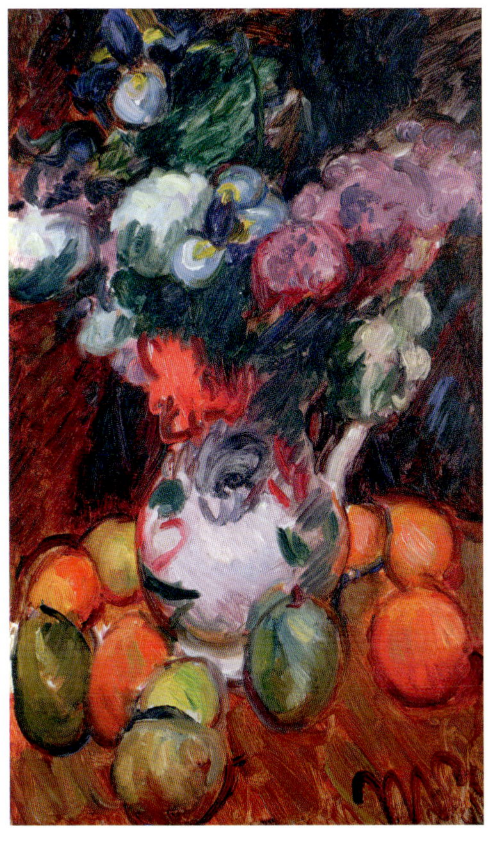

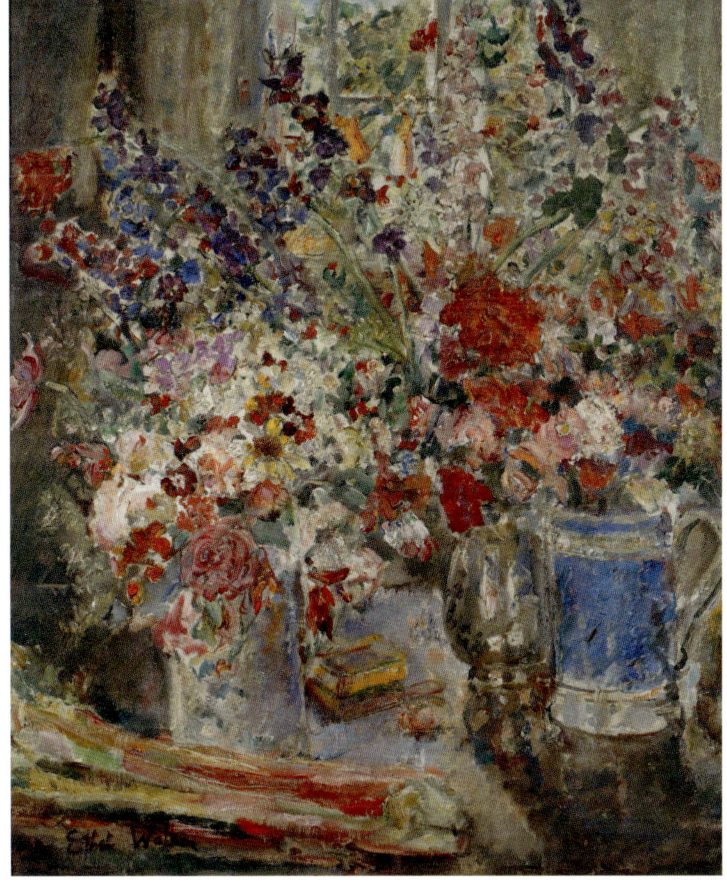

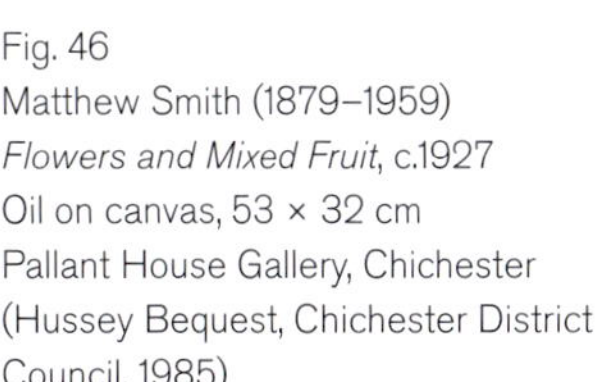

Fig. 46
Matthew Smith (1879–1959)
*Flowers and Mixed Fruit*, c.1927
Oil on canvas, 53 × 32 cm
Pallant House Gallery, Chichester (Hussey Bequest, Chichester District Council, 1985)

Fig. 47
Ethel Walker (1861–1951)
*Flower Piece No. 4*, c.1930
Oil on canvas, 76.7 × 64 cm
The Courtauld, London (Samuel Courtauld Trust)

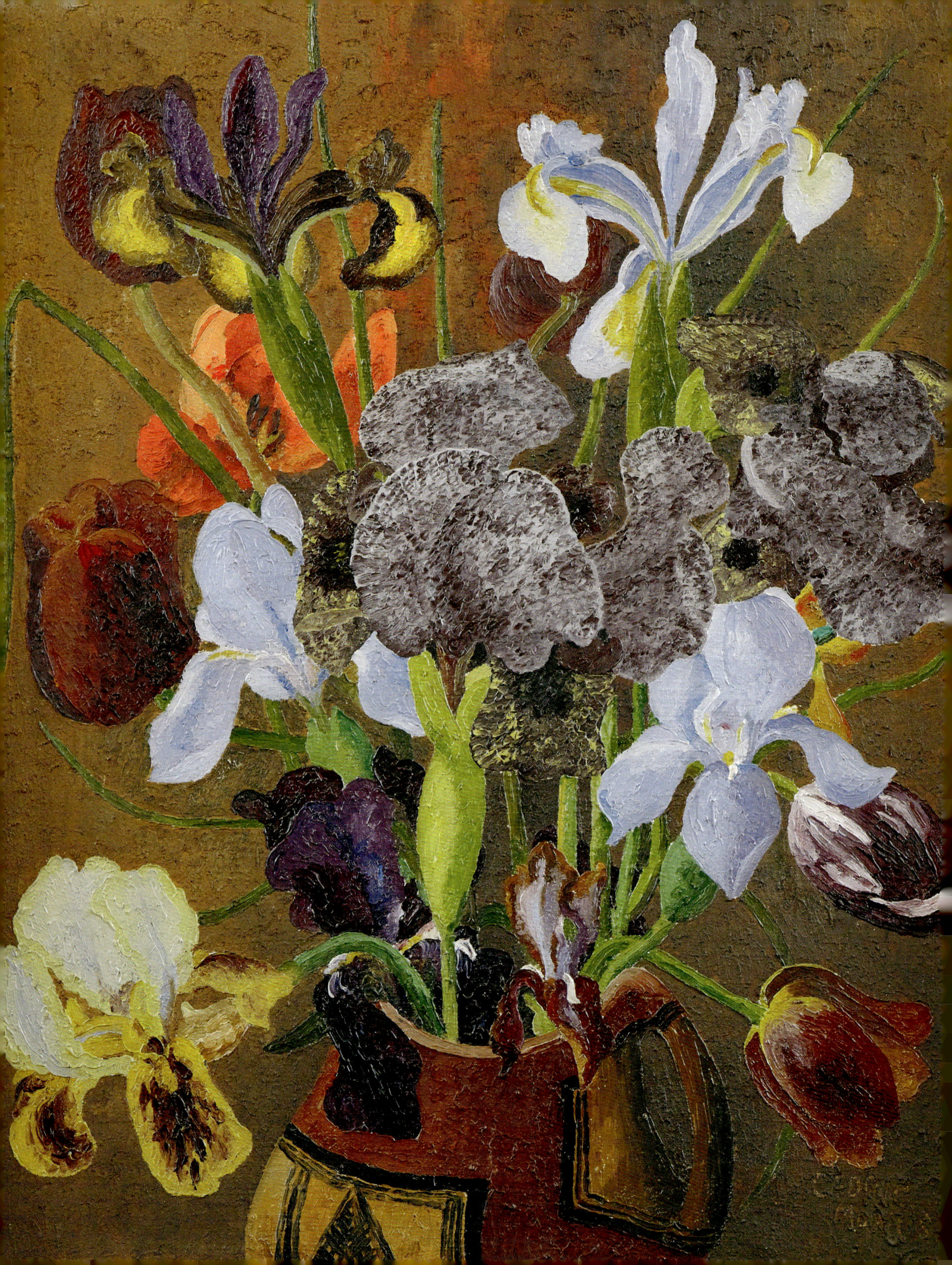

# 3 'Reality and the other thing': Still Life in Interwar Britain

CHLOE NAHUM AND EMMA SHARPLES

Writing in the pages of *The Listener* in 1931, Paul Nash (1889–1946) heralded the demise of the still life. 'The tyrannical reign of Nature Morte is, at last, over', he declared. 'Apples have had their day.'[1] As one of its pioneers through the 1920s and 1930s, Nash's diagnosis of a genre in decline is somewhat surprising and, indeed, misleading: still life stood at the forefront of artistic innovation throughout the period. Yet, rather than denouncing it wholesale, Nash's impatience was with a style that had come to gradual prominence in Britain following Roger Fry's post-impressionist exhibitions of 1910 and 1912. The now moribund apple stood as a tired symbol of the movement, having captivated the Bloomsbury group in the work of Paul Cezanne and become much emulated by British painters.[2]

Distilling what he saw to be the particular ingenuity of Ben Nicholson's (1894–1982) work, in the same article, Nash signalled a new direction in still life painting, stating that Nicholson held 'an intenser regard for the juxtaposition of paraphernalia'.[3] Animating his brief analysis are two ideas that shaped many explorations of the genre in these decades. First is the intensity of design, or 'structural purpose', that Nash would claim to be the mark of a 'contemporary spirit' in 1933.[4] Second is the sense of chance and contradiction contained in the notion of juxtaposition. Impelled by the psychological devastation wrought by the First World War, a resultant interest in dreams and the unconscious mind, as made newly intelligible through Freudian methods of interpretation and free association, became a source of fascination in the early part of the 20th century. These dual concerns – on the one hand a meticulous attention to composition, structure and design, and on the other a dance of obfuscation and ambivalence – reinvigorated still life in the interwar period.

Fig. 48
Cedric Morris (1889–1982)
*Irises and tulips*, 1935
Oil on canvas, 61 × 50.8 cm
Private collection

Caught between two world wars, British society grappled with psychic shocks that were indelibly forged in the wastelands of the first and soon to be reinforced by the next – a keen sense of human fragility and, in bewildering opposition, its capacity to enact unbridled violence. Many artists, most famously Nash, saw both conflicts at first hand. How did these historical circumstances take seats at tables set for still life? Ever capacious in its absorption of manifold concerns, the genre was recharged in this era of worldwide, mechanised conflict.[5] Objects were recruited to many causes: some as a refuge from modern life; others dredged up from the dream world to undermine the seeming rationality of modernity. A genre with a fraught relation to its own gendered implications, artists worked to unravel still life's proximity to the domestic in the wake of newly won emancipation for women.[6] In addition, the medium opened itself out to the possibilities of representation in light of the early 20th-century's self-conscious questioning of gendered categories.

As the First World War raged, so too did debates about its effects on the arts. The opinion of one commentator, writing in 1915, is revealing: 'The Vorticists and the Imagists and the Futurists and the rest of the rabble of literary and artistic lunatics provided slender entertainment for empty days; but our minds are empty no longer; and we have no time to waste on monkeys on sticks'.[7] Such predictions would, to some degree, bear out in the war's aftermath. A new classical quietude had emerged in the visual arts, identified in France in 1919 by the cubist André Lhote (1885–1962) as a '*rappel à l'ordre*', or return to order.[8]

The diminution of a more rabble-rousing modernism seems encapsulated in the Seven & Five Society, which was founded in the same year and held its first exhibition in 1920.[9] The accompanying catalogue did not so much proclaim as whisper the Society's objective: 'merely to express what they feel in terms that shall be intelligible, and not to demonstrate a theory or attack a tradition'.[10] Though 'grateful to the pioneers', the authors believed that 'there has been of late too much pioneering along too many lines in altogether too much of a hurry'.[11] In spite of, or perhaps due to, this mild-mannered and somewhat vague agenda, by the end of the decade it stood as one of the country's leading exhibiting societies. Subject and style adhered to the needs of a society anxious to forget the recent horror of war. Seven & Five artists such as Winifred Nicholson (1893–1981) and David Jones (1895–1974) worked in a lyrical mode often centred upon a still life set before a window, through which a landscape was seen. In the interior tranquillity of such works, a sense of domestic quietude was being shored up against memory of the war's destruction of bodies, nature and things.

This violent annihilation had been experienced by various members of the Society in different ways – for Nicholson as a maker of plaster casts for artificial limbs required for amputee servicemen, and for Jones as a private on the Western Front. Jones's witnessing of war's devastation

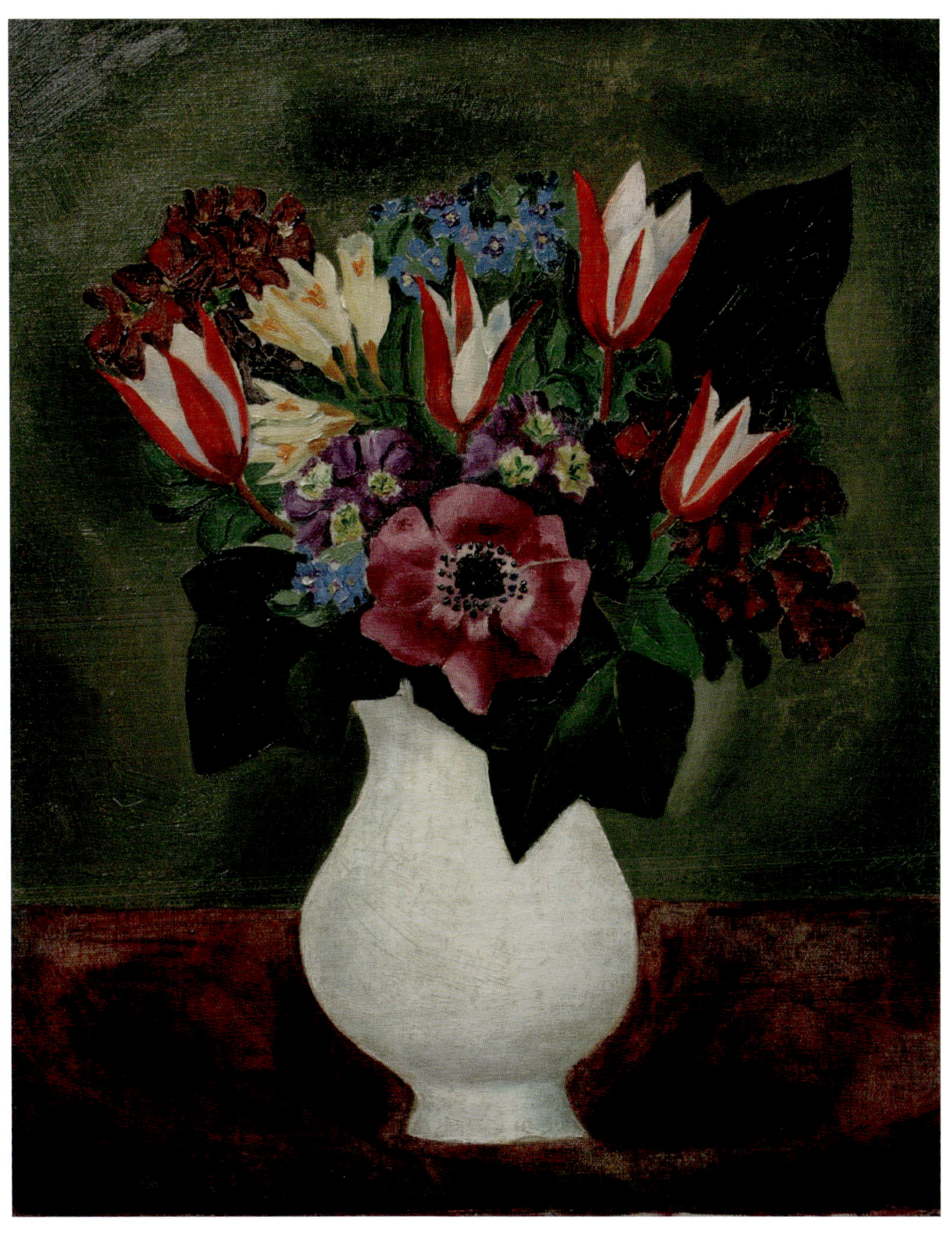

Fig. 49
Christopher Wood (1901–1930)
*The White Vase*, 1930
Oil on canvas on board, 46 × 38 cm
Pallant House Gallery, Chichester
(Bequeathed by Ian Mylles with Art Fund support 2021)

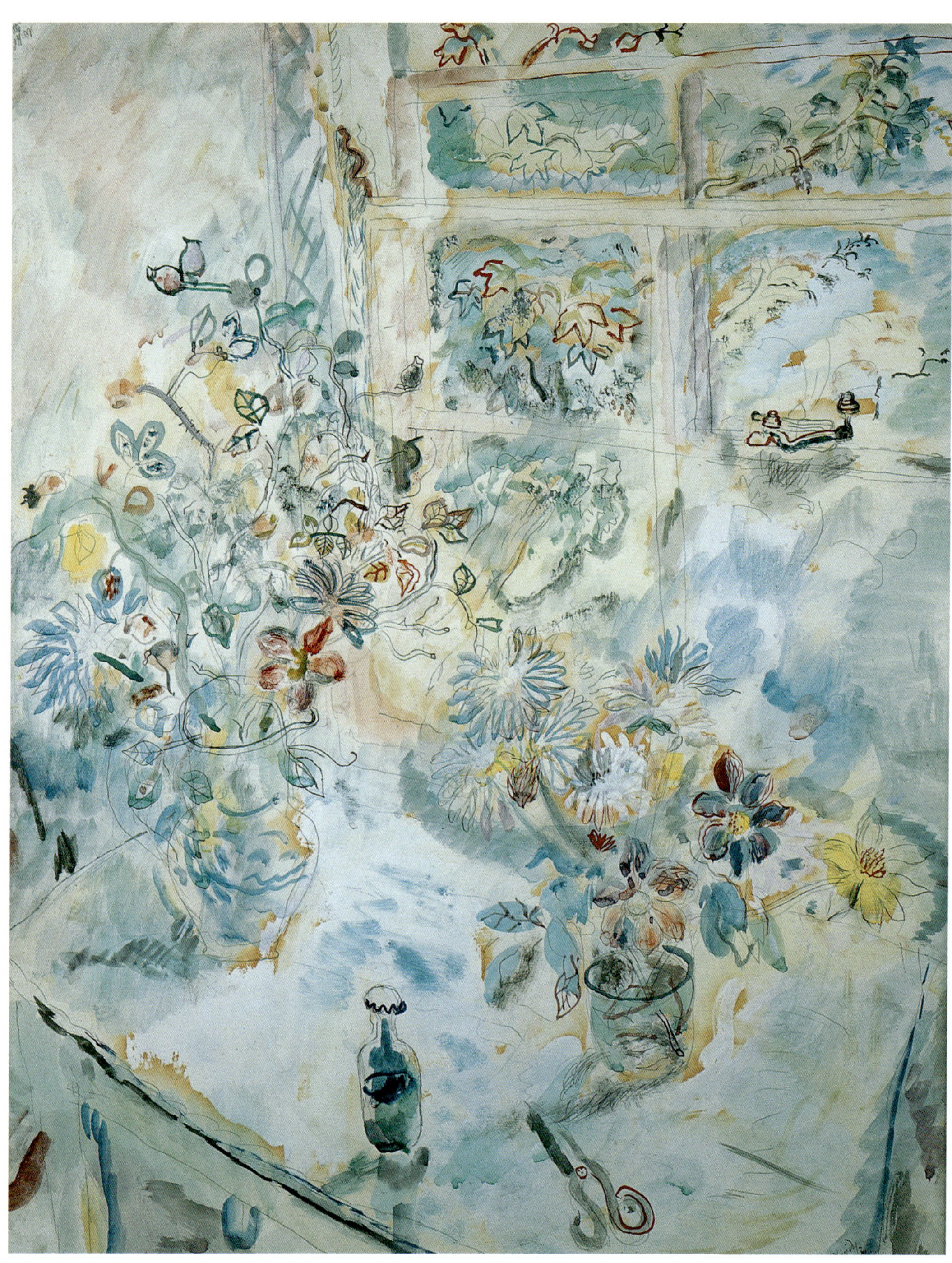

Fig. 50
David Jones (1895–1974)
*July Change*, 1930
Watercolour on paper, 59.5 × 46.7 cm
Pallant House Gallery, Chichester
(Kearley Bequest through Art Fund, 1989)

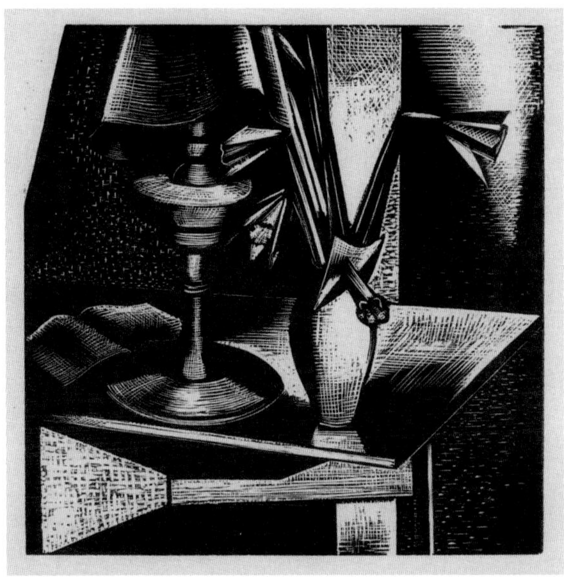

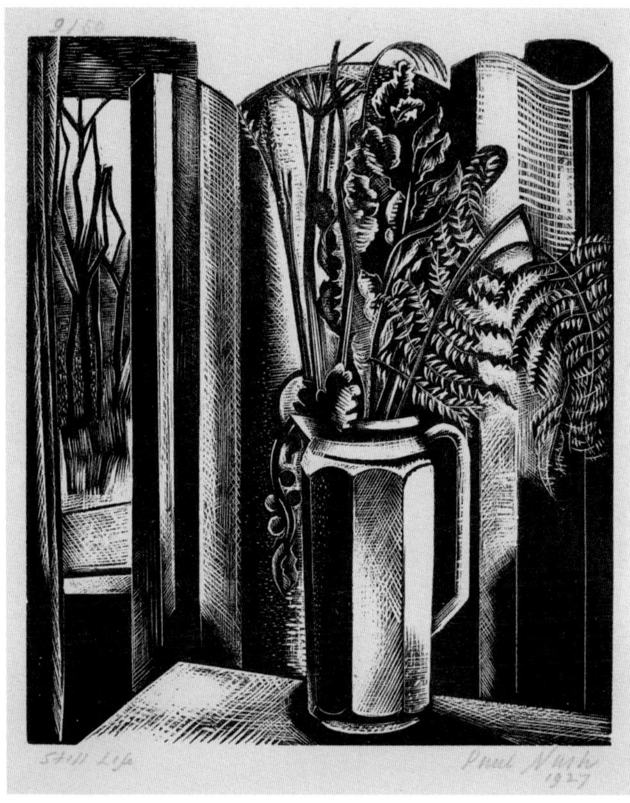


Fig. 51
Paul Nash (1889–1946)
*Still Life No.1*, 1925
Wood engraving on paper, 11.5 × 11.5 cm
Pallant House Gallery, Chichester
(The Clare Neilson Collection Presented by Jeremy Greenwood and Alan Swerdlow through Art Fund, 2013)

Fig. 52
Paul Nash (1889–1946)
*Still Life No.2*, 1927
Wood engraving on paper, 25.5 × 18.2 cm
Pallant House Gallery, Chichester
(The Clare Neilson Collection Presented by Jeremy Greenwood and Alan Swerdlow through Art Fund, 2013)

('relentless, mechanical' as he would remember it),[12] seems inextricable from his retreat into airy, resplendent table-scapes such as *July Change* (fig. 50), made from the 'reasonably sheltered position' in which he favoured working.[13] Indeed, in *July Change* the outside world is subordinate to that which takes place within four walls, for while vegetation is visible beyond the window frame, it becomes amplified and resplendent upon breaking into the interior. Though the painting feels accordingly untroubled by the world beyond the window, a muted memory of that conflict intrudes in a pair of scissors placed in the foreground, reminding us, in the tradition of the *memento mori*, that this luxuriant flora, cut and arranged in jugs, faces imminent decay. Words that Jones would author in his epic war poem *In Parenthesis* (1937), on which he was working at this time, speak pertinently to this in the precarity of the living thing met with the weaponry of war: it is 'disproportionate in its violence considering / the fragility of us'.[14]

Jones untethered line from shadow in his depiction of the object, creating what Paul Hills has described as the 'air shadow' which casts a diaphanous mist over Jones's watercolours.[15] These works shared aesthetic concerns with those of Ben Nicholson, who had nominated Jones for membership in 1928 and whose own innovations in still life greatly excited him in their 'tightrope balancing of representation and

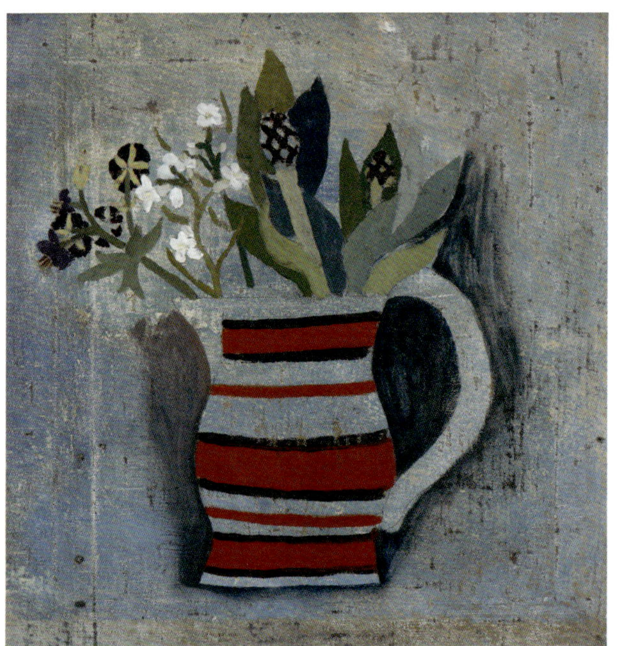

Fig. 53
Ben Nicholson (1894–1982)
*1928 (striped jug and flowers)*, 1928
Oil on canvas, 38 × 37 cm
Private collection

design'.[16] Nicholson had inherited his interest in still life from his father, William Nicholson, both in his deft and extensive handling of the genre and in the considerable collection of 'jugs mugs and goblets' around which he recalled growing up.[17] Yet, in the 1920s, Nicholson departed from his father's interest in the surface of the represented object and moved towards sustained investigation of the surface of the canvas and a cubism-influenced deconstruction of the object. Early inquiry into new ways of representing the object world is visible in the flattening of *1928 (striped jug and flowers)* (fig. 53), the planar surfaces of which presage his reliefs of the next decade.[18] Nicholson's own progression into abstraction would also shape the direction of the Seven & Five, renamed the 7 & 5 Society in 1932, and then Seven & Five Abstract Group under his presidency in 1934 and becoming in turn a conduit for a more patently modern and continental school of art.

With this development came the departure of a number of the group's more figurative artists, including Edward Bawden (1903–1989), Frances Hodgkins (1869–1947) and Cedric Morris (1889–1982). Outside of the Society's parameters, the less ostensibly avant-garde styles pursued by these and other artists remained commercially viable into the 1930s, catering to that section of society insulated from the troubled economic history of the interwar years. Whilst the subject matter of still life was gathered from the ornament and detritus of the domestic interior, these works became commodities in themselves and took their place on the walls of fashionable society homes, becoming, in the words of the critic R.H. Wilenski, 'wall

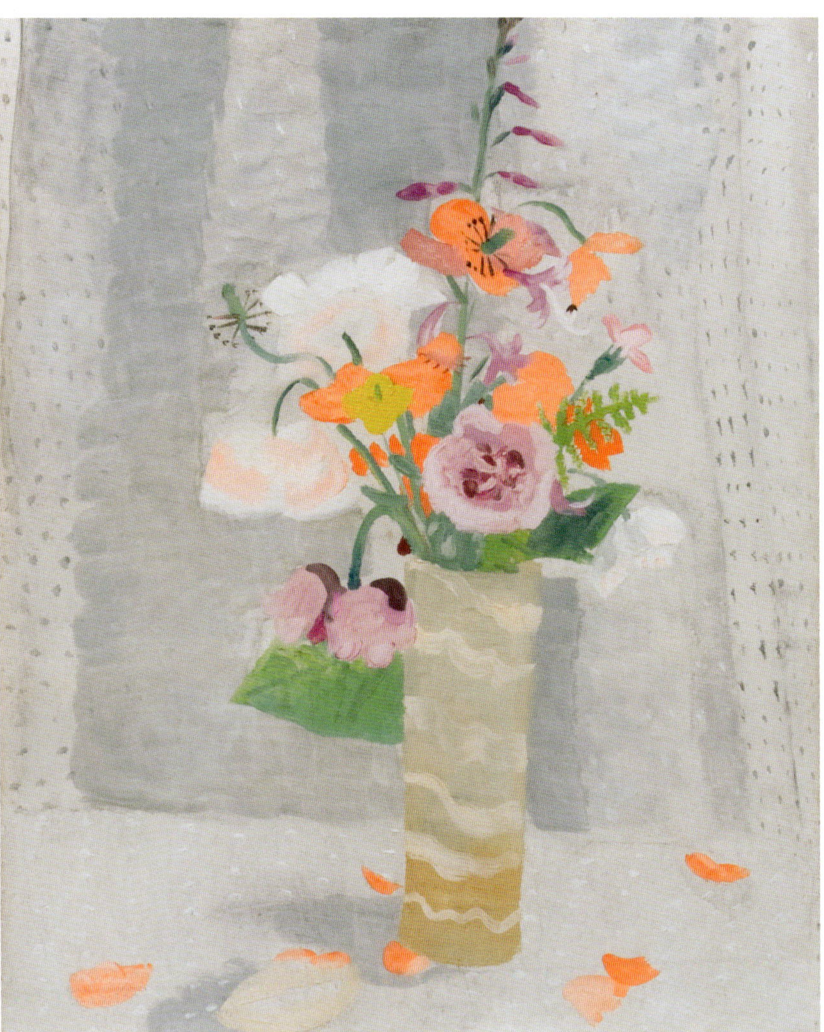

Fig. 54
Winifred Nicholson (1893–1981)
*Vermillion and Mauve*, c.1928
Oil on board, 66 × 54.5 cm
Private collection

furniture'.[19] The all-white interiors popularised by society designer Syrie Maugham threw off the remnants of Edwardian trappings – they were 'Like the countryside after a hard frost … shimmer[ing] with plate glass and chromium steel against pickled or limed panelling, with fabrics in the natural shantung shades of silks and unbleached linen and cotton'.[20] Nonetheless, floral painting could survive this cull of ornament provided it remained clear-hewn in design through the colourful and rhythmical organisation of stems, or offered some novelty, as in the work of Morris, which retained 'something of the child's wonder at ordinary things'.[21]

Morris's contemporary, the painter and sculptor Glyn Philpot (1884–1937), never joined any of the more progressive groups of the 1930s, having been elected a Royal Academician in 1923. However, his departure from the academic and old master traditions of his earlier portraiture into still life coincided with a period of artistic renewal, which led the artist to

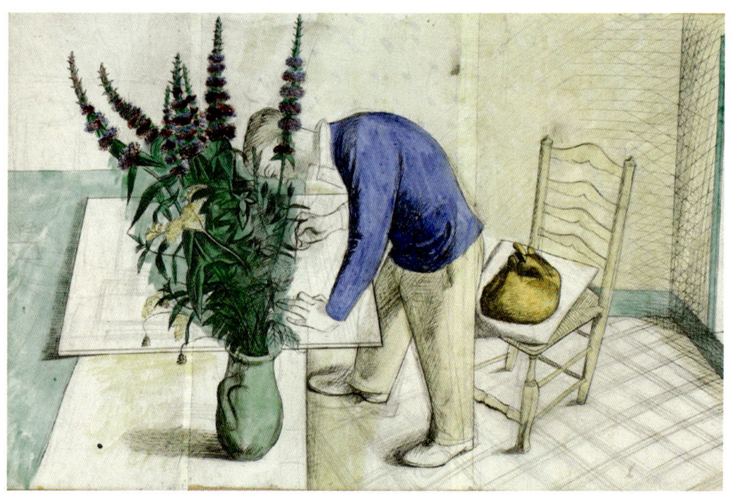

Fig. 55
Edward Bawden (1903–1989)
*The Boy – Eric Ravilious in his studio at Redcliffe Road*, 1929
Watercolour on paper, 42.8 × 66.5 cm
Towner Eastbourne

Fig. 56
Eric Ravilious (1903–1942)
*Ironbridge Interior*, 1941
Watercolour and pencil on paper, 46 × 57.7 cm
Private collection on loan to Towner Eastbourne

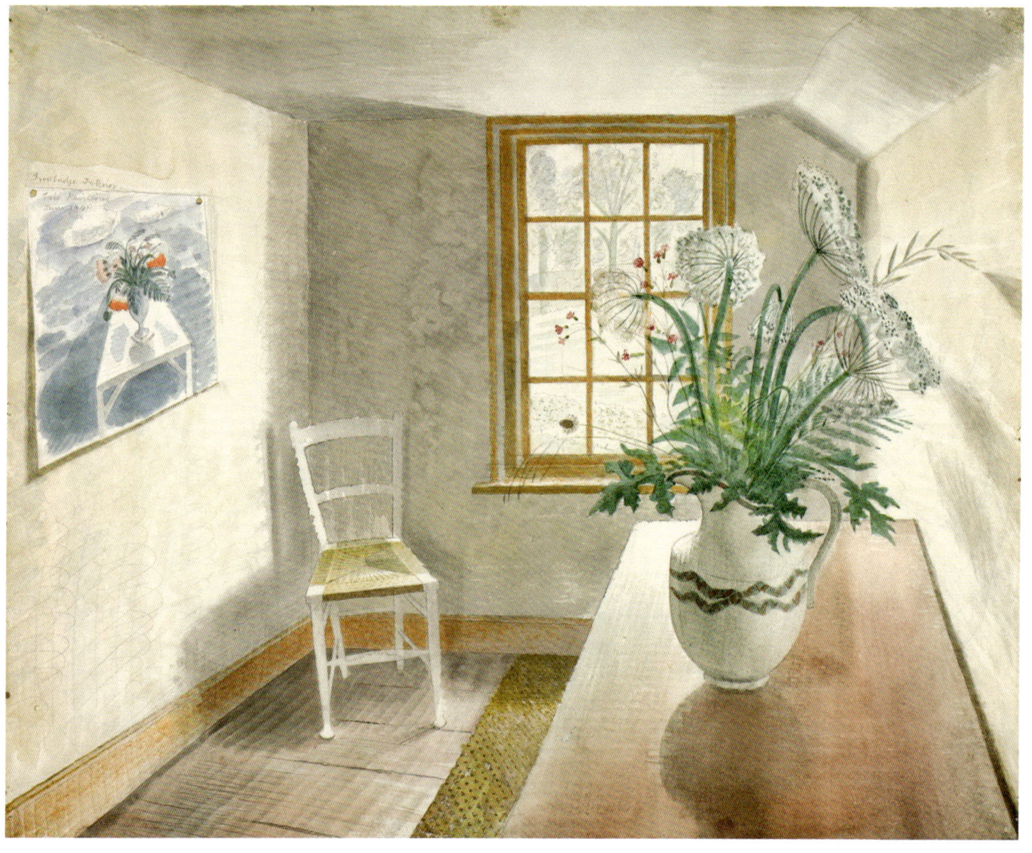

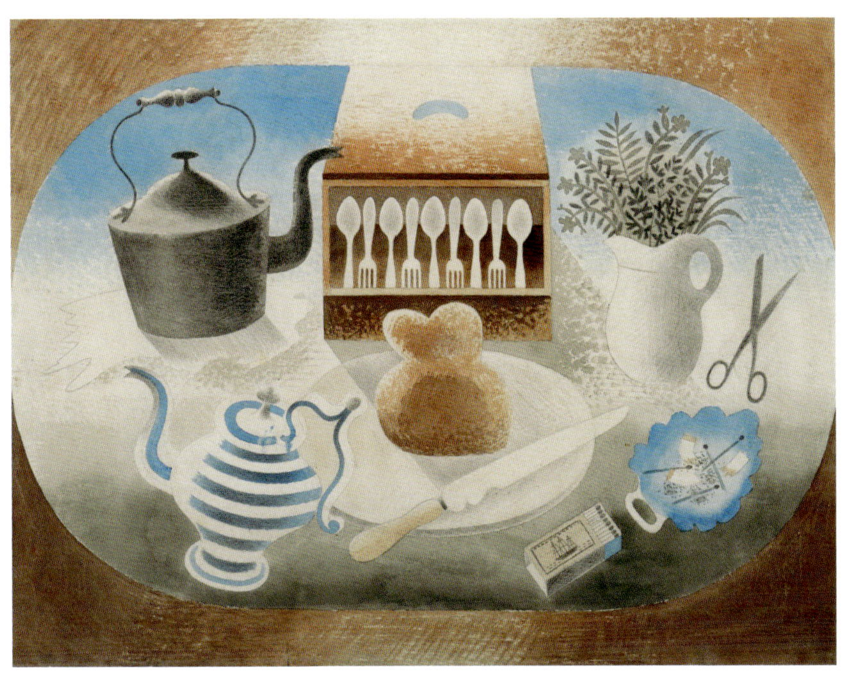

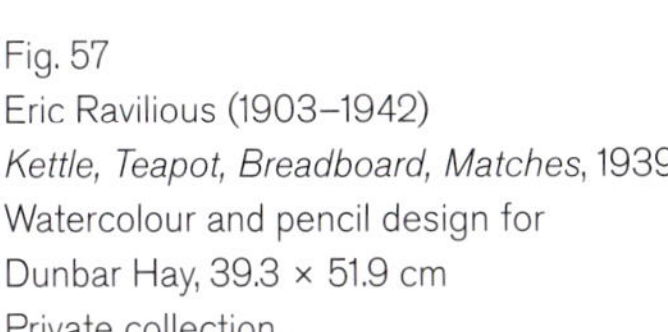

Fig. 57
Eric Ravilious (1903–1942)
*Kettle, Teapot, Breadboard, Matches*, 1939
Watercolour and pencil design for
Dunbar Hay, 39.3 × 51.9 cm
Private collection

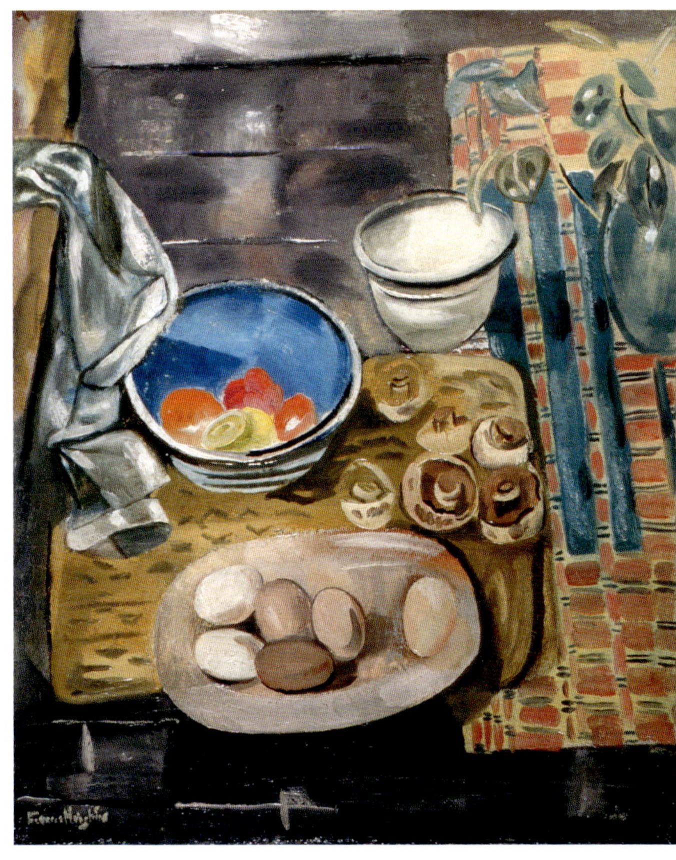

Fig. 58
Frances Hodgkins (1869–1947)
*Still Life: Eggs, Tomatoes and Mushrooms*, c.1929
Oil on canvas, 64 × 53 cm
Brighton & Hove Museums

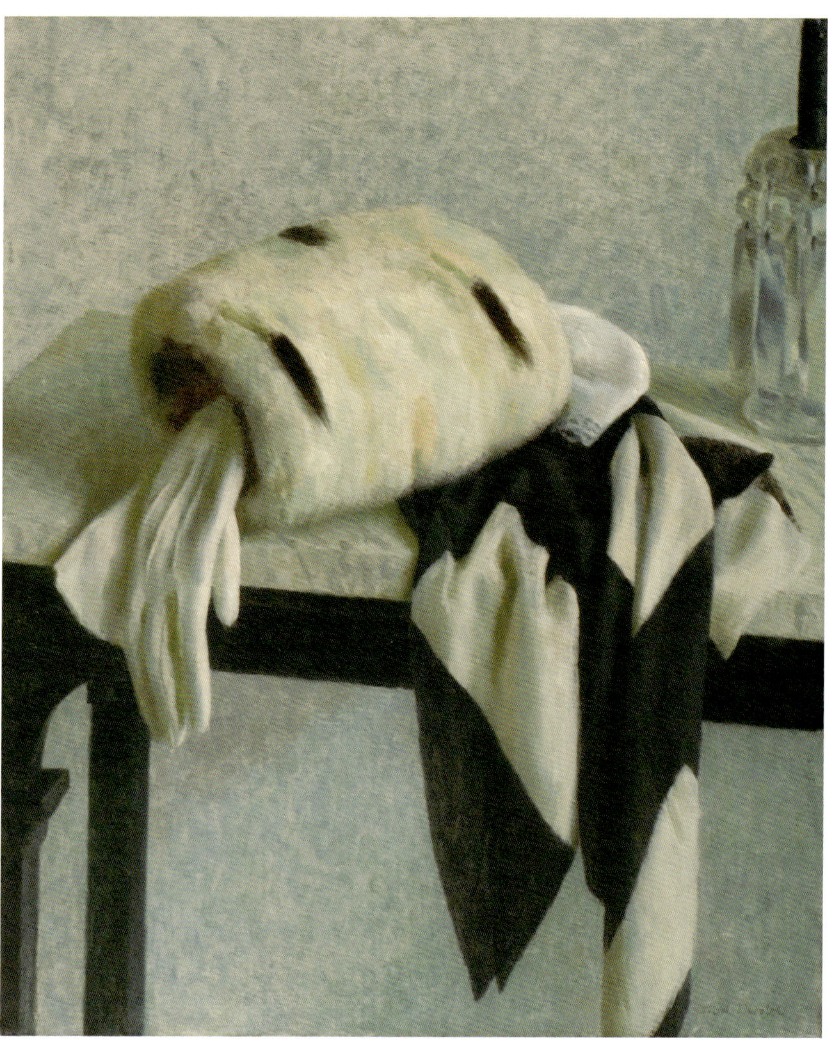

Fig. 59
Dod Procter (1892–1972 )
*Black and White*, c.1932
Oil on canvas, 61 × 50.8 cm
Southampton City Art Gallery

Paris – and, briefly, Berlin – in the early 1930s and to adopt a more modern, painterly style: one which would change the course of his career. Less concerned with meticulous finishes, the composition of *Stachys and Leaves* (fig. 60), is laid bare across a mottled, pigmented ground. As Simon Martin has noted, other still lifes from this period relay the modernist furniture of Philpot's Parisian studio, including the Bauhaus chrome nesting table which can be glimpsed in *Lilac and Black Iris* (1931–2), cultivating a self-sustaining relationship between modernist interiors and the works which would come to adorn them.[22]

Similarly, there were slippages between representation and the real in the creative collaboration of the artist Gluck and her partner, the floral designer Constance Spry, who had been introduced by the interior designer Prudence Maufe early in the decade.[23] Gluck meticulously rendered Spry's cut stem work, painting *Lords and Ladies* (fig. 61) in the

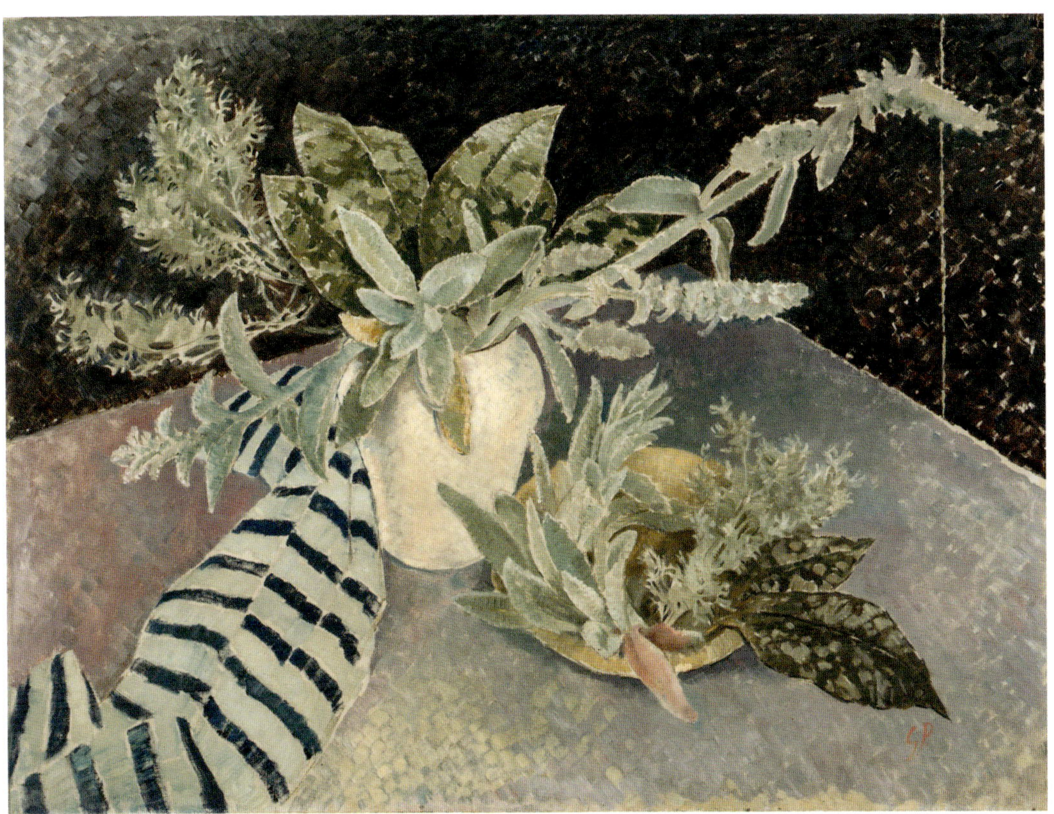

Fig. 60
Glyn Philpot (1884–1937)
*Stachys and Leaves*, 1934–35
Oil on canvas, 89 × 117 cm
Private collection

garden studio of Bolton House, her Hampstead home that had been designed by Prudence's husband, the architect Edward Maufe, as an exercise in 'modernity with manners'.[24] At Gluck's exhibition at the Fine Art Society, London, in 1932, which included a number of the artist's floral still lifes, Spry's arrangements were presented alongside their realisations in paint, enclosed in specially designed architectural, stepped frames: a total environment which brought still life firmly into the realm of modernist aesthetics.[25]

These artists' experiments in still life can be understood within a wider context of design and decorative innovation that was tightly knit to ideas of the modern in the interwar period. The centrality of design, both to the visual arts and as a vital force in its own right, was a central tenet of the short-lived group Unit One, founded by Nash with the intention of furthering modernist interests in architecture, sculpture and painting.[26] Comprising painters John Armstrong (1893–1973), John Bigge (1892–1973), Edward Burra (1905–1976), Nash, Ben Nicholson and Edward Wadsworth (1889–1949), sculptors Barbara Hepworth (1903–1975) and Henry Moore (1898–1986), and architects Wells Coates (1895–1958) and Colin Lucas (1906–1984), the group demonstrates the interleaved nature of art, design and industry at the time, and a broader interest in domestic space that was

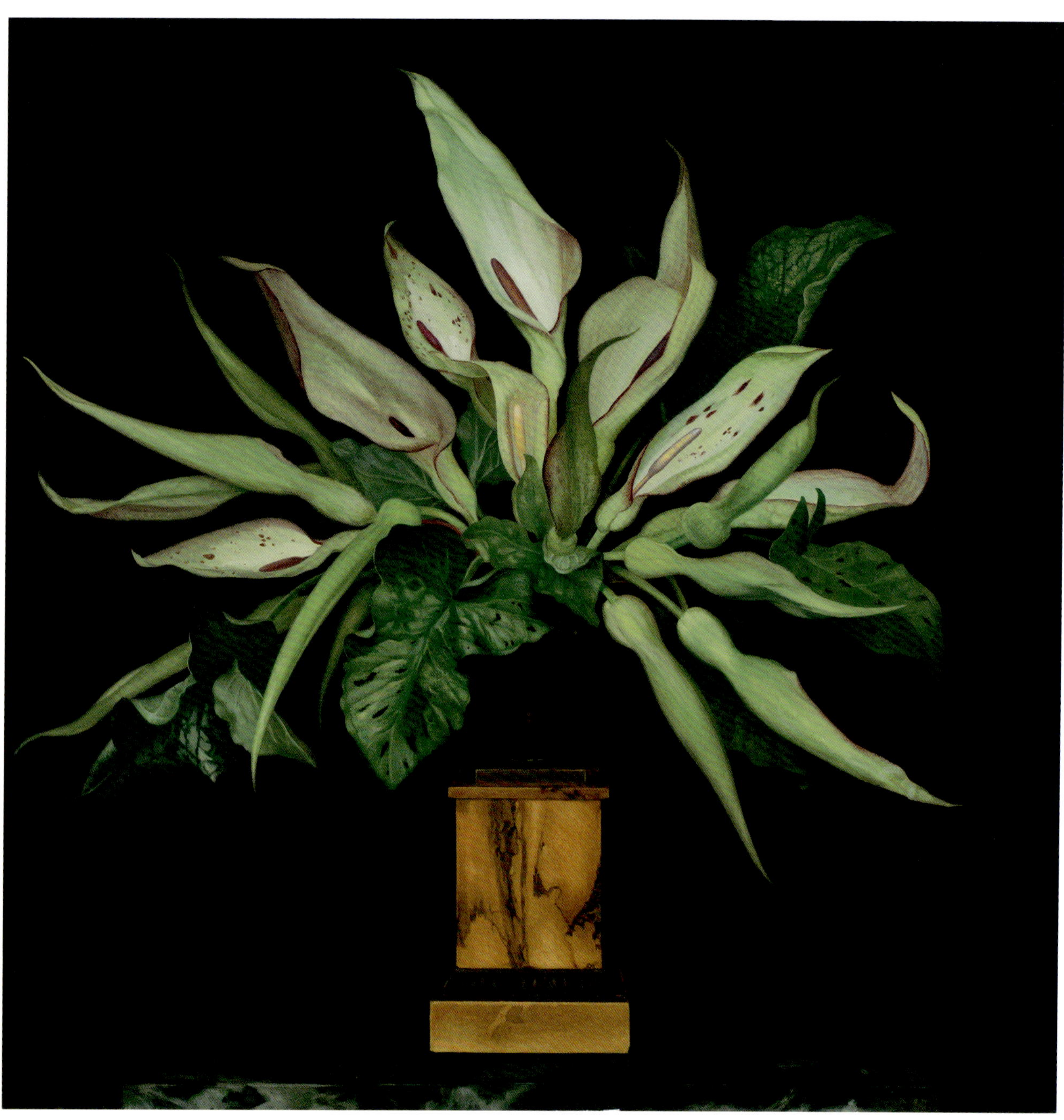

Fig. 61
Gluck (1895–1978)
*Lords and Ladies*, 1936
Oil on canvas, 75 × 75 cm
Private collection, London

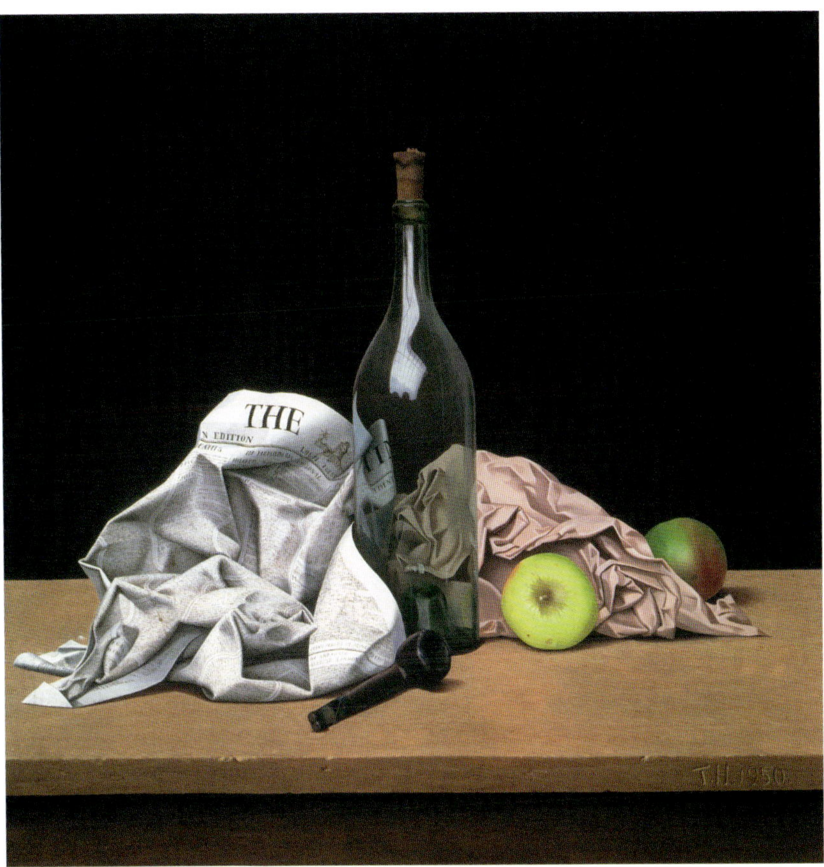

Fig. 62
Tristram Hillier (1905–1983)
*The Green Bottle*, 1950
Oil on canvas, 61 × 61 cm
Southampton City Art Gallery

shared by these artists in their pursuit of the still life.[27] The group looked beyond Britain – as Wadsworth quipped, 'one does not speak of "English" tennis or "English" mathematics'.[28] In early experiments in tempera, such as *Bright Intervals* (fig. 71), his own sympathy with international currents of realism and precision shared, for example, with Neue Sachlichkeit in Germany, are writ large.[29] The luminosity of tempera, clinical in its consistency, was an apt medium for the objective observation also being pursued in Europe. Yet in his concern with maritime instruments and depictions of nautical life, it is possible to detect, in the words of his friend, sculptor Ossip Zadkine (1888–1967), 'the consciousness of an islander'.[30]

The formation of Unit One was announced in a letter from Nash published in *The Times* in June 1933. It was, he explained, 'a method of concentrating certain individual forces, a hard defence, a compact wall against the tide, behind which development can proceed and experiment continue'.[31] Behind this bulwark were two somewhat surprising bedfellows: abstraction ('the expression of structural purpose in search of beauty in formal interaction and relations apart from representation') and a figurative, if tentative, surrealism, which Nash characterised as 'the pursuit of the soul, the attempt to trace the "psyche" in its devious flight'.[32] These

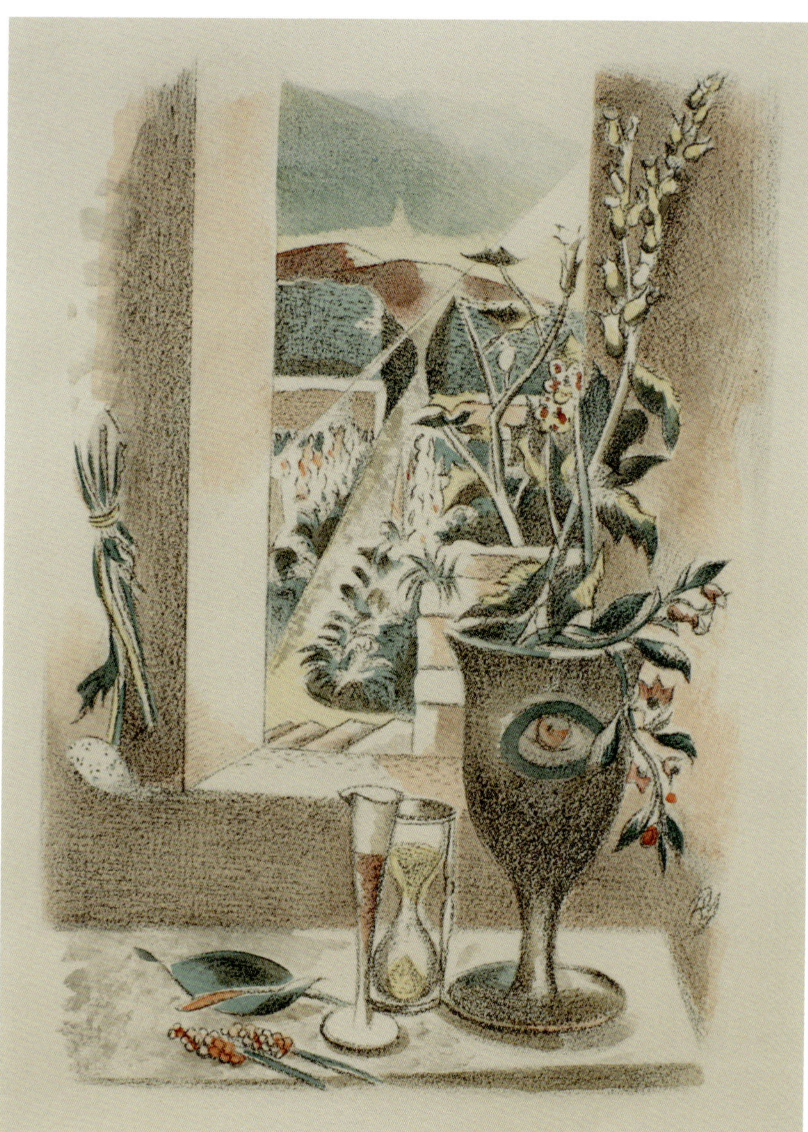

Fig. 63
Paul Nash (1889–1946)
*Poisonous Plants*, from 'For Urne Buriall and the Garden of Cyrus', 1932
Collotype and stencilled watercolour on paper, 31 × 23 cm
Pallant House Gallery, Chichester
(Lucas Bequest, 1995)

two distinct schools were perhaps no such thing for Nash, whose earliest dream memories, recorded in his memoir *Outline* (1949), took a distinctly structural, even abstract, form: 'One was undoubtedly a formal dream of a non-figurative or non-representational idiom. But it was not static. The horror consisted in being hemmed in by vast perpendiculars of changing dimensions, as though the building of walls and columns might begin a deliberate animation, like a slow-motion film, its architectural features changing position, eccentrically.'[33] These childhood nightmares echo through the disorientating dream structures of works such as *Dead Spring* (fig. 66) and *Harbour and Room* (1932–6, Tate), themselves redolent of the uncanny townscapes of Giorgio de Chirico (1888–1978), whose work Nash had first seen and admired at Arthur Tooth and Sons, London, in 1928.

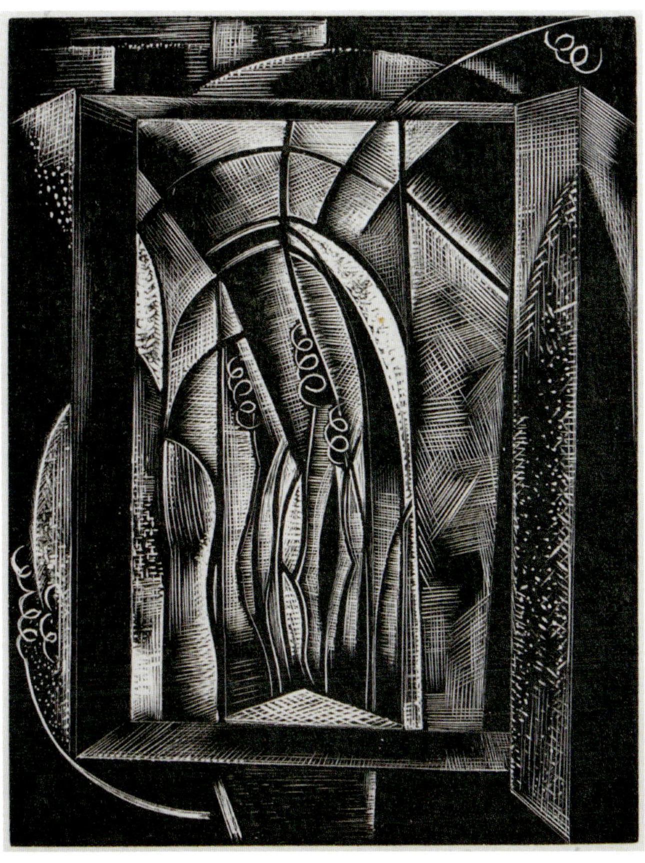

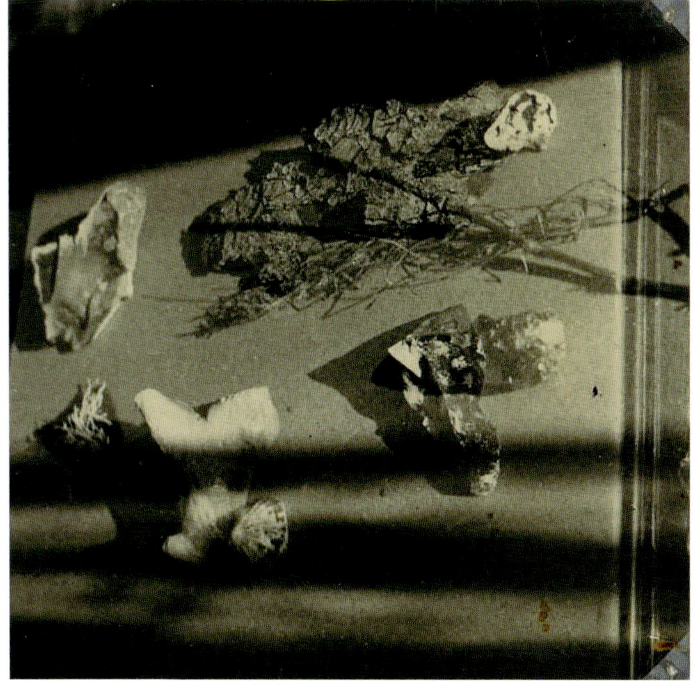

Fig. 64
Paul Nash (1889–1946)
*Coronilla*, 1925
Wood engraving on paper, 11.6 × 9 cm
Pallant House Gallery, Chichester
(The Clare Neilson Collection Presented
by Jeremy Greenwood and Alan Swerdlow
through Art Fund 2013)

Fig. 65
Paul Nash (1889–1946)
*Untitled*, 1934–35
Photograph, silver gelatin print
on paper, 17.2 × 13.9 cm
Pallant House Gallery, Chichester
(The Clare Neilson Collection Presented
by Jeremy Greenwood and Alan Swerdlow
through Art Fund 2013)

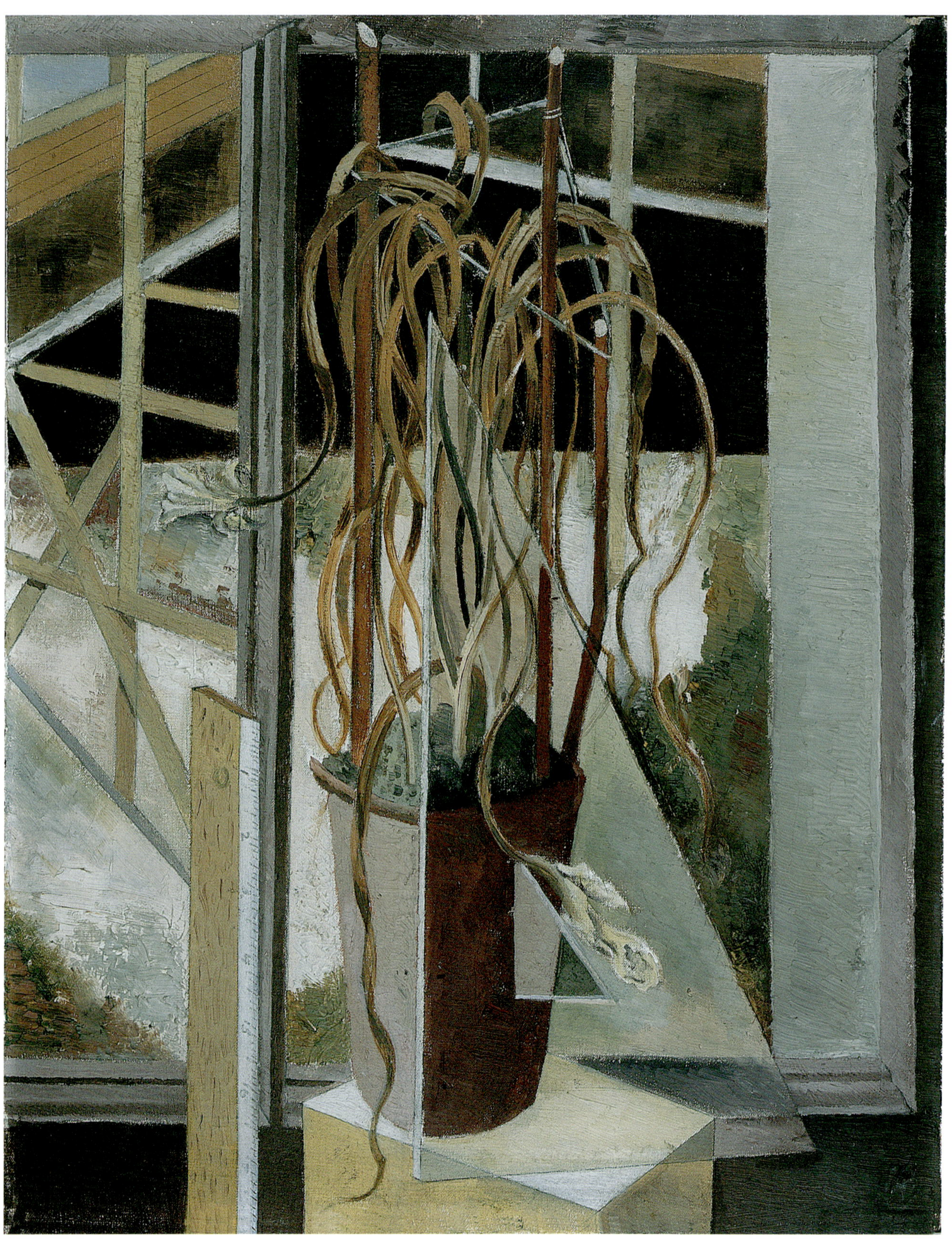

An abiding interest in dreams drew Nash to surrealism, observable in his contention that 'the divisions we may erect between night and day – waking world and that of the dream, reality and the other thing, do not hold. They are penetrable, they are porous, translucent, transparent; in a word they are not there'.[34] But, as Emma Chambers has noted, Nash was 'selective in the aspects of surrealism he adopted', utilising it to develop the strand of metaphysical interest in the landscape which endures from his earliest works.[35] Added to this was the found object, which was critical to the artist's explorations of place: although inanimate, such objects – including shells, driftwood and 'wild stones' – gained mysterious lives of their own as 'object-personages'.[36]

In 1930, Nash's wife Margaret gave him a pocket Kodak folding camera.[37] The objects that offered themselves to Nash during country walks became strangely othered as they passed through its lens, as in *Untitled* (fig. 65). 'It is through the camera that we first discover the optical unconscious, just as we discover the instinctual unconscious through psychoanalysis', wrote Walter Benjamin in the middle of the decade.[38] Moreover, 'many of the deformations and stereotypes, transformations and catastrophes which can assail the optical world in films afflict the actual world in psychoses, hallucinations, and dreams'.[39] The surrealists ran headlong into the possibilities of disturbing the object world through this technology, adding its mechanical estrangements to their catalogue of convulsive automatisms.

Photography's perceived ability to accurately capture reality also supported a surreal agenda: that images were read as truth compounded their sense of the uncanny when, upon further observation, their content upended all expectation. Following a friend's radical mastectomy, Lee Miller (1907–1977) asked the surgeon if she could keep the severed breast and proceeded to photograph it plated upon a laid table between knife and fork. In place of nourishment, a macabre incursion into the domestic sphere prompts reflection on the category of woman as sexual object, to be consumed. For Claude Cahun (1894–1954), too, 'irrational sproutings of flesh' were an extension of the object world, at once a burden in their foreclosure as gendered signifiers and, as a result, something to be rearranged at will, manipulated in the image of the marvellous.[40] 'I have my head shaved, my teeth pulled and my breasts cut off – everything that bothers my gaze or slows it down – the stomach, the ovaries, the conscious and cysted brain. When I have nothing more than a heartbeat to note, to perfection, I will have won.'[41] A series of self-portraits of the artist's seemingly decapitated head in a bell jar compounds this interrogation of the material body and its reticence, under examination, to conform to expectations of gender; the corollary being *Untitled (Objects in a Bell Jar)* (fig. 68), in which Cahun photographed assemblages foregrounding a lay figure (a jointed artist's mannequin) under containment. Between the photographs, as Katherine Conley has pointed out, slippages between the

Fig. 66
Paul Nash (1889–1946)
*Dead Spring*, 1929
Oil on canvas, 48.5 × 40 cm
Pallant House Gallery, Chichester
(Kearley Bequest through Art Fund, 1989)

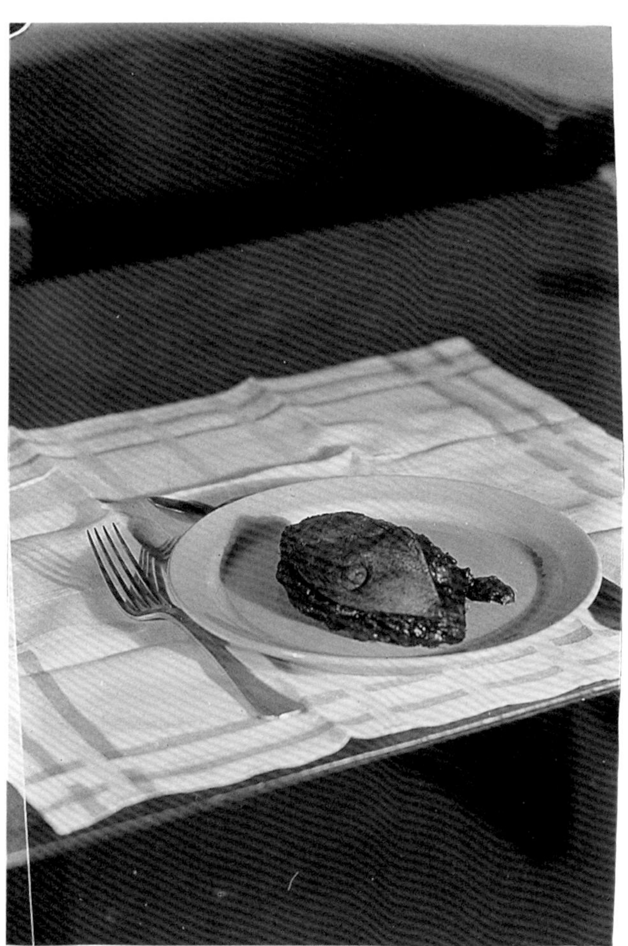

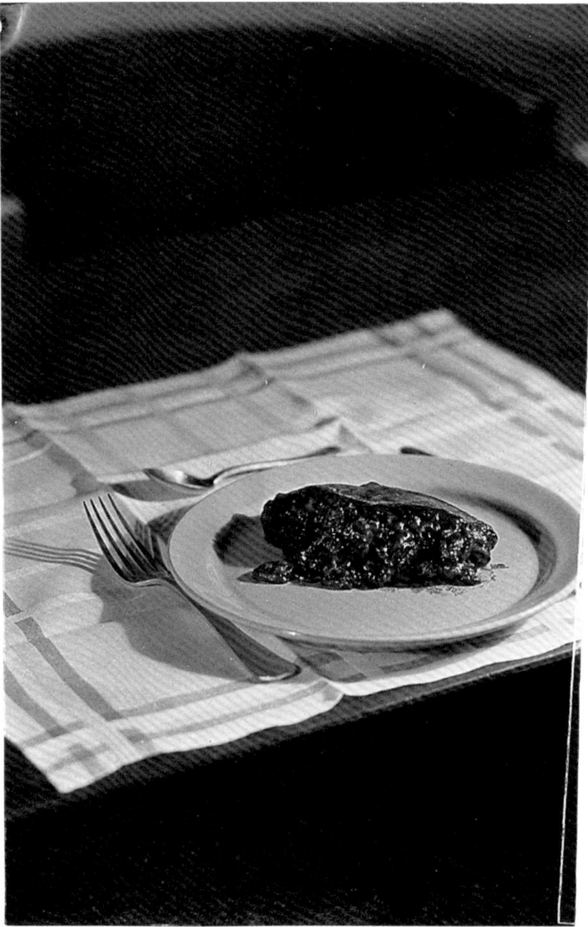

Fig. 67
Lee Miller (1907–1977)
*Untitled [Severed Breast, from radical surgery in a place setting 1 & 2], Paris, France*, c.1929
Photograph, 16.3 × 12.0 cm & 16.3 × 11.8 cm
Lee Miller Archives, East Sussex

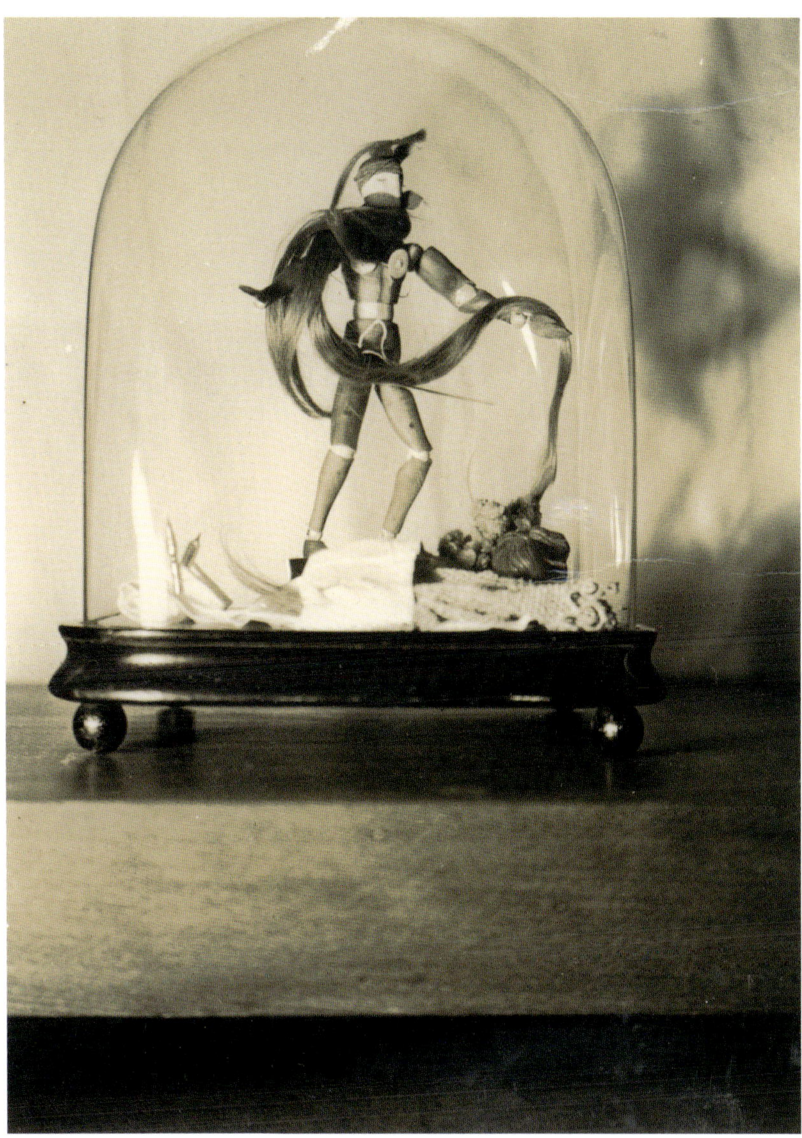

Fig. 68
Claude Cahun (1894–1954)
*Untitled (Objects in a Bell Jar)*, 1936
Photographic print, 23.7 × 17.8 cm
Courtesy of Jersey Heritage

human and the object contribute to their uncanny atmosphere, 'a blurred distinction between what is or is not sentient', as still life metabolises into death.[42]

Cahun also published a text, 'Beware Domestic Objects!' in the special issue of the magazine *Cahiers d'Art* which accompanied the *Exposition surréaliste d'objets* that took place in May 1936 at the Galerie Charles Ratton in Paris. Writing that the 'overproduction of stranger and stranger objects (such as microscopic tweezers, usable only under a microscope) assures us that all around us present-day reality is cracking at the seams', Cahun's text is both a lament and portent of the commodity fetish.[43] Self-devised assemblages were less threatening, talismanic, and could defend against the atrocities of the assembly line. Indeed, something of the subjectivity and essential untouchability of still life seems to call out from the text: 'I could go on and on about those objects: they will speak to you better themselves, and they would speak still better if we could touch them in the dark'.[44]

In 1937, *Surrealist Objects and Poems* opened at the London Gallery, reinscribing the 'sudden efflorescence' brought about by the International Surrealist Exhibition which had taken place at the New Burlington Galleries the previous year. As compared with the 1936 exhibition, *Surrealist Objects and Poems* cemented the liberation of still life from the canvas in the 20th century. As Alyce Mahon has written, the genre 'took on new forms with ... collage, the ready-made object, photography, assemblage and installation art', a point seemingly illustrated by Eileen Agar's (1899–1991) *The Object Lesson* (fig. 69), in which the artist affixed objects – a wicker rack, a lay figure holding a paintbrush-speared cork – to one of her earlier abstract canvases.[45] *The Object Lesson* was used to illustrate 'The Object in Surrealism' (1940) in the *London Bulletin*, in which Conroy Maddox spoke of phantom objects representing 'a systematic plan of disturbance and demoralisation against the commonplace and rational'.[46] At the outbreak of the Second World War, there was little comfort to be found in the relationship between the real and its representation; in Meredith Frampton's (1894–1984) *Trial and Error* (fig. 70), the hyperreal articulation of objects belies their artifice, which the artist often created in facsimile before rendering in paint.[47] In the 'so-called real world', objects were liable to mutate via subjective encounters with the realm of the unconscious.[48] Armed with the potential to disrupt and destabilise reality, at this moment the still life took in the canvas and whole rooms too. Reality was now faced with 'the other thing': another plane, a vast dream world of both fear and comfort, antipathies and antagonisms, at once vital and at a deadly rest.[49]

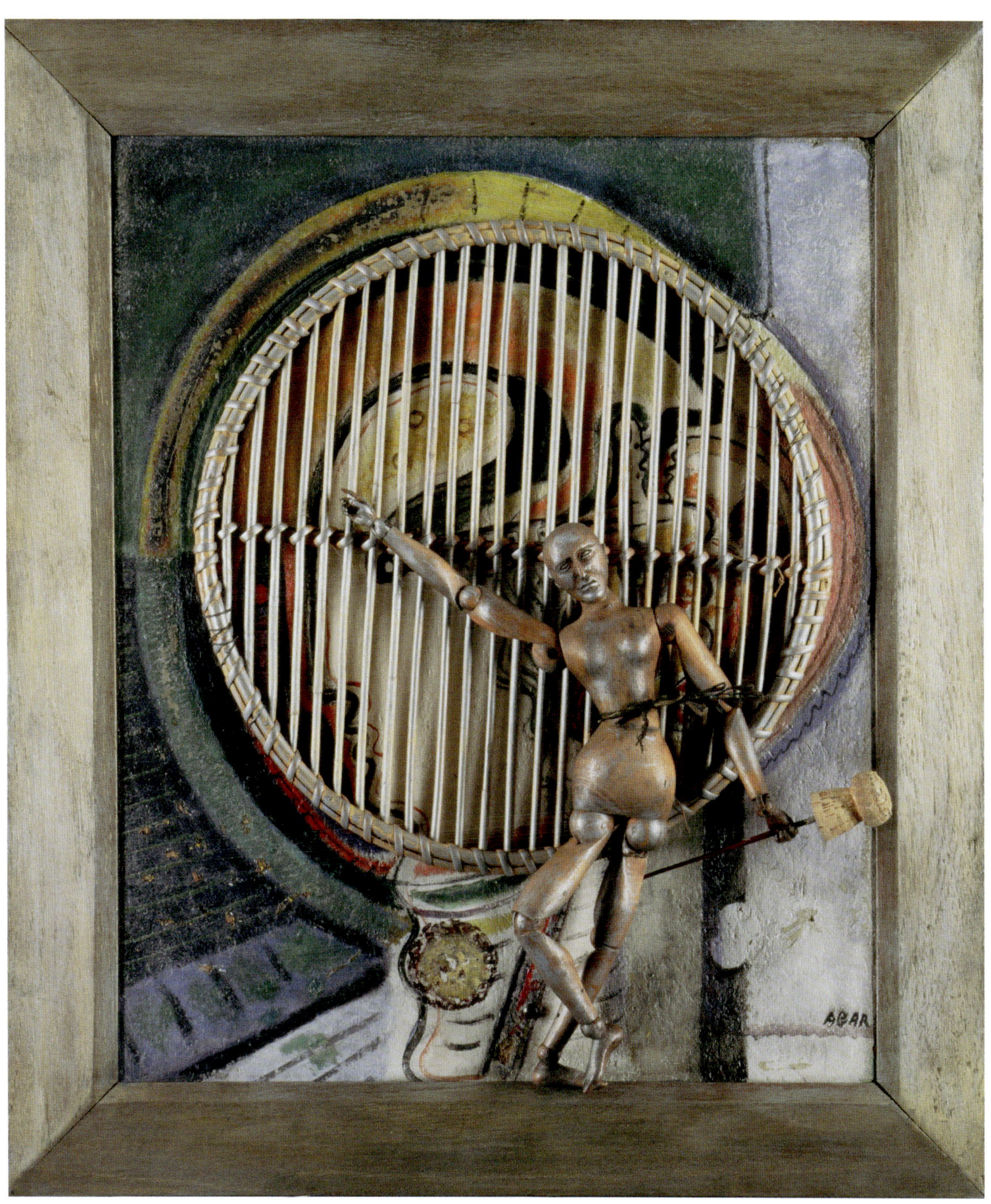


Fig. 69
Eileen Agar (1899–1991)
*The Object Lesson*, 1940
Collage and bodycolour on board,
55.8 cm × 46 cm
Southampton City Art Gallery

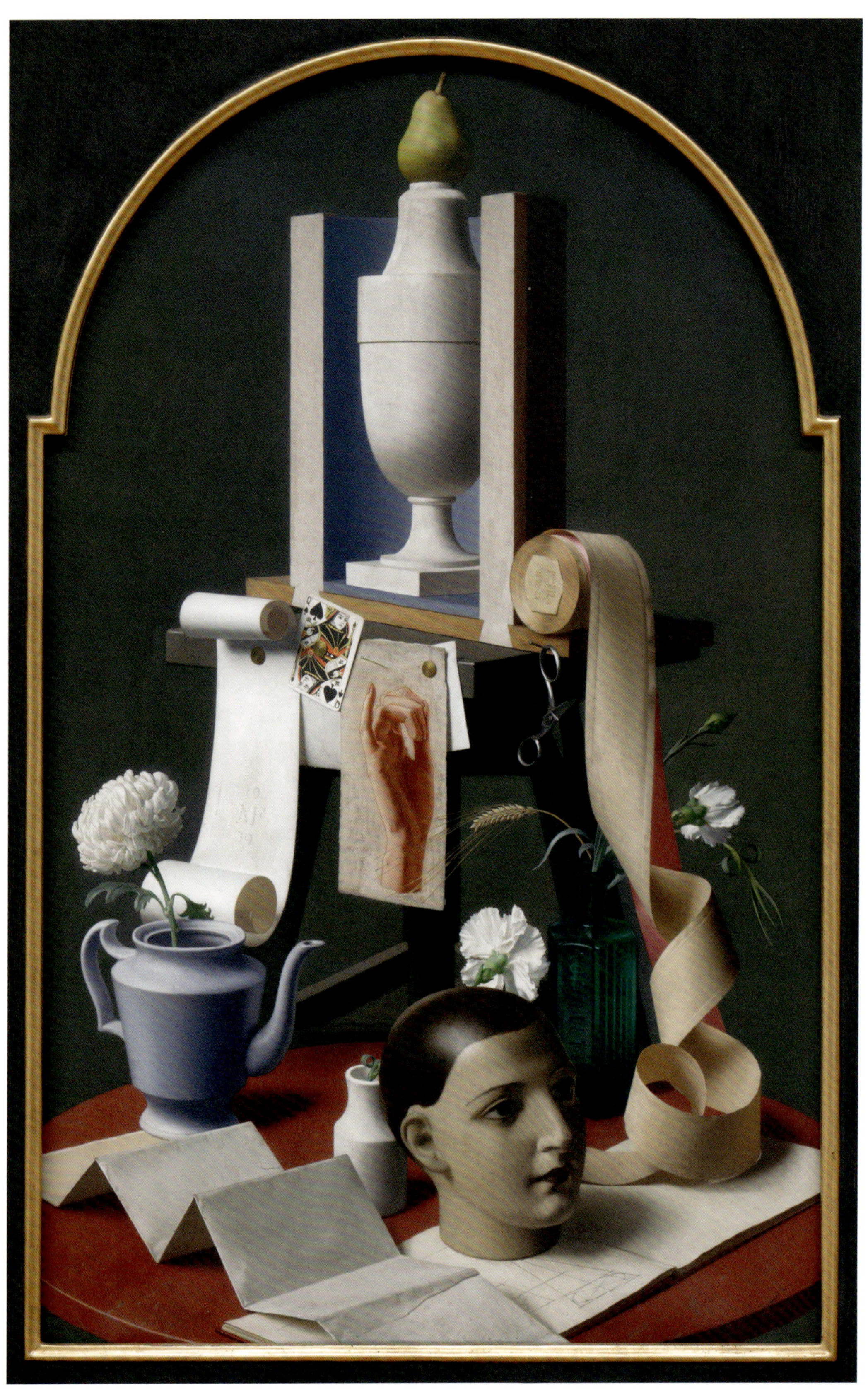

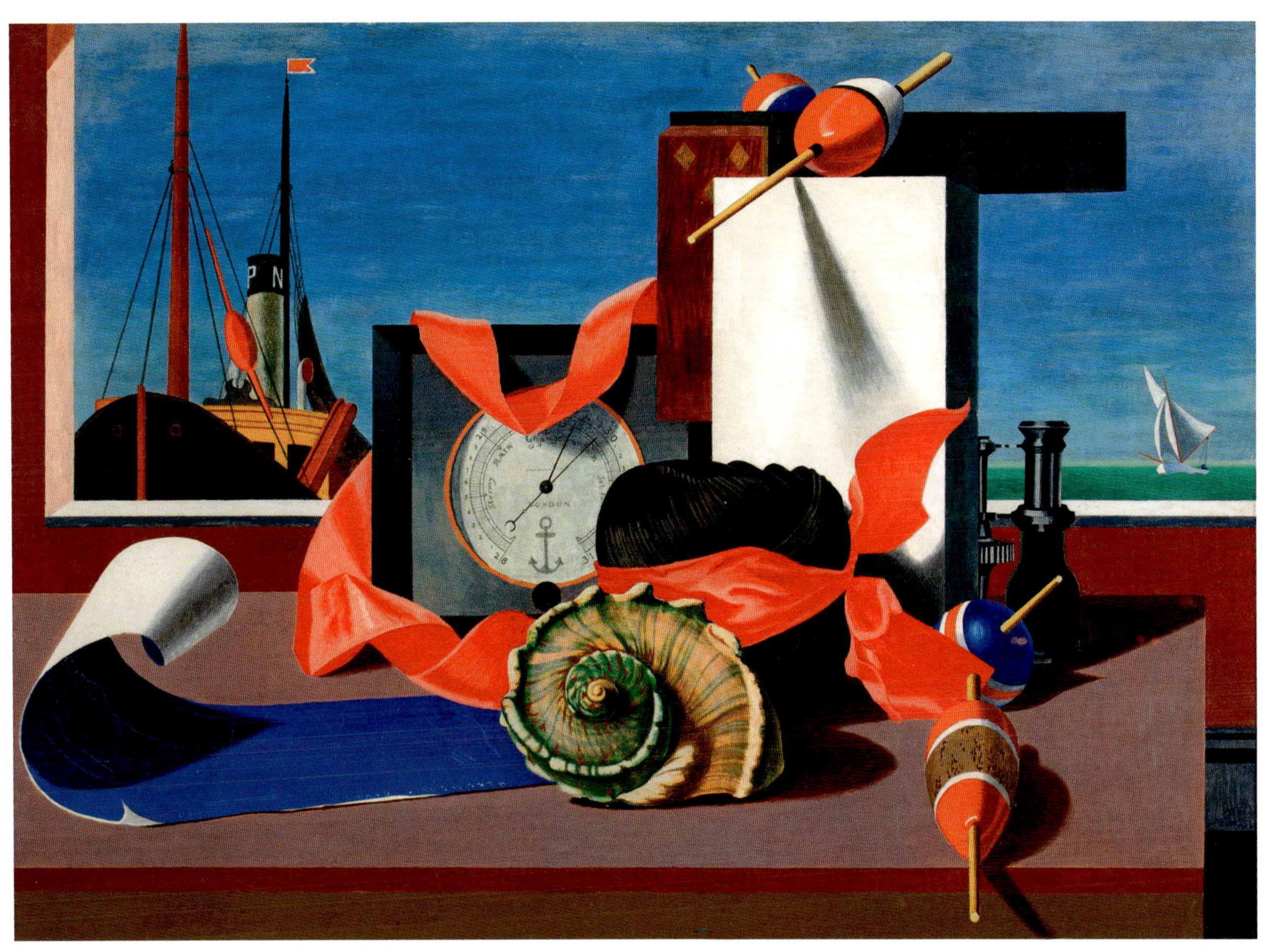


Fig. 70 (opposite)
Meredith Frampton (1894–1984)
*Trial and Error*, 1939
Oil on canvas, 112.7 × 71.4 cm
Tate: Bequeathed by Miss J.B. Dickins 2010, accessioned 2019

Fig. 71 (above)
Edward Wadsworth (1889–1949)
*Bright Intervals*, 1928
Tempera on canvas laid on panel, 63 × 88 cm
Museum and Art Swindon

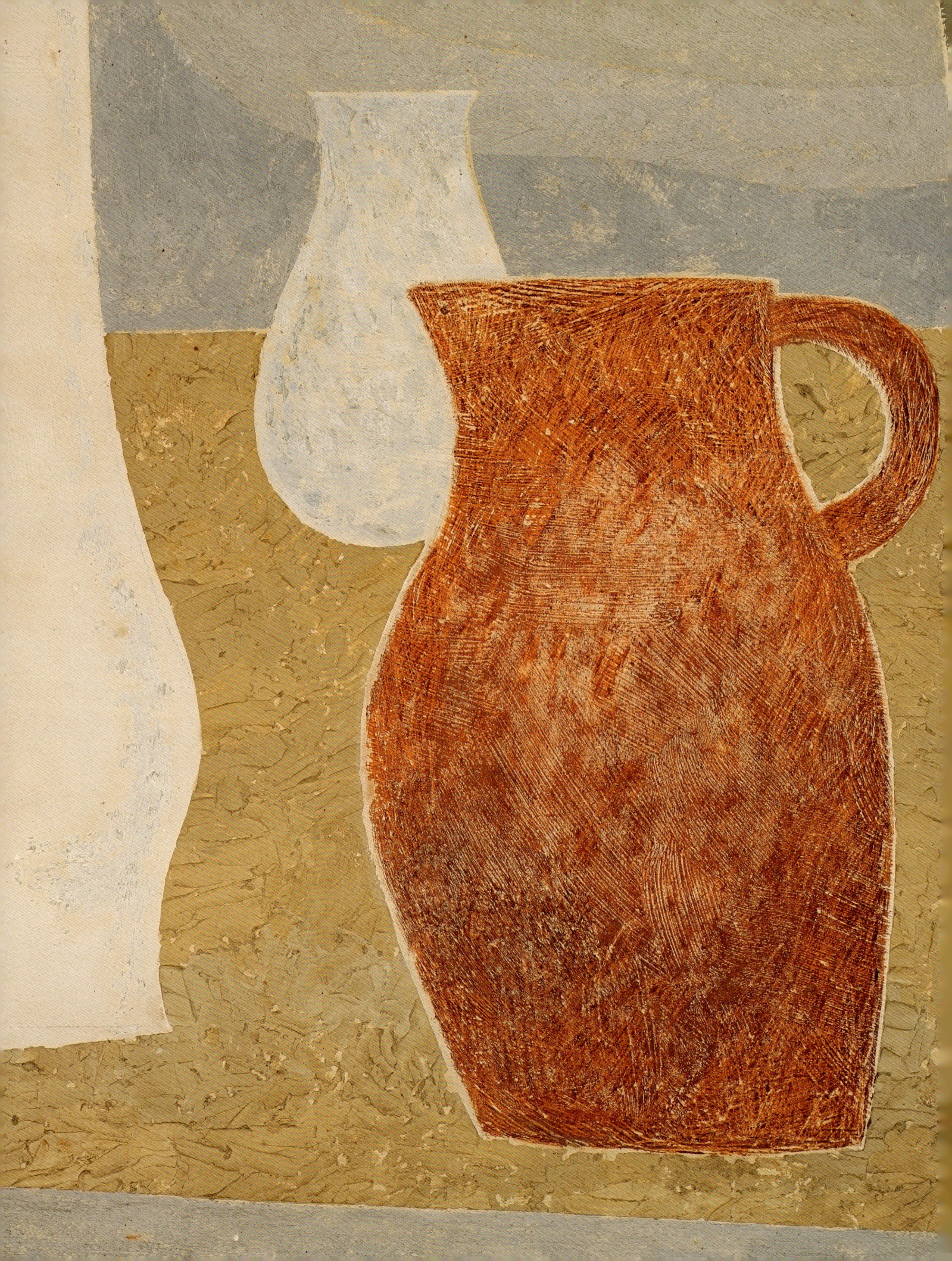

# 4 Paths to Abstraction

MICHAEL BIRD

Summer turns to autumn in 1940; the Battle of Britain segues into the Blitz. Lying awake in bed at Monk's House near Rodmell one night, Virginia Woolf (1882–1941) listens to enemy bombs exploding – so close, it seems, and all around – and the answering anti-aircraft fire from batteries along the Sussex coast. What is it about human nature – more specifically, male nature – she wonders, that impels us to destroy and kill? She takes some comfort from the thought that a contrary impulse towards kindness and harmony is always there, revealing itself whenever it gets the chance. Just recently, for example, she has heard that, when a German plane was downed in a nearby field and the pilot captured, 'an Englishman gave him a cigarette, and an Englishwoman made him a cup of tea'.[1]

A few years later, in 1946, taking the cultural temperature of postwar Britain, George Orwell declared that 'tea is one of the mainstays of civilization in this country'.[2] His much-quoted piece in the *Evening Standard* was titled simply 'A Nice Cup of Tea' – and when you think about what that phrase connotes at times of fear, pain, loss and insecurity, even today, you get a sense of how the large white mug in Ben Nicholson's *1943–45 (St Ives, Cornwall)* (fig. 75) holds out a luminous promise of peace and calm you can almost grasp by the handle. Whatever else is going on in the world, there it stands, centre stage in the domestic theatre of the curtained windowsill, against a placid backdrop of sea and sky, and toylike traditional fishing boats, as if it had won the struggle against the powers of darkness to which the jaunty victory Union Jack, borrowed from a child's sandcastle, seems to refer.

Still life has meant many things to many artists, but in all its incarnations it is pre-eminently an art of peace – peace both as a fact of

Detail of fig. 76
Jessica Dismorr (1885–1939)
*Composition*, c.1935 (detail)

life and as a yearning (like Woolf's) in time of war. For still life to happen, there have to be tables and chairs, rugs and tablecloths, mantelpieces and windowsills, all the physical tokens of an objective reality in which – in the artist's room or studio, at least – order reigns. Although still life by definition admits no people, it is also a strangely sociable art form, inviting us in (like the cup of tea) to share its stillness, which is very different from the lonely stillness you find in some landscape paintings. And there is always someone backstage – there has to be. Jugs, cups, bowls, wine glasses, teapots and vases must be lifted from shelves and cupboards, fruit arranged and flowers picked. The fortunes of war were on the turn in 1943, after Nazi defeat at Stalingrad early in the year, when Ivon Hitchens (1893–1979) painted *Flowers* (fig. 72). The fresh, lyrical colour notes (a vivid contrast to the cubistic earths and whites in the Tate's *Autumn Composition, Flowers on a Table* from 1932) project the kind of optimistic uplift that Nicholson inserted more concisely with his tiny Union Jack. Hitchens in deepest Sussex, Nicholson in furthest Cornwall – both sending still-life votes of confidence in a sociable peacetime world that would survive.

Go back to artists' studios in early 20th-century Paris, however, and still life itself is one of the main battlegrounds – a cultural boxing ring, where long-serving academic conventions of visual representation and choice of subject matter are being dealt a knockout avant-garde one-two by Georges Braque (1882–1963) and Pablo Picasso (1881–1973). Braque, himself a serious amateur boxer, described cubism's re-exploration of pictorial space as a whole-body activity, 'physical painting'; yet a breakthrough work like his 1909–10 *Mandora* (Tate) depicts nothing more sensational than an elegant stringed instrument. Many of the best-known paintings, sculptures and collages of the cubist revolution have quiet titles like *Glass of Absinthe* and *Still Life with Chair Caning* (Picasso) or *Fruit Dish, Bottle and Glass* and *Still Life with Violin* (Braque). The point about the hundreds of prismatic, fractured wine bottles, guitars, tobacco pipes and newspapers that followed in Braque and Picasso's wake, with their *mise en scène* of café tables and ambient hum of cosmopolitan art-talk, is that an artist can work with the most ordinary household objects – the kinds of things we handle every day without a thought – look at them long, see them differently, make them new. This revisioning or re-enchantment of ordinary objects ran on, after the First World War, through surrealist art. In the Freudian-surrealist symbolic dreamscape, a teacup is never *just* a cup: it is an inland sea, a grail, a womb. 'In the burrows of the nightmare,' wrote W.H. Auden, 'the crack in the tea-cup opens/ A lane to the land of the dead.'[3]

As the son of the painter of *The Hundred Jugs* (1916, Walker Art Gallery, Liverpool) and of the beautifully observed, less densely stage-managed still life in this exhibition (fig. 40), Ben Nicholson might have been expected to ditch still life entirely in the cause of 'beginning again in painting', as his first wife, Winifred Roberts, described their shared ambition in the 1920s.

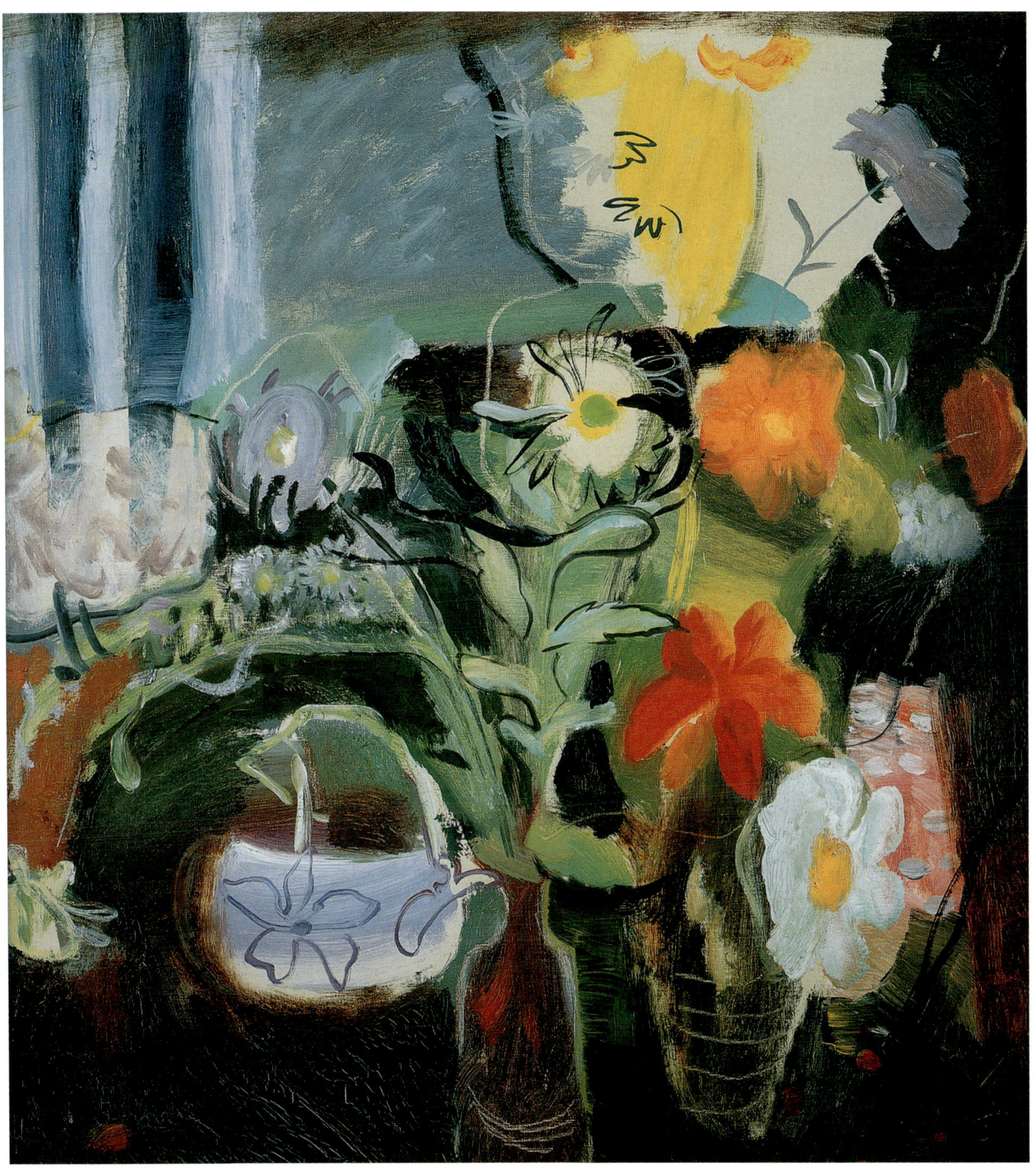

Fig. 72
Ivon Hitchens (1893–1979)
*Flowers*, 1943
Oil on canvas, 61 × 56.3 cm
Pallant House Gallery, Chichester
(Mrs Diana King Bequest presented through Art Fund, 2003)

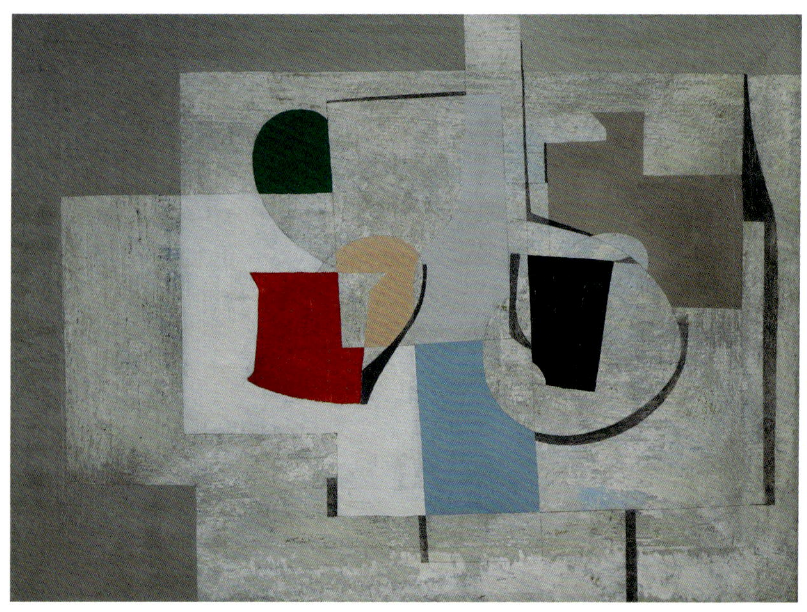

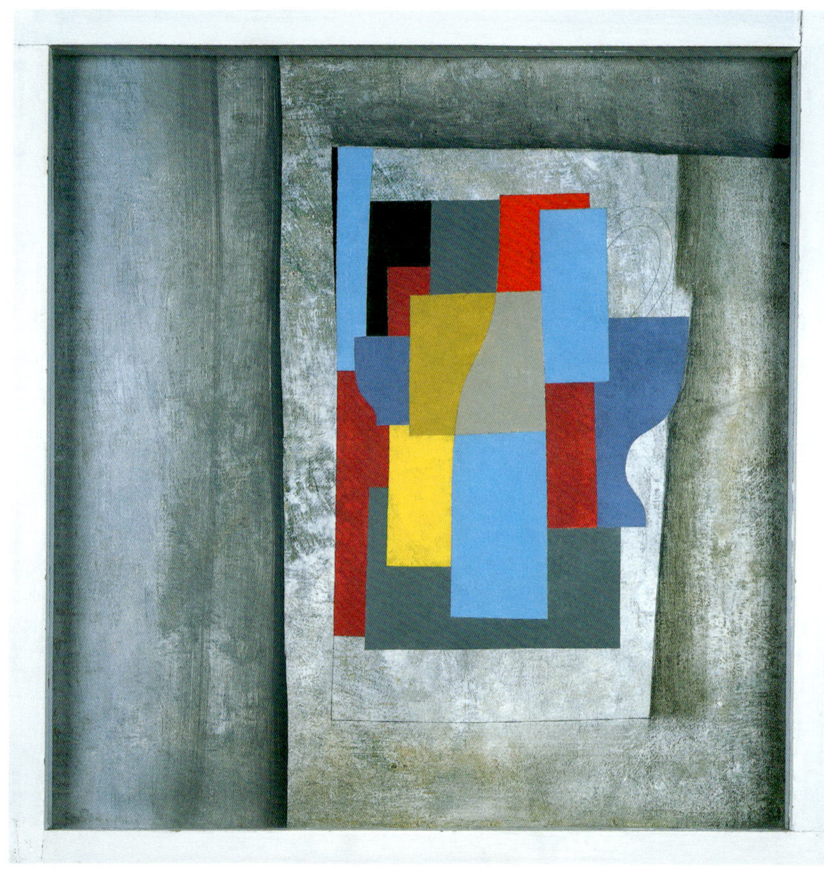

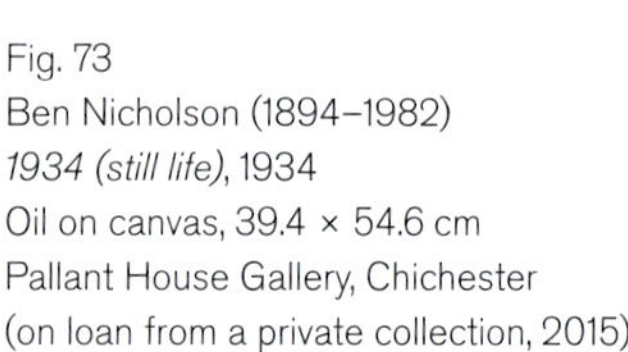

Fig. 73
Ben Nicholson (1894–1982)
*1934 (still life)*, 1934
Oil on canvas, 39.4 × 54.6 cm
Pallant House Gallery, Chichester
(on loan from a private collection, 2015)

Fig. 74
Ben Nicholson (1894–1982)
*1946 (still life, cerulean)*, 1946
Oil on canvas over board, 63 × 61.5 cm
Pallant House Gallery, Chichester
(Kearley Bequest, through Art Fund, 1989)

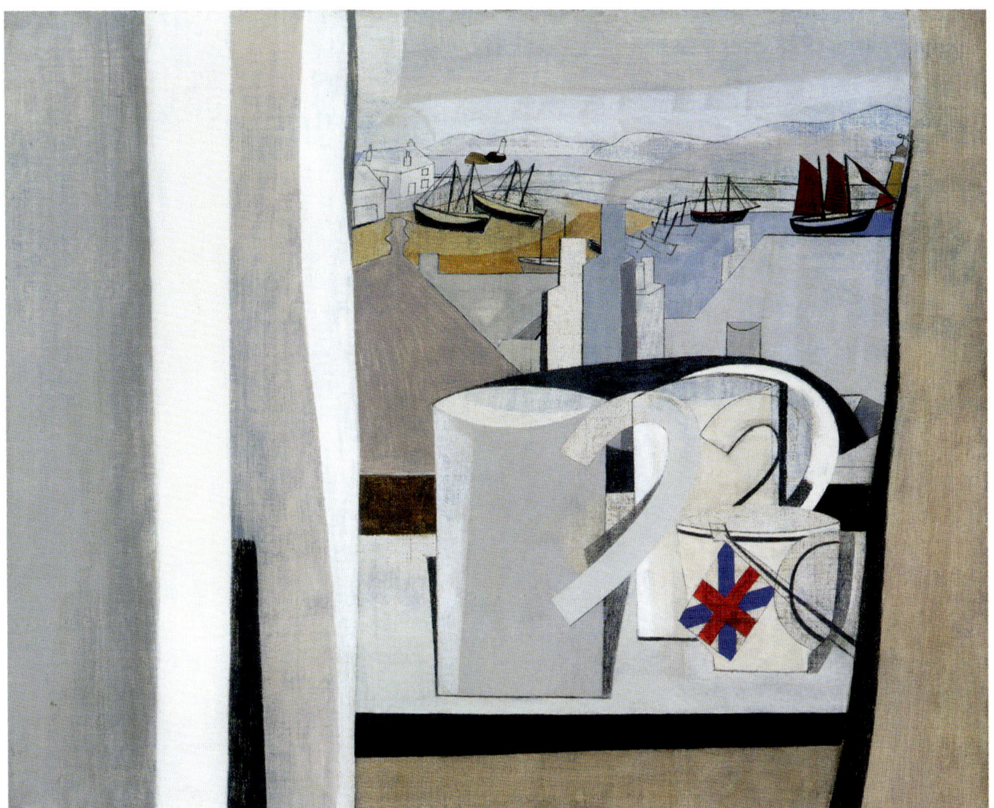

Fig. 75
Ben Nicholson (1894–1982)
*1943–45 (St Ives, Cornwall)*, 1943–5
Oil and graphite on canvas, 40.6 × 50.2 cm
Tate: Purchased 1945

Not so, apparently. 'I owe a lot to my father,' Nicholson would later reflect, 'especially to his poetic idea and to his still-life theme.'

> In my work, this theme did not originally come from cubism ... but from my father – not only from what he did as a painter but from the very beautiful striped and spotted jugs and mugs and goblets, and octagonal and hexagonal glass objects which he collected.[4]

Yet there is no ignoring Nicholson's debt to cubism, which dates from another emotional epoch in his life. By the early 1930s, he had left Winifred and their two children, and was to-ing and fro-ing between London and Paris with his new love, Barbara Hepworth. The still-life paintings he saw in Parisian galleries and studios owed nothing to Edwardian bric-à-brac, but they did validate still life as a central theme in avant-garde practice. In a still life Nicholson painted in 1934 (fig. 73), the two streams merge. Against a configuration of pale abstract-geometrical forms, which feels like an homage both to Piet Mondrian's (1872–1944) work and to his rue du Départ studio – a carefully curated, large-scale white still life – float the shapes of a red jug and black mug, objects of the kind whose contours,

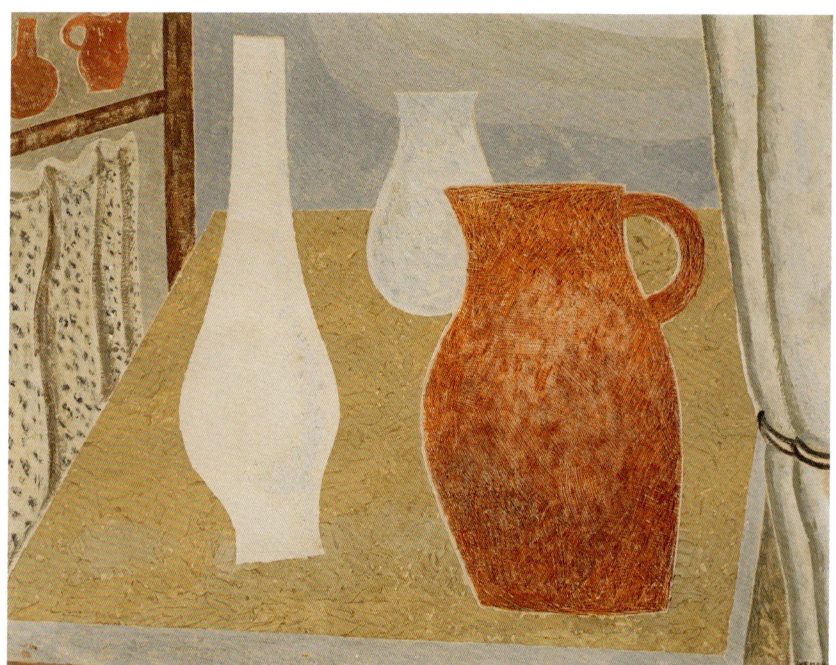

Fig. 76
Jessica Dismorr (1885–1939)
*Composition*, c.1935 (detail)
Oil on card, 46 × 59 cm
Ömer Koç Collection

colours and sheer homely *thereness* had been 'an unforgettable early experience' of Nicholson's childhood.[5] Still life was sometimes, literally, the raw material with which he worked: around this time, he also made a pure abstract, white relief, sculpted from the top of a vintage dining table picked up in a junk shop on the Portobello Road.

All the while, there was a developing tendency among a small but highly serious and articulate sector of the European avant-garde to establish firm intellectual credentials for abstract art. Briefly, they sought to frame it as an art of essential structures and relationships as opposed to contingent surface details. With the rise of fascism in the 1930s, abstract art – which the dictators hated – became identified with the political left and with utopian ideals of transnational unity and brotherhood. For British artists in the mid-1930s, whatever kind of work they had previously been producing, ideas associated with abstraction exerted a magnetic pull. The reddish-brown jug and ghostly vases in Jessica Dismorr's (1885–1939) *Composition* (fig. 76) are on the cusp of transformation into the flat, monochromatic painted and collaged shapes that would fill her pictures in the next few years. As early as 1930, a 27-year-old Hepworth was confidently positioning her work on a mid-point 'between pure representation and the abstract', explaining:

> Generalisation ... is nearer to the abstract than particularisation, which is a faithful portrayal of an individual object.
>
> My trend is towards generalisation; but I have not dispensed with representation entirely; as I find that it is possible to take a pebble

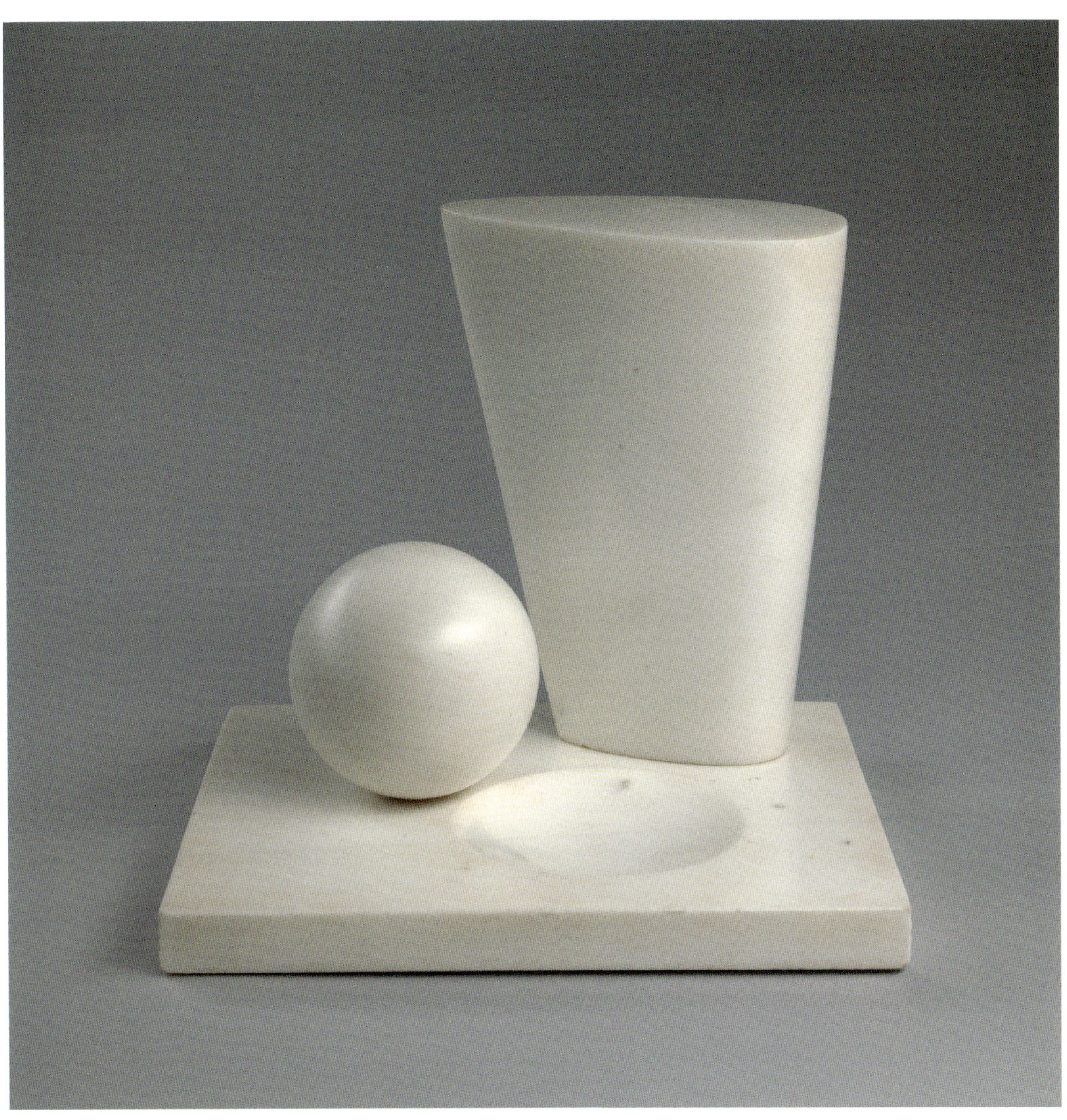

Fig. 77
Barbara Hepworth (1903–1975)
*Conoid, Sphere and Hollow III*, 1937
Marble, 32 × 35.5 × 30.5 cm
UK Government Art Collection

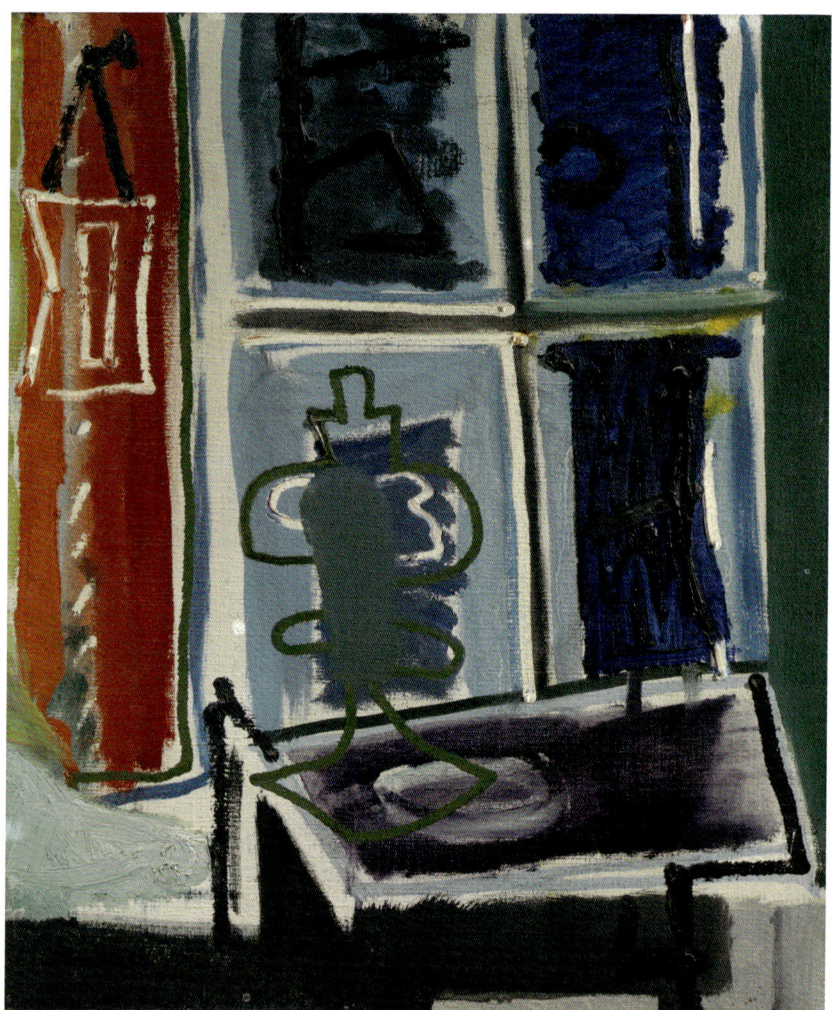

Fig. 78
Patrick Heron (1920–1999)
*Still Life*, c.1948–9
Oil on canvas, 50 × 30 cm
The Courtauld, London
(Samuel Courtauld Trust)

> of fine and simple shape and carve in addition a sequence of planes suggestive of the human form, thus giving it an added significance of emotional value.[6]

Hepworth's 1937 tabletop sculpture *Conoid, Sphere and Hollow III* (fig. 77) could almost have taken its cue from this statement. Are her two abstract vertical and spherical marble forms 'suggestive' of tree and stone, adult and child, female and male, or the balance between opposites – or all or none of these things? And does it matter what these shapes suggest, since everyone who encounters them is likely to make different associations? In this case – and here is the heart of inter-war abstract art's utopian social agenda – the viewer's personal freedom of interpretation is entirely compatible with the austere formal order created by the artist. In the same year Hepworth carved her sculpture, Le Corbusier foretold that 'machine-made civilization', embodied in modern art and architecture,

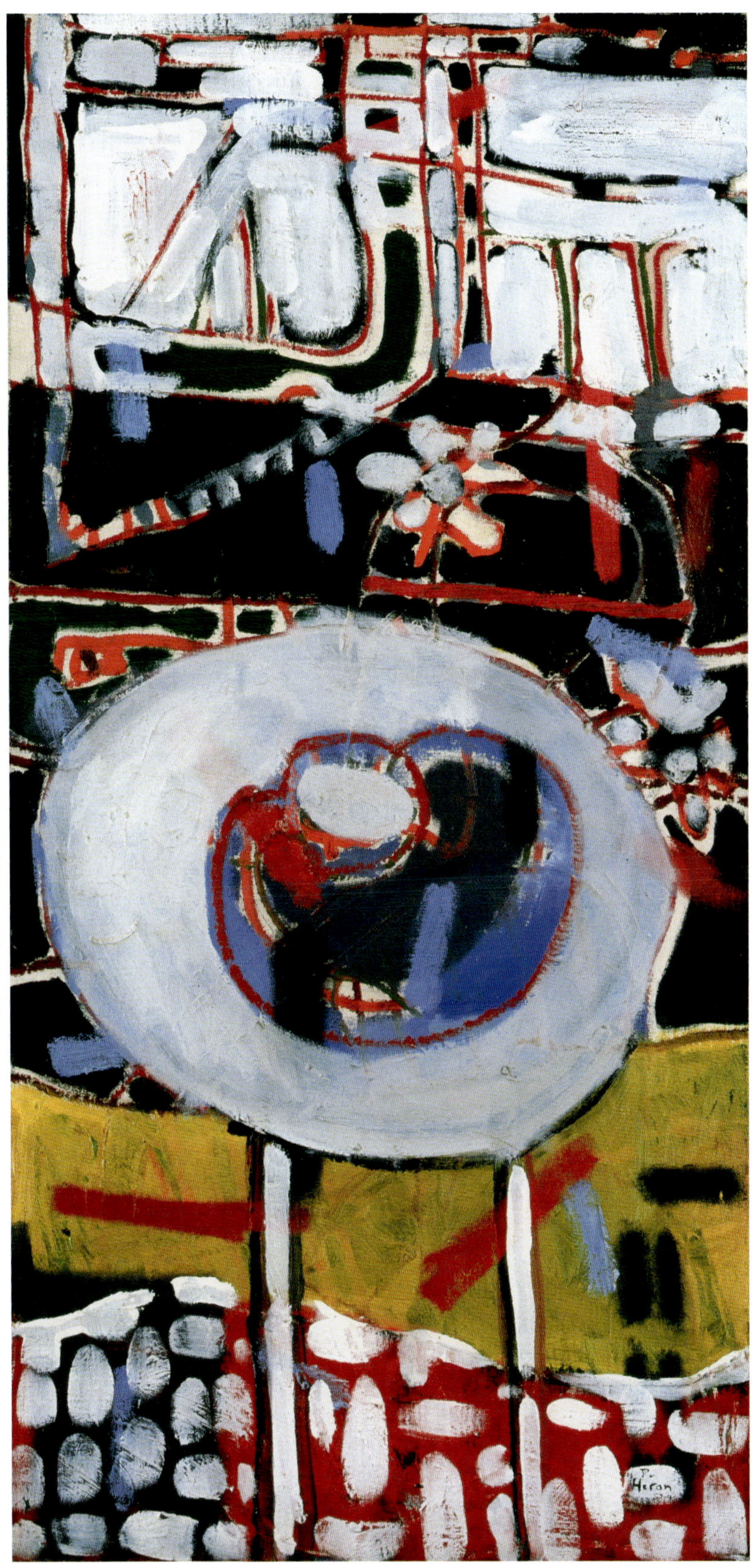

Fig. 79
Patrick Heron (1920–1999)
*Round White Table: St Ives: 1953–1954*,
1953–54
Oil on canvas, 91.4 × 45.7 cm
Katharine Heron and Susanna Heron

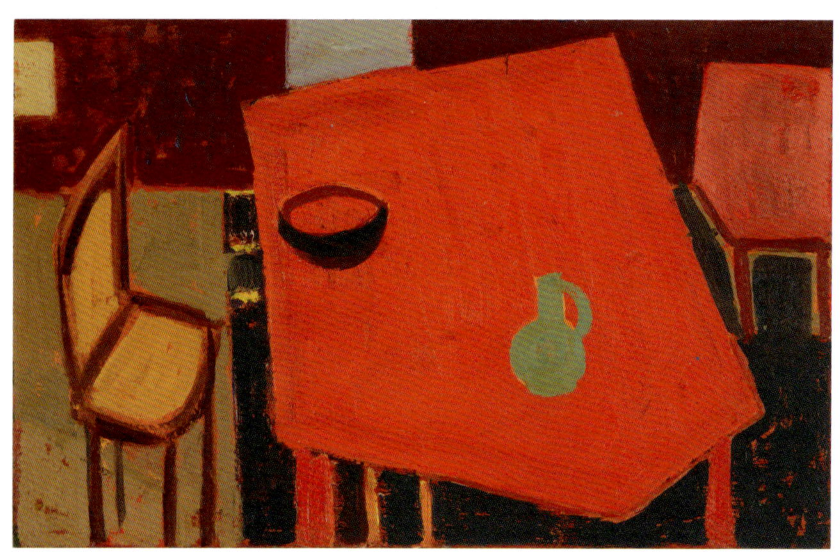

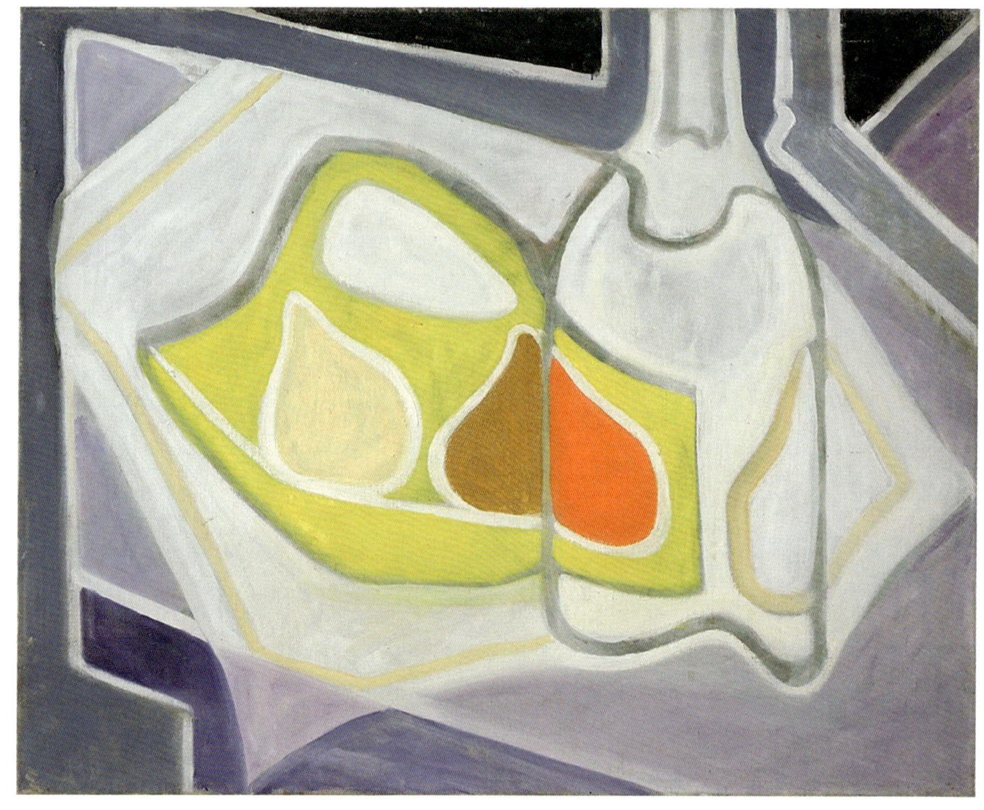

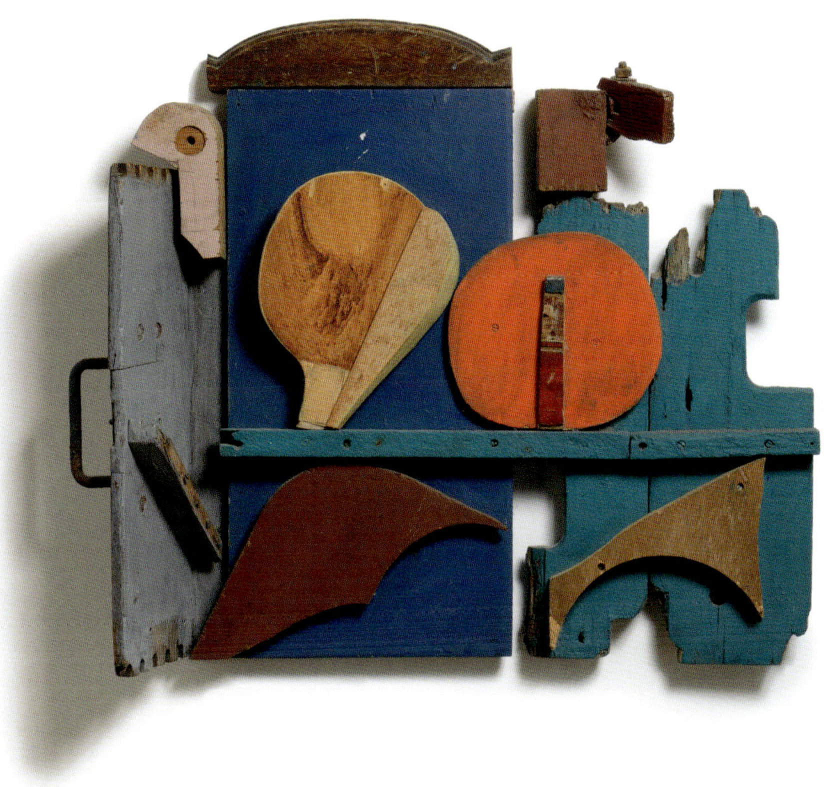

would 'give us happiness and a greater individual liberty, combined with ... collective vitality'.[7] For his part, Nicholson was much less excited than his new partner by abstraction's conceptual poetics. On the question of abstract-versus-representational, he was at best a fuzzy theorist and reluctant statement-maker, prone to tying himself in verbal knots:

> It must be understood that a good idea is exactly as good as it can be universally applied, that no idea can have a universal application which is not solved in its own terms[8]

Fig. 80 (opposite, above)
Wilhelmina Barns-Graham (1912–2004)
*Red Table*, 1952
Oil on canvas, 12.3 × 20 cm
Wilhelmina Barns-Graham Trust

Fig. 81 (opposite, below)
Margaret Mellis (1914–2009)
*Yellow Basket with Bottle*, 1952
Oil on canvas, 51 × 63.5 cm
Estate of Margaret Mellis.
Courtesy of The Redfern Gallery

Fig. 82 (above)
Margaret Mellis (1914–2009)
*Toy cupboard (thirty)*, 1983
Driftwood construction, 54.6 × 59 cm
Estate of Margaret Mellis.
Courtesy of The Redfern Gallery

There was something about the specific shape of this jug or that wine glass that spoke to him more directly, suggested more 'good ideas', than the generalised notion of a conoid or a sphere.

Forward to 1946; travel to Europe is again possible and the art market slowly returning to life. Nicholson's pre-war desire to align his work with international abstraction is reasserting itself. His *1946 (still life, cerulean)* presents another tabletop, another gathering of domestic objects – a wine glass, a cup – and another almost playful juggling of abstract, coloured shapes. This time, however, everything is transposed into a still-life register that Nicholson had made his own – a fusion of bright, flattened pattern-making with the atmospheric depth of landscape, a symptom of the seven years this dapper metropolitan artist had by now spent in the

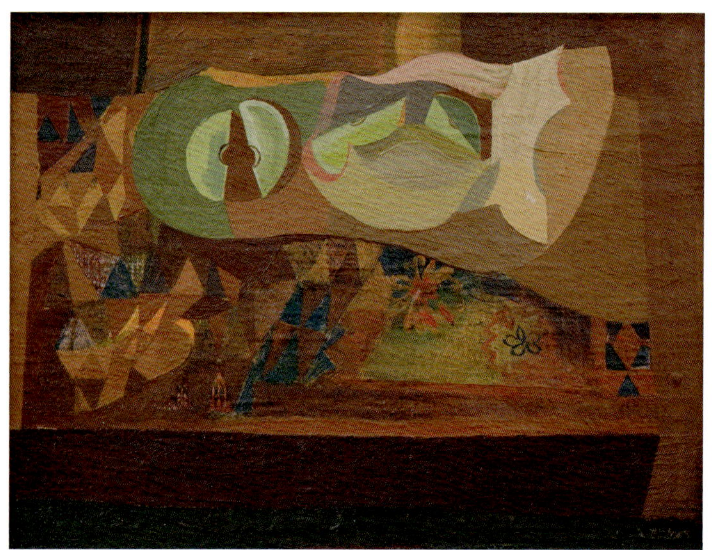

Fig. 83
Robert MacBryde (1913–1966)
*Apples on Paper*, n.d.
Oil on board, 30 × 39.5 cm
Pallant House Gallery, Chichester
(Kearley Bequest through Art Fund 1989)

rough-hewn natural environment of West Cornwall. If still life as a genre had retained, thanks to cubism, its international modernist credentials, landscape painting had been the only field, pre-Henry Moore, in which British artists had won serious recognition abroad. And there is a sense in which, in contrast to European cubism, landscape continued to infiltrate Modern British still-life painting – an intuition, often, of natural light and atmosphere, an acknowledgement of the world outside the window.

A thread that links the earliest and latest of Nicholson's three works in this essay, intravenously connecting Parisian cubism to contemporary British art through the quasi-abstract treatment of still life, can also be traced through the work of his younger contemporary Patrick Heron (1920–1999). In June 1949, Heron was in Paris, where he visited Braque in his studio. Braque had remained in Paris during the Occupation, producing still lifes in which he sometimes gave familiar cubist tabletop objects a sombre twist by the addition of a skull. In 1946, Braque had an exhibition of his wartime still lifes in London; together with the *Picasso and Matisse* show at the Victoria and Albert Museum in winter 1945, this belatedly introduced the British public, including a generation of artists who had reached adulthood during the war, to three legendary figures of the European avant-garde. Braque's recent work, wrote Heron, revealed him to be the 'greatest living master of still life';[9] it 'brought something that we could not have had previous experience of – a new development in an immensely powerful art'.[10] This new development represented 'the most powerful fusion so far made of the abstract and the representational – two aspects of art which, isolated, either from the other, can only impoverish the painting of our time'.[11]

Begun after he had seen the 1946 exhibition and completed the year of his visit to Paris, Heron's *Still Life* (fig. 78) shows him exploring exactly the 'powerful fusion' he had discovered in Braque. The representational still-life elements – a mirror on the wall, a tabletop, an oil lamp, a window frame – are painted in outline or silhouette, with broad areas of colour that seem to occupy the same plane, rather than suggesting background surfaces. And in Heron's colour, 'emotional value' (to borrow Hepworth's phrase) weighs stronger than observational accuracy; the window frame's four rectangles, for example, contain four different combinations of pale blue- and lilac greys, blacks and midnight blues.

By the time he painted *Round White Table: St Ives: 1953–1954* (fig. 79), Heron was spending long summers in St Ives with his young family, in

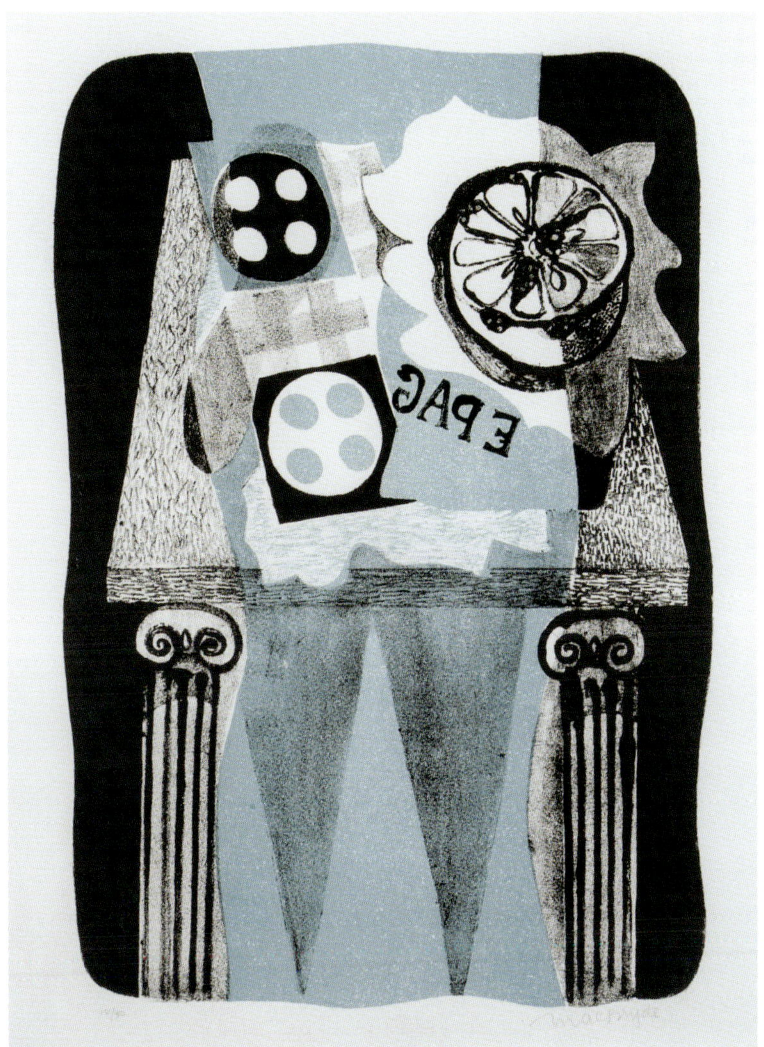

Fig. 84
Robert MacBryde (1913–1966)
*Still Life (with Ludo Board and Lemon)*, c.1950
Lithograph in colours, 55 × 39 cm
Pallant House Gallery, Chichester
(The Golder – Thompson Gift, 2021)

close proximity to Hepworth and Nicholson, and his direction of travel towards abstraction was even more pronounced. The white table shape – both actual table and abstract oval – is anchored by its legs in what you then start to try to read as an interior: *that* shape is definitely a flower, and that is probably a window, and maybe the thick white brushstrokes against red at the bottom are a rug. Or possibly, whether or not there was a real-life rug on the floor, Heron simply decided to create a pattern that would work with the yellow, red, blue and black section above. His description of the way in which Braque's 1940s still lifes seemed to make the distinction between abstract and representational painting redundant was also, of course (and perhaps primarily), a description of what Heron now wanted to achieve: a focus on, an immersion in 'the picture itself; alive, mysterious, full of sensuous refinement; yet durable in its substance and timeless in its impact and effect'.[12]

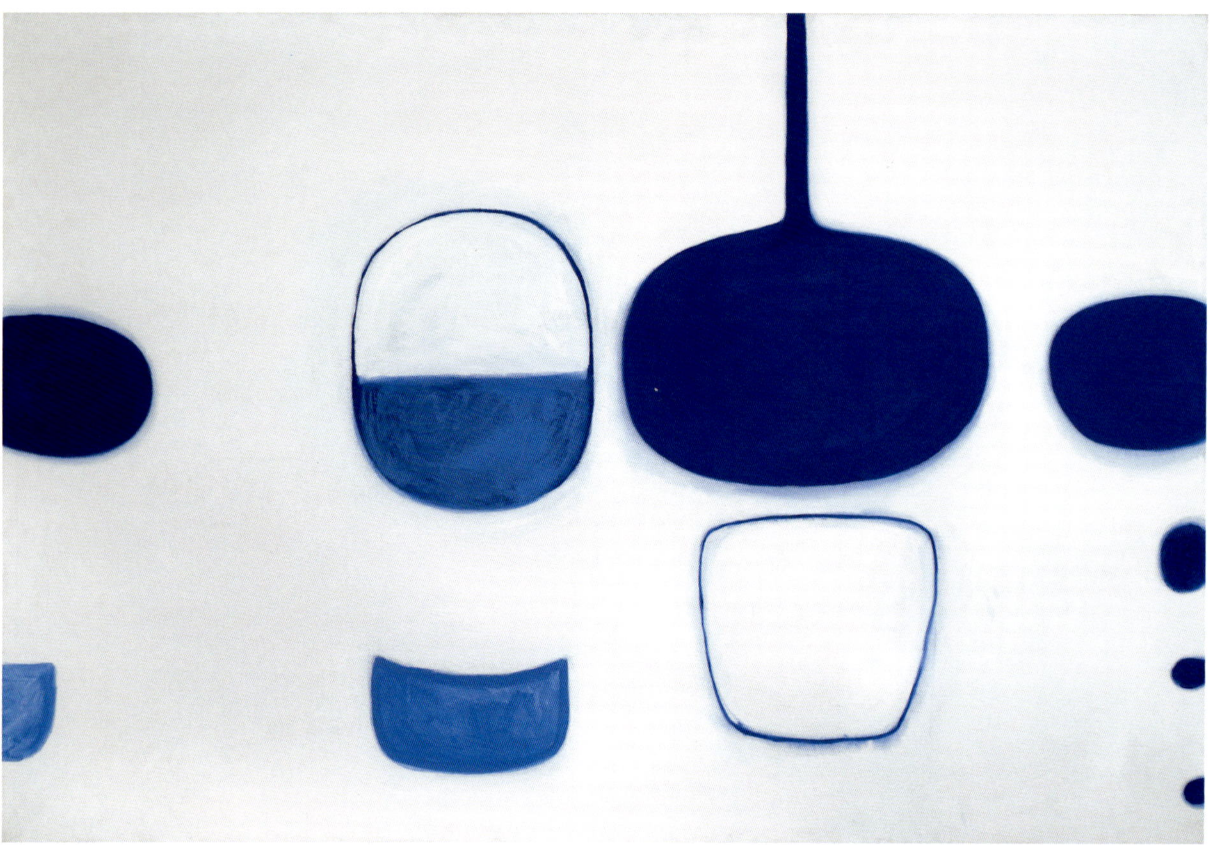

Fig. 85
William Scott (1913–1989)
*Still life variations 2*, 1969
Oil on canvas, 121.9 × 182.9 cm
Private collection

Between 1939, when Hepworth and Nicholson had arrived in St Ives on the eve of war, and the mid-1950s, when British artists' excitement about American abstract expressionism pushed the earlier dialogues with cubism, constructivism and European abstract art in general into the shadows, St Ives was where the push-and-pull between representation and abstraction was most consistently put to the test. After painting *Red Table* (fig. 80), which is, like Heron's *Round White Table*, an orchestration of abstract shapes and colours (were the tabletop and the contents of the bowl really that solid, in-your-face scarlet?), Wilhelmina Barns-Graham (1912–2004) reprised the arrangement based on a central tetrahedron with a balancing semicircular shape in a series of abstract works. Her friend Margaret Mellis (1914–2009), who in 1946 had left St Ives for France, then moved to rural Suffolk in 1950, was walking a similar path between abstract forms and recognisable objects. The tabletop in her *Yellow Basket with Bottle* (fig. 81) owes something to Braque in its outline silhouettes; something to Picasso in the bodily liveliness of the basket's contents; and a lot to the memory of Côte d'Azur sunshine in its colour.

For British artists in general, the early 1950s were a time when it was possible to shake free of the pre-war dominance of Paris, New York was not

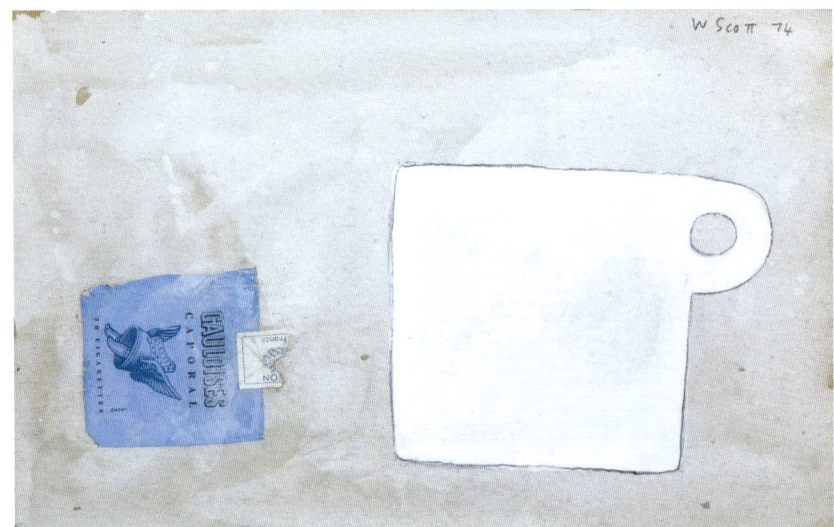


Fig. 86
William Scott (1913–1989)
*Cup*, 1974
Gouache and collage on paper,
20.4 × 32.6 cm
Pallant House Gallery, Chichester
(The George and Ann Dannatt Gift, 2011)

yet in the ascendant, and the art market was still in a postwar process of renewing and reinventing itself. If brilliant opportunities had not quite yet opened up (as they would do for David Hockney, b.1937, and his contemporaries in the 1960s), many things seemed seriously, confidently possible. Two still lifes by Robert MacBryde (1913–1966) (figs. 83 and 84) present the kind of objects – tilted-up tabletop, fruit dish, typographic snippet, board game – that would have been at home in 1900s Paris. They remind us that MacBryde's louche celebrity in wartime London had much to do with his sombre, slightly gothic take on cubism, which felt all the more impressive in the absence of any chance to see Braque and Picasso's originals. Postwar, his crisper, more illustrative line and brighter colour are in tune with his parallel career in stage set design – an art form in which still life often acts as a physical prop. Newly arrived at the Slade School of Art from Lahore in 1956, Anwar Jalal Shemza (1928–1985) destroyed much of the work he had brought with him to London, where he found zero interest in contemporary Pakistani art, and embarked on a new phase, under the guiding star of Paul Klee (1879–1940). In a painting from 1957 (fig. 88), Shemza marries the glowing nocturne of a Klee dreamscape with a collection of still-life cups and bowls that are already half-way towards his pure abstract practice of the 1960s.

This is Britain in the mid-century. By the 1970s and 1980s, the heat had transferred from the abstract-versus-figurative debate to arguments about conceptual art. The 'death of painting' was widely touted. But painting, as we now know, did not die. If the poise and poetry of William Scott's (1913–1989) still lifes (figs. 85 and 86) looked a touch *passé* in the conceptual 1970s, they hold their own today; as Heron wrote of Braque, it is still true that (among other qualities) 'permanence, grandeur, deliberation, lucidity and calm are paramount virtues of the art of painting'.[13] So too is the ability of still-life painting to make space for the fragile, the evanescent, the easily ignored or missed. Few people paid much attention to Margaret Mellis or had any idea about her long artistic career when, in the 1980s, she beachcombed an enormous store of wooden flotsam on the Suffolk coast, assembling bits and pieces that caught her eye into three-dimensional still lifes (fig. 82). And what was Howard Hodgkin thinking about when he painted his *Still Life* in 1987–90 (fig. 87)? It feels like a coded diary entry about an intense still-life moment – the taste of a strawberry, a slip of sunlight falling through leaves onto a table, glimpsed in a rear-view mirror, telling us that still life is perhaps always a journey from the actual, the specific to some other plane of experience.

Bottles spill, cups break, tables burn, flowers fade. Luckily, though, we have paintings. Presenting his television series *Ways of Seeing* in 1972 – the dawn of the personal-computer information age – the artist-turned-writer John Berger (1926–2017) observed that 'paintings are silent and still in a sense that information never is ... the silence and stillness permeate the actual materials, the paint'.[14] Berger and Heron, who agreed on very little else, agreed on this. Today, navigating the data-saturated landscape of information overload, it is as much of a lifeline as it ever was to catch hold of the handle of a Ben Nicholson mug or swim into Anwar Jalal Shemza's washed-silk blues – whatever works for you in the never-more-urgent quest for stillness, lucidity and calm.

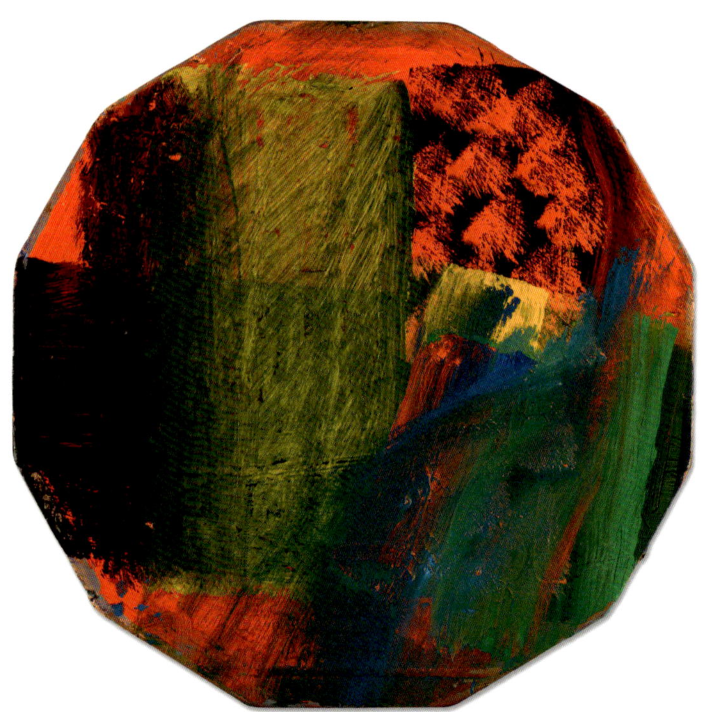

Fig. 87 (right)
Howard Hodgkin (1932–2017)
*Still Life*, 1987–90
Oil on wood, 37 cm diameter
Private collection

Fig. 88 (opposite)
Anwar Jalal Shemza (1928–1985)
*Still Life*, 1957
Oil on fibreboard, 64 × 46.4 cm
Estate of Anwar Jalal Shemza

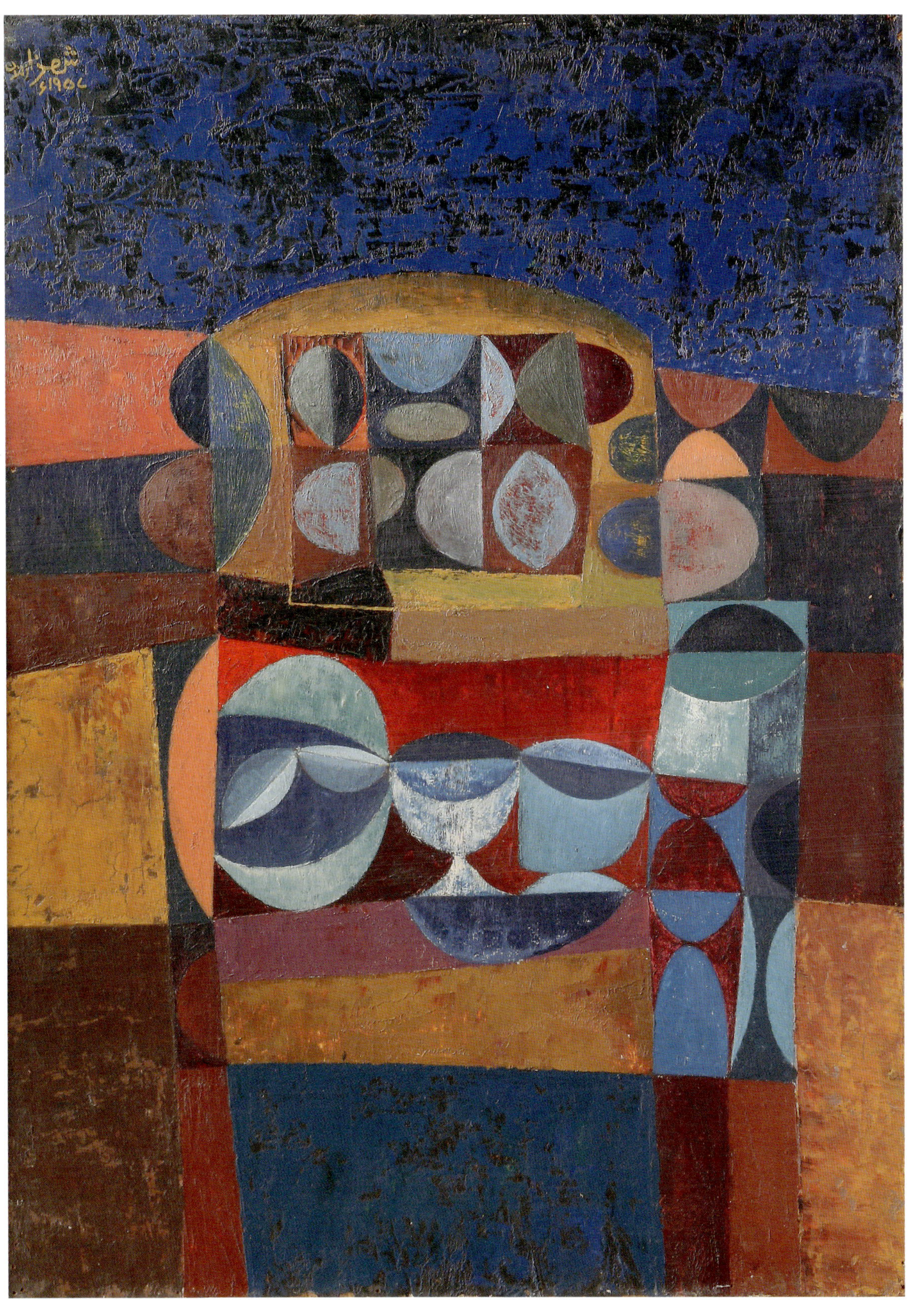

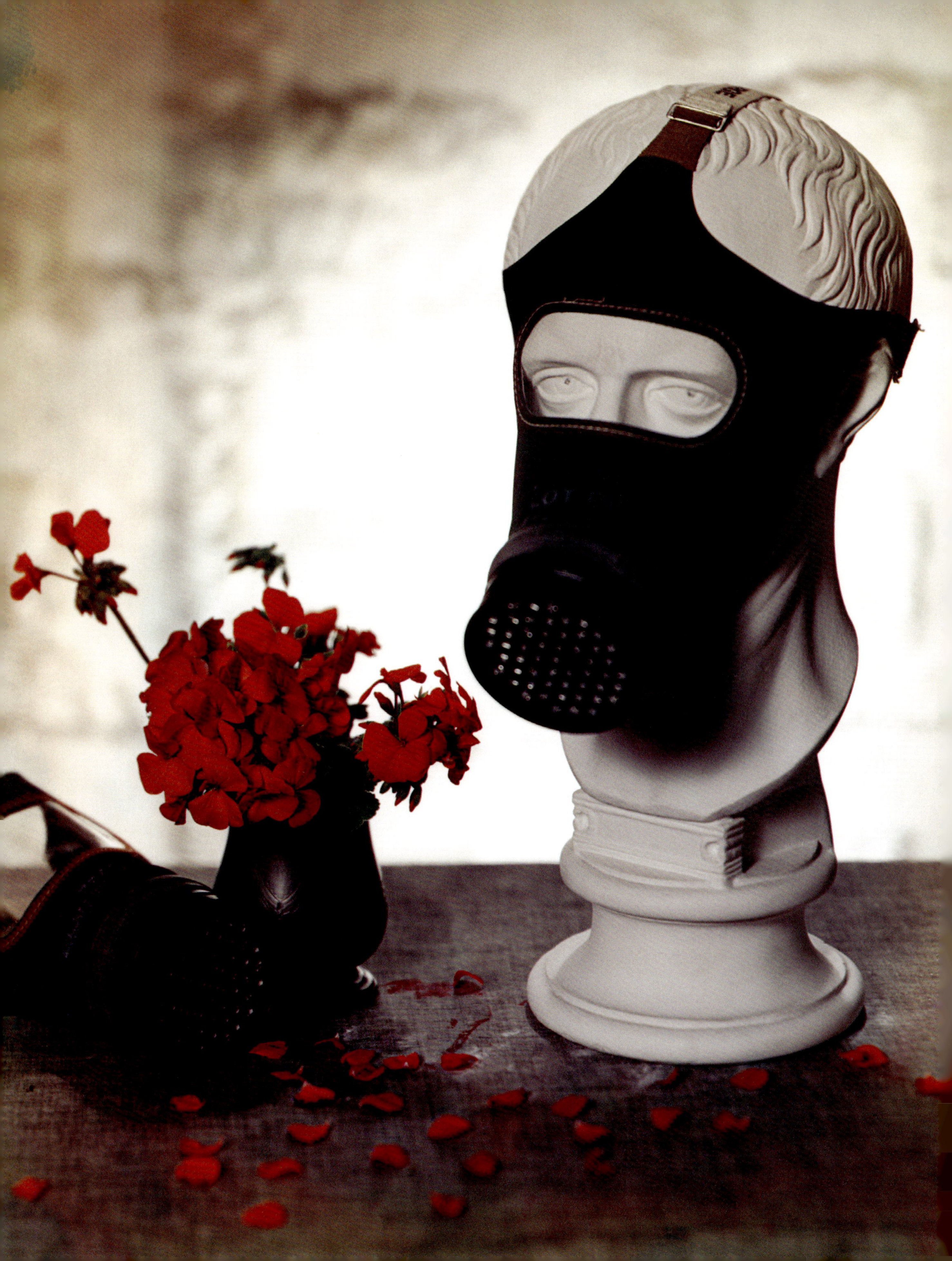

# 5 'The World Is Still Dark': Death and Existentialism in British Still Life, 1939 to Now

MELANIE VANDENBROUCK

When, in May 1933, the German artist Hans Feibusch (1898–1998) emigrated to Britain, he was fleeing persecution in Nazi Germany. Following Adolf Hitler's appointment as Chancellor, it was Nazi policy to ban the work of Jewish artists from museums or to display them as 'degenerate art'. Like many other Jewish artists, it was these events that had precipitated his decision. Feibusch had considered moving to Italy, but as he was engaged to be married to Sidonie Gestetner, a British woman, London was a natural choice. Painted the year of their marriage in 1935, an untitled still life (fig. 90) evokes the sense of uncertainty and uneasiness at a time of escalating international tension. A sculpted head, candle, vase and shell are tightly arranged alongside each other on a single plane. The profile of the head, shown from the neck up, resembles Feibusch himself. The scene is lightly illuminated by a flickering candle, a common still-life motif, which may symbolise the breath of life and the fragility of human existence. It may also evoke light in darkness, a symbol of hope in uncertain times.

If still life had long represented the inescapable fact that everything that lives will die, this fundamental truth about the human condition was brought into much sharper relief by the Second World War: the butchery at the front, the carnage of indiscriminate bombings, the sense of isolation, the belated discovery of the horrors of the death camps, wartime and postwar rationing, the return of servicemen suffering post-traumatic stress-disorder. And then, from 1947, the years of 'the high cold war',[1] the ever-present threat of nuclear annihilation, the remapping of the world order, and Britain's international status shaken to its core by the decline of empire, accelerated by the decolonisation movement.

Fig. 89
Yevonde (1893–1975)
*Crisis (ARP)*, 1939
Photographic print, 38.1 × 30.5 cm
National Portrait Gallery, London

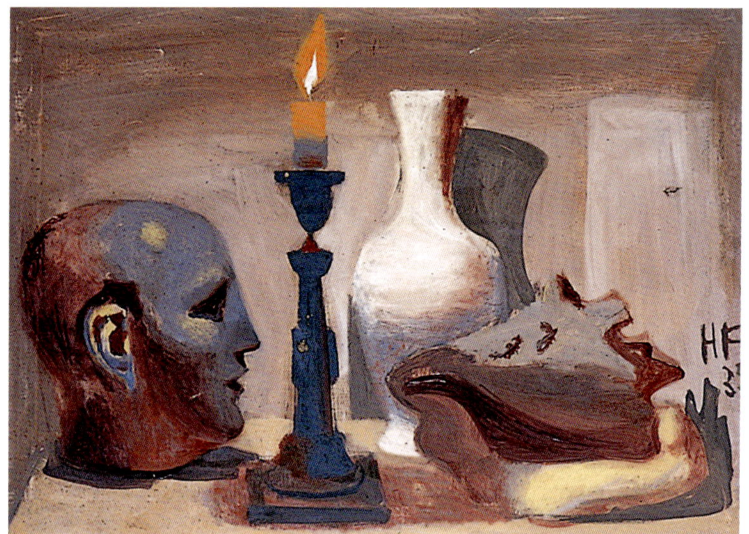

Fig. 90
Hans Feibusch (1898–1998)
*Still Life of a Bust, a Candle, a Vase and a Shell*, 1935
Oil on canvas, 53 × 73.5 cm
Pallant House Gallery, Chichester
(Feibusch Studio, Gift of the Artist, 1997)

As the likelihood of war with Germany increased in the late 1930s, so did the fear of aerial warfare and the bombing of civilians. In 1937, the British government passed the Air Raid Precautions Act (ARP), with the aim of preparing local authorities for air attacks. It was believed that such attacks might include poison gas, and from the the following year the entirety of the British population was issued with gas masks. As Britain entered into war with Germany on 3 September 1939, air raid sirens resounded over London. (In fact, though these became part of Londoners' everyday life, German air raids would not start until June 1940 and, thankfully, poison gas was never used.) *Crisis (ARP)* (fig. 89) by pioneer of colour photography and society portraitist Madame Yevonde (1893–1975), evokes the menace and isolation, the resolve but also resignation, that was felt with the outbreak of the war. Adept at striking juxtapositions, Yevonde adorned a bust of the Roman emperor Julius Caesar (a recurring character in her 'surrealist' still lifes) with a gas mask. Another mask rests to the left of the picture, perhaps expressing the readiness to put one on, or symbolising a body no longer there. Between them, a jar contains a small bouquet of geraniums shedding blood-coloured petals. This had been a year of personal grief for Yevonde, whose husband had died of cancer in the spring. This was also one of her last colour photographs, as the company which produced the Vivex technology she favoured became an early casualty of the war.

In some ways, colour left British art during this period. While some artists served at the front, others, whether conscientious objectors or dispensed from service due to age or ill health, were involved in the war effort through the War Artists Advisory Committee. Some of them, loosely described as neo-romantics – among them Paul Nash, Michael Ayrton, John Craxton, Lucian Freud, John Minton and Graham Sutherland – produced brooding pastoral scenes mingling introspection with a mystic devotion to the British landscape. They also experimented with still lifes, including themes redolent of wartime isolation and *mal-de-vivre*.

Death looms large in the early work of Michael Ayrton, perhaps in part inspired by the death of his father when he was still a teenager. In 1941, he and his friend Minton (1917–1957) were commissioned by Sir John Gielgud to create the designs for a new production of *Macbeth*, staged in 1942. These were marked by the use of 'decaying walls, tattered curtains and rags, dramatic lighting and deep shadows', apposite to the sinister narrative of

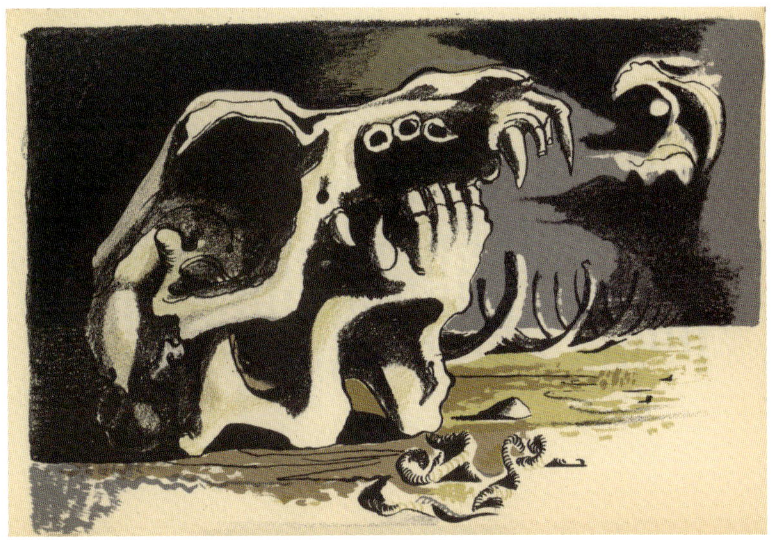

Fig. 91
Michael Ayrton (1921–1975)
*Illustration for Poems of Death*, edited by Phoebe Pool, published by Frederick Muller Ltd, 1945, Pallant House Gallery, Chichester

the play and the context of wartime.[2] Invalidated from the RAF in 1942, Ayrton spent much of the rest of the war teaching at Camberwell School of Art. Around that time, he painted his *Temptation of St Antony* (1942–3, Tate), a disturbingly macabre scene which reveals his profound preoccupation with death. This dark tendency was further expounded in his nightmarish *Skull Vision* (private collection) of 1943, the bestial skull as impressive for its monstrous monumentality as it is for the revulsion it conjures. While the work has been read by some as symptomatic of Ayrton's interest in the occult, the apocalyptic red glow that reflects on the bone surface also recalls the incendiary bombs that pounded London at the time.[3] Ayrton produced a somewhat dislocated version of this skull for his lithographic illustrations of Phoebe Pool's anthology, *Poems of Death* (1945) (fig. 91); if less horrific than *Skull Vision*, the collapsed bones, missing teeth and black hole of the gaping eye socket form a potent evocation of the desolation of wartime, and the ruination of buildings as well as lives.

In comparison, the depictions of dead animals that the young John Craxton (1922–2009) and Lucian Freud (1922–2011) produced around the same time seem relatively restrained. Dead game and 'meat stuff' had been a major subject of still life across centuries; symbolically charged with the reminder of death, but also as expressions of wealth and status at periods when meat was reserved to the ruling class. At a time of heightened awareness of mortality, as well as strict food rationing, it is impossible not to read the subtext of war in the decomposition of flesh in Freud's detailed *Dead Bird* (fig. 93) (an exact draughtsmanship which may owe to the example of Albrecht Dürer, with whose work he was familiar since his childhood in Berlin) or in Craxton's *Hare on a Table* (fig. 94), with its unsettling blue eye, limbs and ears stiffened by death. Craxton saw in the hare – formerly agile and bouncing, now reduced to a lifeless corpse – a representation of himself, trapped in locked-down Britain. He only completed the painting as the war ended and, the borders reopened, he was free at last.

As Margaret Garlake writes in *New Art New World: British Art in Postwar Society*, the role of women in society had changed little since pre-war times. Despite their contribution to the war effort, women were not encouraged to join the workforce, or indeed the arts (as Frances Spalding puts it, a 'vocation for art worked against likelihood of marriage and domestic harmony'), and so the postwar period is predominantly

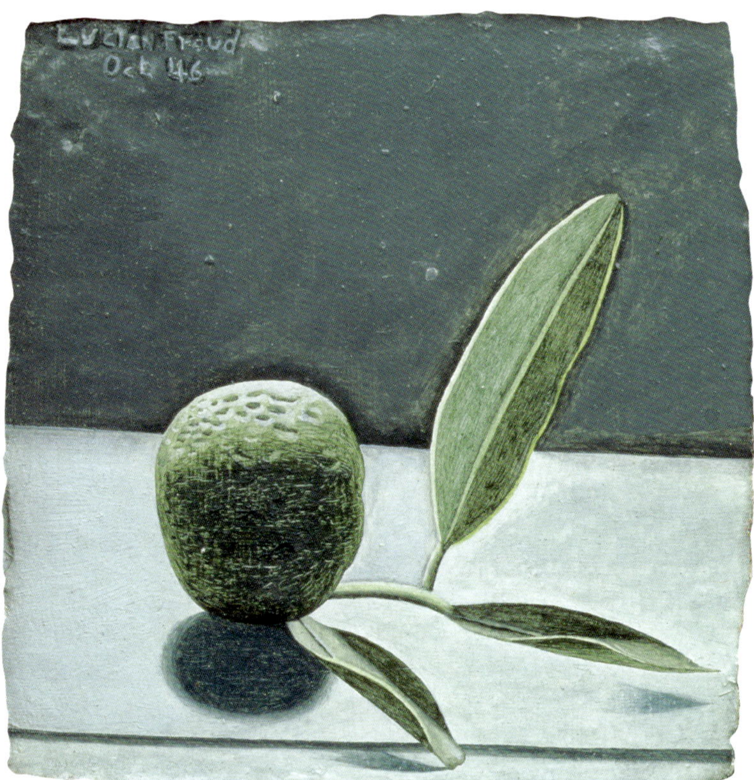


Fig. 92
Lucian Freud (1922–2011)
*Unripe Tangerine*, 1946–47
Oil on board, 9.3 × 9 cm
Pallant House Gallery, Chichester
(Wilson Loan, 2006)

marked by the work of male artists.[4] One of too few notable exceptions was Prunella Clough (1919–1999). Trained in design, life drawing and sculpture at Chelsea School of Art from 1937, as war broke out, she was conscripted by the Ministry of Labour to do clerical work, eventually drawing maps for the Ministry of Information and working as assistant art editor for the Office of War Information. Clough thus found little time to paint but, as war ended, she returned to art full time. Working in London in 1946–9, she soon became associated with the neo-romantics, with whom she socialised. During that period, she largely painted still lifes, featuring cabbages, nets, anchors, roots and dead birds seen during excursions to the beaches and harbours of Suffolk or at home. Her *Dead Plants in a Greenhouse* (fig. 95) is characteristic in its quietly intense observation of her surroundings. With a small, nondescript figure busying herself in the background, Clough pairs the matter-of-fact decay of collapsing organic matter in the thick-rooted plants (possibly parsnips, a staple of British diets and kitchen gardens during rationing) that lie flat and lifeless, yet monumental. Reviewing Clough's exhibition of 35 works at Roland, Browse and Delbanco, London, in 1949, which included this painting, Patrick Heron commented: 'Nothing could be calmer or – almost – more self-effacing than these truly accomplished paintings of still life … There is no sign of short cuts; she goes the hard way and doesn't jump, arbitrarily, from reality to

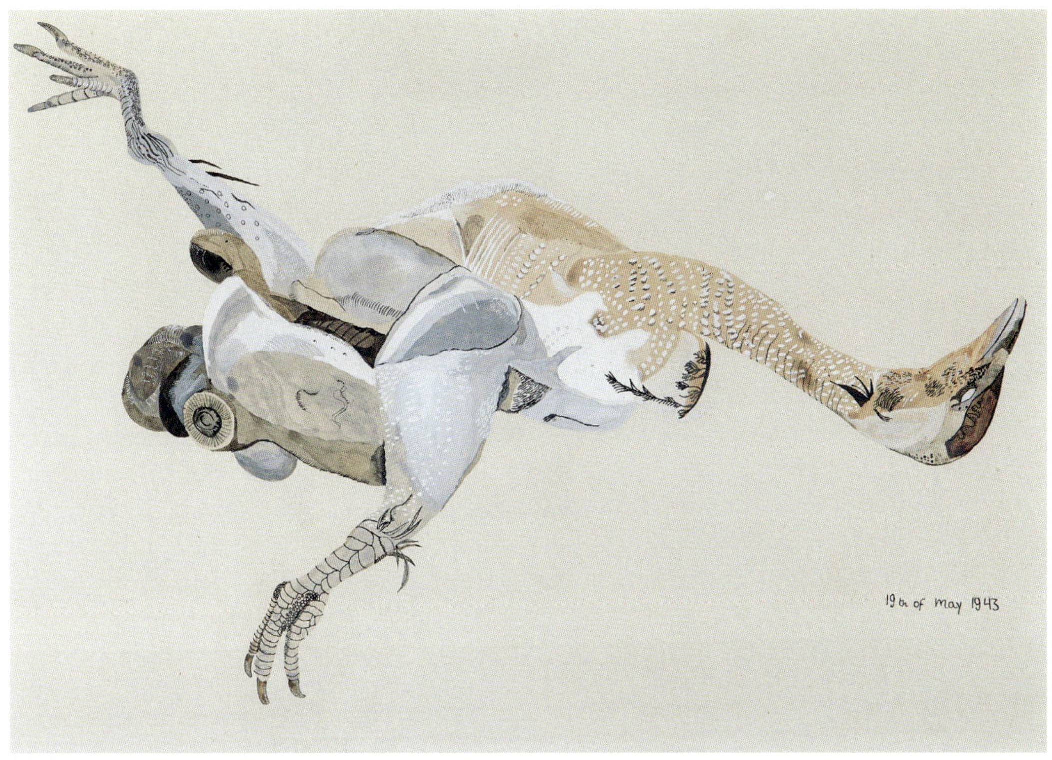


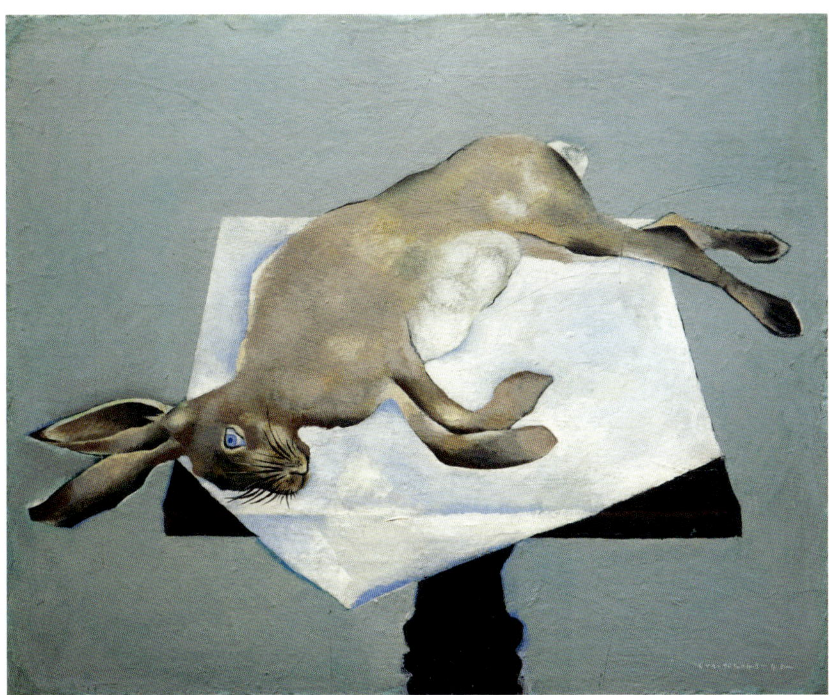

Fig. 93
Lucian Freud (1922–2011)
*Dead Bird*, 1943
Ink, gouache and watercolour
on paper, 27.5 x 39.5 cm
Pallant House Gallery, Chichester
(on loan from a Private Collection 2019)

Fig. 94
John Craxton (1922–2009)
*Hare on a Table*, 1944–46
Oil on canvas, 51 × 63.4 cm
Pallant House Gallery, Chichester
(on loan from the John Craxton Estate)

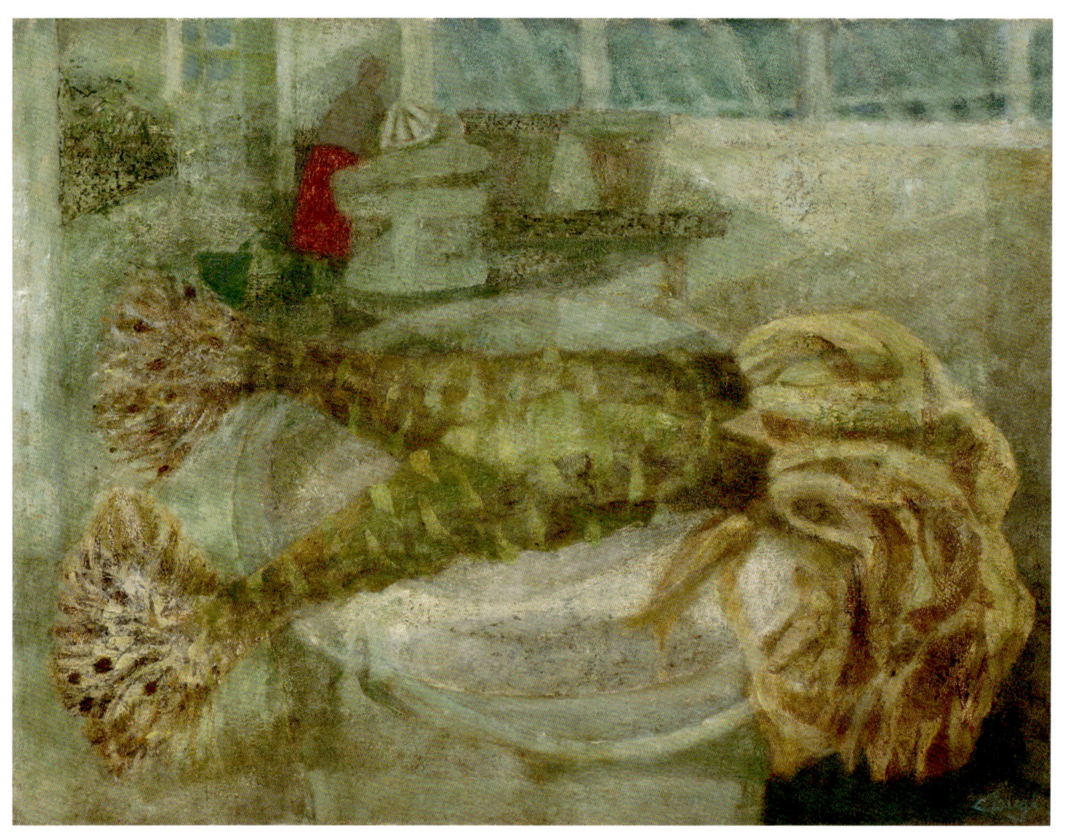

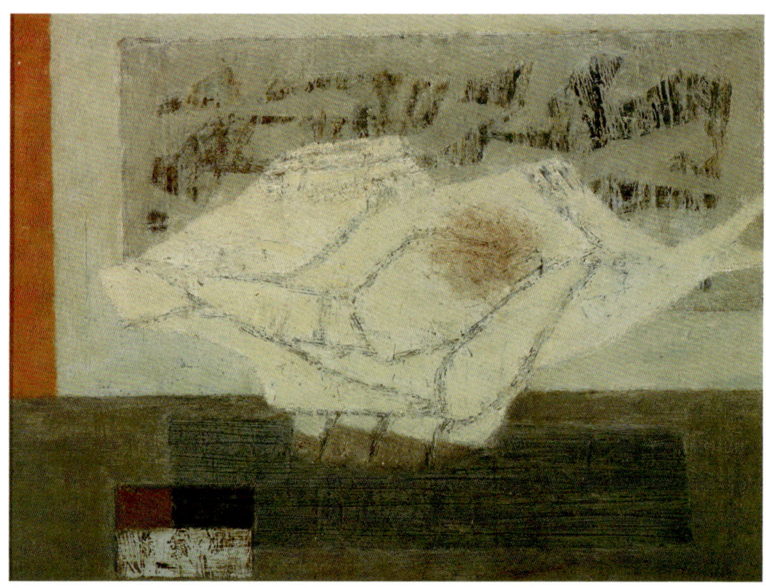

Fig. 95
Prunella Clough (1919–1999)
*Dead Plants in a Greenhouse*, 1947
Oil on canvas, 48 × 60 cm
Private collection of Amanda Posey & Nick Hornby

Fig. 96
Prunella Clough (1919–1999)
*Bone Drawing*, 1949
Oil on board, 25.5 × 33 cm
Private collection

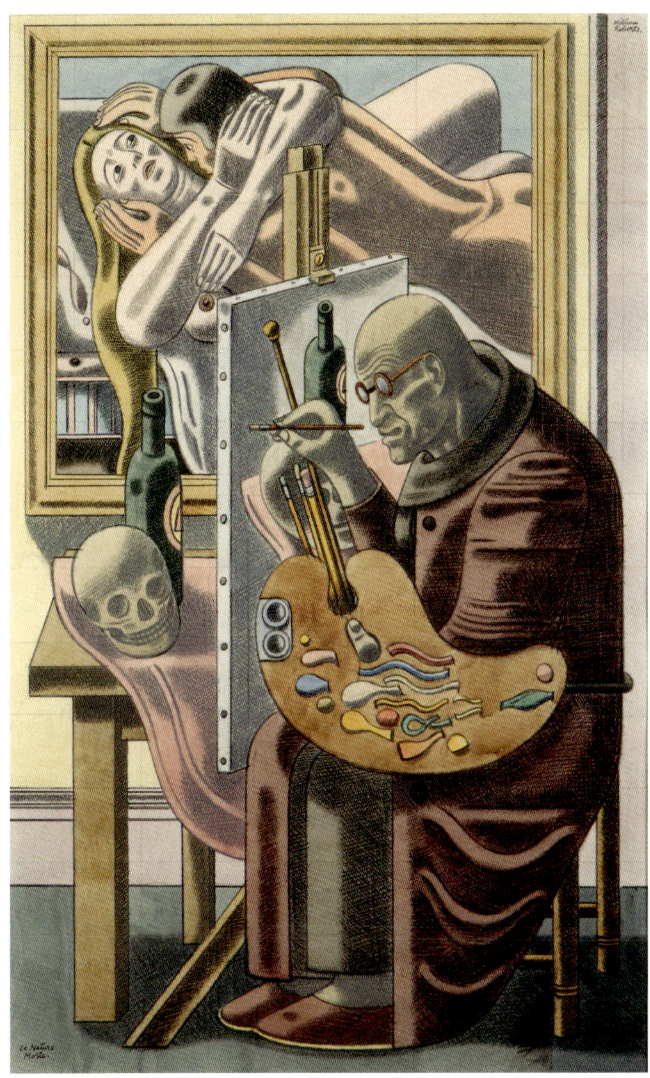

Fig. 97
William Roberts (1895–1980)
*La nature morte*, c.1948
Watercolour on paper, 49.5 × 31.8 cm
Museum and Art Swindon

abstraction. Her abstraction is condensed from her subject'.[5] In both this and *Bone Drawing* (fig. 96) from the following year (another oil painting, despite its title), Clough's restrained colour palette and tight focus on the physical presence of objects that take up most of the picture plane become a formal exercise more than a narrative or symbolic one. In the latter painting, Clough focuses on the primeval solidity of her subject, which manifests the aura of a tangible relic of something past. As the art critic John Berger observed in 1953, 'above all, she is interested in the material, the density, the tactile "feel" of the objects she paints'.[6] Her attention to the structure and the bleached surface betrays her interest in sculpture (the discipline she had studied before the war) but this painting already evidences the predilection for texture and subtle gradation of colour that would mark Clough's later, more abstract work.

For all the dampened optimism of austerity, the end of the Second World War also heralded a return to life and what would be later called a 'baby boom'. In his *La nature morte* (fig. 97) (the French title an affectation perhaps mockingly directed at collectors' enduring taste for French art), William Roberts (1895–1980) rather satirically reminds us that the corollary of death is life, the inevitable association of Eros and Thanatos that was a long staple of European culture. In what could be read as a self-portrait, Roberts presents a be-gowned painter at his easel, preoccupied with the act of painting. Across the easel is a table on which rests a bottle of Bass Ale and an object in dangerous proximity to the edge: the skull, this most archetypal of *memento mori* motifs, a reminder of one's fate. Beyond, hung on the wall, is a picture of a nude couple, caught in the act. The gaping eye-sockets of the skull mirror the hard lenses of Roberts's spectacles, while the jaws and cheeks of the skull in turn mirror the bone structure of the artist's face. The meeting of several planes – the plane of the painting in the background, that of the table, of the canvas in the process of being painted and the picture plane of the artwork itself – expresses the coalescence of several registers. Roberts is playing with genres, operating a kind of double portrait – a portrait of the artist at the easel, the skull as the artist's own – an erotic picture as a backdrop, while ostensibly making this watercolour about still life and the making of still life. In his comical association of lovemaking with the

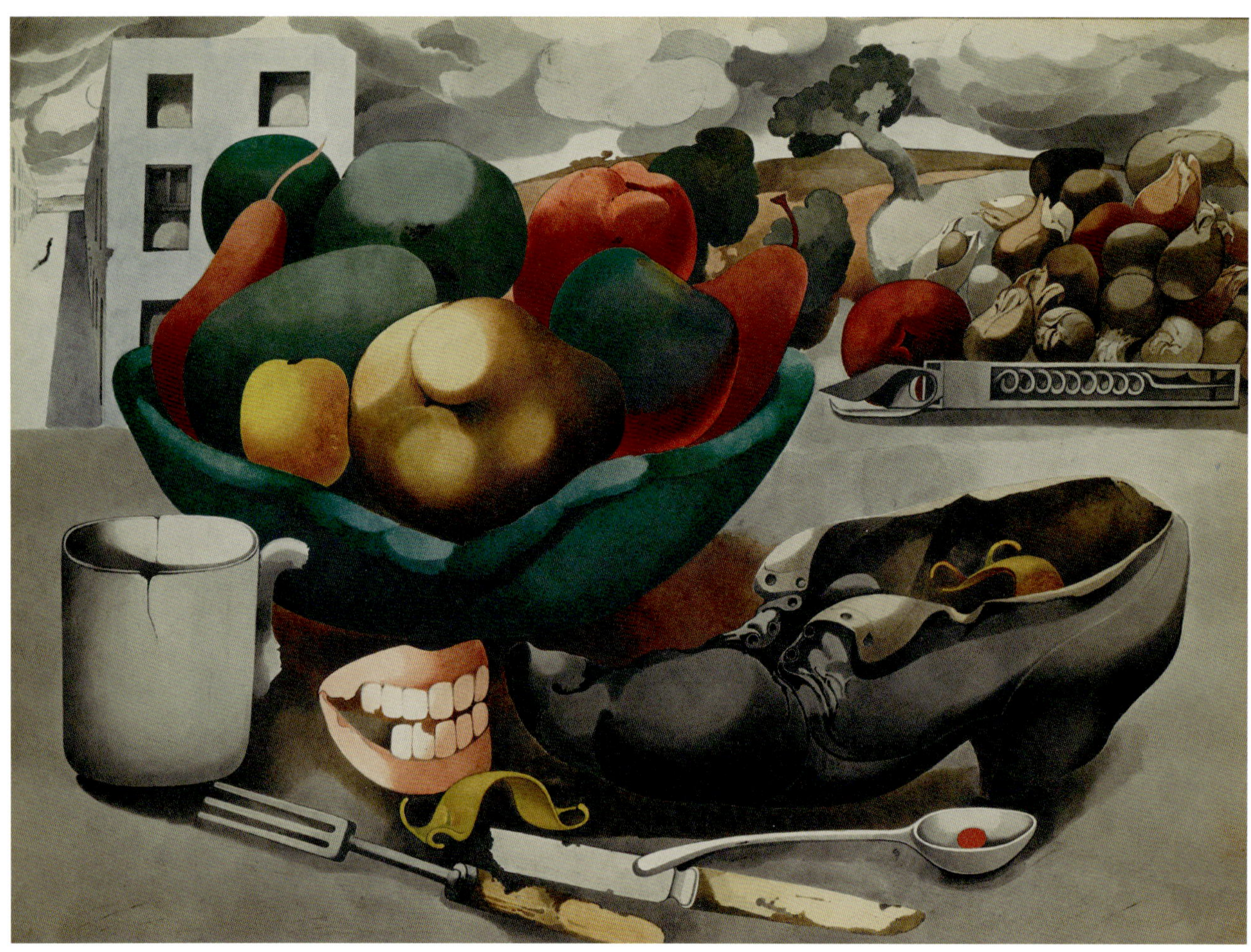

Fig. 98 (above)
Edward Burra (1905–1976)
*Still Life with Teeth*, 1946
Pencil, watercolour and gouache
on paper, 56 × 76.5 cm
Private European collection

Fig. 99 (opposite)
Valentine Dobrée (1894–1974)
*Composition with Skull and Shells*, n.d.
Oil on board, 55.5 × 44 cm
Reproduced with the permission of Special
Collections, Leeds University Library,
[University Art Collection], [LEEUA 1993.018]

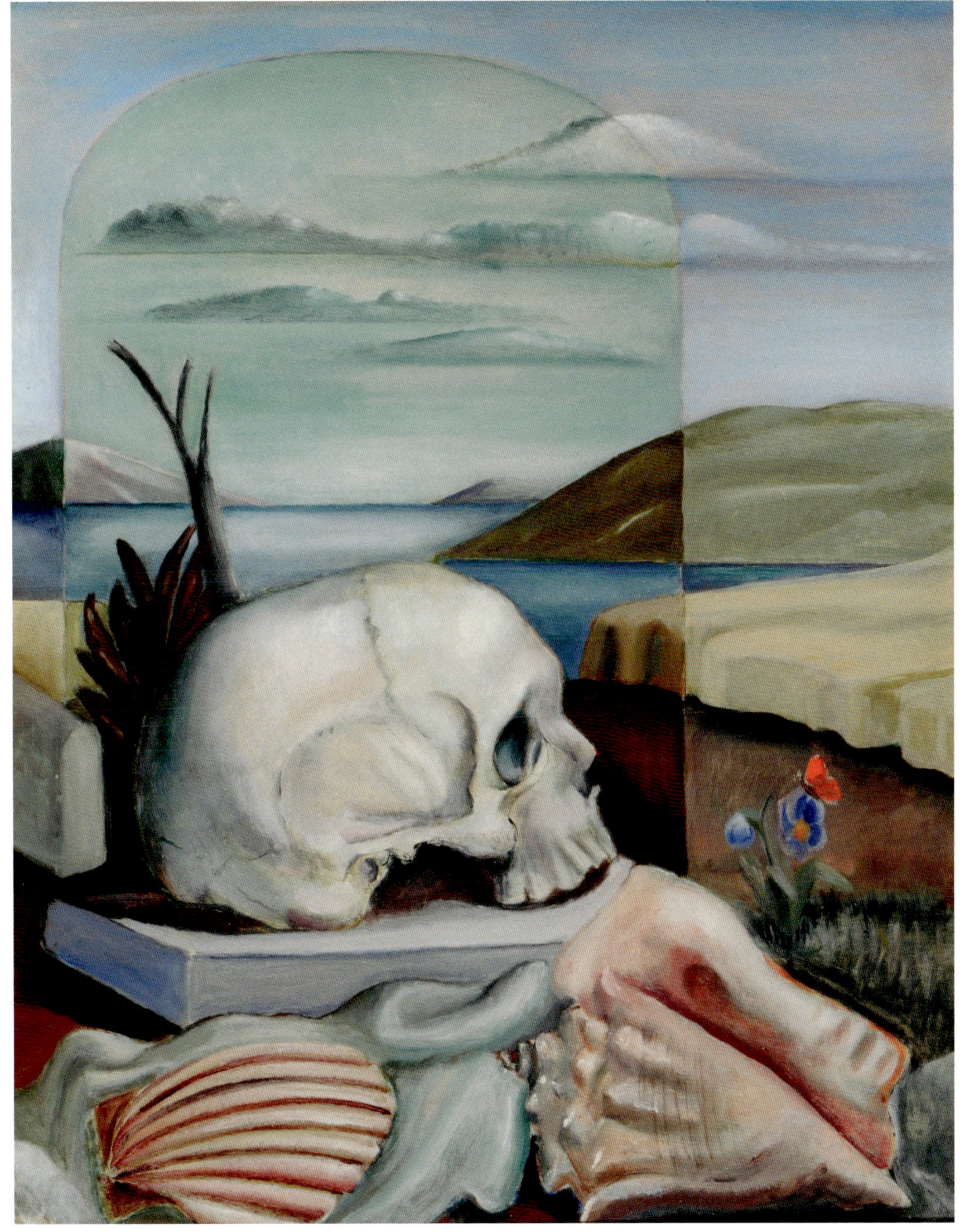

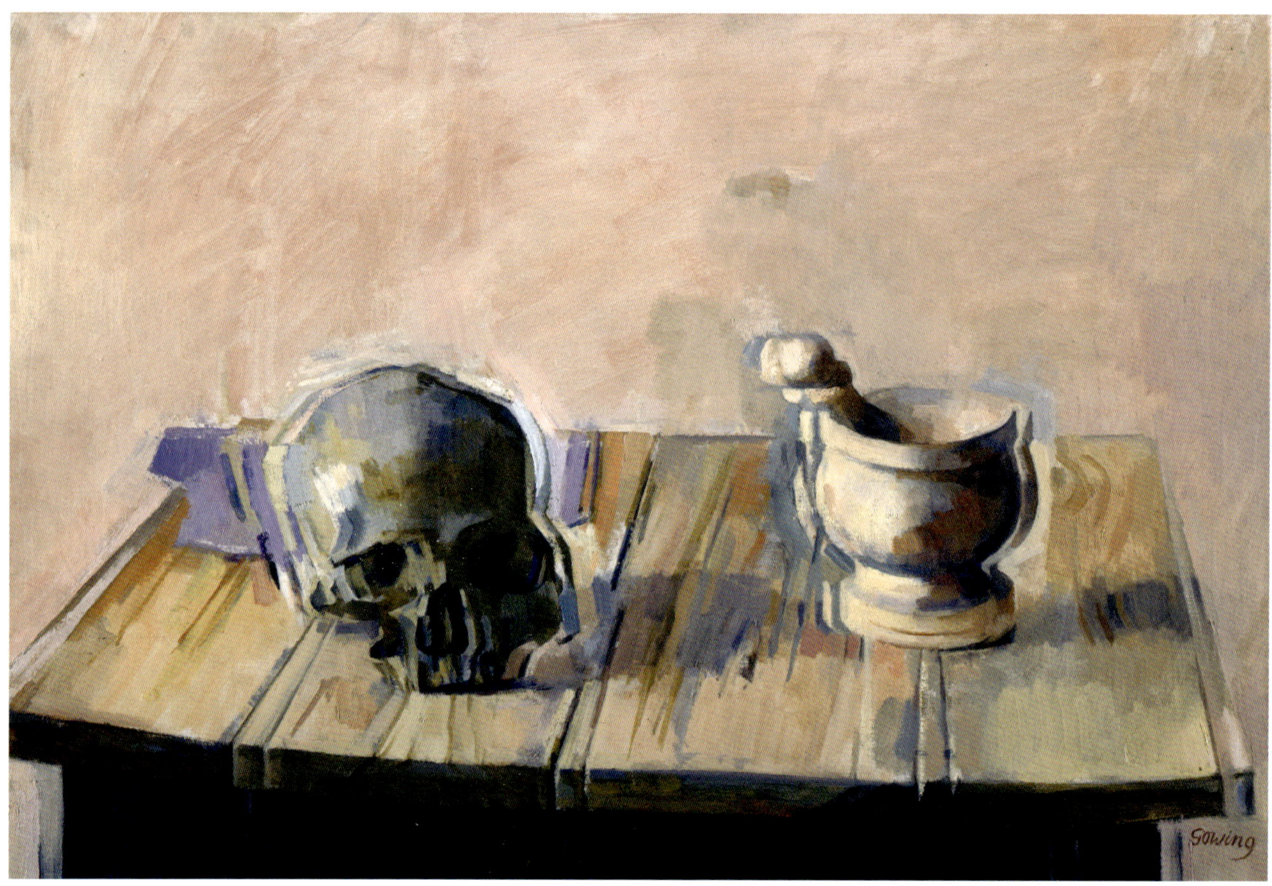


Fig. 100
Lawrence Gowing (1918–1991)
*Still Life: Vanitas*, 1979
Oil on canvas, 51 × 76 cm
Lent by Royal Academy of Arts, London

grinning skull, Roberts seems to tell us that, after all this wartime thinking about death, it is time to get on with life.

This focus on the act of painting and the place of still life within art is also the subject of Lawrence Gowing's (1918–1991) *Still Life: Vanitas* (fig. 100), painted three decades after Roberts's watercolour. In this work, Gowing proclaims his allegiance to Cezanne in the rendering of the shadows in colour; the play with perception in the blurred, dual vision; the 'honest' wooden table rejecting any artifice. Skull and mortar are here about painting; the skull as the indispensable studio prop (Cezanne, for that matter, kept several in his studio) and object of focus in art academies and schools; the mortar as the instrument for the crushing of pigments, so essential in the work of a colourist.

If some artists met the end of the war with relief or exaltation, others teetered out of years lived in darkness without finding the light. Thus, on 20 September 1945, Keith Vaughan recorded in his journal the end of wartime blackout: 'Today I saw a streetlamp. I suppose it must have been five years since I saw the last ... The lights go on and everyone mistakes them for light. But they are not light. There is no true illumination. There is just a garishness everywhere. The world is still dark'.[7] This darkness did not leave Vaughan. In 1948, he wrote in his journal: 'I became aware of this growing sense of doom ... almost as though I was under a sentence of death'.[8] The subject of death and Vaughan's own mortality recurs in his journals (going as far as musing about taking his own life, in which he would eventually succeed). Vaughan's existentialist mindset, inspired by the writing of philosophers Søren Kierkegaard and Jean-Paul Sartre (the latter's writings enjoying particular traction among cultural circles in Europe at the time) is reflected in his fleeting engagement with the genre of still life in the early 1950s. A number of sketch studies in the Tate collection show his interest for arrangements of bottles and fruits on tables. They also include a skull as their main subject, diversely surrounded with fruits and a coffee grinder, close up or on a tall-legged table, together with annotations about light direction and colour. These studies resulted in *Still Life with Skull* (fig. 101), the solid lines, tight focus and powerful composition lending authority to this otherwise conventional subject. The motif of the skull on a table, the angularity and strong contrasts also betray the influence of Pablo Picasso, whom Vaughan greatly admired, having seen the *Picasso and Matisse* exhibition at the Victoria and Albert Museum in 1945–6, along with his friends and fellow neo-romantics Robert Colquhoun (1914–1962) and Robert MacBryde. The skull, a perfect expression of the body turned object, suited Vaughan's unsentimental existentialism as well as the prevalent mood of 1950s Britain.

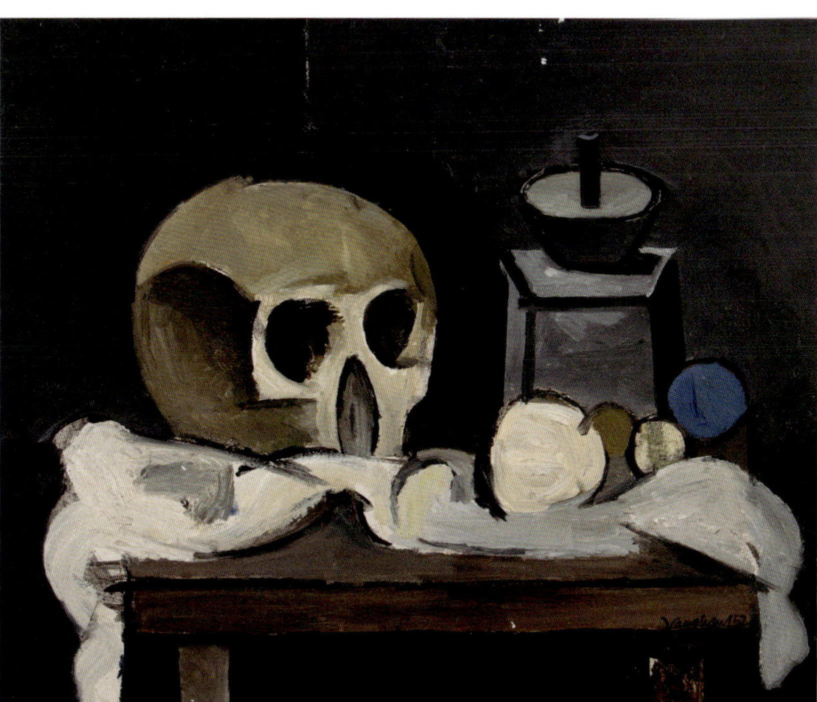

Fig. 101
Keith Vaughan (1912–1977)
*Still Life with Skull*, 1952–3
Oil on canvas, 35.5 × 43.5 cm
Collection of Antony Wright, London

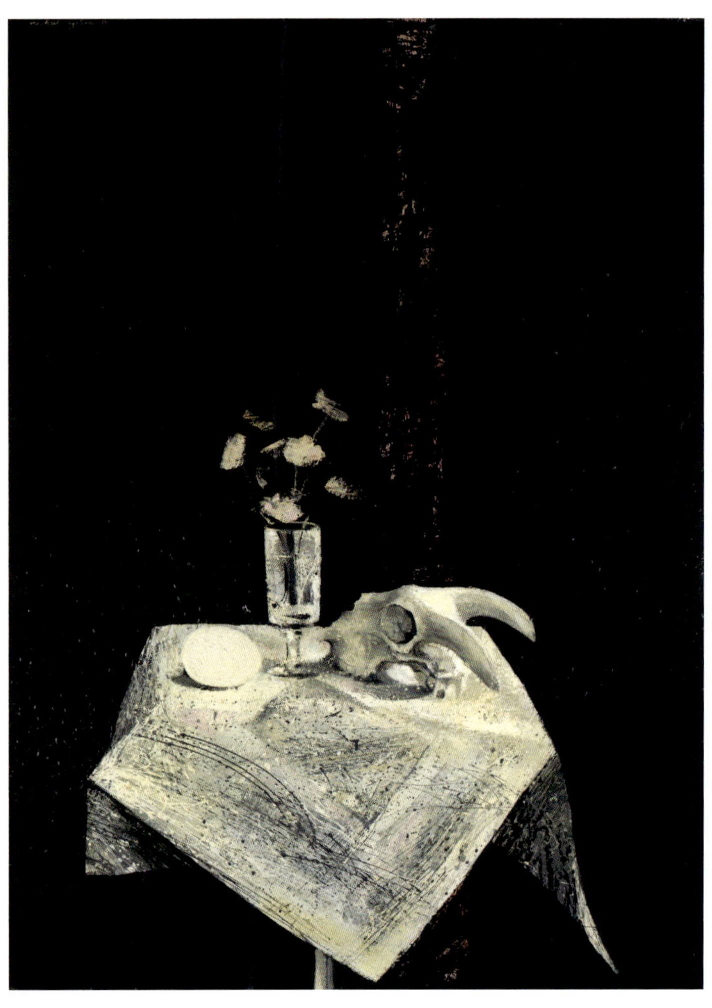

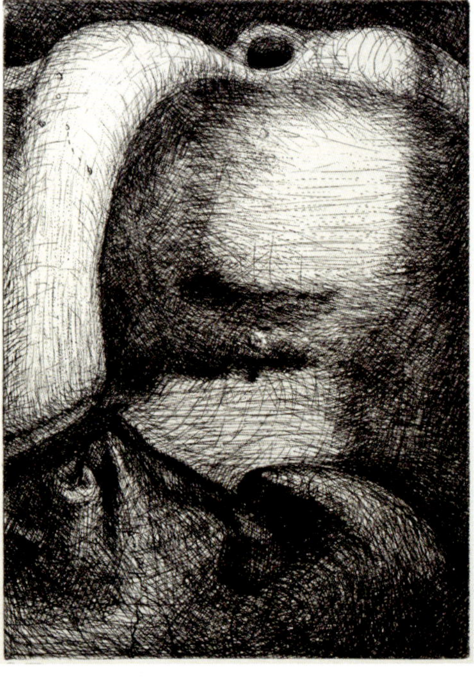

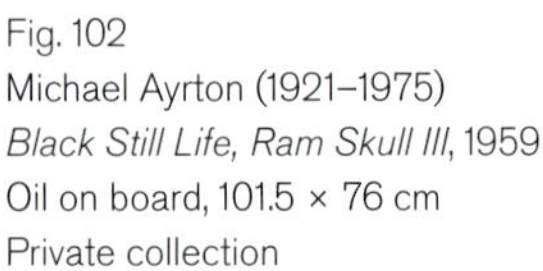

Fig. 102
Michael Ayrton (1921–1975)
*Black Still Life, Ram Skull III*, 1959
Oil on board, 101.5 × 76 cm
Private collection

Fig. 103
Henry Moore (1898–1989)
*Elephant Skull, Plate XIX (Cramer 132)*, 1969–70
Etching on paper, 23.5 × 31 cm
Pallant House Gallery, Chichester (Hussey Bequest, Chichester District Council, 1985)

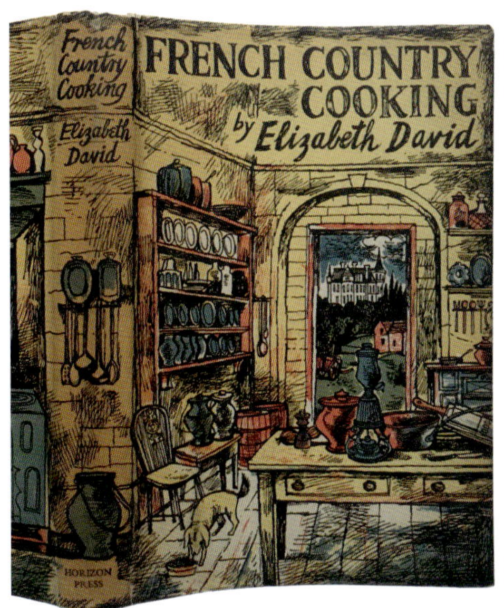


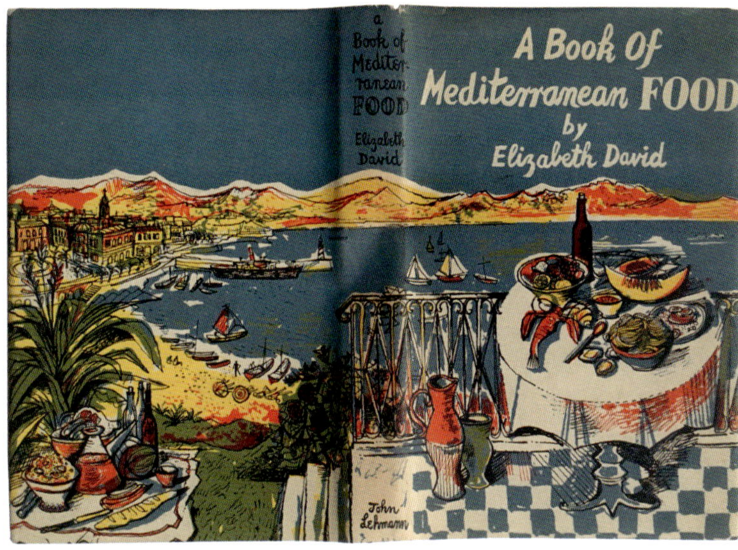


Fig. 104
John Minton (1917–1957)
Cover design for *French Country Cooking* by Elizabeth David, published by John Lehmann, 1951
Private collection

Fig. 105
John Minton (1917–1957)
Frontispiece for *A Book of Mediterranean Food* by Elizabeth David, published by John Lehmann, 1950
Private collection

At that time, Ayrton too returned to the motif of the animal skull, but in a perhaps appeased version compared to his wartime works. So it was with *Winter* (1950, private collection), where the expanse of the picture plane is largely taken up by a window, on the sill of which rests a small animal skull, or in his two-tone exploration of the motif of the ram skull in *White Still Life* and *Black Still Life, Ram Skull III* both from 1959 (fig. 102) According to Ayrton biographer Justine Hopkins, the black and white versions were, respectively, reflections on the light of East Anglia, where he lived, and Greece, which he first visited in 1957. Both versions are almost identical in composition, their stark difference lying in the striking contrast of the white table, skull, egg and bouquet of flowers emerging out of a darkness so deep it feels solid. Most remarkable is Ayrton's handling of paint, his conscious attention for figuration met with a form of gestural dripping and splatter that lends the painting texture and relief, reflecting the developments in American Abstract Expressionism, which were felt like a storm in London with a series of exhibitions in the late 1950s.[9] There is a sculptural quality, too, to the ram's skull, with the bleached, pitted bone recalling the texture of marble, in keeping with the interest in sculpture that Ayrton was developing at the time. The painting retains the unsettling pathos particular to Ayrton, who said:

> 'The term still life is common enough. At first sight it is a bold, flat designation ... yet those two words imply an undercurrent of meaning at once poignant and vital, suggesting objects ... curiously related to each other, silent, composed in tranquil, even ominous association. Alive, even lying in wait for the spectator'.[10]

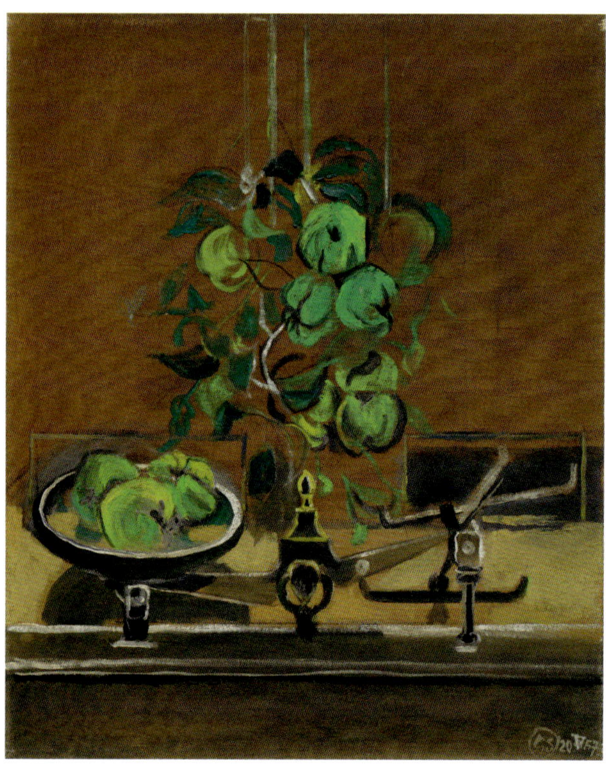

Fig. 106
Graham Sutherland (1903–1980)
*Still Life with Apples and Scales*, 1957
Oil on canvas, 65.4 × 54.6 cm
Private collection

As the war ended, so did travel restrictions, and as borders opened British artists began to escape the harsh realities of postwar Britain. Craxton and Freud sought the Mediterranean light in Greece – the latter bringing his piercing gaze to the island of Poros where he painted *Unripe Tangerine* (fig. 92), tart to the eye if not to the taste. With its cool, blueish green tones, the diminutive painting calls for a double-take: the unripe fruit is as unlike a tangerine as one can imagine for the word instantly conjures a bright orange. The limpid precision speaks of Freud's debt to Netherlandish art as much as his intense scrutiny, capturing all the pits and asperities of the fruit's skin. Meanwhile, John Minton gorged on the light and warmth of Corsica in 1947, before depicting the abundance of Mediterranean and French country cooking for Elizabeth David's cookery books (figs. 104 and 105), which invited British readers to experiment with recipes that were far out of their reach in rationed Britain. The vividly coloured table spread on the cover of *A Book of Mediterranean Food* is laid with fruits, shellfish and a bottle of wine, at odds with Minton's increasingly despondent mood. His last works were the designs for two murals for the Reed Paper Group at the Packaging Exhibition, Olympia, one of them displaying a profusion of food, wine and games, with festive tables laden with bottles and glasses. Two days before the exhibition opened, Minton took his own life on 20 January 1957.

Having spent much of the war in Wales, Graham Sutherland (1903–1980) undertook the first of many visits to France in the late 1940s, eventually buying a villa near Menton, in the south of France, in 1955, which would be his principal residence until 1961. There, according to Rosalind Thuillier, he found light, sunshine, French food and people, but also 'freedom after the incubation of war'.[11] He also looked at the work of Cezanne, Matisse and Picasso afresh. For Sutherland, the period signalled a new approach to colour: brighter, like the light of the south, but also a more frontal, flattened articulation of the pictorial space.[12] His painting of nature also changed, from the romantic, almost mystical darkness of Pembrokeshire to Mediterranean subjects: vine pergolas with datura flowers, palm and banana tree motifs; cacti or branches of trees heavy with fruits, his predilection for landscapes making space for fragments of nature and still life. His work from the 1950s is marked by hanging, swinging or rotating forms, as in the symmetrically ordered *Still Life with Apples and Scales* (fig. 106). While Sutherland's prior focus was on landscapes or natural subjects seemingly devoid of human intervention, here its presence is suggested by the table and scales. Whether

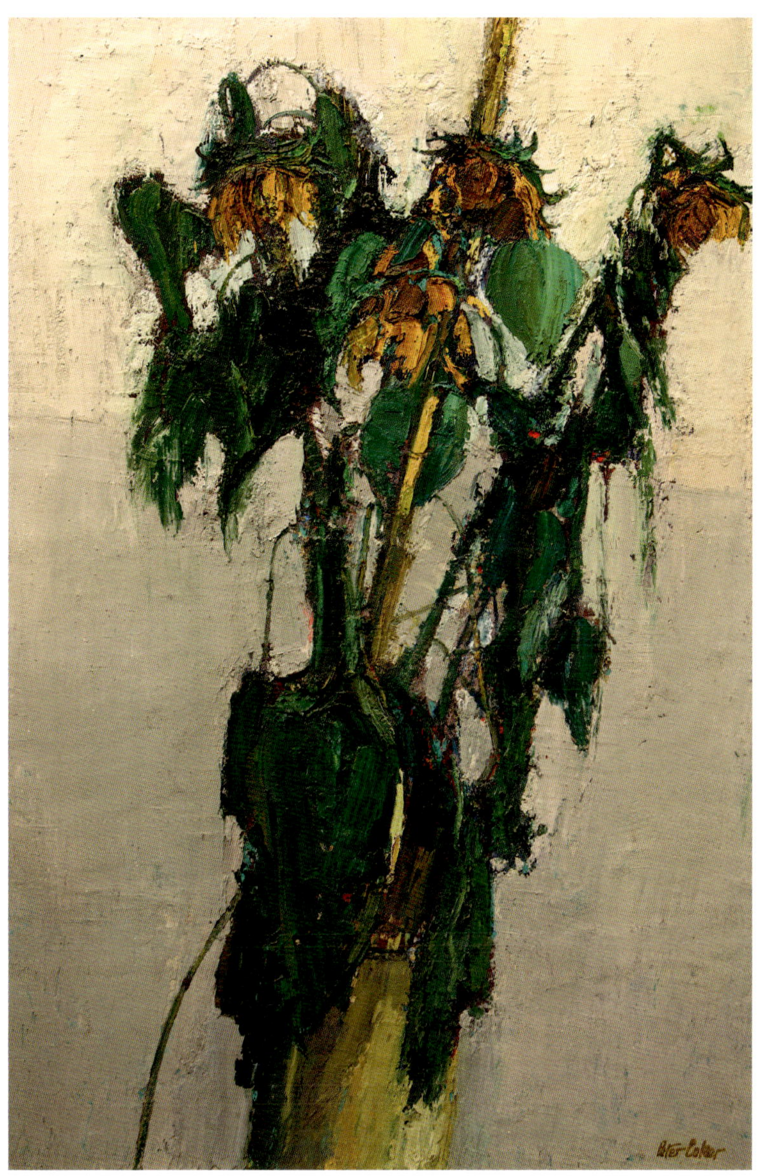


Fig. 107
Peter Coker (1926–2004)
*Sunflowers*, 1961
Oil on board, 121.9 × 81.3 cm
Pallant House Gallery, Chichester (Bequest of Mrs Vera Coker in memory of Peter Coker, 2014)

these are purely decorative or hold symbolic significance (a 1961 painting of scales by Sutherland in the Tate collection has been interpreted as holding a religious significance) is difficult to say, but placed in sunshine they offer sophisticated interplay of shadow and light.[13] The composition and subject project a sense of equilibrium and harmony, the apples deftly suggested with heavy brushstrokes of rich emerald and viridian greens offset by a dun-coloured, undefined background.

The influence of French art would endure in the work of artists like Vaughan, Sutherland or the younger Peter Coker (1926–2004) whose painting of decaying sunflowers (fig. 107) is marked by the vigorous handling of dense slabs of paint sliced with a palette knife, showing the influence of Nicolas de Staël (1914–1955). But it would decline among the new vanguard that came to prominence during the 'Swinging Sixties', as American art took over with Abstract Expressionism and Pop. So Vaughan glumly mused in 1964, after seeing the *New Generation* show at the Whitechapel Gallery in London, which included works by Derek Boshier (b.1937), Patrick Caulfield and David Hockney: 'after all's one thought and search and effort to make some sort of image which would embody the life of our time, it turns out that all that was really significant were toffee wrappers, liquorice allsorts and ton-up motorbikes ... I understand how the stranded dinosaurs felt'.[14] As Miriam O'Connor Perks shows in her essay in this volume, the 1960s replaced the gloom of postwar austerity with the abundance, excess and plenty of a new consumerist era; and yet, existential threats had not altogether disappeared from the art of the period.

In 1960, Jean Cooke (1927–2008) painted a seemingly innocuous still-life arrangement (fig. 108) of potted pansies and 'sweet William' flowers alongside a bouquet of foxgloves, peonies, irises, pelargoniums and dahlias in a glass jar. Yet the title, *Through the Looking Glass*, suggests that all is not what it seems. In the background, mostly concealed by the

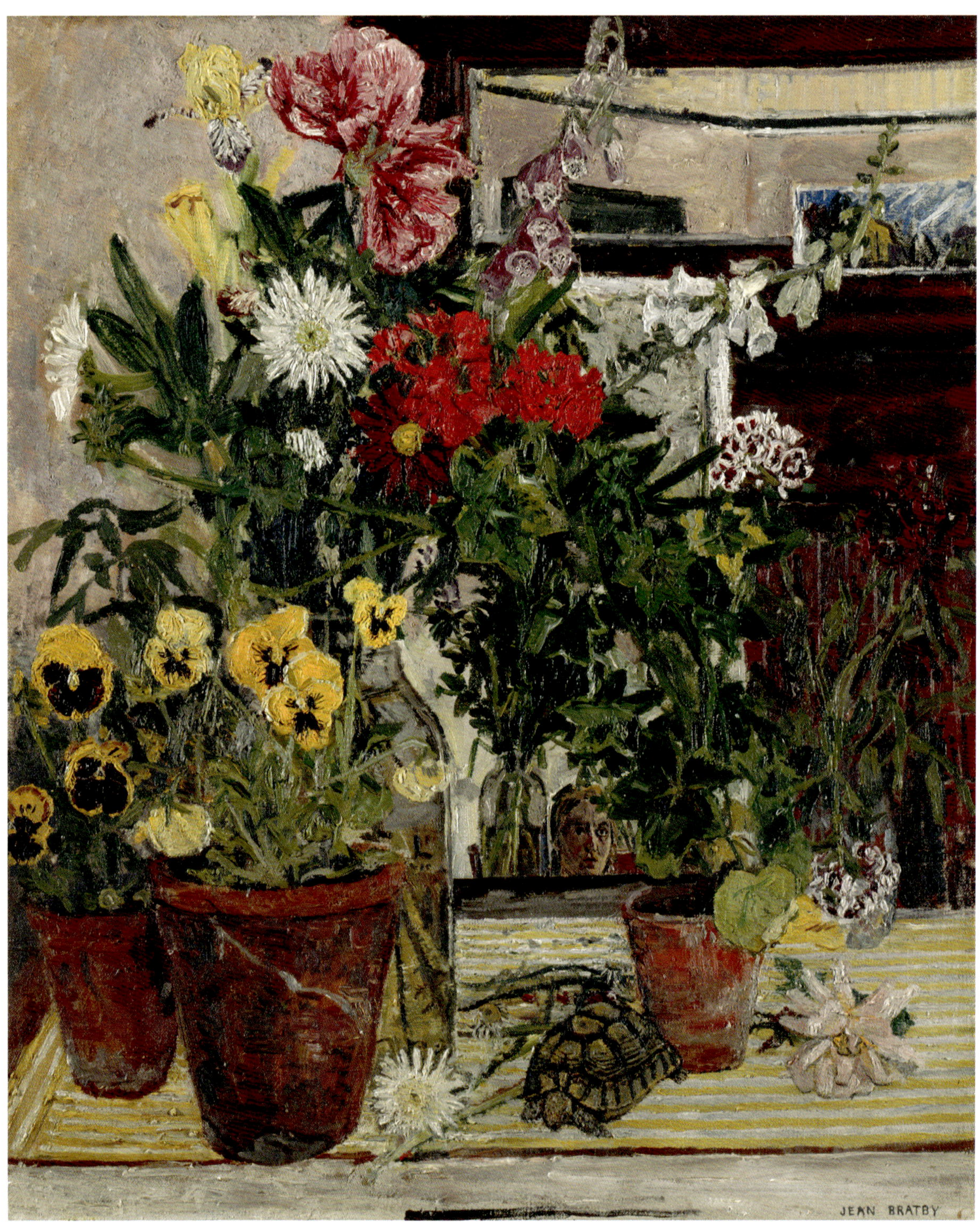


Fig. 108
Jean Cooke (1927–2008)
*Through the Looking Glass*, 1960
Oil on canvas, 60.8 × 50.8 cm
Lent by Royal Academy of Arts, London

*She's got*
*seven ears*
*like*
*her mother*

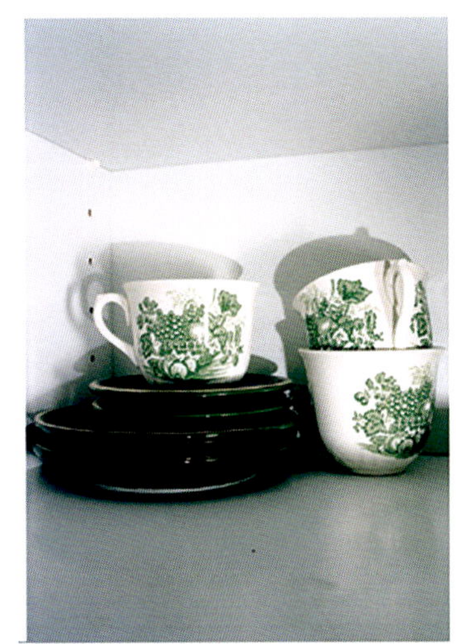

*I'm going to*
*put her under the grill,*
*i wouldn't*
*cover her in butter,*
*i'm going to*
*cover her in grease,*
*and*
*fry her*

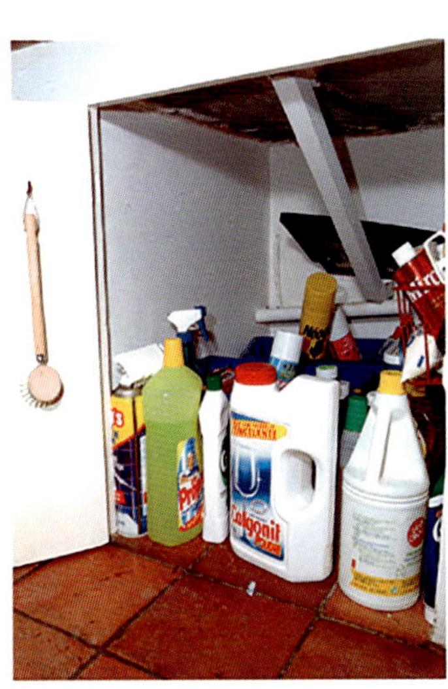


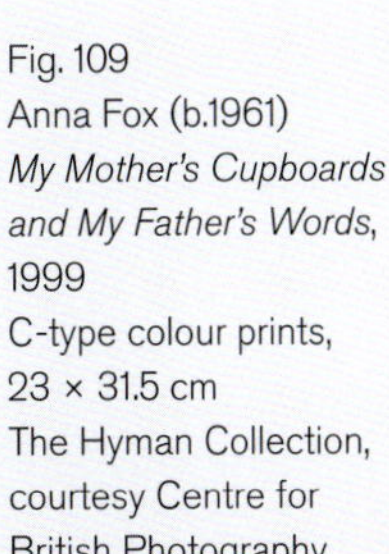

Fig. 109
Anna Fox (b.1961)
*My Mother's Cupboards and My Father's Words*, 1999
C-type colour prints, 23 × 31.5 cm
The Hyman Collection, courtesy Centre for British Photography

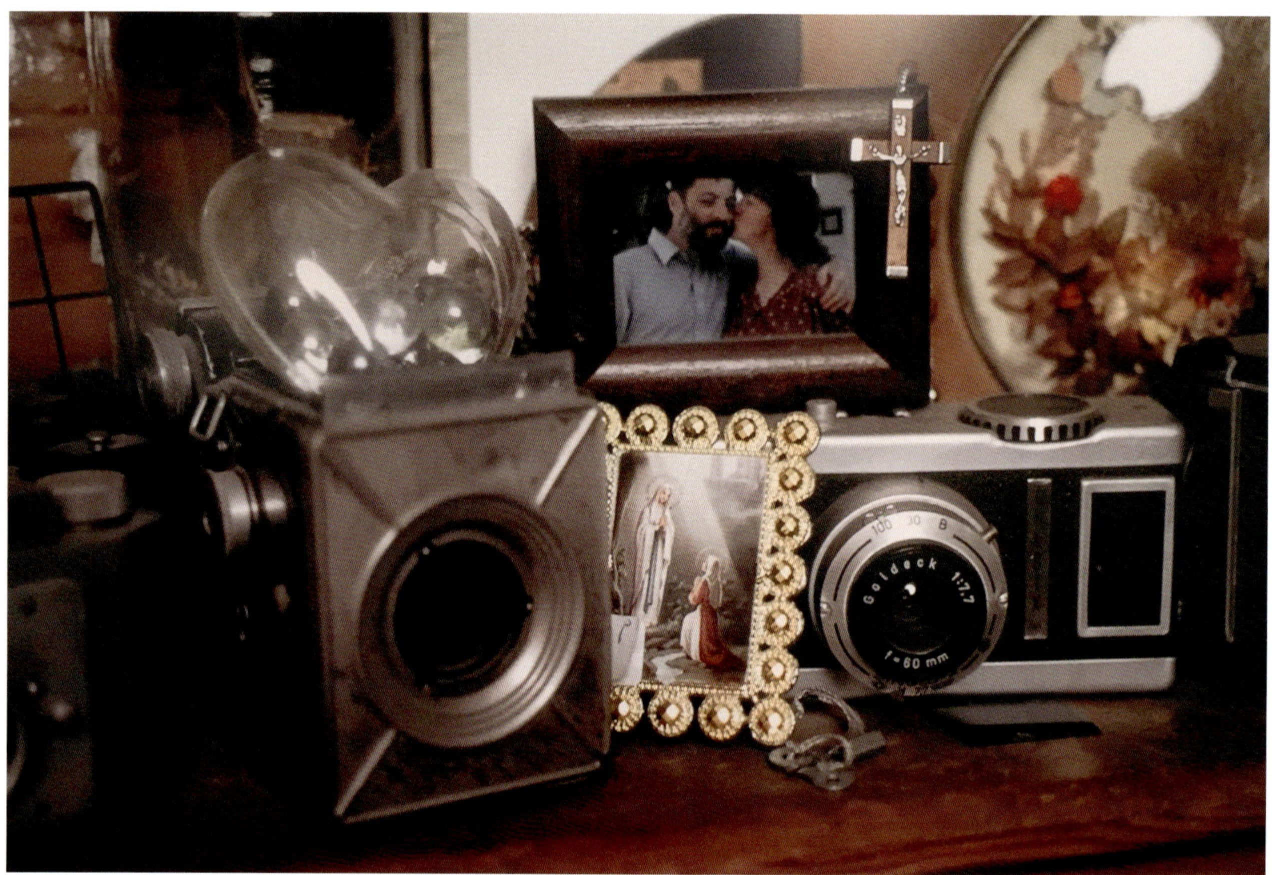


Fig. 110
Jo Spence (1934–1992)
*[Shrine]*, from the series *The Final Project*, 1991–92
Digital print from medium format negative, 89 × 134 cm
The Estate of Jo Spence, courtesy Richard Saltoun Gallery, London and Rome

summer flowers, the bottom edge of a mirror reflects a face, from the chin up, peering back at us: Cooke herself. This scene likely takes place in her studio: the only room her abusive husband, the painter John Bratby (1928–1992), allowed her to paint in, because he had judged the room too unsafe for his own use (the ceiling being unsound). This is one of few paintings from that period that survive, the domineering Bratby being in the habit of destroying or painting over her work while allowing her only three hours of practice per day. It is tempting to read the small tortoise in the foreground (a visitor from a neighbouring garden) as a symbol of strength and self-protection. Here, Cooke is in her safe space, her unblinking stare resolutely proclaiming 'here I am, despite everything'. A survivor.

There is something defiant in this simple statement of presence, similarly found in Anna Fox's (b.1961) *My Mother's Cupboard and My Father's Words* (fig. 109), an uncompromising expression of domestic violence, trauma and alienation. In this photographic book, Fox unravels a claustrophobic narrative in which her father's verbally violent eruptions against mother and daughter are paired with photographs of her mother's neat cupboards. Here, the matter-of-fact presence of objects such as crockery, linen, detergents and beauty products speak not so much of gendered domesticity, but of resilience and order amid the outbursts. Fox's mother may not be in control of her situation, trapped as she is in caring for an ailing and volatile husband, but she has control over these hidden, enclosed, self-contained spaces.

The documentary language of Fox's series recalls the radical gaze of photographer and activist Jo Spence (1934–1992). Having danced with death through a decade living with breast cancer in the 1980s, Spence eventually succumbed to leukaemia in 1992, but not before documenting her own slow, terrible death. She met her illness with a robust sense of agency, experimenting with alternative medicines and applying her pioneering concept of phototherapy which, borrowing from techniques of co-counselling, used the healing potential of photography in reclaiming one's own narrative. *The Final Project* (1991–1992), which chronicles the last two years of her life, is poignant in its honesty yet also at times derisive and humorous. Taking inspiration from cultures that embrace death as part of life, it includes still-life arrangements of dolls and masks as her version of the Egyptian shabti figurines that followed the dead in the afterlife and smiling skeletons borrowed from the Mexican Day of the Dead. The series brings these together with staged photographs of the artist's body in the landscape, portraits of herself superimposed with images of cells, as well as a visual diary of her illness and treatment. She used these objects and montages of her life to counter her impending absence:

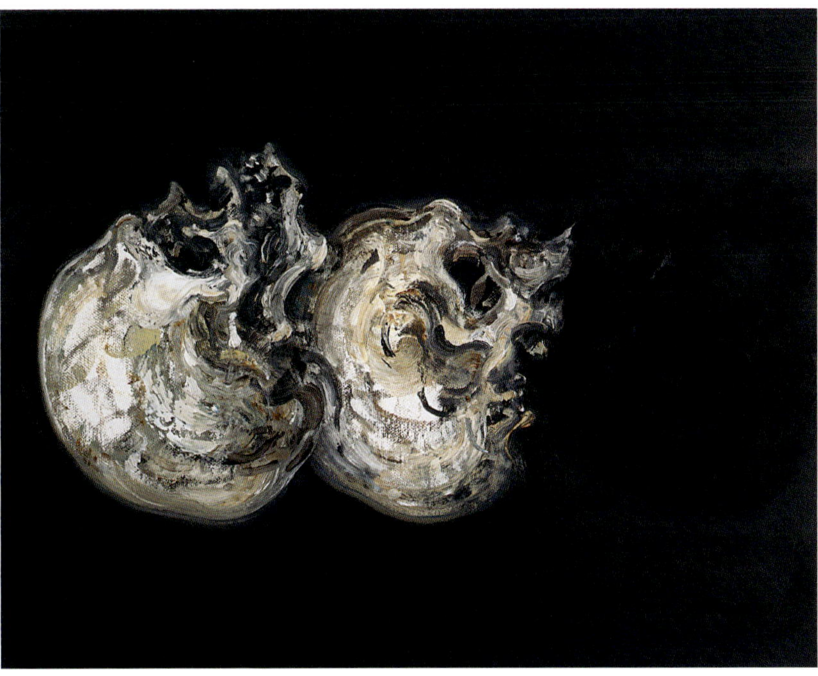

Fig. 111
Maggi Hambling (b.1945)
*Cuddling Skulls*, 1995
Oil on canvas, 40 × 50 cm
Collection of the artist

'I was there', the pictures seem to say. As her long-time collaborator Terry Dennett explained, 'the therapeutic intention of this work was to "get to know death" so as to reduce the fear of the subject'.[15] *The Final Project* could be seen as a form of *ars moriendi* (the art of dying well), a practice of preparing for death that found currency in late medieval Europe in response to a wave of epidemics including the Black Death. One picture from the series, *[Shrine]* (fig. 110), acts as a kind of memorial: arranged together on a shelf are some of her cameras, as extensions of the artist self; framed pictures, including Mary Magdalene praying to the Virgin Mary, and Spence and her husband David Roberts embracing; a pendant crucifix; a heart-shaped box and tableau of dried flowers; a radiator key. Dust has settled on these objects; the stillness of the image is still as death itself. Spence's series is a dignified reminder that illness and death are part of life. This same sentiment is echoed in Maggi Hambling's (b.1945) *Cuddling Skulls* (fig. 111), the result of her trip to Mexico in 1993. Hambling found that, far from the taboo, out-of-sight and behind-closed-doors attitude to death in Britain, in Mexican culture she felt 'death seems to be a friend rather than an enemy. It's so visibly celebrated', embraced as part of life. There is humour in the oxymoron of the title – where 'cuddling' conjures a warm and fuzzy feeling while 'skulls' speaks of the perceived hardness of death – but also a reflection that, in Mexico, life and death are cheek by jowl. As she said: 'it's there, like the flip side of the coin, life and death together'.[16] But death is also a necessary part of art. In an interview, Hambling revealed that '[Francis] Bacon always said he thought of death every day. I think any serious artist bears it in mind all the time'.[17]

*

How flat a water bottle looks when empty, devoid of substance, lifeless. How rotund, taut and solid when full. In Rachel Whiteread's (b.1963) *Untitled (Pink Torso)* (fig. 112), the object becomes body. The absence within the bottle is made solid, replacing the absence of the body it is designed to comfort, to better signal its existence, its implied presence. Whiteread makes use of plaster – a material ubiquitous in art schools' drawing rooms, but also humble, common, absorbent and absorbing – as a blank canvas to explore the profundity of life. *Untitled (for Frank)* (fig. 113), the imprint of three full bookshelves, their volumes felt in reverse, the books symbols of a well-read life, is suggestive of what is not there – the reader. Porous, the white plaster has picked up irregularities from the objects themselves, absorbing pigments and dust impregnated within the spines and the pages' edges. The rawness of the plaster is redolent of the rawness of these imprints, their history exposed. These are objects that have been leafed through, their pages dog-eared, the covers warmed by the touch of hands, fingers turning the pages. The empty space is pregnant with presence, the silence filled with invisible words and the books' contents frustratingly out

Fig. 112
Rachel Whiteread (b.1963)
*Untitled (Pink Torso)*, 1991
Pink dental plaster and wax
9.5 × 17 × 23.5 cm
Private collection

Fig. 113
Rachel Whiteread (b.1963)
*Untitled (For Frank)*, 1999
Plaster, polystyrene and steel in three parts, 26 × 90 × 26 cm
Pallant House Gallery, Chichester (Accepted under the Cultural Gifts Scheme by HM Government from Frank Dunphy and allocated to Pallant House Gallery, 2018)

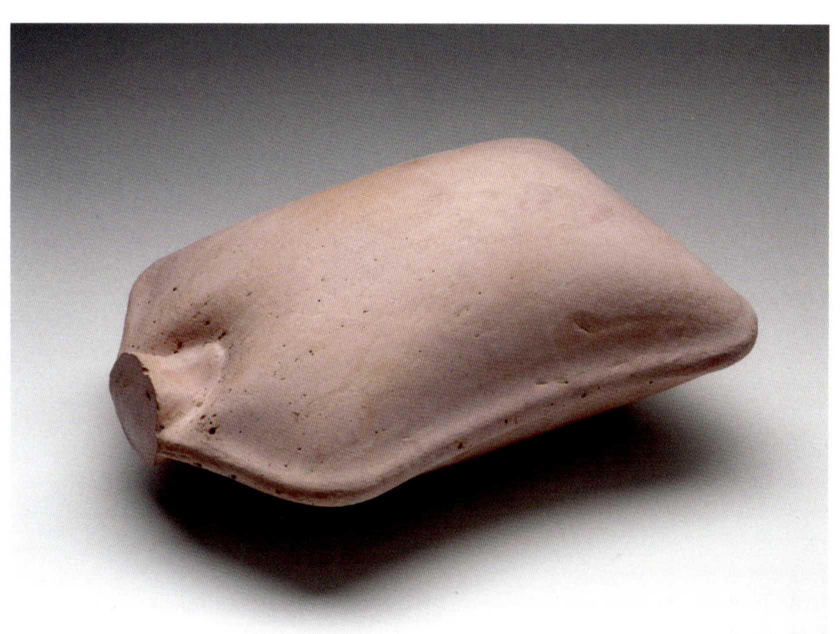

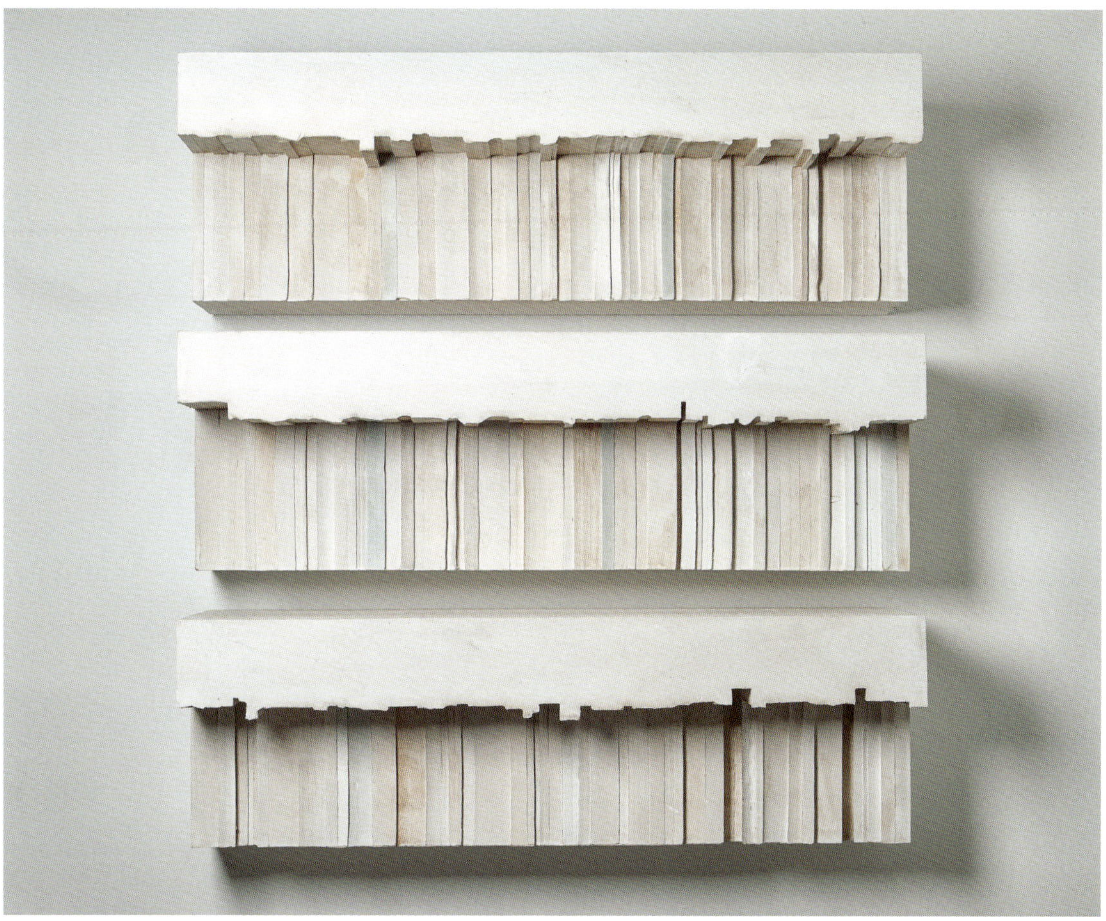

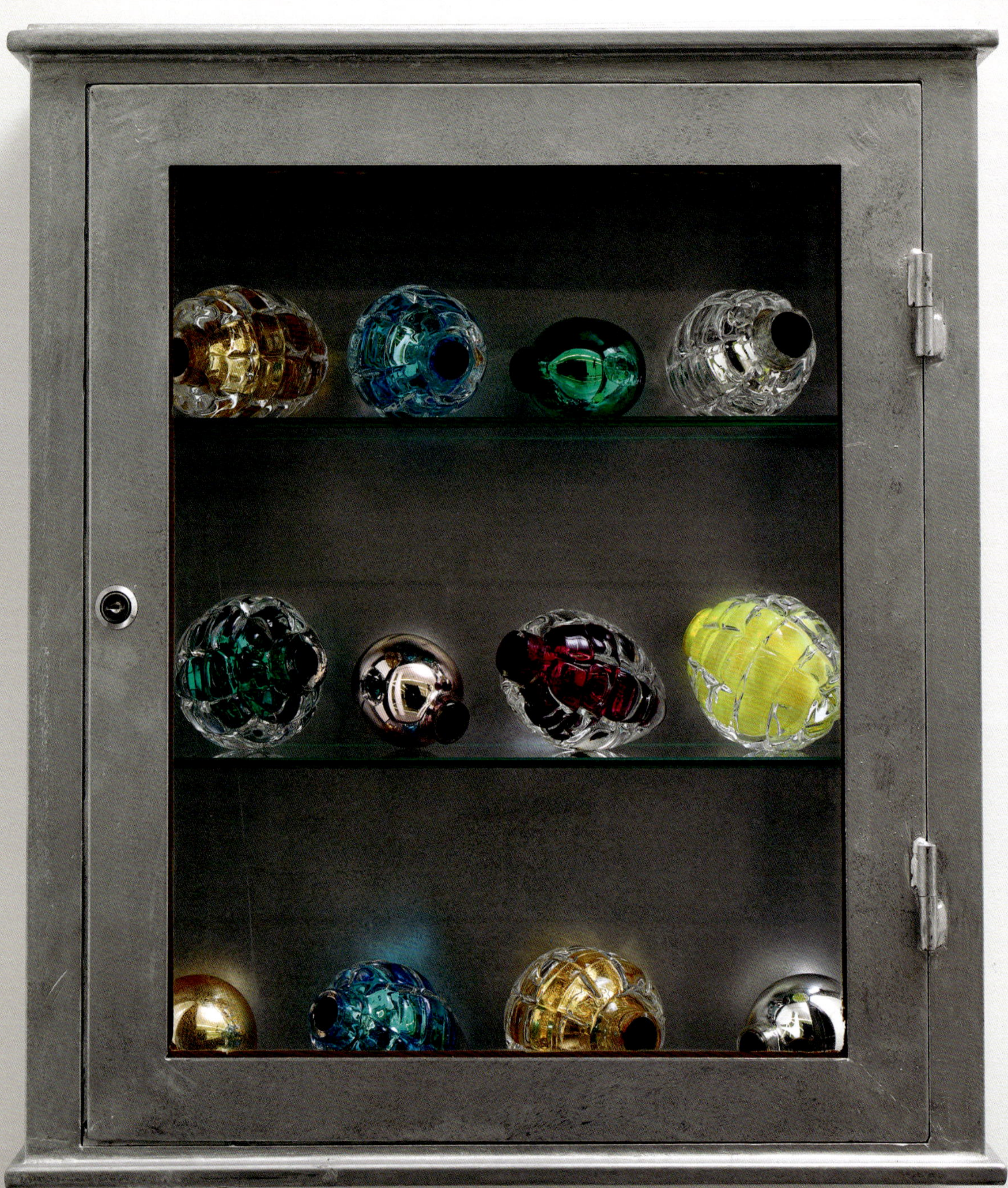

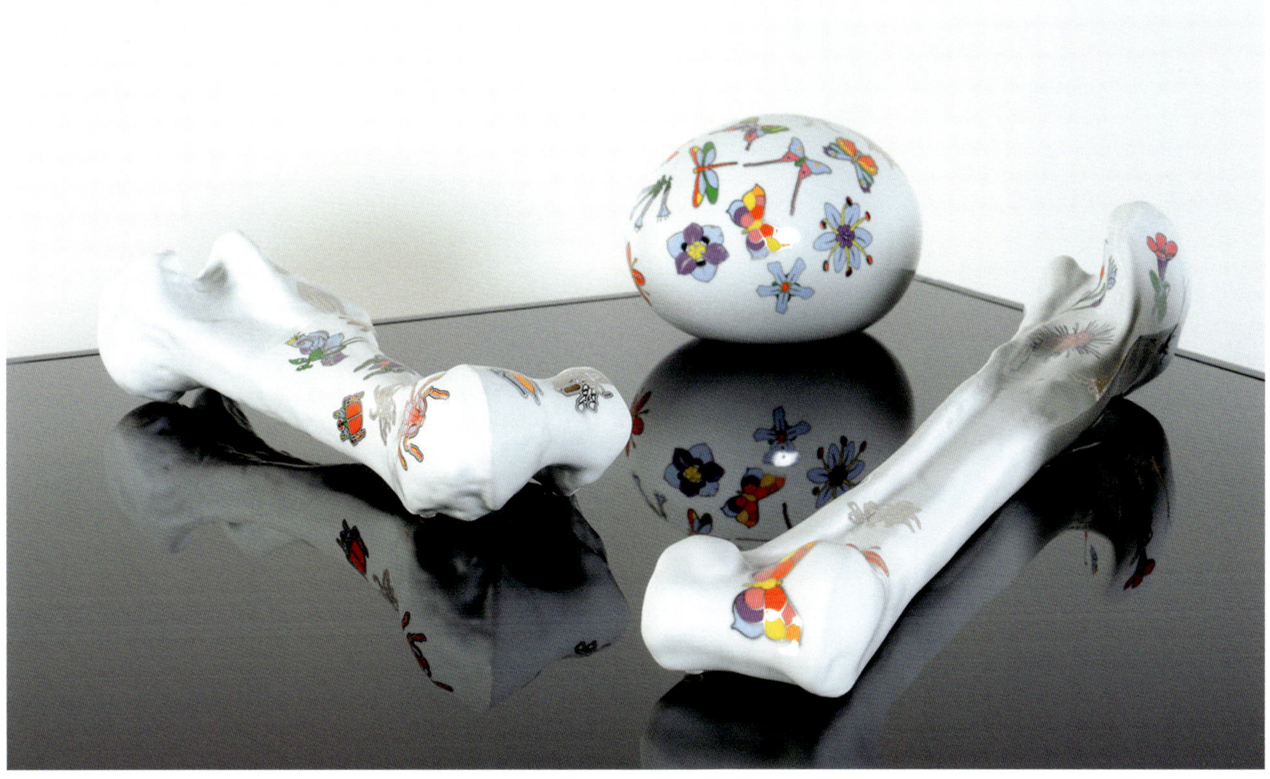

Fig. 114 (opposite)
Mona Hatoum (b.1952)
*Natura morta (medical cabinet)*, 2012
Murano mirrored glass, steel and glass cabinet, 61.5 × 54 × 17.5 cm
Courtesy of Mona Hatoum Foundation

Fig. 115 (above)
Lucy + Jorge Orta (b.1966 & b.1953)
*Amazonia Collection:*
*Palaeomastodon (humerus bone, Egypt)*, 2010
*Aepyornis (Elephant bird egg, Madagascar)*, 2010
*Gallimimus (fossil limb bone, Mongolia)*, 2010
Royal Limoges porcelain fossil cast, enamel and platinum drawings, unique piece, Certificate Perpetual Amazonia, dimensions variable
Courtesy Lucy + Jorge Orta

of our reach; like the artwork itself (though dedicated to the art dealer Frank Dunphy), they remain untitled to our eyes. The silent books' poignancy is also found in Whiteread's *Judenplatz Holocaust Memorial* in Vienna (completed in 2000), her monument to expunged lives, commemorating in concrete the unspeakable horrors of the Shoah, the spines of thousands of library books turned inwards, irremediably shut and unread.

Like much of her work, Mona Hatoum's (b.1952) *Natura morta (medical cabinet)* (fig. 114) speaks of brutal conflicts, a theme whose tragic currency, at the time of writing, is showing no sign of abating. The work consists of a cabinet in clinical stainless steel, laden with deliciously colourful handblown Murano glass pieces in the shape of grenades. Hatoum has spoken in relation to another work of 'working with certain material properties which amplify the concept'.[18] Throw a glass grenade, and rather than detonating an explosive, it will shatter into thousands of pieces. Conflating the fragility of glass with the brutality of war is only one of an unsettling set of dualities that lend the work its potency: the medicine cabinet (healing) and the grenade (death); the clinical hardness of the cabinet's shelves and the soft curves of the grenades; the translucency of the glass and the opacity of violence; the candy colours of the pieces and the darkness of war; the minimal aesthetic and the messiness of conflict; body fragility and state violence; seductive and threatening. The fragility of the material and its enticing colours only add to the emotional charge of the work.

Lucy + Jorge Orta's (b.1966 and b.1953) *Amazonia Collection* (fig. 115) addresses another kind of violence: that perpetrated on nature. In 2009, the duo joined a scientific expedition in the Peruvian Amazon rainforest, where they observed the astounding biodiversity and vulnerability of an imperilled environment endangered by extractive practices, deforestation and the needs of capitalist societies thousands of miles away. Here, they cast in white porcelain specimens from extinct species – the fossil bone of dinosaur Gallimimus, the Oligocene era elephant ancestor Palaeomastodon, and the egg of the elephant bird Aepyornis – which they adorned with colourful Amazonian flowers, insects and butterflies. In tracing these delicate drawings on the brittle porcelain, they overlay one mass extinction onto another – the fifth, at the end of the Cretaceous 66 million years ago, onto the sixth, ongoing today. In so doing, they alert us to the urgency of action. With the Amazon rainforest's influence on both regional and global climates, the work reminds us of the interconnectedness of world systems, the impact of consumer choices and the necessity for systemic change.

Katie Paterson's (b.1981) *Endling* (fig. 116) is a colour wheel divided into one hundred sections, each painted with pigments made from the dust of crushed specimens that represent the history of our planet, from pre-solar times, 5 billion years ago, to the offspring of Gingko trees that survived the atomic bomb that fell on Hiroshima. The design is reminiscent of a clock, where the birth of our solar system occurs at '12 o'clock' and the Anthropocene era, here defined as 1945 to now, marked at roughly ten to midnight.[19] In this way, it is also redolent of the Doomsday Clock created in 1947 by scientists involved in the Manhattan Project to warn humanity against the existential threat caused by the advent of a nuclear age. Set yearly, this metaphorical clock now considers threats as varied as nuclear warfare, pandemics, climate change and artificial intelligence (AI), with midnight representing hypothetical human-made global catastrophe. (In recent years, it has been dangerously close to midnight.) *Endling* is the ultimate *memento mori* painting in its evocation of everything that ever was, since the birth of our planet, from inert rocks to the most destructive of human inventions, from the first glimpses of life to the extraordinary resilience of species threatened by human intervention. Together with Paterson's related work *Requiem* (2022), *Endling* is 'an elegy to a disappearing world, a lament', a reminder that the climate crisis is the greatest existential crisis ever faced by humankind.[20] One inspiration behind Paterson's practice of deep-time thinking and radical hope, is philosopher Roman Krznaric's concept of the 'good ancestor', in that we have the choice to lead our lives with future generations in mind and, as data scientist Hannah Ritchie now proposes, be 'the first generation to build a sustainable world'.[21]

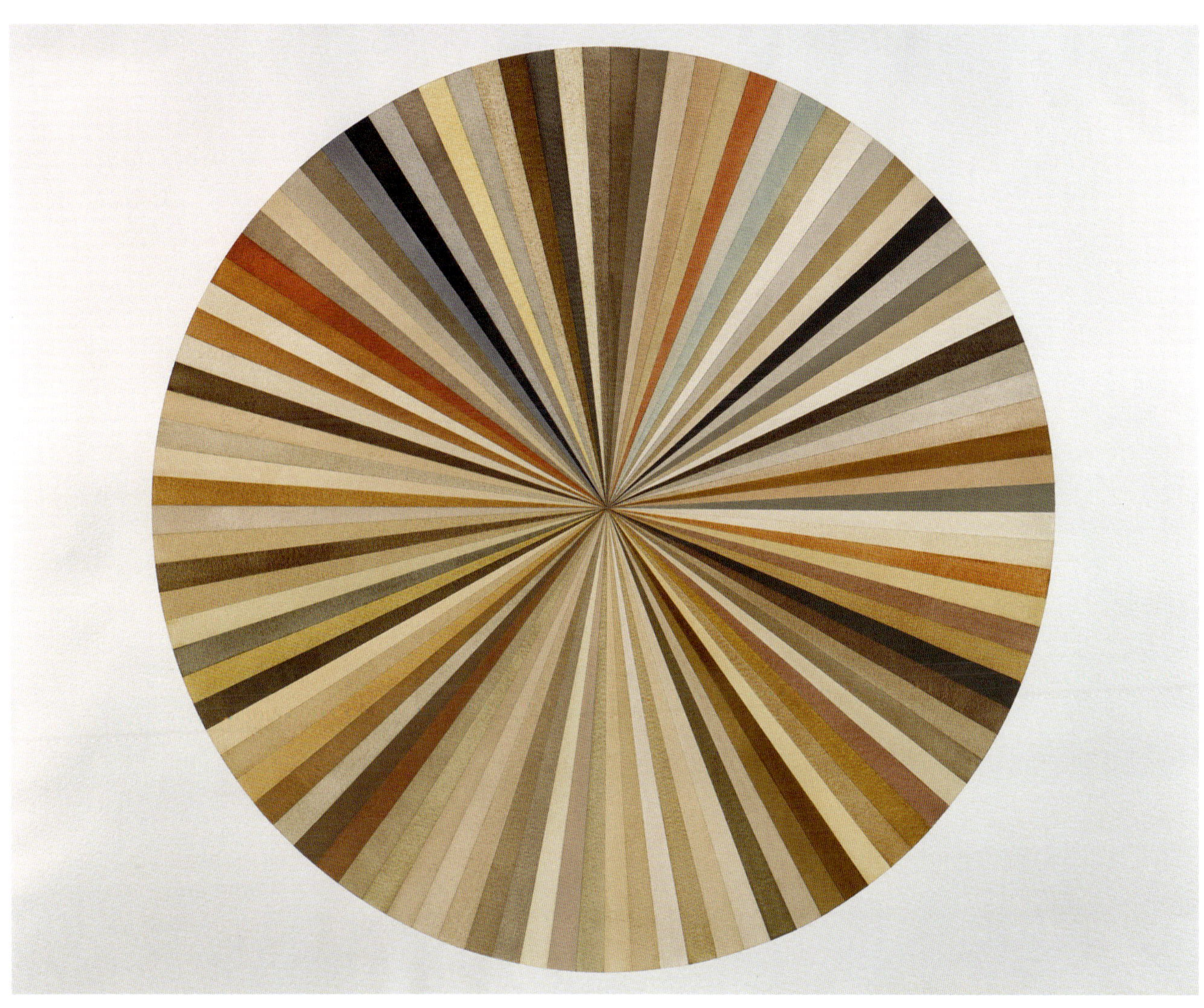

Fig. 116
Katie Paterson (b.1981)
*Endling*, 2022
Mixed media in 100 pigments ground from the pre-solar dust of 5 billion years ago to the ginkgo trees of Hibakujumoku, 92 × 92 cm
Courtesy of the artist

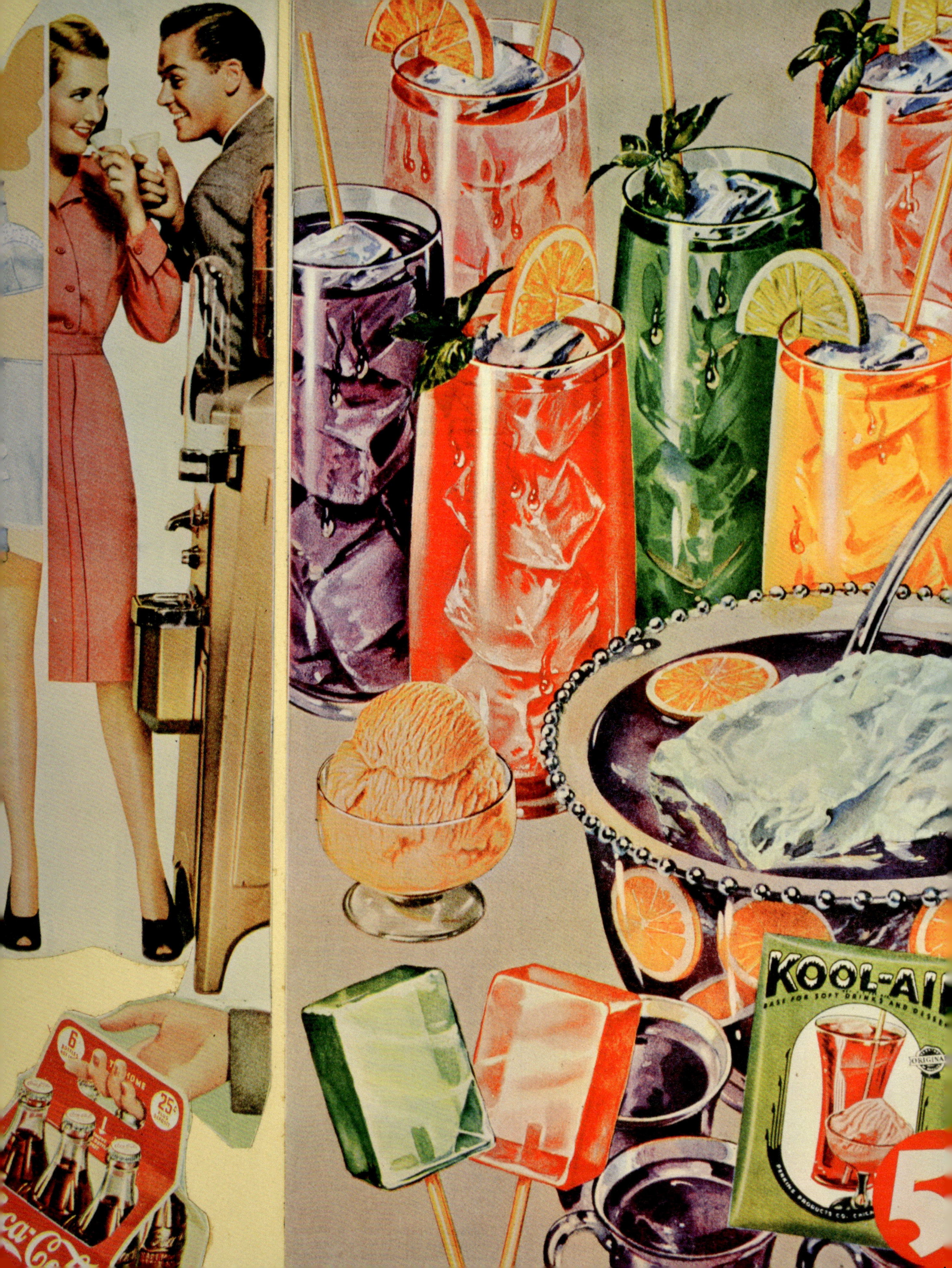
KOOL-AI

# 6 Accelerated Decay: Consumer Culture and Still Life

MIRIAM O'CONNOR PERKS

> The Pop Art of today, the equivalent of the Dutch fruit and flower arrangement, the pictures of second rank of all Renaissance schools, and the plate that first presented to the public the Wonder of the Machine Age and the New Territories, is to be found in today's glossies bound up with the throw-away object.
>
> Alison and Peter Smithson, 'But Today We Collect Ads', 1956

In their article celebrating the effects of mass media on art, architecture and new ways of living, British architects Alison (1928–1993) and Peter Smithson (1923–2003), drew a compelling comparison between still-life painting in the Netherlands in the 17th century and the proliferation of consumer products, and the reproduction of these in magazine adverts. It was written in 1956, the same year as the radical and highly influential *This Is Tomorrow* exhibition at the Whitechapel Gallery in London, which featured collaborations between artists, architects and critics and took inspiration from popular and commercial culture such as advertising, movies, science fiction and pop music. Contributing artists included Eduardo Paolozzi (1924–2005) and Richard Hamilton (1922–2011), long seen as the progenitors of British pop. Paolozzi and Hamilton, alongside other artists associated with the British pop art movement, were fascinated with the growing influence of American consumer culture and how advertising companies promoted products, turning to popular commodities such as baked beans, cigarettes or packets of tea as subject matter for their art.

As the Smithsons astutely pointed out in 'But Today We Collect Ads', the links between consumerism and still life had their roots in

Detail of fig. 120:
Eduardo Paolozzi (1924–2005)
*Refreshing and Delicious*
from *Bunk!*, 1947–72

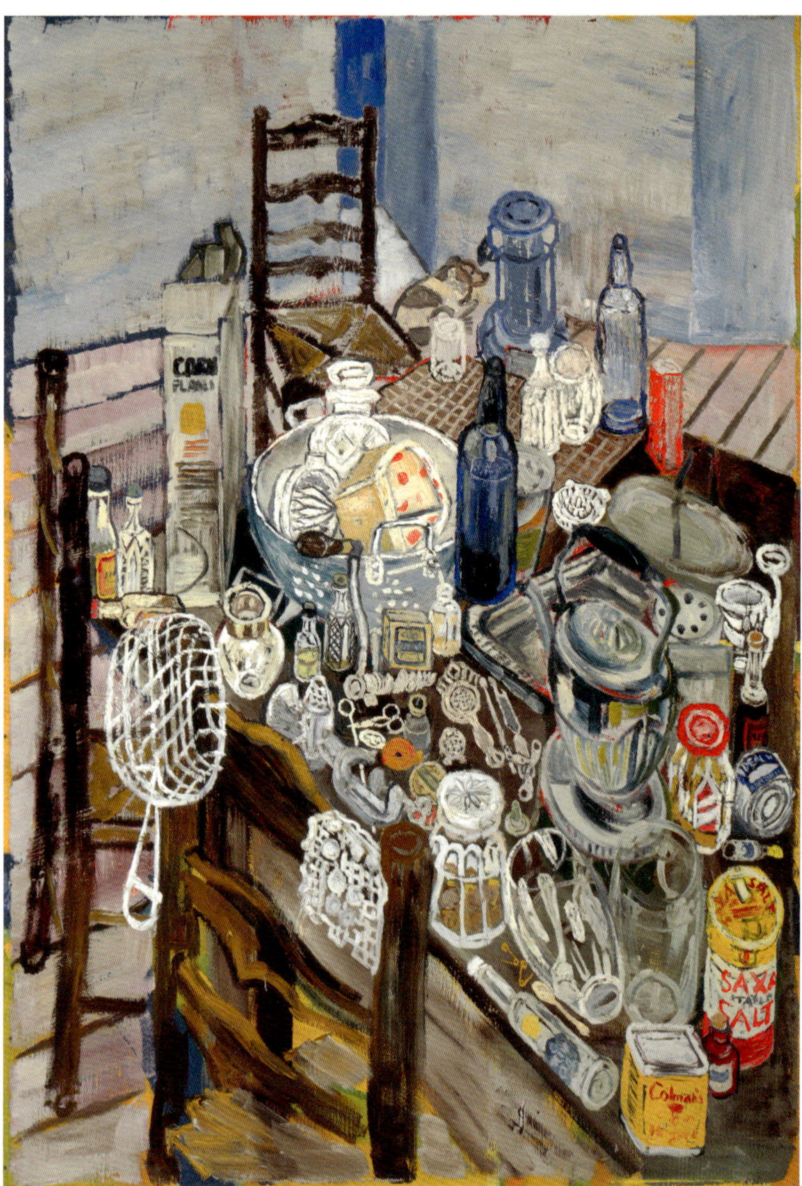


Fig. 117
John Bratby (1928–1992)
*Still Life with Chip Frier*, 1954
Oil on canvas, 131.4 × 92.1 cm
Tate: Presented by the Contemporary Art Society 1956

the mercantile society of the 17th-century Netherlands.[1] This was the first European society to experience the problem of oversupply and consumption, and the still-life genre boomed reflecting this newfound affluence and its products. The ways in which Dutch artists represented this new wealth was bound up in Protestant morality; at the time, ethics and economics were inseparable.[2] Pop art has often been criticised as cynically appropriating consumer culture, and the question of whether these artists were celebrating or undermining the powers of the marketplace has been much debated.[3] However, through the isolation and stylisation of commodities, pop artists highlight their latent symbolic content: these are items that will help us live a better life, or so we are told. As in 17th-century Dutch society, late capitalism puts a value judgement on rapid consumption: it is good to buy goods.

Linda Nochlin wrote in her essay 'Running on Empty' about the society of consumption, that 'despite its emphasis on plenty, even plenitude, there is actually never enough. Nothing, for the consumptionist imaginaire, is ever enough, nor is it meant to be'.[4] This has strong parallels with the highly influential critique of consumer culture written by American social critic Vance Packard in *The Hidden Persuaders*, published in the UK in 1962. The book looked at how advertising companies used psychological techniques to induce desire for products. It was the first critique to use the term 'built-in obsolescence' – the idea that products are designed to have a limited lifespan or to become unfashionable. This is a form of accelerated decay – a modern concern that runs throughout works by British pop artists.

Although there has been some exploration of the relationship between still life and pop art in such exhibitions as *The Pop Object: The Still Life Tradition in Pop Art* held at the Acquavella Galleries in New York in 2013, these have tended to focus on the contribution of artists from the United States.[5] British pop artists have a markedly different relationship to consumer culture, resulting from the experience of postwar austerity Britain. The 1950s was a period of great reconstruction, with both people and cities recovering from the devastating effects of the Second World War. Rationing had only ended in 1954. The era was marked by a need to restore idealism, and the optimism of consumer culture presented an opportunity. British pop art, pop music and mass media were inextricably linked in the 1960s, and all were used by advertising companies to promote a new British identity that was modern, hip and aspirational.[6]

John Bratby's *Still Life with Chip Frier* (fig. 117) reflects the complexities and ambiguities inherent in British art's response to the rise of consumer culture, and the 'Americanisation' of British society, an important precursor to British pop's handling of contemporary commodities. John Bratby was associated with the 'Kitchen Sink' painters and the Angry Young Men writers, a group of cultural figures disaffected with the socio-political order of British society. Bratby's painting demonstrates a shift from traditional representations of food and earthenware found in still life, towards mass-produced goods such as the chip pan or processed foods like Kellogg's Corn Flakes. The table is heaving. It is an image of abundance but also of disorder: bottles lie on their side, items jumbled and hoarded. *Still Life with Chip Frier* problematises the masculine individual's conflicted position in the postwar home. As Gregory Salter argues in *Art and Masculinity in Post-War Britain: Reconstructing Home*:

> this developing connection of masculinity to the home was seen as conformist and met with resistance from some men, just as, outside

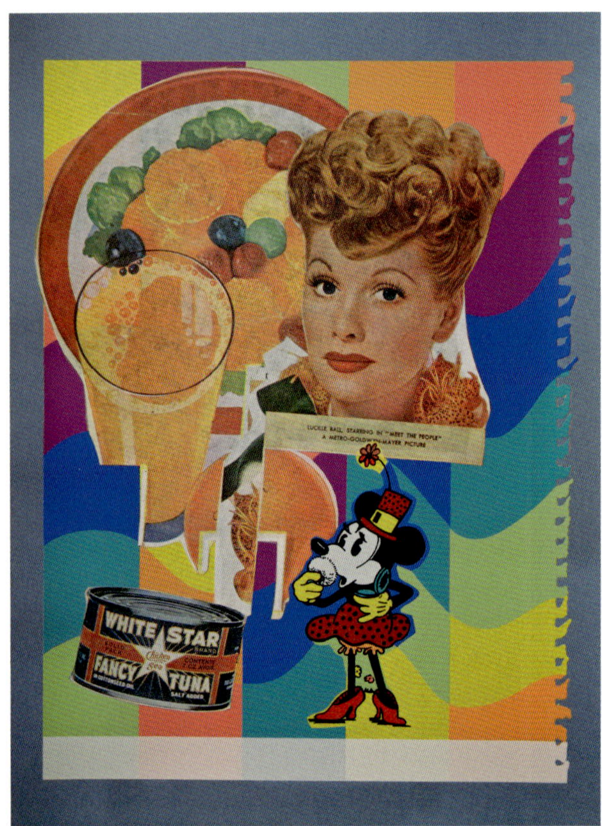


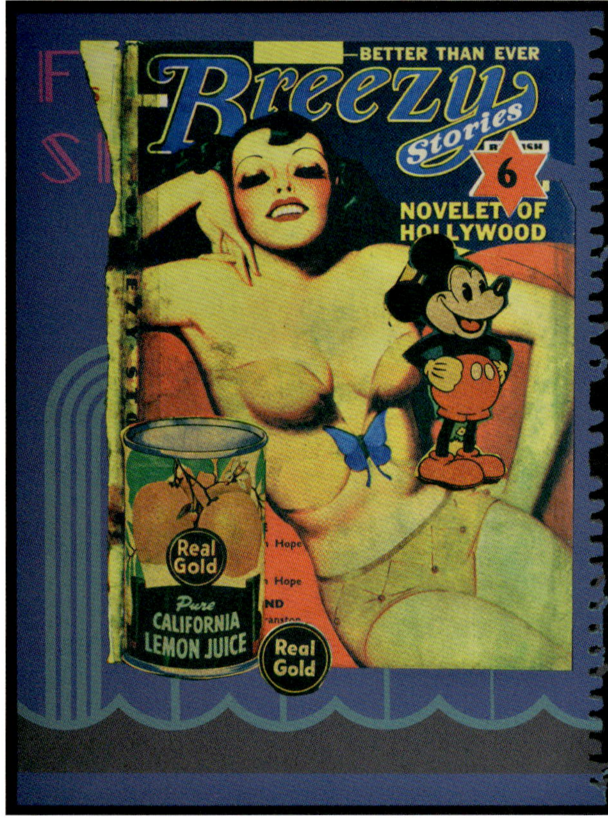


Fig. 118
Eduardo Paolozzi (1924–2005)
*Meet the People* from *Bunk!*, 1947–72
Lithograph on paper, 34.7 × 25.9 cm
Pallant House Gallery, Chichester
(Wilson Gift through Art Fund, 2006)

Fig. 119
Eduardo Paolozzi (1924–2005)
*Real Gold* from *Bunk!*, 1947–72
Lithograph on paper, 31.8 × 24.2 cm
Pallant House Gallery, Chichester
(Wilson Gift through Art Fund, 2006)

Fig. 120
Eduardo Paolozzi (1924–2005)
*Refreshing and Delicious* from *Bunk!*, 1947–72
Lithograph on paper, 37.8 × 28 cm
Pallant House Gallery, Chichester
(Wilson Gift through Art Fund, 2006)

> of the family, the rise of mass culture, consumerism and an increasing 'Americanisation' of British culture were interpreted as threats to male individuality as well as contributing to the feminisation of society in general.[7]

*Still Life with Chip Frier* reflects Bratby's psychological state in the place where he lived and worked with his wife, the artist Jean Cooke. The claustrophobic atmosphere speaks of the violence Bratby inflicted on Cooke and his home, the objects becoming symbolic of the anonymising effects of consumer society on the fragile male psyche. John Bratby's paintings are deeply unsettling but confront us with the presence of violence within the postwar home.

Male pop artists occupy an interesting position in relation to ideas around gender and consumerism. Writers in the early 1960s criticised pop art for its femininity and domesticity. In many ways, women were the primary agents of consumerism, in that they were the individuals out shopping, buying shiny new goods such as vacuum cleaners, push-button appliances and ready-made cake mixes. Hamilton observed:

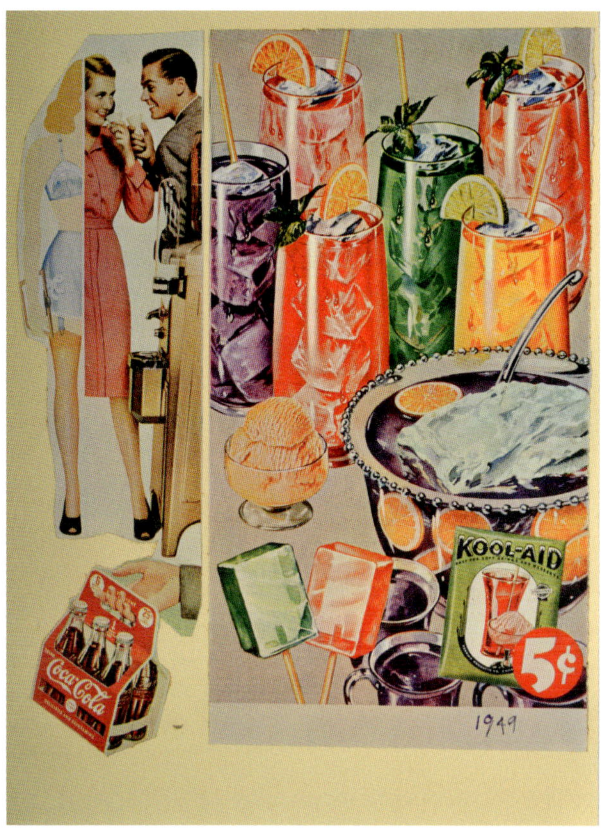


> The worst thing that can happen to a girl, according to the ads, is that she should fail to be exquisitely at ease in her appliance setting – the setting that now does much to establish our attitude to woman in the way that her clothes alone used to. Sex is everywhere, symbolised in the glamour of mass-produced luxury – the interplay of fleshy plastic and smooth, fleshier metal.[8]

Hamilton explored these ideas in *Hers is a lush situation* (1957) and *Hommage à Chrysler Corps* (1957), both works play on the conflation of female bodies and car bodies in advertising. Paolozzi's collage series *Bunk!* (1947–52) also comments on this tendency, in which women are targeted as consumers but also turned into objects of desire by advertising agencies. One collage, *Meet the People* (fig. 118), juxtaposes Lucille Ball's perfectly styled red pin curls with a glistening fruit salad, while in *Real Gold* (fig. 119) the lemons on the tin of juice mirror the pin-up girl's acid-toned bikini. In the advertising world, women are trapped between two choices: what to buy or how to be sold.

A seminal moment in the history of British pop, Paolozzi first presented *Bunk!* as a lecture-performance at the Institute of Contemporary Arts, London in 1952. Using only a projector, Paolozzi presented consecutive images taken from postcards, magazine clippings and science fiction comics. The lecture was an onslaught, with Paolozzi mimicking the mass proliferation of images in this new age, progressing at speed.[9] Images of automobile adverts would be followed by pin-up girls followed by Coca-Cola adverts in rapid succession. There is some debate as to where Paolozzi got the title for his collage series, many believing it to be a reference to an idea expressed by American industrialist Henry Ford, along the lines of 'History is more or less bunk ... we want to live in the present'.[10] Through collecting and presenting these new forms of domesticity and technological progress, Paolozzi was arguing that the material and visual culture of the present was of as much aesthetic value as what was considered fine art.

On closer inspection of the series, it is clear that Paolozzi makes no attempt to hide the images' well-worn appearance. The edges of the paper are frayed and discoloured, providing a sharp contrast to the promise of things that are brand new. Paolozzi cherished the low, the ephemeral, the decaying waste of the new consumer society, representing a 'nostalgia for now' which differentiates the approach of British artists to mass contemporary culture from their American counterparts' intentionally

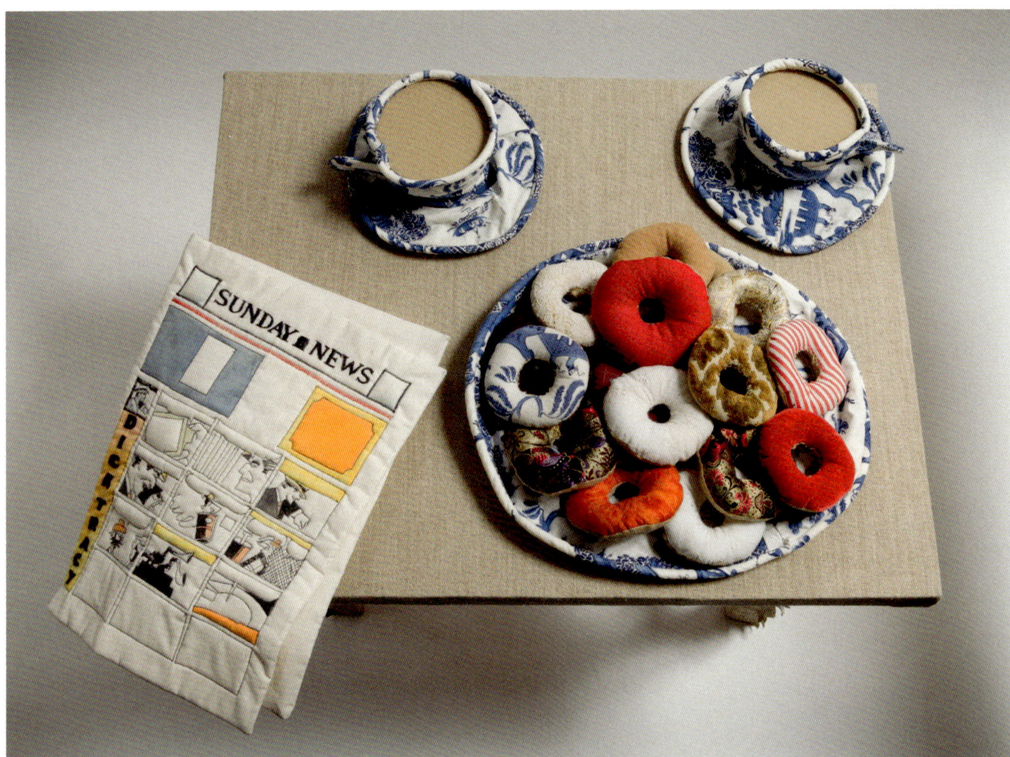


Fig. 121
Jann Haworth (b.1942)
*Donuts, Coffee Cups and Comic*, 1962
Fabric, thread and kapok, 65 × 69 × 54 cm
Wolverhampton Art Gallery

impersonal approach.[11] The work of Jann Haworth (b.1942) also occupies an interesting space in between these approaches; as a US artist in Britain she exploited stereotypes from her own culture. Her revolutionary handmade soft sculptures present a wry satire of the detached, mechanised ways that consumer goods or pop icons are sold. *Donuts, Coffee Cups and Comic* (fig. 121) provides a kitsch take on the serious genre of still life, taking inspiration from the breakfast that Haworth would buy at The Big Donut Drive in North Hollywood when she was a teenager. Her choice of medium was also political, as she stated in relation to the male students she studied alongside at the Slade: 'I was determined to better them, and that's one of the reasons for the partly sarcastic choice of cloth, latex and sequins as media. It was a female language to which the male students didn't have access.'[12]

A significant development in the history of sculpture in the 20th century, soft sculpture as characterised by the use of cloth, fibre and sewn elements was utilised by many women artists during the 1960s including Yayoi Kusama (b.1929), Marisol (1930–2016) and Patty Mucha (b.1935) whose collaborations with her husband Claes Oldenburg (1929–2022) pioneered the new genre. Artists such as Haworth highlighted the expendability of cloth, subverting the sculpture tradition through an ephemeral material and devalued craft. It also has resonance with American vernacular culture, such as quilt making, borrowing from popular culture both old and new.

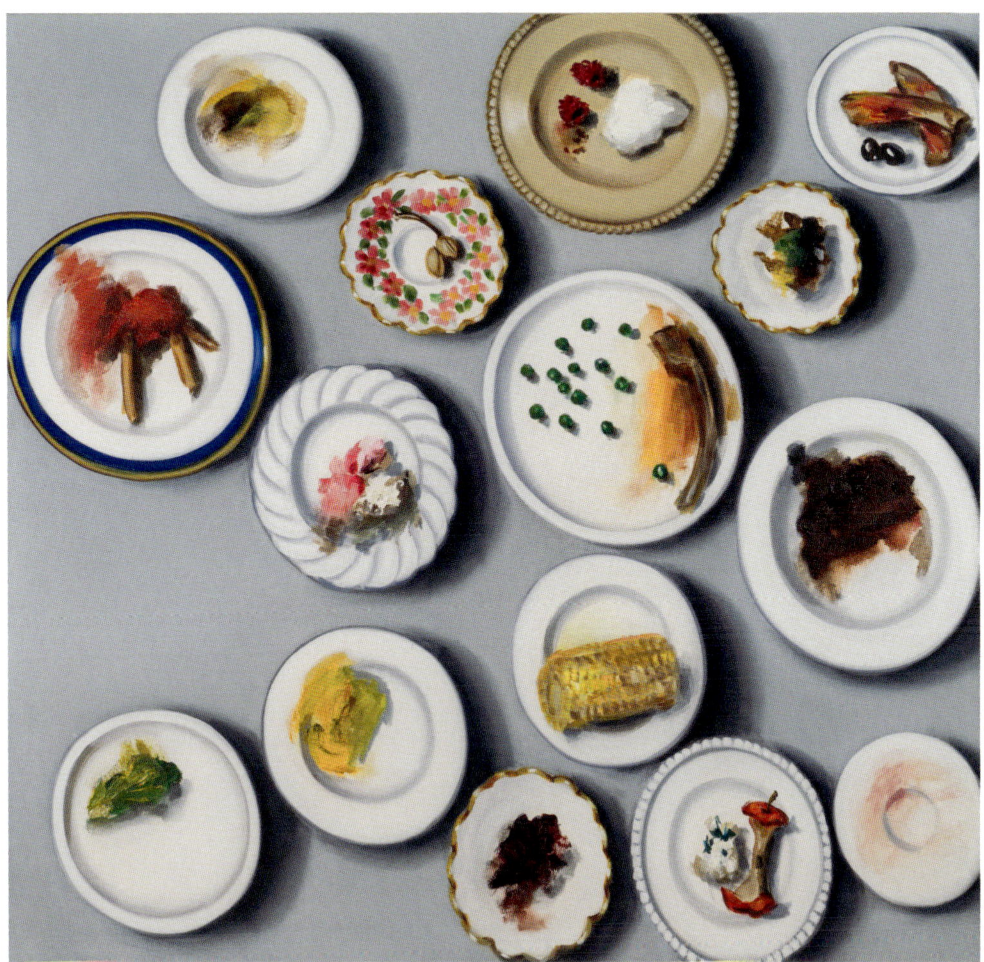

Fig. 122
Lisa Milroy (b.1959)
*Plates No. 1*, 2018–23
Oil on canvas, 119.5 × 116.5 cm
Courtesy of the artist and
Kate MacGarry, London

As Erica Battle describes it, 'this tendency represents a kind of *holding on* to the detritus of the present, and so giving these things a greater subjectivity and symbolic meaning'.[13]

This can certainly be said for Peter Blake (b.1932), whose work is characterised by a deep affection for his subject matter, including pop music pin badges, circus performers, Hollywood stars and packaging. Blake's painting from 1959–60, *Cigarette Pack* (fig. 123), demonstrates his attraction to popular ephemera and branding, through depicting a discarded packet of Belga cigarettes. Blake makes not only the logo, but also the torn piece of plastic, the focus of the painting. Through his attachment to overlooked detritus and things that look lived-in, his work is set apart from the American pop treatment of commercial packaging, as a more personal and tender approach to mass-produced objects. The open pack provokes the memory of the person who smoked the last cigarette. Blake exploits the flatness of the green floor to foreground the discarded packet, subverting the usual presentation of objects within a traditional still life.

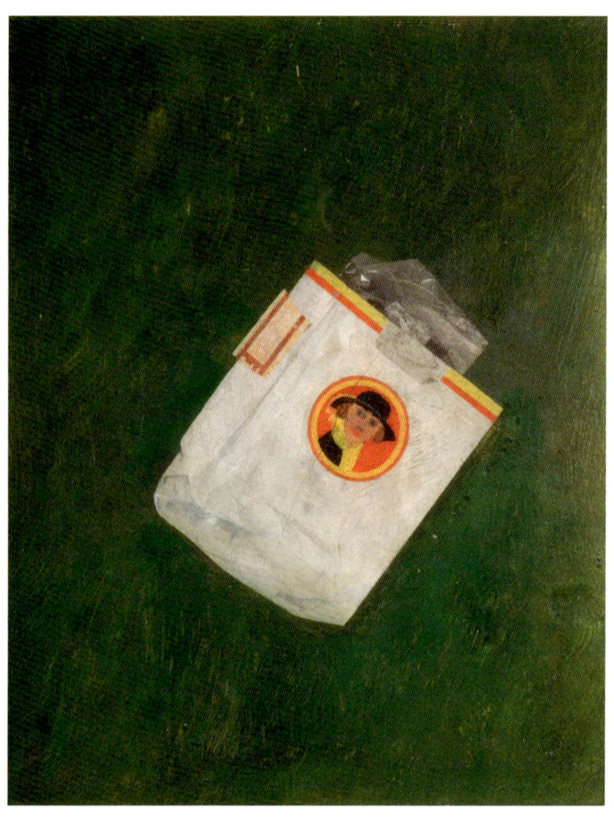

Fig. 123
Peter Blake (b.1932)
*Cigarette Pack*, 1959–60
Oil on canvas, 18.5 × 16 cm
Wolverhampton Art Gallery

Fig. 124
Peter Blake (b.1932)
*Love*, 2007
Enamel, wood and found objects on panel, 97.8 × 156.8 × 10.1 cm
Pallant House Gallery, Chichester
(Accepted under the Cultural Gifts Scheme by HM Government from Lorna Dunphy and allocated to Pallant House Gallery, 2018)

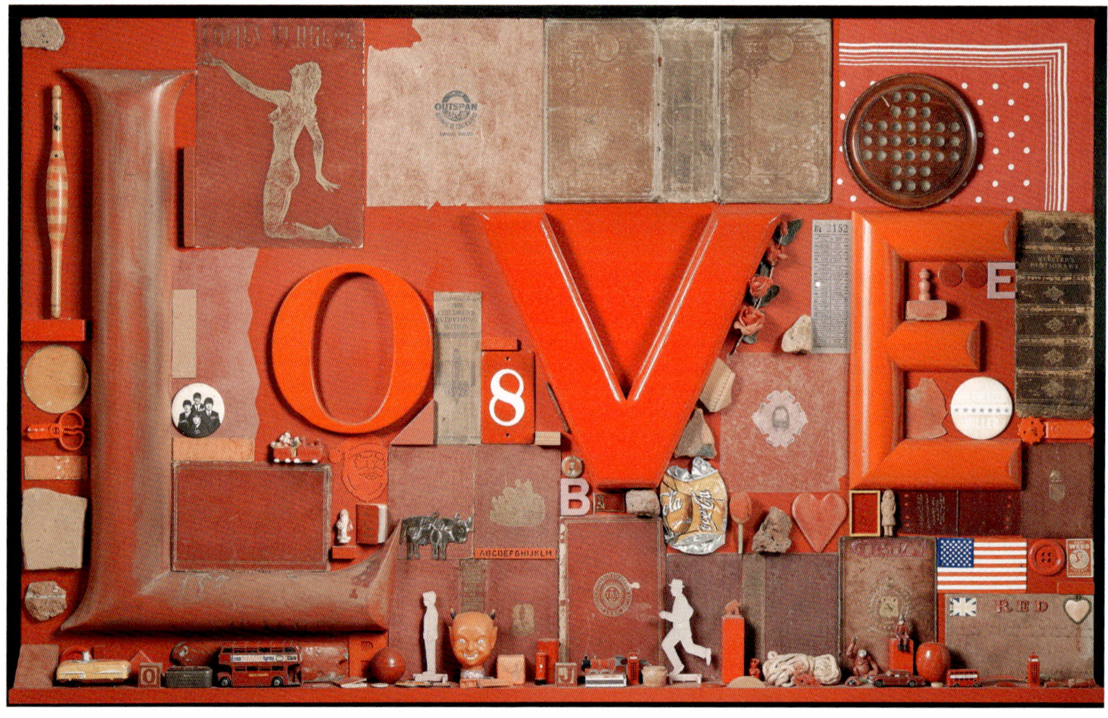

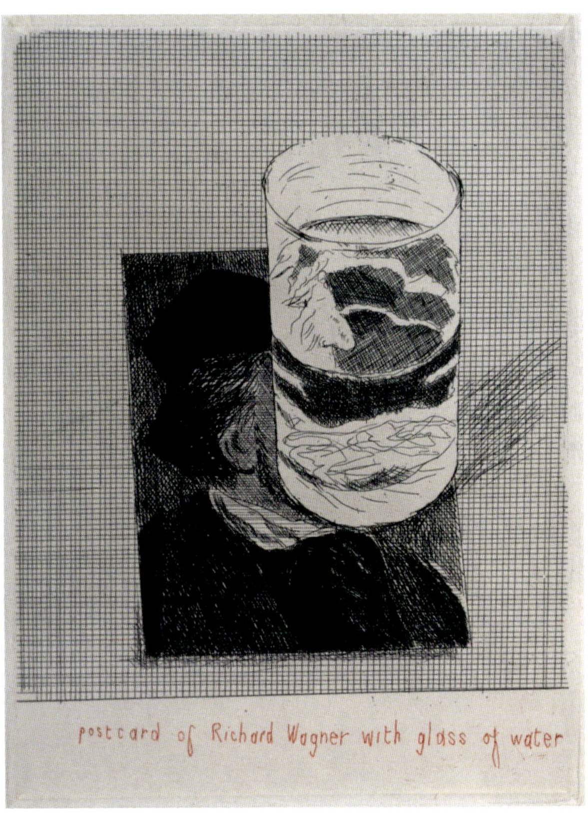


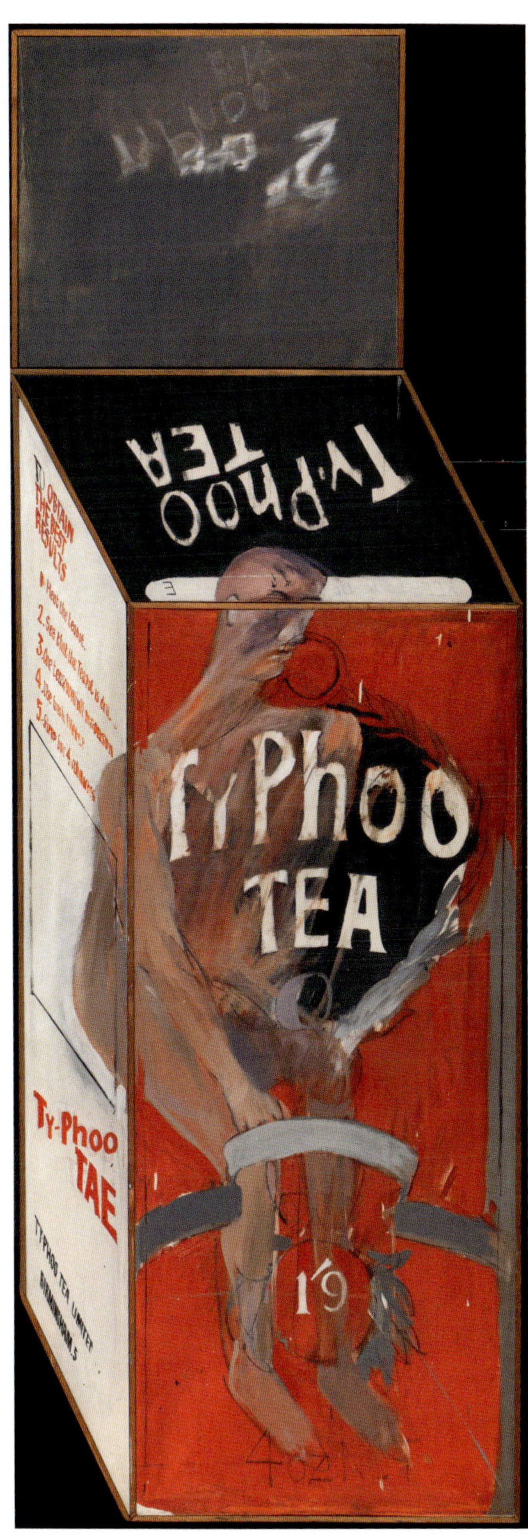


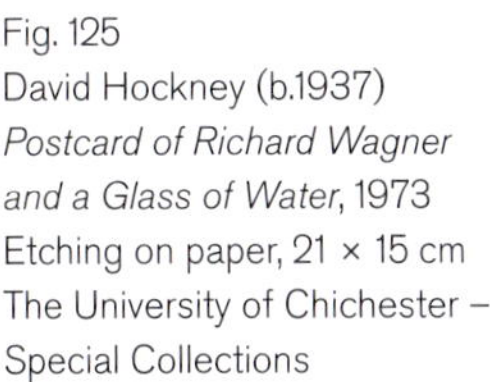

Fig. 125
David Hockney (b.1937)
*Postcard of Richard Wagner and a Glass of Water*, 1973
Etching on paper, 21 × 15 cm
The University of Chichester – Special Collections

Fig. 126
David Hockney (b.1937)
*Tea Painting in an Illusionistic Style*, 1961
Oil on canvas, 232.5 × 83 × 3.8 cm
Tate: Purchased with assistance from the Art Fund 1996

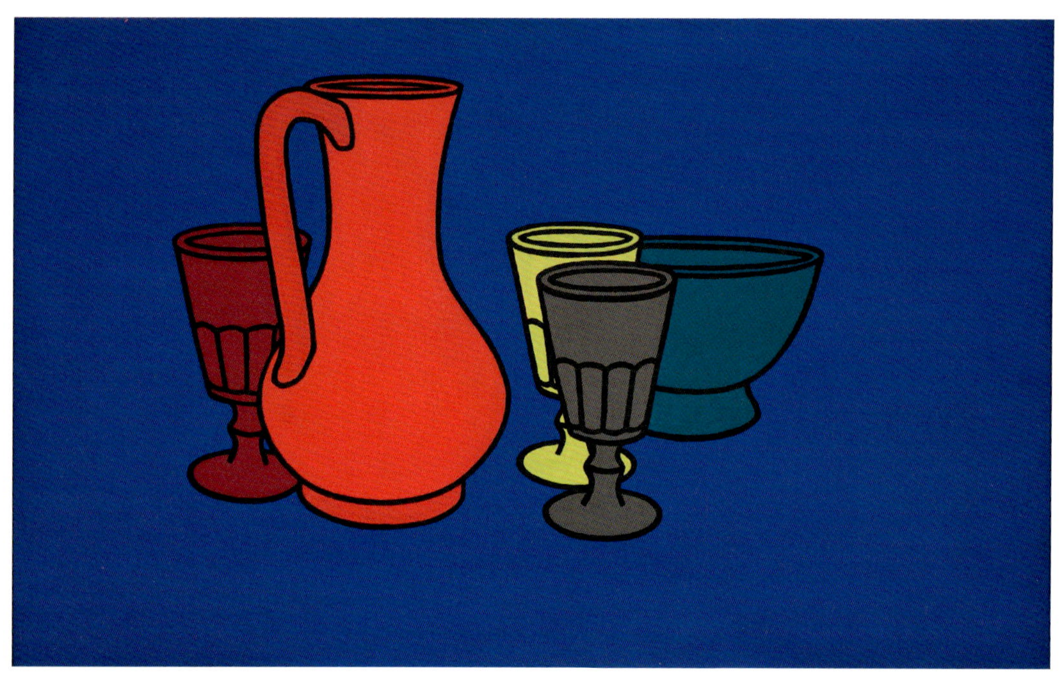

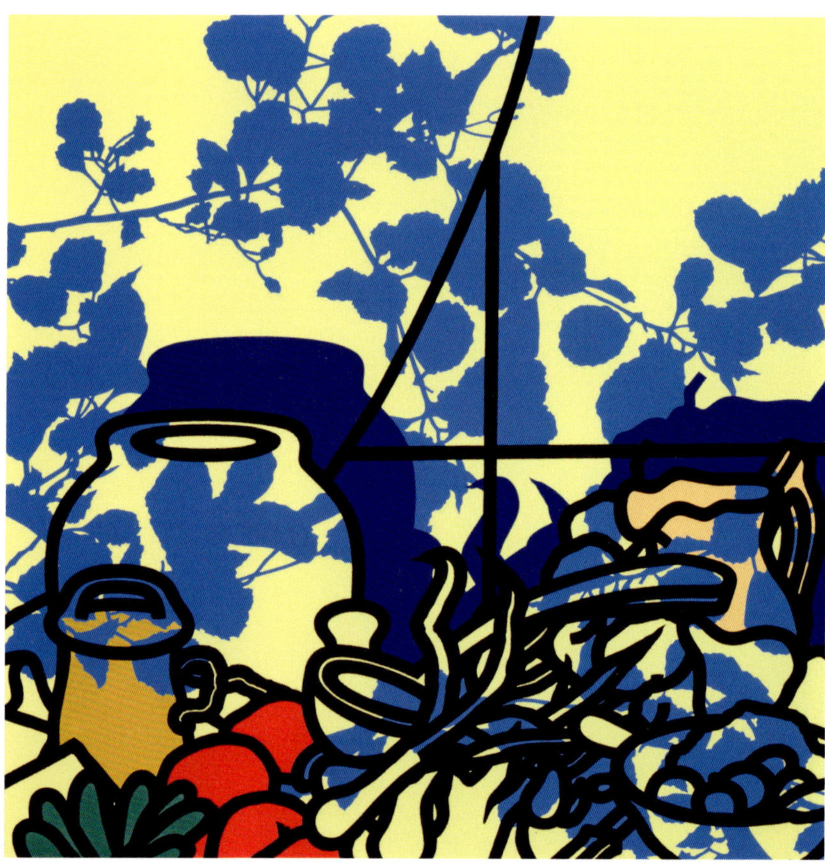

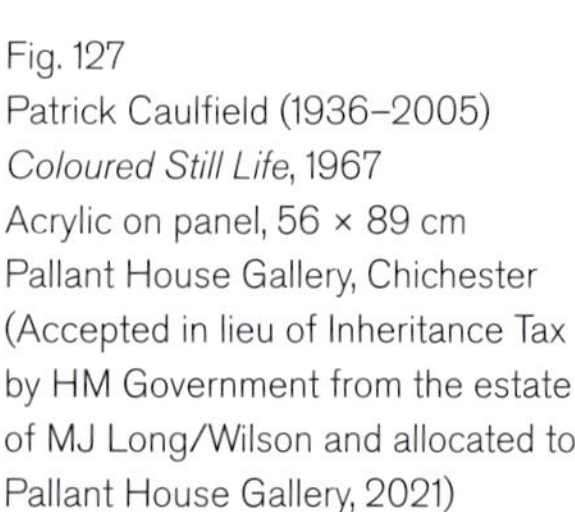

Fig. 127
Patrick Caulfield (1936–2005)
*Coloured Still Life*, 1967
Acrylic on panel, 56 × 89 cm
Pallant House Gallery, Chichester
(Accepted in lieu of Inheritance Tax by HM Government from the estate of MJ Long/Wilson and allocated to Pallant House Gallery, 2021)

Fig. 128
Patrick Caulfield (1936–2005)
*Still Life Ingredients*, 1976
Screenprint on paper, 71.1 × 71.1 cm
Pallant House Gallery, Chichester
Wilson Loan (2006)

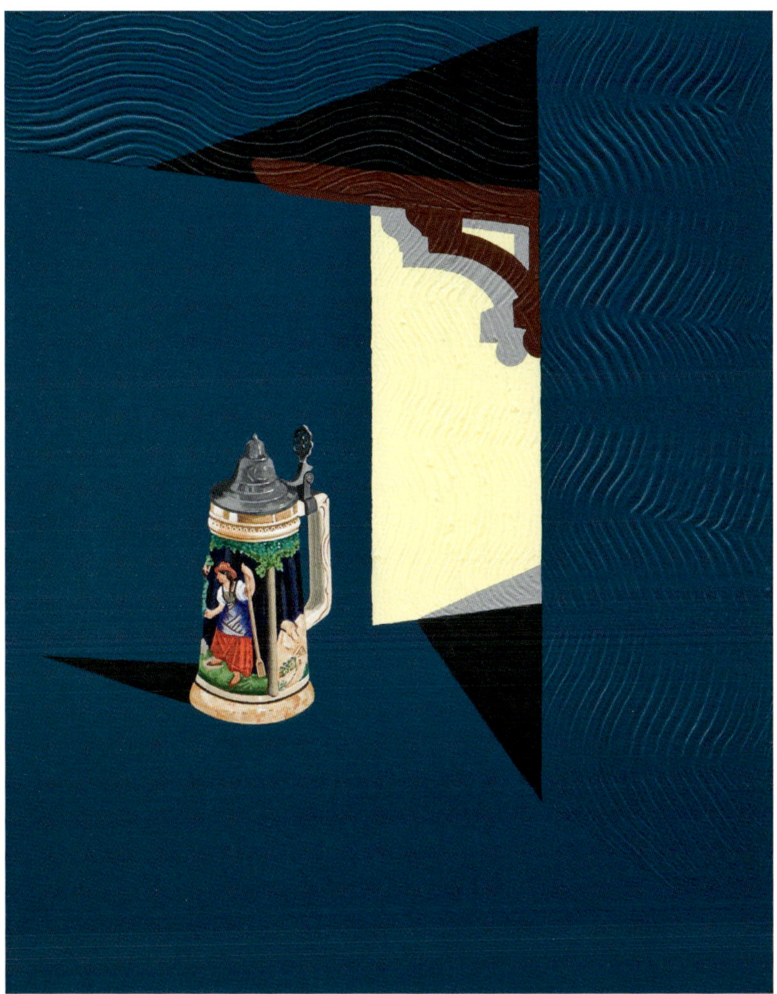

Fig. 129
Patrick Caulfield (1936–2005)
*Kellerbar*, 1997
Acrylic on canvas, 76.8 × 61.6 cm
Pallant House Gallery , Chichester
(Accepted in lieu of Inheritance Tax by HM Government from the estate of MJ Long/Wilson and allocated to Pallant House Gallery, 2021)

American critic Leo Steinberg talked of the 'flatbed picture plane' which he understood to be 'the characteristic picture plane of the 1960s', citing surfaces such as table tops, studio floors and bulletin boards as the backgrounds upon which objects are scattered.[14] The legacy of the flat picture plane can be seen in the work of Lisa Milroy (b.1959), whose practice is as much about the social value of everyday objects as about painting itself. Her paintings have an ambiguous position in relation to the *meaning* of objects. The seriality and minimal backgrounds seem to anonymise things, such as her motifs of plates, clothing and shoes, but each item is often painted individually, with pleasure and care. Through an attention to the flatness of the canvas and the repetition of objects, Milroy's work can be seen in relation to Jasper Johns's *Flag* paintings which use 'an image that is also an object in a way that *both recognises and empties out its everyday meanings*'.[15]

David Hockney similarly exploits the flatness of the picture plane to reimagine contemporary still life with his *trompe l'oeil* work *Tea Painting in an Illusionistic Style* (fig. 126). Hockney's choice to stretch the canvas into the shape of a Typhoo tea packet was radical at the time, and demonstrates how British artists in the 1960s were expanding the genre of still life to comment on the proliferation of consumer goods and shifting economies. This work was created while Hockney was a student at the Royal College of Art in London, his studio providing the inspiration for the painting, with its packets of tea piled up among tubes of paint, surrounded by postcards, pictures of Cliff Richard and newspaper photographs pinned to the walls. He commented that most works of art he encountered were through reproductions, saying 'the idea that paintings should be rectangular or square was so fixed in every student's mind that even Italian paintings of the Crucifixion, constructed in the shape of the cross, still appeared in my memory as rectangular'.[16] To create a more illusionistic painting, Hockney changed the shape of the canvas in order to paint it in a flat style. It reveals the artificiality of the reproduced image, a key concern

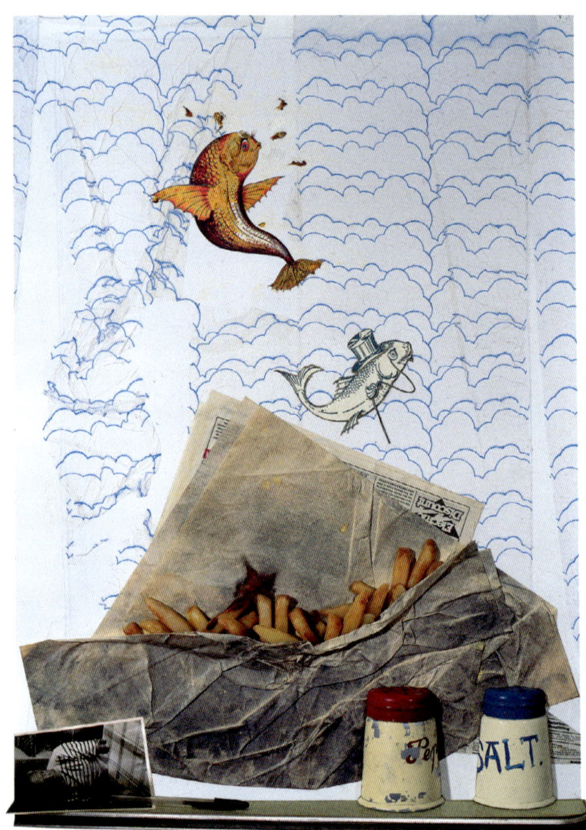


Fig. 130
Colin Self (b.1941)
*The Fishy Tale of the Battered Still Life*, 1987
Multimedia collage, 77.2 × 54 cm
Private collection

within postmodern thought which is closely connected to the age of late or consumer capitalism. As Fredric Jameson argued: 'If there is any realism left here, it is a "realism" which springs from the shock of grasping that confinement and of realising that, for whatever peculiar reasons, we seem condemned to seek the historical past through our own pop images and stereotypes about that past, which itself remains forever out of reach'.[17]

British pop artists frequently 'recycle' images, with little distinction between reproductions of fine art and glossy adverts in contemporary magazines. Although Patrick Caulfield would not describe himself as a pop artist, his still-life paintings and screenprints could be seen as representing postmodern modes of representation, such as pastiche, montage and fragmentation, in that they take from a variety of different sources, including postcards, the world of advertising and the work of Cubist artists such as Fernand Léger and Georges Braque. Works by these artists had become so familiar by the 1950s through reproduction that they had taken on the value of the pop images.[18] Caulfield subverts the language of advertising; through his affection for the devalued or dated motif, he makes us see the familiar with fresh eyes. While works such as *Coloured Still Life* (fig. 127) borrow heavily from the still-life tradition, Caulfield's bold, simplified forms, outlined in black demonstrates the influence of commercial sign painting which he argued guaranteed 'an immediacy for the image'.[19] Like Caulfield and Hockney, Richard Hamilton's work uses pastiche through appropriating tropes from art history, as well as finding new inspiration from the world of design.

By the late 1960s, Hamilton's approach to consumer culture had developed. While images such as *Just what is it that makes today's homes so different, so appealing?* (1956, Kunsthalle Tübingen) and *Hommage à Chrysler Corp.* (1957, Tate) had a kitsch, slightly sarcastic take on aspirational products, his later works looking at Braun conveyed a seriousness, treating industrial design with the same reverence as high art.[20] There was an explicit tension between the elite in Britain, which had always had a deep mistrust for mechanisation, and an emerging working-class culture, focused on modern materials, technology and attitudes, as exemplified by Hamilton's approach. He said of one of the most prominent designers at Braun: 'My admiration for the work of Dieter Rams is intense and I have for many years been uniquely attracted towards his design sensibility; so much so that his consumer products have come to occupy a place in my heart and consciousness that Mont Sainte-Victoire did in Cézanne's.'[21]

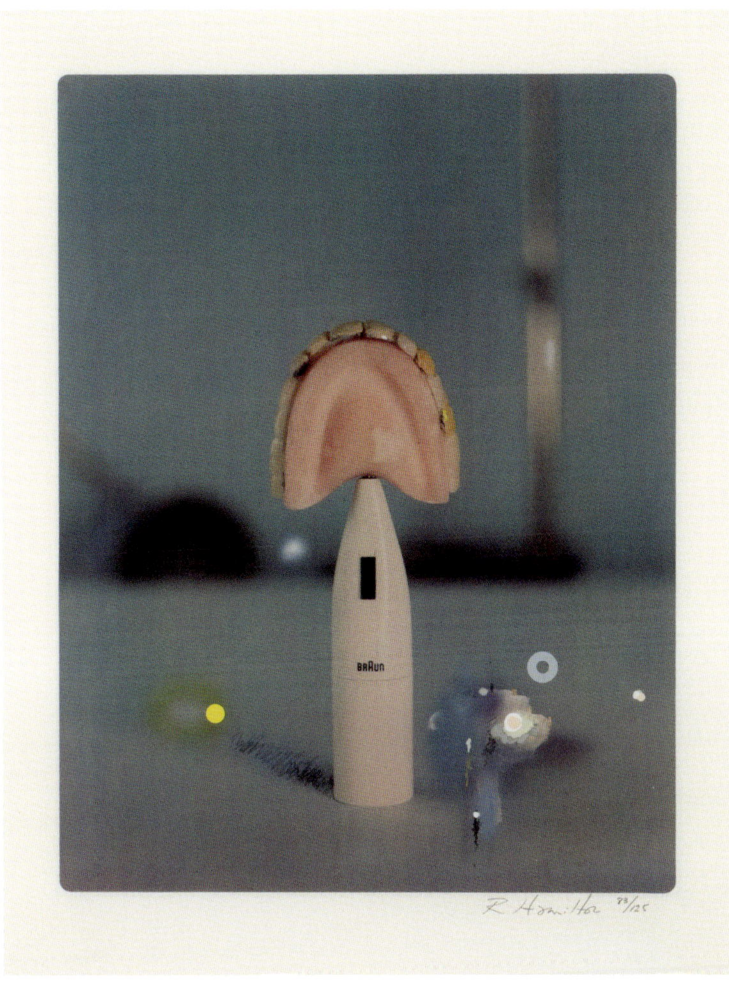

Fig. 131
Richard Hamilton (1922–2011)
*The Critic Laughs*, 1968
Laminated screenprint and lithograph with collage and hand additions, 34.2 × 26.4 cm
Pallant House Gallery, Chichester
(Wilson Gift through Art Fund, 2006)

Through Hamilton's treatment of household items of design as fine art objects, he undermines the threat of planned obsolescence, bestowing the aura of singularity upon mass-produced goods. A Braun electric grill became the subject of Hamilton's *Still-life* in 1965, which revelled in the cool, minimalist aesthetic, and consequently the same treatment was given to an electric toothbrush in *The Critic Laughs* (fig. 131). This screenprint originates from an assemblage Hamilton made from an oversized set of teeth cast in sugar mounted onto the neck of his Braun electric toothbrush. In this work, Hamilton pays homage to Jasper Johns's *The Critic Smiles* (1969, National Gallery of Art, Washington), a grim sculpture portraying human teeth on a toothbrush, in embossed lead, tin and gold. It is a unique take on the *memento mori* but instead of making reference to human mortality, Johns and Hamilton allude to the death of an artist's reputation. *The Critic Smiles* was made in response to bad reviews, becoming a comment upon the commodification of the artist, who is at the mercy of art critics and the marketplace.

Among all the artists discussed here, Hamilton approaches the effects and influence of consumer culture with perhaps the greatest ambiguity and self-consciousness, precipitating the strategies of artists associated with the YBAs, such as Gavin Turk. Turk's practice, which looks to question the function of the artist in terms of creativity, originality and authority, makes deliberate reference to art history, recycling modernist ideas such as the readymade. In his work *Dump* (fig. 132), Turk recreates a full rubbish bag out of painted bronze – echoing Jasper Johns's *Painted Bronze (Ballantine Ale)* (1960, Kunstmuseum Basel) – to make a comment on the commodity value of things and works of art. Here, waste is made precious through an expensive sculptural material – bronze. Turk returns again and again to the language of waste to reflect upon contemporary society's attitude towards value.

Artists now are aware of the fact that consumer culture's rate of growth is not sustainable; the production of goods is at the expense of human labour and finite environmental resources. Contemporary photographer

Maisie Cousins's (b.1992) saturated images of congealing rubbish (figs. 133 and 134) occupy a space between attraction and revulsion with regards to indulgent consumption. They represent 'where the polite rules of resemblance and reference fall apart' – an entropy of plastic bags, takeaway boxes, rotting flowers and sweets.[22] While the British pop movement was born out of the mass proliferation of images and goods in the postwar era, the accelerated rate of consumption in the present moment could be seen as even more overwhelming. There is a paradox at play in the engagement with, and representation of, the objects in consumer culture by the artists discussed here. On the one hand these objects represent aspiration and growth; on the other waste and decay. Despite the cool cynicism often directed at these artists' appropriation of mass culture, their depictions of everyday consumer items do have symbolic meaning, reflecting attitudes and ways of living in the contemporary world.

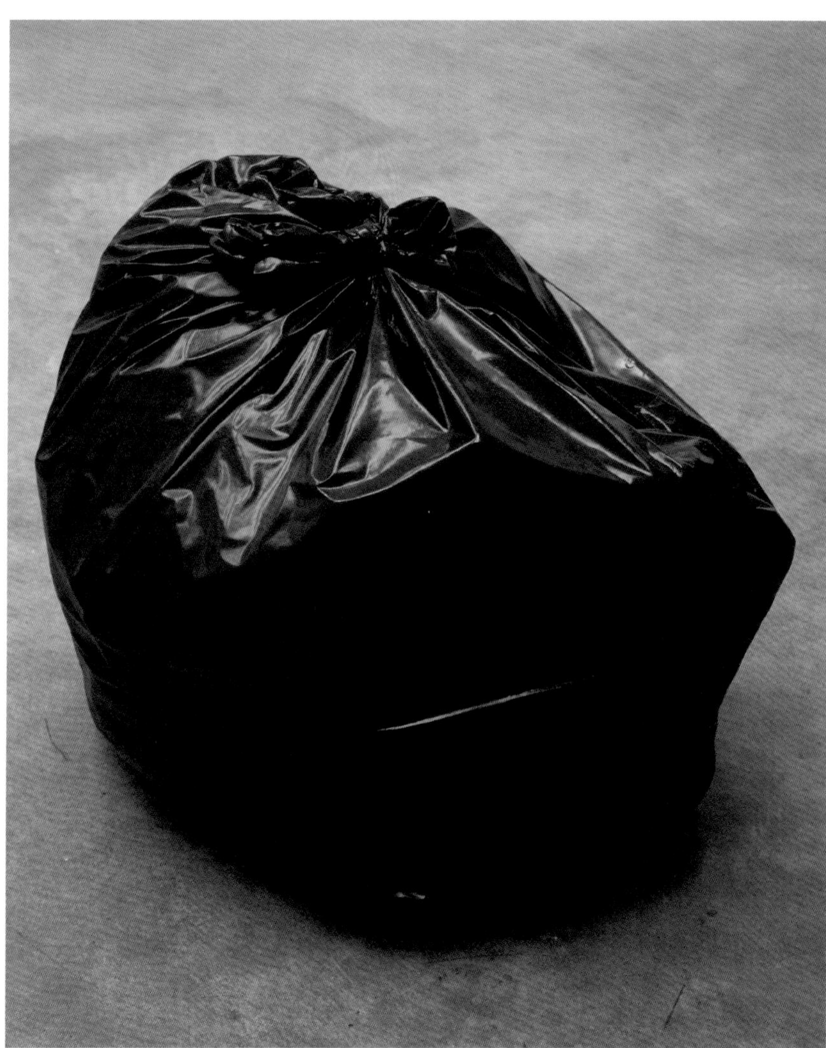

Fig. 132
Gavin Turk (b.1967)
*Dump*, 2004
Painted bronze, 43 × 47 × 61 cm
Pallant House Gallery, Chichester
(Accepted under the Cultural Gifts Scheme by HM Government from Frank Dunphy and allocated to Pallant House Gallery, 2018)

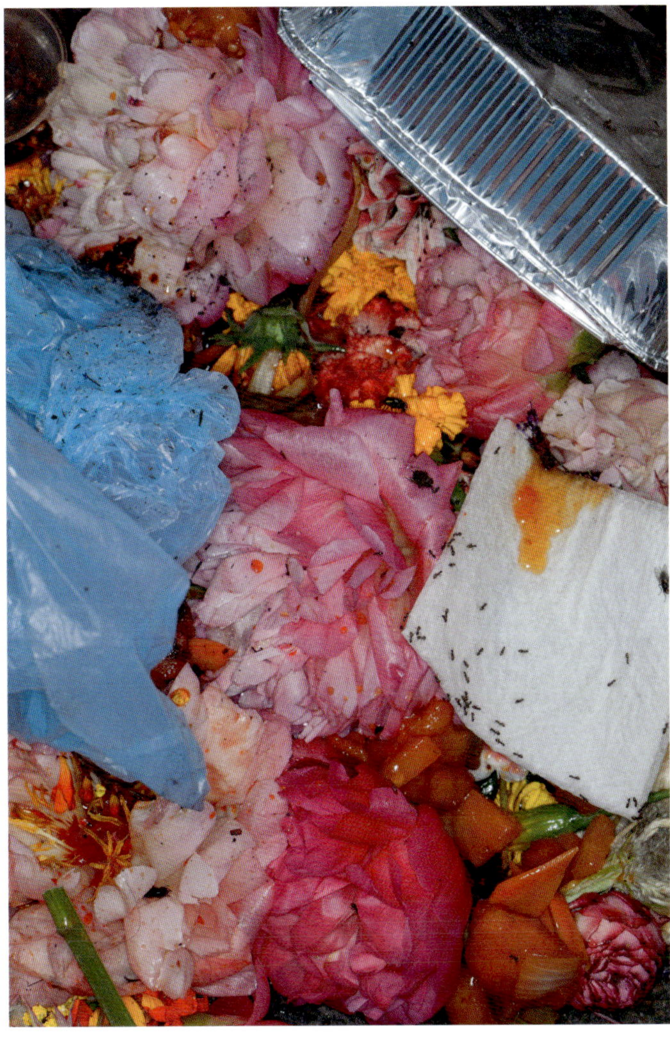

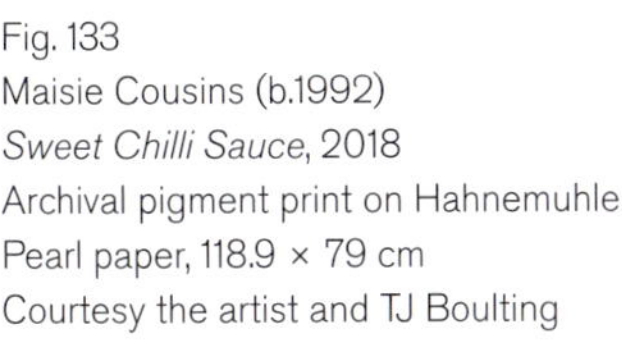

Fig. 133
Maisie Cousins (b.1992)
*Sweet Chilli Sauce*, 2018
Archival pigment print on Hahnemuhle
Pearl paper, 118.9 × 79 cm
Courtesy the artist and TJ Boulting

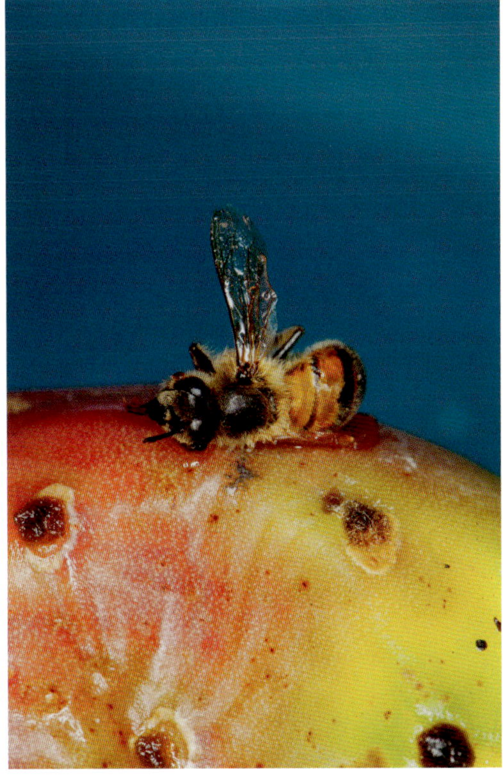

Fig. 134
Maisie Cousins (b.1992)
*Wasp*, 2017
Archival pigment print on Hahnemuhle
Pearl paper, 29.7 × 42 cm
Courtesy the artist and TJ Boulting

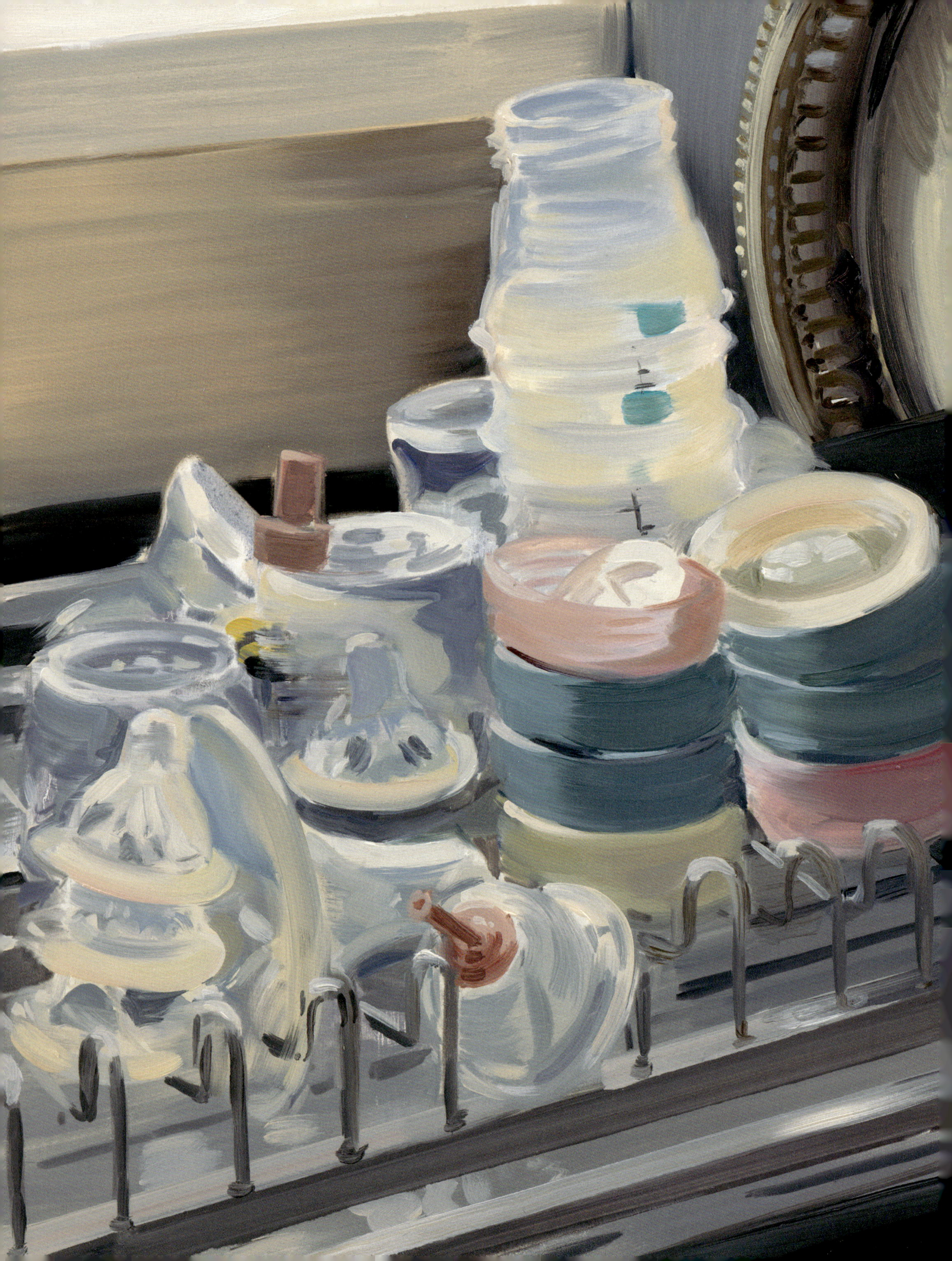

# 7 'It doesn't shout – it whispers': On the Quietness of Still Life

MELANIE VANDENBROUCK

Motherhood, particularly in its early days, weeks and months, seldom rhymes with stillness – instead, one may readily picture sleepless nights, bodily fluids and wailing. Caroline Walker's (b.1982) quietly matter-of-fact *My Bottles and Pumps* (fig. 135) offers a glimpse of respite amid the relentlessness of an infant's needs. This is a personal piece (Walker describes it as a self-portrait, as it is her own experience of motherhood depicted here), and yet it will ring true for many mothers, not least those juggling parental care, paid work and the other responsibilities life may throw at them. For centuries, maternal devotion has been depicted with women cradling children, infants suckling at the breast. Here, it is conveyed in breast pump valve, flange and cap, stacked-up silicone teats and bottle screw rings; the clinical plastic's curves and translucency rendered in deftly loose, milky oil brushstrokes. If still life has often been equated to women's work, expressing mother's milk into bottles is most definitely 'women's work', with all its unglamorous, practical and dull repetitiveness. Many viewers will recognise here a moment of calm, perhaps even solitude, in the ritualistic, meticulous washing of each implement of the breast-pumping apparatus and baby feeding paraphernalia, soaped, sterilised in boiling water, and then carefully laid out on a dish-drying rack, perhaps looking out of the kitchen window while busying oneself at the sink. Time stands still, if even for a brief moment.

For all its mundanity and portrayal of humble objects, still life has the capacious ability to express the human condition and shared experience, a manifest of the time and society in which it was made. It is perhaps in this, that still life acquires its contemplative, reflective qualities.

Fig. 135
Caroline Walker (b.1982)
*My Bottles and Pumps*, 2024
Oil on board, 41 × 33 cm
Courtesy the artist; Stephen Friedman Gallery, London and New York; GRIMM Gallery and Ingleby Gallery, Edinburgh

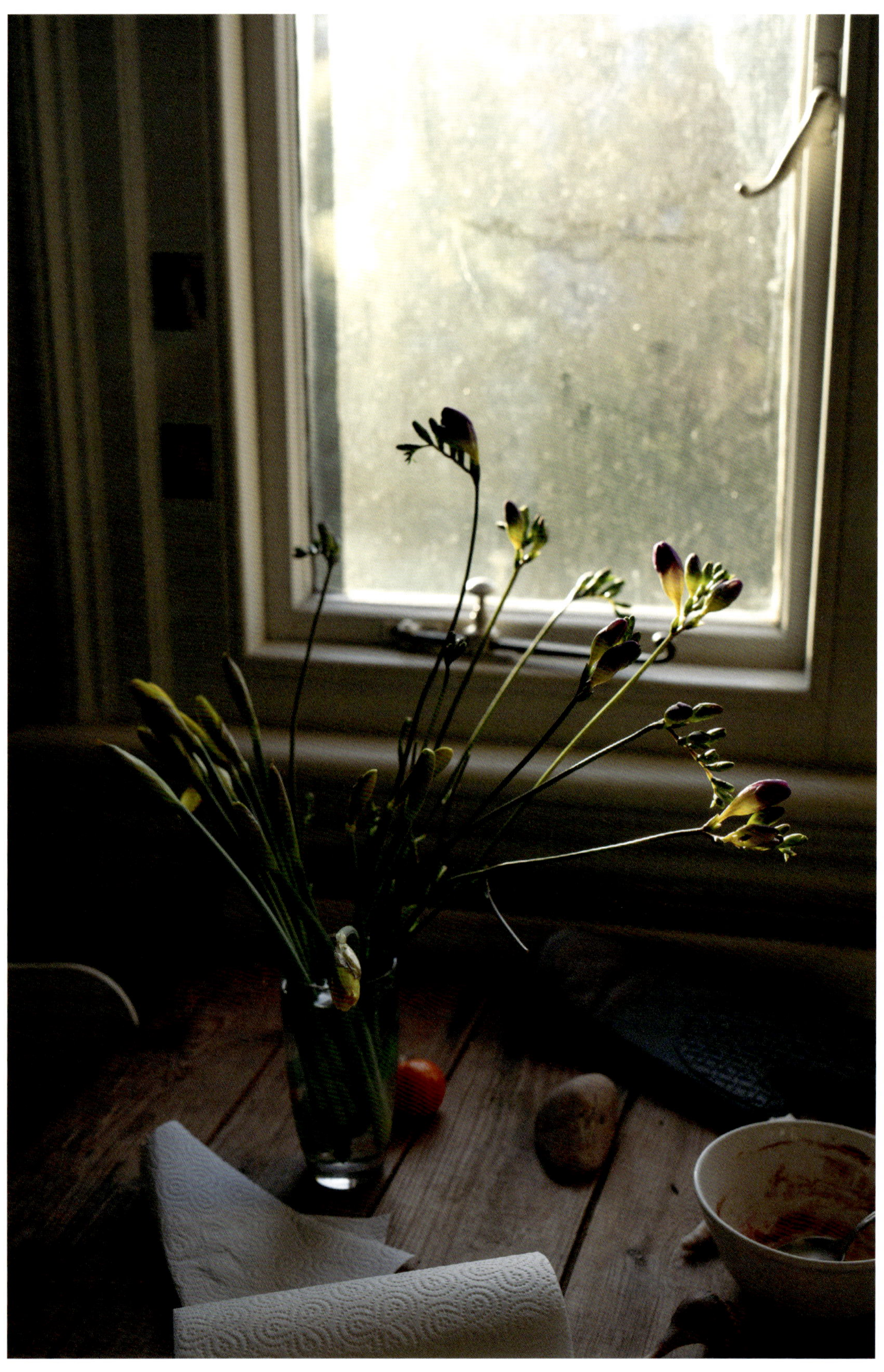

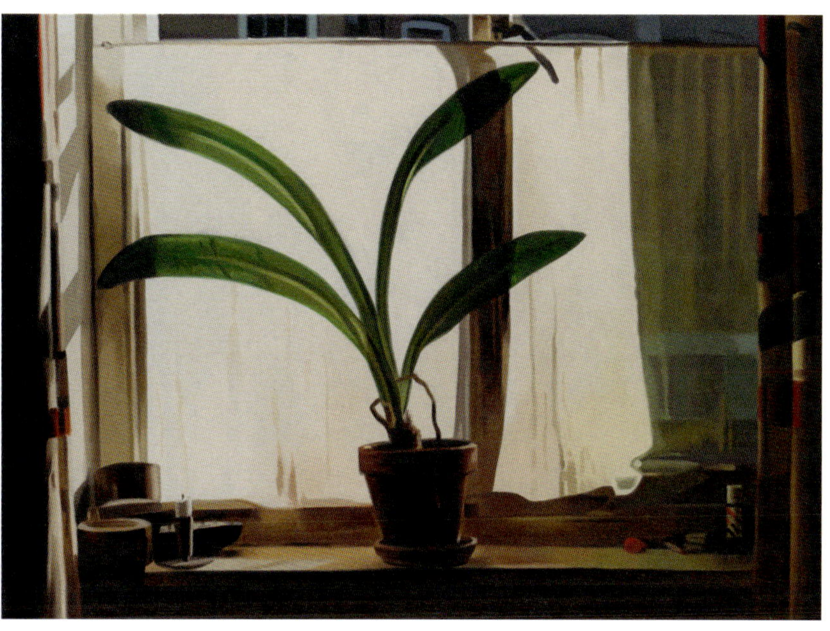

Fig. 136 (opposite)
Wolfgang Tillmans (b.1968)
*Hampstead still life*, 2020
Inkjet print, 206 × 138 cm
Maureen Paley, London

Fig. 137 (above)
Mike Silva (b.1970)
*Window Light*, 2023
Oil on canvas, 66 × 91.4 cm
Courtesy the artist and
The Approach, London

*Hampstead still life* (fig 136), by Wolfgang Tillmans (b.1968), evokes lockdown during the COVID-19 pandemic. For many, this time when life was unexpectedly stilled, often tragically, was a time of heightened awareness – of human mortality, of one's vulnerability, both physical and emotional – perhaps also tinged with loneliness. Without the distractions of the usual everyday routine, it also became a time of renewed sensitivity. In the newfound peace of roads devoid of roaring cars, birdsong emerged from this silence. As air pollution dissipated, ambient scents felt more pronounced. Within the confines of one's home, one became aware of the most subtle shifts of light. Tillmans's photograph captures equally the material qualities of the objects haphazardly gathered on a dining table – the imprint of lacelike motifs on a kitchen roll, a bowl smeared with the dried remains of a meal, the textured rubber of an oven glove – but it is to the light falling on the delicate stems and not yet bloomed buds of a bouquet of spring flowers that our eye is attracted. This is a bouquet alive with possibilities, delicate yet captivating; a picture of time passing slowly.

Another picture of a plant backlit before a window, Mike Silva's (b.1970) melancholy *Window Light* (fig. 137) expresses a kind of longing. As with other works based on 1990s photographs shot by the artist, decades later he is reflecting on moments gone and the relationships these conjure up. While the focus is ostensibly on the houseplant with its graceful silhouette clearly detached against a sun-drenched curtain, the real protagonist here is the light. Like memory, light can be equally fleeting and affecting. Here it endows the scene with warmth, the sheltered intimacy of an enclosed, domestic space. By contrast, Mohammed Sami's (b.1984) *Sunday* (fig. 138)

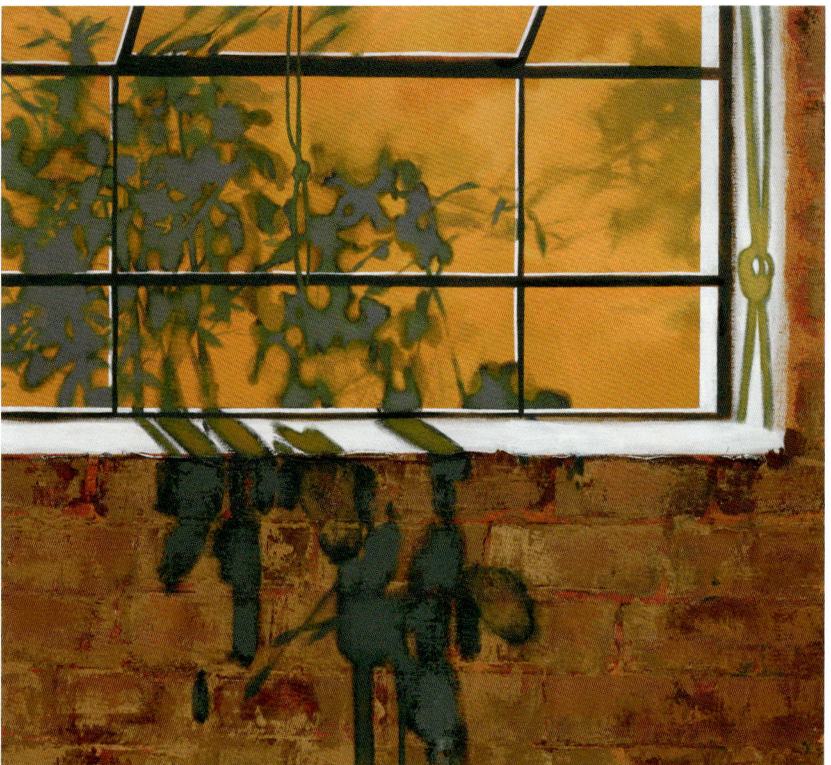

Fig. 138
Mohammed Sami (b.1984)
*Sunday*, 2019
Acrylic on linen, 90 × 100 cm
Courtesy the artist and private collection

carries an irrepressible sense of foreboding. It revolves around a tree framed by a window; its foliage silhouetted outside, its shadow creeping into the space inside, drip-like and expansive, like the bloodstain from a live wound absorbed and spreading on clothing fabric. The atmosphere, too, is unsettling: if the brick wall seems realistic in tone, texture and wear, then what is one to make of the mustard-coloured sky and the bleak, oblique light falling onto the windowsill? It is only after registering the stain-like shadow and the troubling light/colour effect, that comes to the viewer's attention the double motif of a noose-like cord or rope – perhaps that of a blind or the window's shutting mechanism – near the right edge of the canvas, and hanging against the central windowpane. Adding to the scene's disquiet, once seen, the nooses/cords cannot be unseen. While Sami rejects facile attempts to interpret his work through his biography (that of a young painter under Saddam Hussein's regime, who after the US-led invasion of Iraq found asylum in Sweden before coming to study and work in Britain), or to read it as a retelling of traumatic events, his paintings explore the shifting nature of memory, how it grips the senses in recollection, dream or nightmare. As Amy Sherlock writes, 'Sami is a painter of atmosphere rather than action ... In place of the event, he conjures its premonition or aftermath ... Inference is much spookier than evidence'.[1] We may not see it, but we feel it.

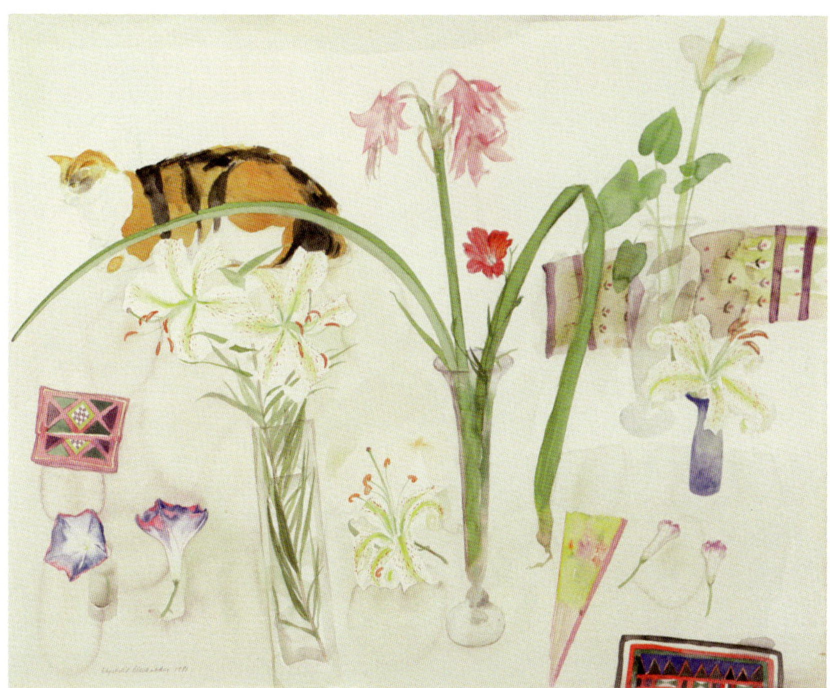

Fig. 139
Elizabeth Blackadder (1931–2021)
*Cat and Flowers*, 1981
Watercolour on paper, 76.2 × 95.8 cm
Fleming Wyfold Art Foundation

At the other end of the emotive spectrum, a sense of quietude emanates from Elizabeth Blackadder's (1931–2021) lyrical still lifes. From a young age, Blackadder was fascinated with flowers, which she collected, pressed in albums and meticulously catalogued. While in her early career she experimented with a variety of subjects, the natural world remained a key source of inspiration and, from the 1960s onwards, it was for her floral compositions that she became best known. Following a period of illness in the late 1970s which made working in oils more challenging, she increasingly focused on the freer mediums of watercolour and drawing, in which she broke away from traditional perspective. *Cat and Flowers* (fig. 139) is a typical if particularly felicitous example, the composition arranged on a flat, undefined background, with negative space rather than a detailed environment binding the objects together. Free from the distractions of a cluttered background, our attention is drawn to the particularities of each flower. Blackadder's precise, almost scientific rendition recalls the visual language of botanical florilegia as well as her youthful practice. The addition of a cat, snoozing amid the bouquets of morning glory, lilies and amaryllis, contributes to the tranquillity of the scene, while the folded fan and cloths embroidered with colourful geometric patterns, objects probably collected during her many travels, speak of her curiosity for the world.

Like Blackadder, Charlotte Verity (b.1954) finds in her garden the source material for her work, in which she explores the passing of time through seasonal cycles. Bringing the outside in, lovingly tended garden flowers are extracted from their environment and set in the abstracted space of the

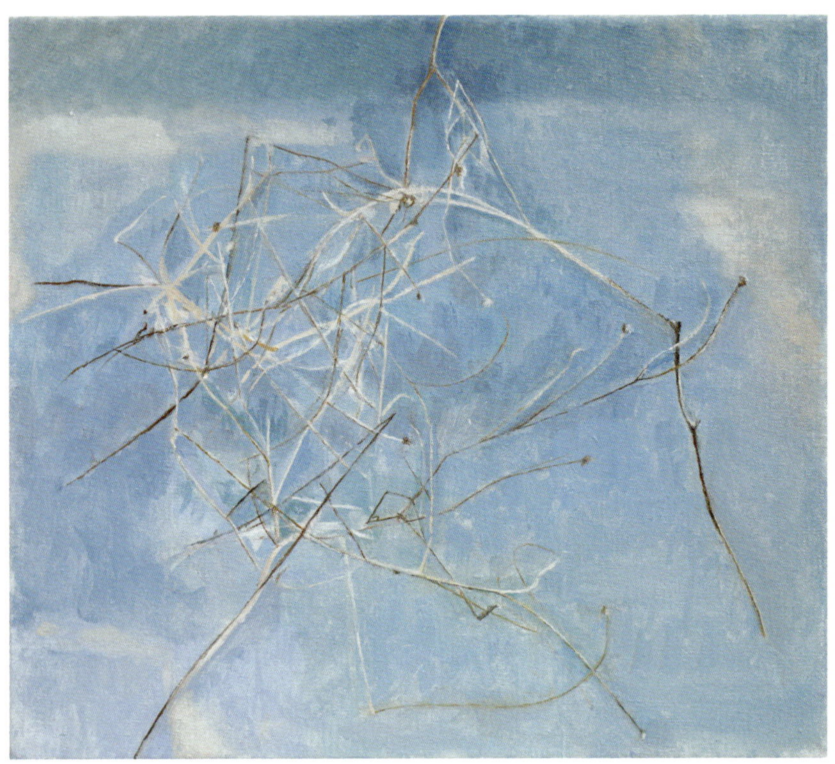

Fig. 140 (left)
Charlotte Verity (b.1954)
*Spent Stems*, 2014
Oil on canvas, 30.5 × 40.5 cm
Courtesy of the artist Charlotte Verity

Fig. 141 (below left)
Jean Baptiste Oudry (1686–1755)
The White Duck, 1753
Oil on canvas, 95.3 × 63.5 cm
Stolen from Houghton Hall, Norfolk, 1992

Fig. 142 (below right)
Euan Uglow (1932–2000)
*Duck*, 1965
Oil on panel, 75 × 48.8 cm
Private collection

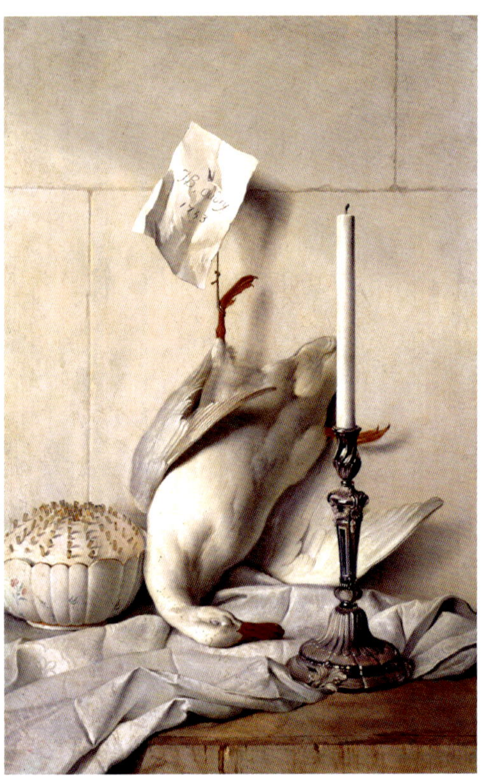

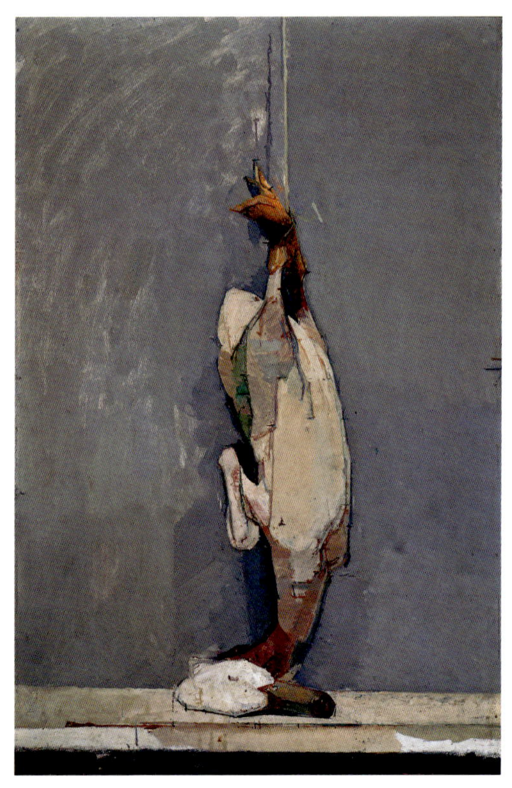

studio, for Verity to observe their every detail, the particularity of their structure, how they respond to light. Although painted slowly, over weeks and sometimes months, her still lifes seize the ephemerality of the organic elements they depict. *Spent Stems* (fig. 140) emerged almost by accident, in the summer of 2014, as she painted *The Day's Eyes* (private collection), a large still life with bunches of small daisies. Verity's working process is one of intense, slow, close looking; one during which flowers may shrink and shrivel, to be replaced by others until the painting is finished. She explains:

> As the painting came to an end, I became intrigued by the small pile of discarded stems that had accumulated. Being so close to the window, they caught the light and became miniature illuminated pathways; the blue cloth felt celestial. I wondered if I could make a painting from this fragile motif and began to untangle the stems with my brush as it were, noting and tracking their change of width and direction and the way they took the light. They are specific, minutely so, but I hope they speak to other fleeting things that are glimpsed as one goes about: flashes of sunlight on rivers, trees, paths or roads, or other moments that pass and that one longs to keep hold of or to remember.[2]

In the months it took for it to be painted, *Spent Stems* acquired a melancholy tinge and almost wintry quality, summer turning into a November light. In observing the simple elegance of the tangle of brittle stems, Verity's precise stillness is meditative, precious.

Although distinct in his approach, the work of Euan Uglow (1932–2000) shares with Verity the profound absorption applied to the act of painting. Few of Uglow's still lifes can be as 'nature morte' as his depictions of dead animals. Among these, *Duck* (fig. 142) shows a bird hung by the feet on a wall, its stiffened body weighed by gravity, its head limply resting on a ledge. In its subject and composition, this painting brings to mind a celebrated 18th-century *nature morte*, Jean Baptiste Oudry's *The White Duck* (fig. 143; now lost, formerly at Houghton Hall from where it was stolen in 1992).[3] Oudry's symphony in white is a *tour-de-force* in *trompe l'oeil*, flaunting the painter's skill at capturing varied textures: the crease of the paper carrying his signature and the folds of patterned fabric loosely spread onto a table; the soft feathers of the duck's rotund breast and open wings; the contrast between the smooth shaft of a candle and the flat ruggedness of a stone wall; the Kakiemon pot holding a cream and almond pudding.[4] By comparison, Uglow's two-toned painting, albeit equally muted, focuses entirely on the duck which shares the picture plane with an undefined grey wall and a modest ledge. Uglow's painterliness is quiet, absorbed; yet the considered simplicity of his composition does not conceal the laborious, mathematical precision of his working method:

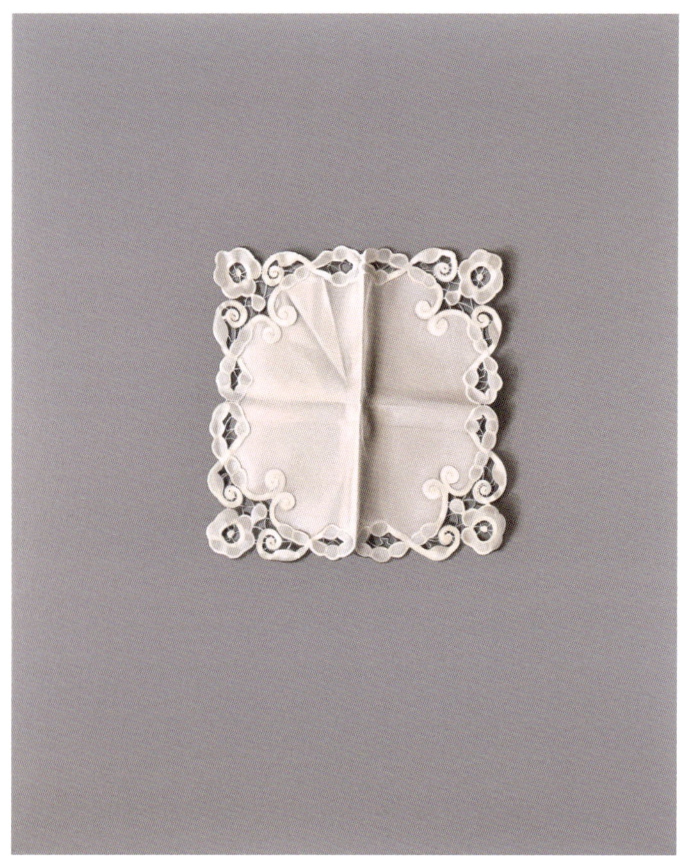

traces of his methodical measurements of proportions remain. Neither polished nor invisible, Uglow's heavy brushstrokes are no less controlled, systematically applied. Compared to Oudry's magnificent bird, Uglow's may be lean and austere, but it is charged with the textural possibilities of painting. Ultimately, his duck is not about death, but stillness, paint and light.

Another conversation across centuries takes place in Alison Watt's (b.1965) paintings inspired by works by the great 18th-century portraitist Allan Ramsay (1713–1784), from which she extracted details or attributes – a flower, a ribbon, a book – to reflect on the practice of painting and on the construction of identity through objects. In several of her works, including *Wemyss* (fig. 143), Watt focused on Ramsay's sitters' linen handkerchiefs (or more accurately, neckerchiefs), to present these unfolded, flat on a neutral picture plane, capturing the lace edgework, the fold creases, the weight of the fabric. Of still life, Watt says, 'It does things quietly, it doesn't shout – it whispers'.[5] These are objects that have been crafted, washed, neatly folded and worn. A symbol of courtship and marital fidelity, handkerchiefs were, in 18th-century Britain, expressive of their sitter's modesty, designed to be folded over the shoulders or covering the bosom. They were, too, a marker of wealth. Lifted from their owner's bodies, taken out of their context, essentialised in the whiteness and delicateness of the detailed lacework, made into still life, the fabric still carries their sitter with them. Still life, Watt goes on to say, 'reflects us. So, by its very nature, it is linked to the portrait. It is a portrait without likeness'.[6]

Hurvin Anderson's (b.1965) *Still Life with Artificial Flowers* (fig. 144) also conveys a sense of identity, that of making a home, planting roots. Commissioned as a print edition for display in British diplomatic buildings around the world, it speaks of Britain through the lens of the African-Caribbean diaspora experience. Described as 'a snapshot of the artist's mother's front room in Birmingham',[7] it depicts the bouquet of artificial flowers that sits in Anderson's family home, placed in a glass vase his mother brought with her from her native Jamaica. Rich in colour and pattern, with its cascading flowers, striped vase and doily set against a vibrant flock wallpaper, Anderson's print radiates with joyful, intricate complexity. (The printmaking itself was a complex process, requiring 15

Fig. 143 (above)
Alison Watt (b.1965)
*Wemyss*, 2020
Oil on canvas, 75.5 × 62 cm
Private collection

Fig. 144 (opposite)
Hurvin Anderson (b.1965)
*Still Life with Artificial Flowers*, 2018
Screenprint on paper, 75.2 × 56 cm
Courtesy of the artist and
Thomas Dane Gallery

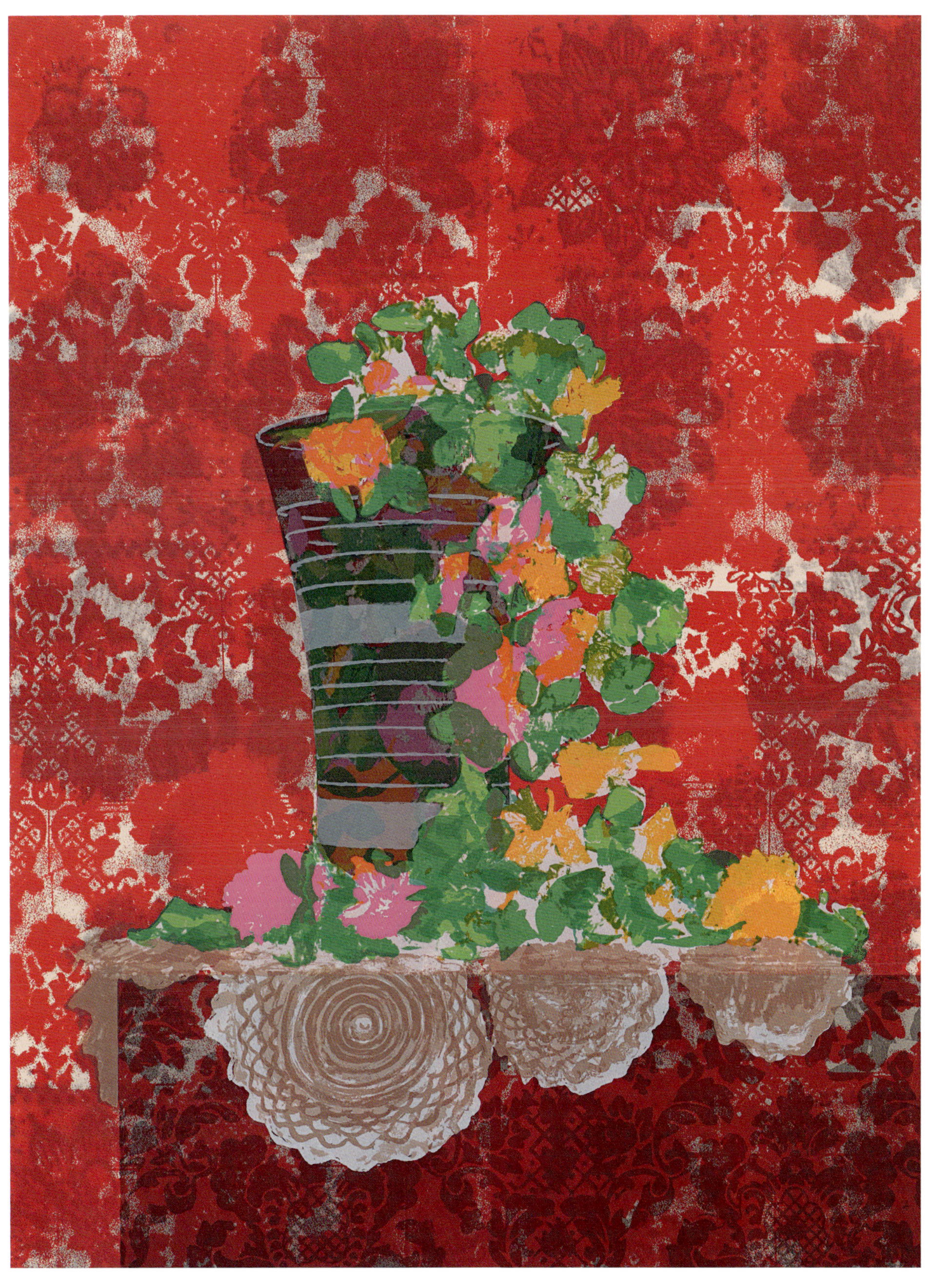

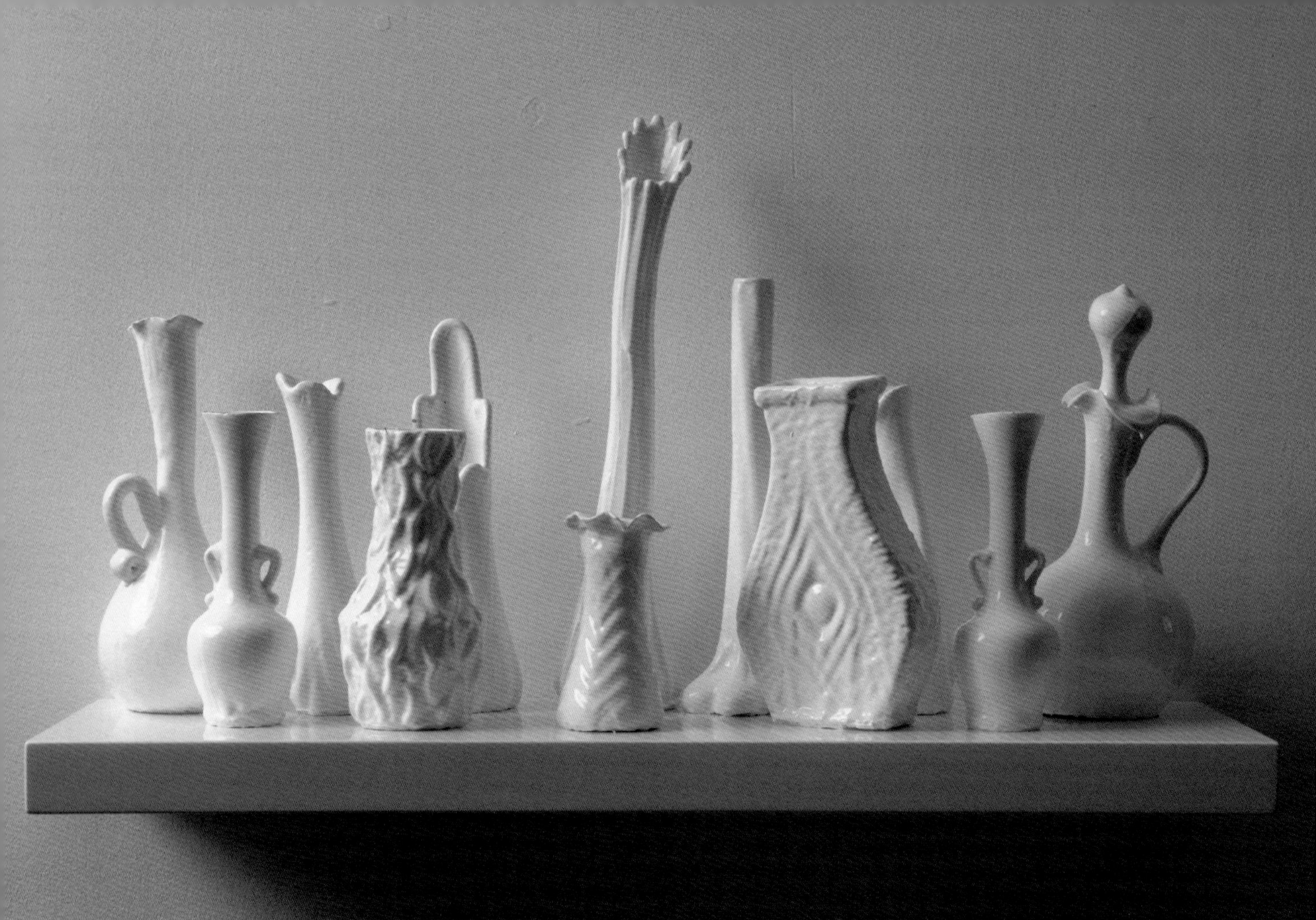

Fig. 145
Jane Simpson (b.1964)
*Our Distant Relatives*, 2004
Silicone rubber, glass, wood and polyester lacquer, 54.7 × 85.5 × 26 cm
UK Government Art Collection

stencils over 21 layers, from master printmaker Kip Gresham.) Artificial flowers and homemade furnishings, like crochet doilies, are common features of West Indian family interiors.[8] A personal work, Anderson's print is also about collective history, a celebration of the 'Windrush generation', citizenship and what it takes to make a home.

Indebted to the formal arrangements of Giorgio Morandi, Jane Simpson's (b.1964) *Our Distant relatives* (fig. 145) is expressive of the tension and vulnerabilities of human interactions, how we are affected by the mood and the contact of others. As the art critic Louisa Buck puts it, 'her arrangements of objects present themselves like family portraits, their interrelationships suspended in time'.[9] Here the family members are vessels of different sizes, shapes and ceramic styles, representing several generations and relationships. The vessels are also not what they seem: what the eye identifies as porcelain in the smooth, milky, almost reflective surface, is in fact rubber, a material which behaves differently from porcelain. Instead of a hard, cool surface and ponderous solidity, recast in rubber, the formerly inanimate objects are imbued with human qualities. Though firmly grounded on their shelf, they quiver in response to the footsteps of people walking nearby. Their instability is relatable. They acquire a slight droop, they wobble. Clustered together, they react in unison. Spirited, the rubber vessels seem to camp their wrists on their waist, as if in disapproval, or tilt their head to better listen. They may appear vulnerable and brittle, but unlike porcelain they will not break in a fall. There may be pathos in how their surroundings affect them, but there is plasticity and resilience in their make-up. As Simpson says, 'my objects are never static'.[10] These floppy doppelgangers are no longer functional vessels but have acquired a mind of their own.

In the early 1970s, Rodrigo Moynihan (1910–1990) started painting series of luminous still lifes showing objects such as bottled turps, palette knives, sponges and rolled paper, informally strewn on single shelves hung on bare walls. Unencumbered by superfluous details, these resonate with silence. There is a clear-sightedness in the simplicity of *White Plastic Container behind Plywood Board* (fig. 146), with its restricted chromatic range and minimalist composition. Known in the 1930s for abstract paintings of gestural qualities whose subject was painting itself, here Moynihan paints the tools of the artist's craft. Around the same time he was creating his studio still lifes, Moynihan was painting a series of searching self-portraits, and one cannot help but see a consideration of artistic identity in these two concomitant bodies of work. Moynihan had termed his pioneering early abstract work Objective Abstraction; this return to figuration shows another kind of 'objectivity'. Rather than a symbolical or artfully formal arrangement of objects, his studio still lifes show these painted as he found them. Moynihan, the art critic John Russell writes, 'would just go into the studio, settle down in front of a collocation of objects no matter how glum, and begin work'.[11] One of the most pared down in its prosaic simplicity, this example presents a synthesis of Moynihan's abstract and figurative tendencies. As Russell recognises, it is Mondrianesque in its 'off-centre distributions', grid-like arrangement of lines, while nodding to the work of contemporary American artists like Barnett Newman, in the 'not-quite-vertical and not-quite-central division of the canvas'.[12] With its tonal realism, it displays a certainty which is not clinical, but softened by the adjoined planes of the pellucid grey wall and the umber plywood. These 'shelf-pictures', the Royal Academician Lawrence Gowing would write for Moynihan's 1978 retrospective, are 'the most specific of his works, which are also the purest and the most austere'.[13]

There is a similar kind of quiet intensity, served by geometric order and purity of line, in the work of Edmund de Waal (b.1964). In a pristine white box-shelf, de Waal has arranged a single porcelain vessel together with two gilded porcelain tiles and an alabaster block (fig. 147): four small objects, closely grouped together in one corner of their enclosure, with what feels like a vast expanse of nothingness above. Four clear notes in the silence;

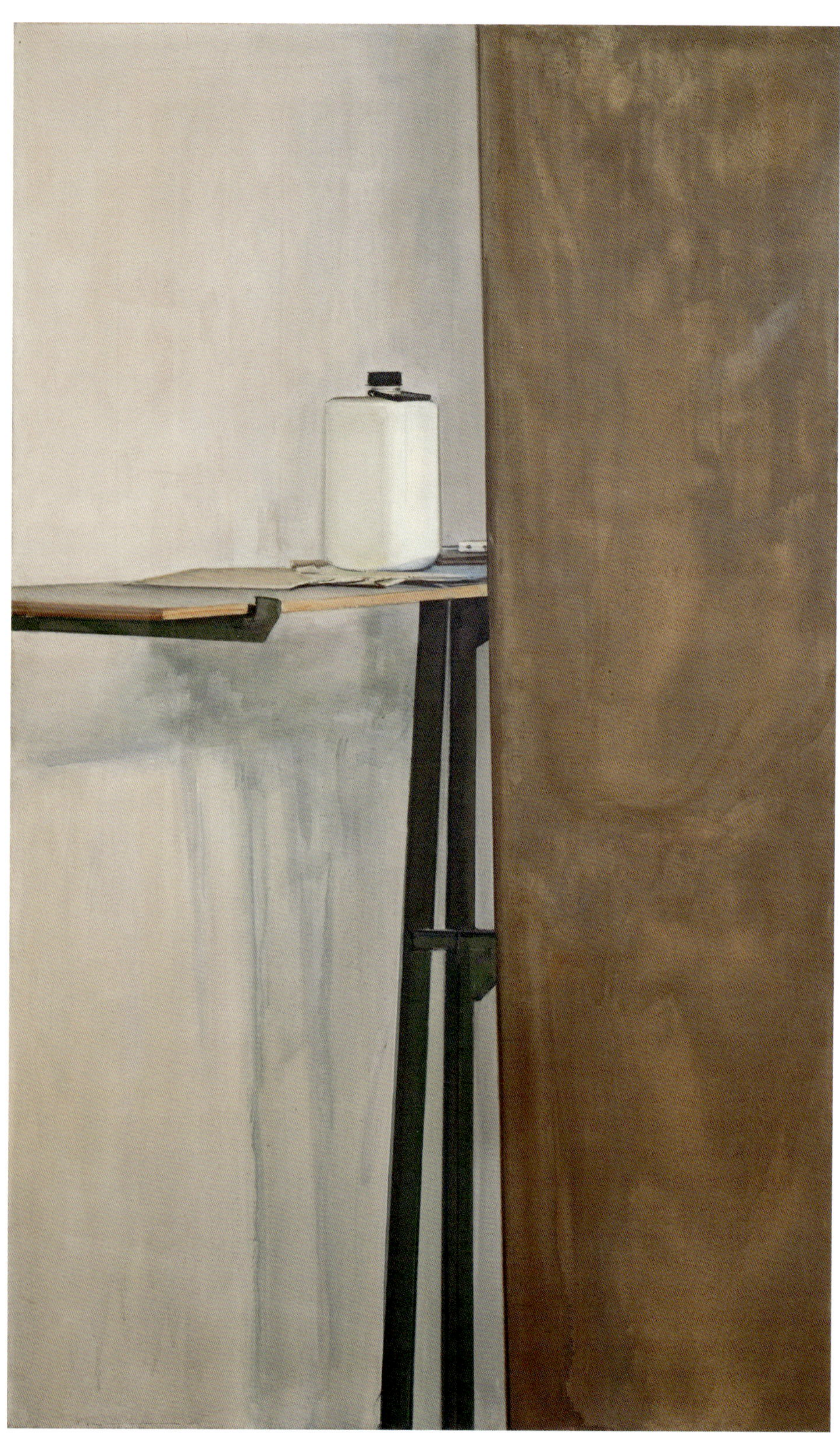

Fig. 146 (left)
Rodrigo Moynihan (1910–1990)
*White Plastic Container behind Plywood Board,* 1973
Oil on canvas, 177.8 × 119.4 cm
Private collection

Fig. 147 (opposite)
Edmund de Waal (b.1964)
*September Song, II,* 2020
Porcelain, gilded porcelain, alabaster, aluminium and plexiglass, in 5 parts,
70 × 42 × 10 cm
Courtesy the artist and Gagosian

the small interstices between them, one senses, pregnant pauses. Having, in the past two decades, created monumental installations congregating hundreds of pots in sophisticated, staccato scansion, the succinctness of his *September Song, II* has an elegiac quality. Thus assembled, these four objects denote opacity, glimmer, translucency. There is a richness and depth to these singular forms, a transfiguration through the kiln, gilding brush and chisel, that evinces de Waal's profound engagement with materiality. The alabaster a petrified thought. The vessel self-contained. The gold absorbing and reflective. Together, an abstracted presence of memory that is musical in its muteness.

Set in the winter Sussex light, Poppy Jones's (b.1985) *Water Glass & Thistle* (fig. 148), calls for a moment of pause. A thistle, its spiny leaves rendered in crisp detail, rests on an open illustrated book. It awaits the return of the reader, their facetted water glass, half full, also on the clothed table. Beyond, the room is lightly touched by the sun, made all the more mysterious by diaphanous, curtain-like layers of light, and the slight distortion of space seen through glass. The parchment-like quality of the image, mono-printed onto suede cloth and watercolour painted, gives the scene a nostalgic aura. Dream-like, as if arrested in time, it could have been made at the beginning of the last century, rather than the winter of 2024. Who is the reader? Why have they gone? What is their book about? The scrutiny of the familiar through still life invites mindful, close looking, to find beauty and meaning in the mundane, quietude in the absorption of the everyday.

The artworks discussed in this essay speak of the eloquence of objects. However insignificant these may seem, the life of objects reveals our own. They ultimately represent us and contain us, as tangible fragments of our selves.

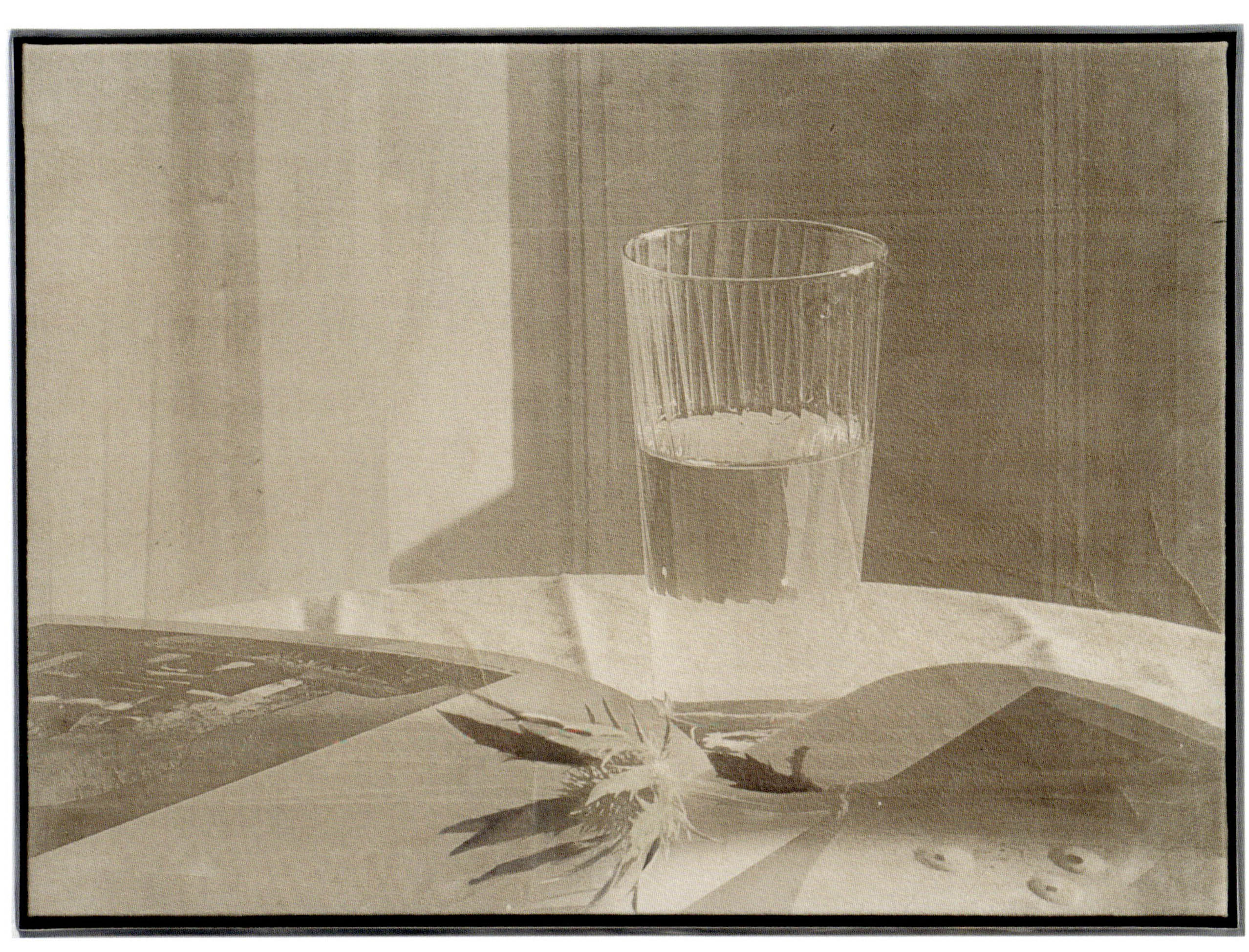

Fig. 148
Poppy Jones, b.1985
*Water Glass & Thistle*, 2024
Oil and watercolour on suede, soldered aluminium frame, 30 × 43 cm
Courtesy of the artist and Herald St, London

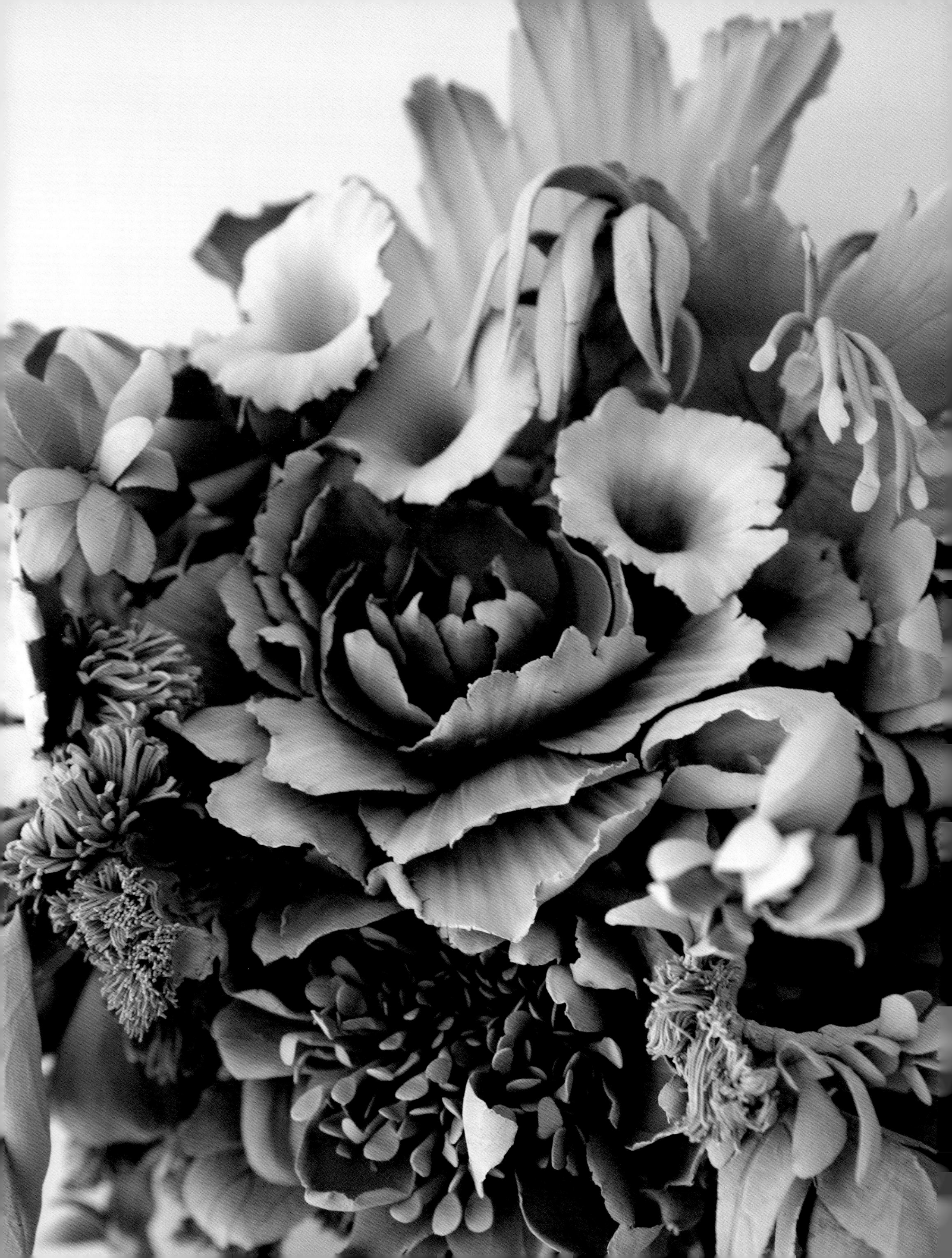

# 8 I Hear Myself with My Throat

PHOEBE CUMMINGS

> Now, too, the rising sun came in at the window, touching the red-edged curtain, and began to bring out circles and lines. Now in the growing light its whiteness settled in the plate; the blade condensed its gleam. Chairs and cupboards loomed behind so that though each was separate they seemed inextricably involved. The looking-glass whitened its pool upon the wall. The real flower on the window-sill was attended by a phantom flower. Yet the phantom was part of the flower, for when a bud broke free the paler flower in the glass opened a bud too.
>
> Virginia Woolf, *The Waves*, 1931

Life is not still.

At the atomic level, all things vibrate. Constantly. 'Like crystal, like metal, and many other substances, I am a sonorous being, but I hear my own vibration from within; as Malraux said, I hear myself with my throat.'[1] Objects, buildings, landscapes, plants, people – all perpetually become and disintegrate at different rates, over different timescales. While painting, drawing or photography are more typically considered the media for still life, we might also observe how it is formed in literature and film.

Towards the end of Yasujirō Ozu's 1949 film *Late Spring*, the camera cuts back and forth to the far side of the room. We are left, twice, for several seconds, with the image of a large vase standing beside a pillar; the silhouettes of plants outside move gently on the paper screen behind. It is quiet but not entirely still, yet the scene gives us the chance to be still with the emotional transitions of the characters. Through Virginia Woolf's

Fig. 149
Phoebe Cummings (b.1981)
Detail of work in clay, 2020

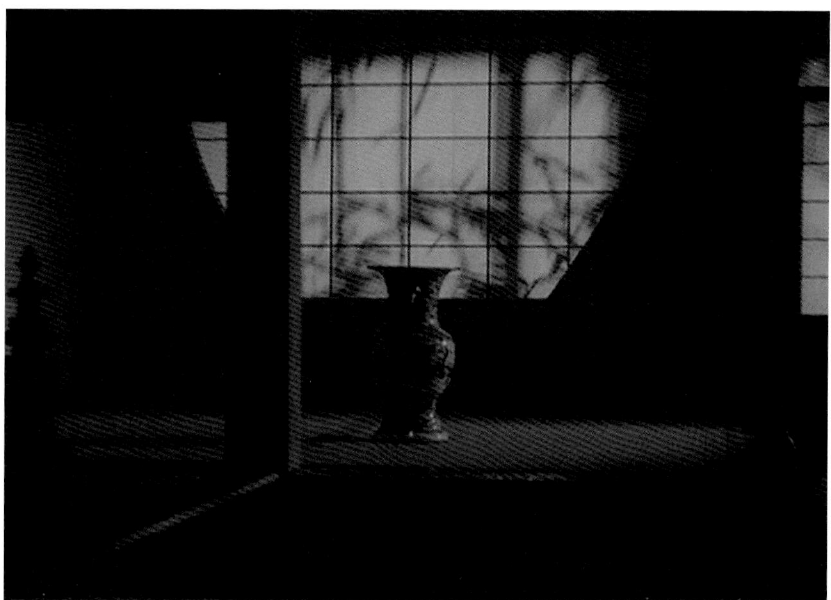

Fig. 150
Film still from *Late Spring*, 1949, directed by Yasujirō Ozu (1903–1963)

acute description above, we witness a room and its objects across a brief moment in time. Similarly, it allows us a space of stillness and absorbency. Reflections and shadows are immaterial yet nevertheless part of lived experience and significant to the ways in which objects and their images coexist. Still life appears prolonged and more active as it extends across the time of reading or viewing. The inanimate becomes animated by changes in light, movement, sound, interaction. The same could be said of sculpture, especially that which is ephemeral, which is never really separate from its place in time and space.

What happens before and after the moment depicted in a still image is imagined. Paintings of the Dutch Golden Age, such as Jan Brueghel the Elder's *Flowers in a Wooden Vessel* (1606–7, Kunsthistorisches Museum Wien), confront us with a moment at its fullest: an explosion of flora, which in reality is quite impossible, given that the different species would never all bloom at the same time. Only at the bottom of the vase do we see things disintegrating, insects moving in. We are mostly left to imagine the petals falling, the slow rotting and dust settling. Life, death and our relation to the natural and made world are implied through the arrangement of things in a still life. In a work made of raw clay, human existence is imprinted onto its every surface: the object arrives from physical labour and direct contact with the skin. Mirrors and photographs are also the surfaces in which we see ourselves disintegrating.

*I Hear Myself with My Throat* is constructed within rooms that mirror one another. The rooms exist as architectural reflections in their proportions and interior features. We see two plants extend down from symmetrical ceiling roses, duplicate in form but unidentical in detail; a profusion of growth flowers at the end of each umbilical stem, projecting into the air, eye to eye with the viewer. Each cluster is an amalgamation of botanical accuracy and ornament. A flowering of night and day is intimated, at once plant and human. The archway between the interlinked rooms becomes an imagined plane between constructed reflections, an invisible surface. Rather than freezing a moment, the work invites the viewer to observe the active present from a position of stillness.

But where does sculpture begin and end? Its borders are softer and more porous than we might imagine. Works are not neatly contained within the limits of their materiality. Sculpture possesses atmosphere and exists as much in memory as in space, its thresholds always a negotiation between bodies. Its images are perpetually adrift, never truly still.

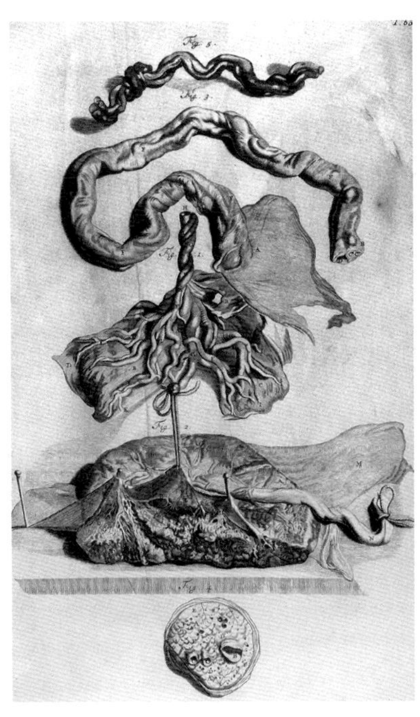

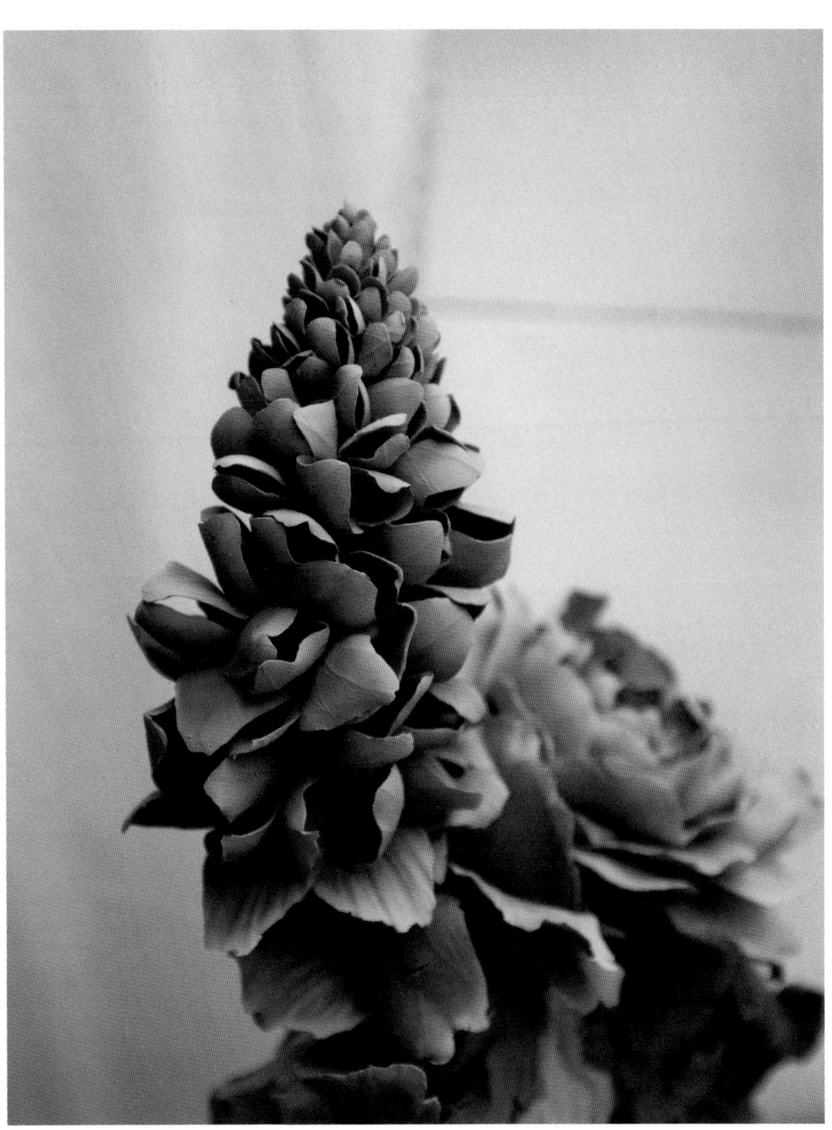

Fig. 151
William Cowper (1666–1709)
*Anatomy of Humane Bodies*, 1698
Medical illustration
Wellcome Collection, London

Fig. 152
Phoebe Cummings (b.1981)
Detail of work in clay, 2024

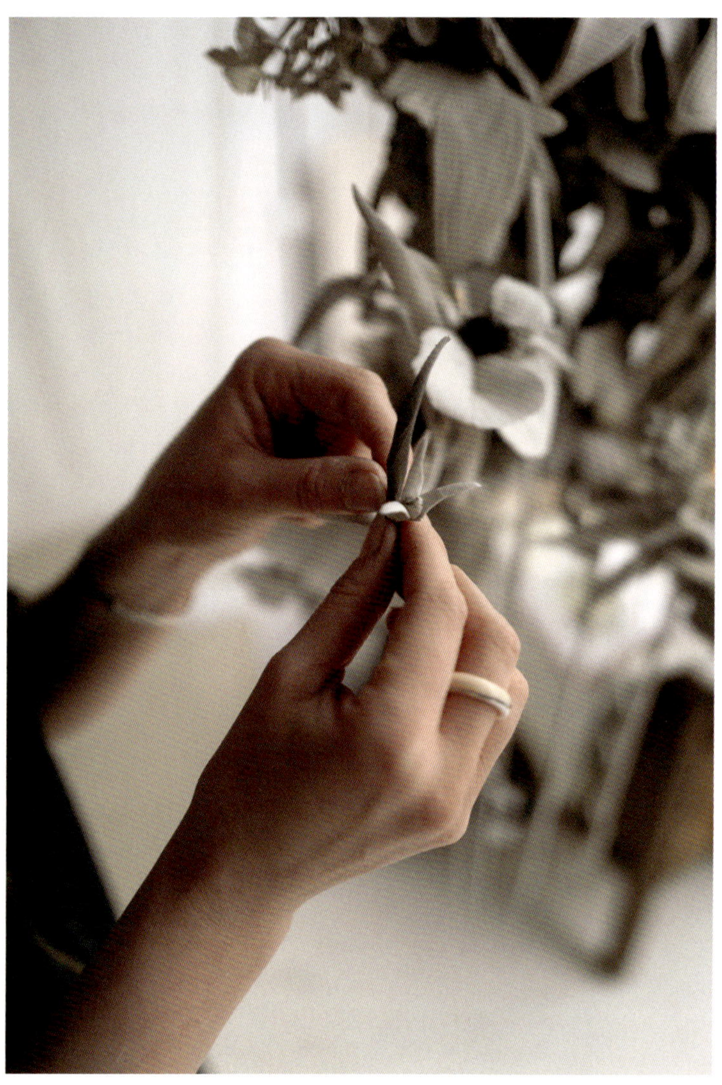

Fig. 153
Phoebe Cummings photographed by Sylvain Deleu

*

Since 2005, I have worked almost entirely with raw clay. It was an abrupt shift in approach after declaring bankruptcy shortly after graduating from an MA in ceramics and glass at the Royal College of Art. To work with clay in its raw state offered me a way to continue without the requirement of a studio and kiln. It also meant the same material could be endlessly dissolved and reformed. Existence is not necessarily a theme in the work but it is enacted by the material itself and the cycles of creation and destruction it requires.

We might consider the fact that the human body is composed of 60 percent water, with specific organs, such as the brain and heart, holding a greater percentage still. Similarly, in its plastic state, clay typically contains 40 percent water. If water can be understood as an element common, and vital, to all living things, then this too might extend to clay. While not a living material, clay echoes certain live characteristics, with behaviour and capabilities largely defined by its water content. In its soft condition, there is not only a shared chemical composition between clay and the human body, but it also puts us in direct conversation. The material feeds back, shaped by where we are, taking on the form exactly where we are not. The reciprocity of human-clay interactions is significant to its use as an artistic medium. Direct manipulation requires no tools other than touch, a quality that separates clay from other traditional materials of sculpture, such as stone, bronze or wood.

When our body enters a sculptural environment constructed from raw clay, there is shared breath. We are immersed in a visceral interaction. To stand in sculpture's atmosphere is to inhale and exhale one another – an inescapable intimacy. 'External perception and the perception of one's own body vary together because they are two sides of a single act.'[2] We are not external in our experience of viewing sculpture. To close our eyes in this space is still to sense it: materials and objects affect acoustics, humidity is felt on the skin. The environment of a sculpture fluctuates in response to the physical characteristics of its location, though it also performs slightly aside of reality.

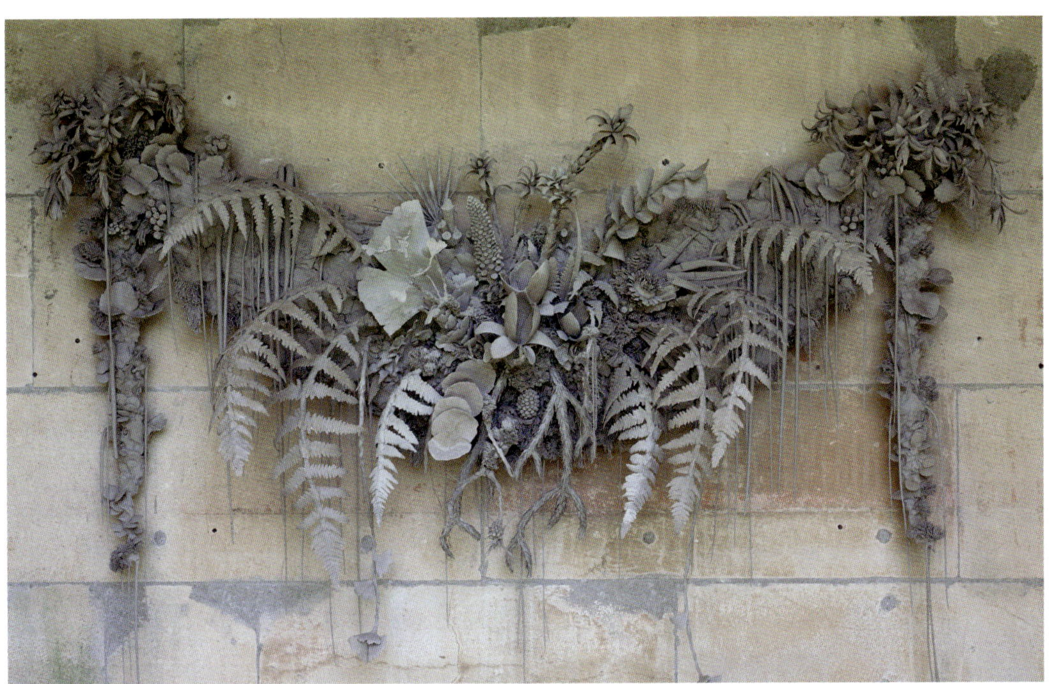

Fig. 154
Phoebe Cummings (b.1981)
*Antediluvian Swag*, 2016
Clay, wire, steel, 180 × 100 × 40 cm
New Art Centre, Hampshire
Photo by Sylvain Deleu

Evaporation results in contraction. Shapes crack and fracture, objects are pulled inwards from the volume they first occupied, leaving behind a residue or traced outlines. Close proximity to the clay formations reveals how all material has been touched through the processes of making. There are recognisable finger and palm prints, the profile of a gripped fist and ridges ploughed by the dragging of fingers. Touch is described visually rather than invited physically, something we also experience frequently through film, a medium where all senses beyond sight and sound rely on translation. 'Cinematic perception is not merely (audio)visual but synesthetic, an act in which the senses and the intellect are not conceived as separate. Thus, it makes sense to talk of touch participating in what we think of as primarily a visual experience, if we understand this experience to be one of the lived body.'[3] It is perhaps helpful to understand both sculpture and our perceptual encounter of it as lived bodies. Neither are entirely separate, but are active and interactive vital components, feeding, and feeding from, the whole.

Flowers, too, act as mirrors, whether they are real or clay duplicates. While their surfaces are not reflective, we tend to see our own existence and emotions reflected in their being, playing and replaying life and death in fast-forward. The sheer variety of structure, appearance, colour and scent of flowers is remarkable. They show us beauty, delicacy, tenacity and vulnerability. They show us birth, sex, aging and death, but they do not resort to a singular narrative or system, and neither do they promote a singular definition of normal. A 'perfect' flower is the term for a bisexual specimen, containing both stamen and carpels; a bramble, on the other hand, is asexual, capable of cloning itself. Flowers suffer a heavy burden of association and symbolism, most of which shoots short of reality (or maybe I mean truth). It can be hard to wade through all the stylising, gendering and romanticisation. Their visual appeal has frequently left them underestimated and dismissed as a subject of limited intellectual substance. Yet plants are, in fact, the convergence of science, history, culture, myth, spirituality and so many other aspects of life, death and procreation.

In the foreword to her 1937 book *Some Flowers*, Vita Sackville-West discusses the difficulty of writing about flowers, praising the prose of Reginald Farrer and D.H. Lawrence, who

> write with violence and not sentimentality. To them both, a flower is a vibrating, living thing, endowed with qualities which are far beyond the reach of mere botany. To Farrer, his gentian burns 'as if it had a light inside'. To Lawrence, the anemone 'issues the red colour, perfectly pure and unknown of earth'. They both, in short, approach the flower as though it were a mystical thing, reflecting on earth some strange beauty which is to be found in perfection only in another, unknown world.[4]

Fortunately, flowers remain indifferent to all our tendencies. They are the product of something inherently determined to live. They make no judgments and require no encouragement beyond earth, water and light. They are also unapologetically sexual, and our encounters with them deeply sensuous, even if we are always the uninvited guest.

*Puya castellanosii* has delicate pale turquoise flowers, a very particular colour on the brink of phosphorescence. This plant takes years to flower, sometimes just once in its lifetime, pushing out an impressively large spear from its leaves, densely covered in flowers with stamen smothered with bright orange pollen. Deep in the throat of the flower is a sweet black nectar, which is attractive to birds, who are vital for pollination. A few years back, a friend's Puya flowered for the first time in 20 years, after it was collected from an expedition in Argentina. It was extraordinary, in the true sense of the word. I did not see it so much as experience it and, like birds, we dipped our tongues in. The thick ink tasted like molasses. It was heady to be around the improbability of its brief glory. Of course, the flower merged with the day, which was seen, heard, touched, tasted, smelled – now remembered. Sculpture can operate in much the same way, sensed as well as seen, impossible and real at the same time, ultimately remembered not possessed.

Ceramics lends itself to mimesis; it can model and replicate easily. There is a long tradition of modelling flowers from clay within the decorative arts. The lavish porcelain bouquets produced by Vincennes/

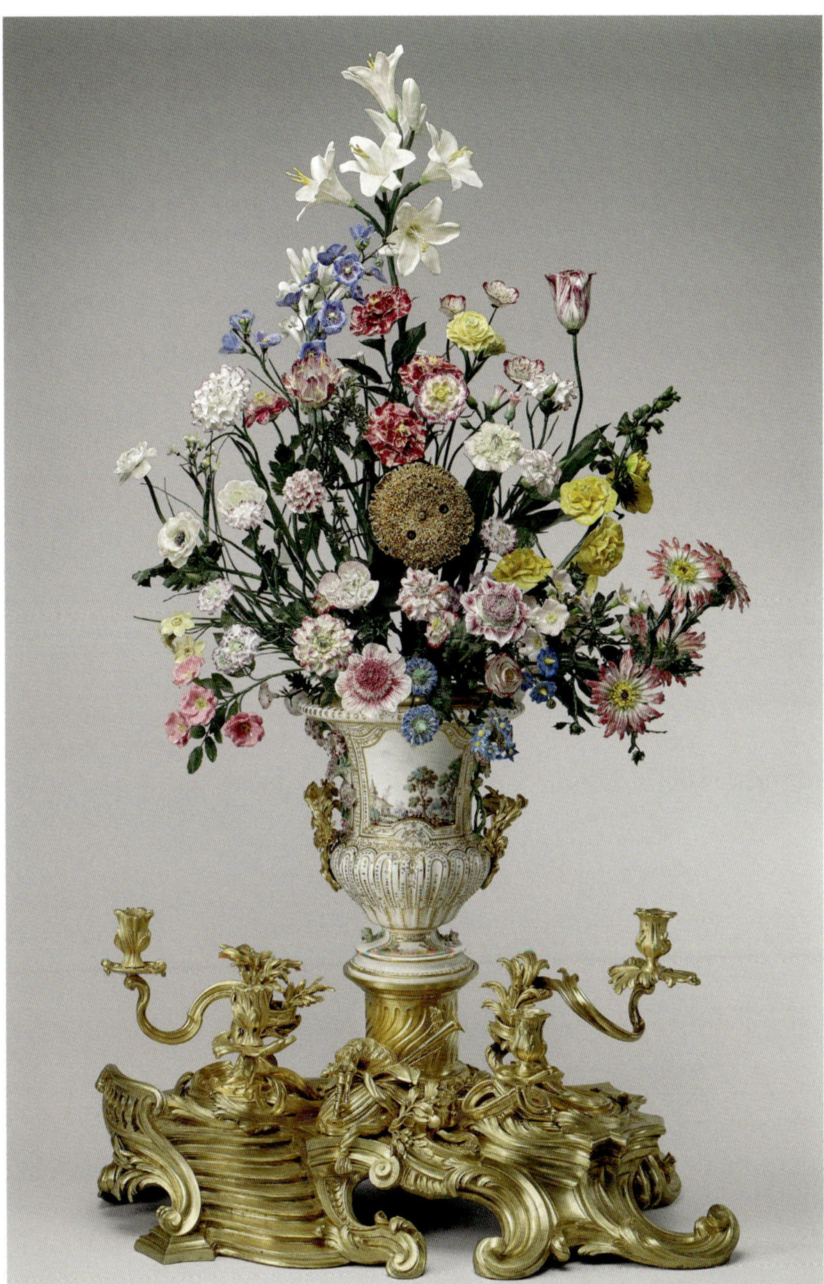

Fig. 155
Vincennes Porcelain Factory (1738–56)
*The Sunflower Clock*, c.1752
Gilt, bronze, copper alloy, soft paste porcelain, wire, lacquer, painted ceramics, 105.4 × 66.7 × 54 cm
Royal Collection Trust

Sèvres in the 18th century act as a literal form of still life, holding a floral arrangement indefinitely at its peak. These objects were also often fragranced and would have been designed for use at different times of day, and in different locations within the interior. They speak directly to a human desire to still time. Perhaps flowers always speak to and of desire.

During the 18th century, the painter and designer Jean-Baptiste Pillement (1728–1808) created an extensive series of illustrations of fantastical flowers. They clearly demonstrate his deep understanding of plants and patterns of

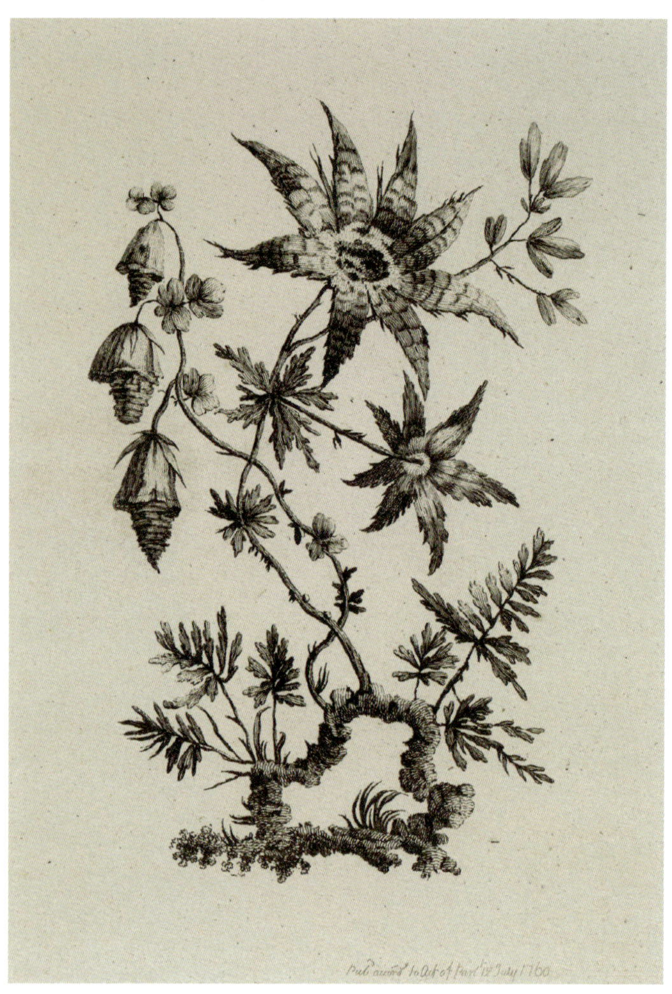

growth, but they also give way to imagination. Foliage ruptures into feathered bells, organic parasols and shells, yet these imagined species are rendered with a sensitivity that is beguiling. Mutability is a significant aspect of Baroque and Rococo design, and also intrinsic to ephemeral sculpture.

It could be further considered that science and fiction go hand in hand in the development of industrially produced European decorative ceramics in the 18th century. Manufacturers such as Meissen, Sèvres and Wedgwood all relied on technological and scientific innovation to develop the materials (and mastery of them) necessary for production. Meissen porcelain is often extreme in its decorative excess, flamboyant or theatrical like the occasions and interiors for which the objects were intended. Like literary science fiction, elements of reality are pressed up against each other in new, hitherto unknown ways. Historically, humans have invested on an industrial scale to make their dreams solid and still enough to keep a hold of.

Artists including Leonora Carrington (1917–2011) and Dorothea Tanning (1910–2012) extend the tradition of imagined plants and flowers in the 20th century. Joan Fontcuberta's (b.1955) photographic series *Herbarium* from 1983 also generated fictional exotic flowers, assembling found materials, including industrial detritus and plant and animal parts. Georgia O'Keeffe's (1887–1986) paintings and Karl Blossfeldt's (1865–1932) photographs can reveal flowers and plants in a way that feels utterly unknown and new. Working with clay, for me, is always a form of fiction. As with written language, something emerges that is vivid and felt. Within the process of making there are moments when my body and the material are inseparable. Flowers arrive from the contact and pressure of my hands, wrists, elbows, feet and jaw in earth. Doubled but not identical, the profusion of growth in the work, made specifically for the rooms of the gallery, leads us to see where the mirror slips. The reflection is imperfect and everything is built in the shadow of inevitable loss. 'Science fiction properly conceived, like all serious fiction, however funny, is a way of trying to describe what is in fact going on, what people actually do and feel, how people relate to everything else in this vast sack, this belly of the universe, this womb of things to be and tomb of things that were, this unending story.'[5]

Fig. 156
Pierre-Charles Canot (c.1710–1777)
After Jean Pillement (1728–1808)
*Recœil de fleurs de caprice inventé et dessiné par jean pillement*, 1760
Engraving on paper, 24.1 × 16.2 cm
Victoria and Albert Museum, London

Fig. 157
Phoebe Cummings (b.1981)
detail from a work in clay, 2022
Thomas Dane Gallery, Naples

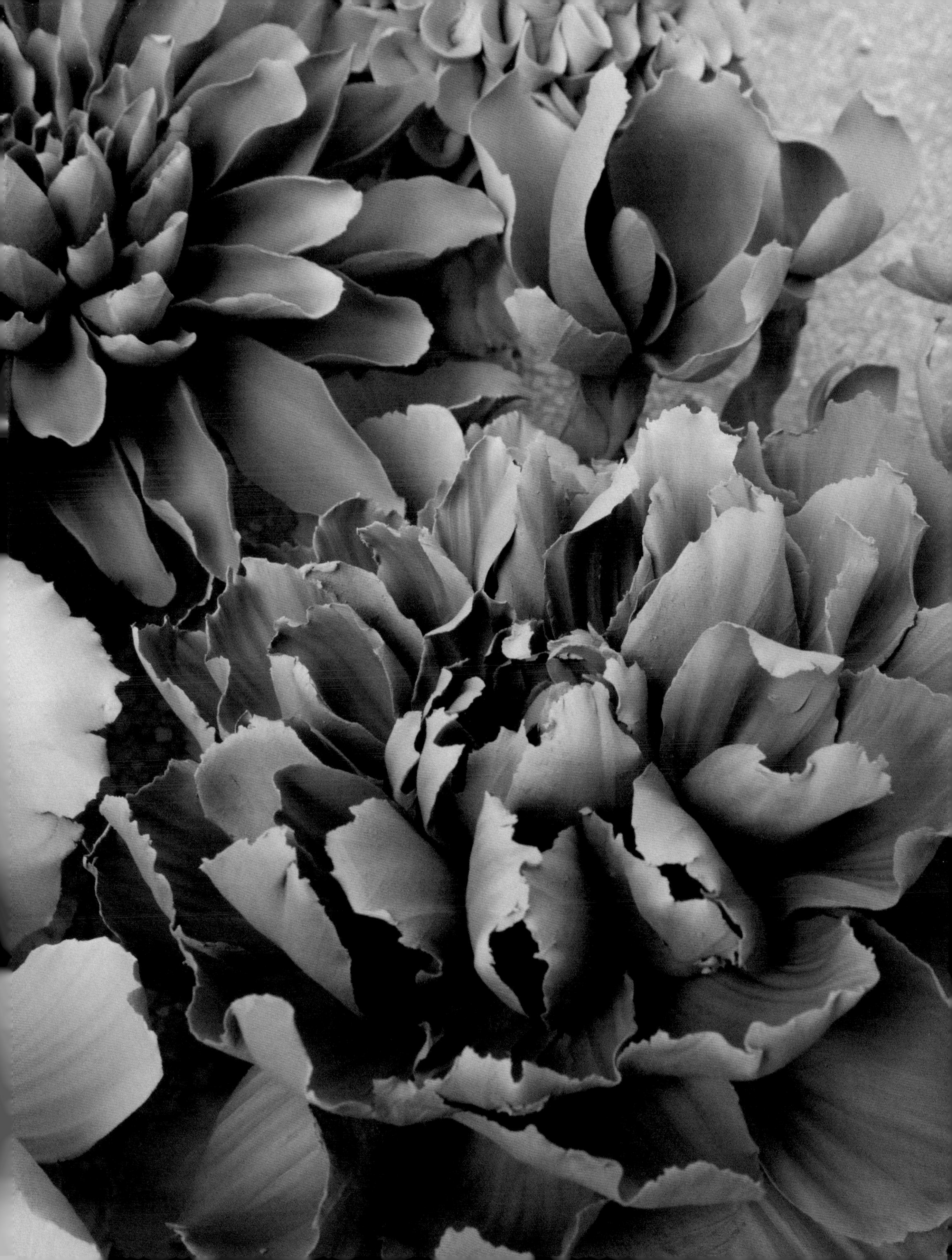

# Notes

## Foreword
SIMON MARTIN

1. Christopher Wood, letter to his mother, 29 May 1922, Tate Gallery Archive TGA 773.2.
2. Ben Nicholson, Statement, January 1957, in Maurice de Sausmarez (ed.), *Ben Nicholson: A Studio International Special*, Studio International, London and New York, 1969, p.40.

## 1. History Repeating: Still Life Between Past and Present
SIMON MARTIN

1. Robert Latham and William Matthews (eds.), *The Diary of Samuel Pepys*, vol.IX, London, 1976, pp.514–15.
2. Pliny the Elder, *Natural History, Volume IX: Books 35–36,* (Loeb Classical Library no. 394), translated by H. Rackham (vols. 1–5, 9), Harvard University Press, Cambridge Mass., 1989, p.65.
3. Charles Stirling, *Still Life Painting from Antiquity to the Present Time*, Universe Books Inc and Éditions Pierre Tisné, New York and Paris, 1959, p.43.
4. This format was informed by the earlier Dutch still life painter Willem van Aelst (1627–1687).
5. This work was incorrectly titled as *Roses, columbine, and poppies in a glass vase on a marble ledge with some grapes* in Christie's Old Master Paintings and Sculpture sale, 17 December 2020, lot 247
6. Gerard de Lairesse, *Groot schilderboek*, vol.II, Haarlem, 1740, p.356; quoted in Alan Chong and Wouter Kloek, *Still-life Paintings from the Netherlands 1550–1720* (exh. cat.), Amsterdam, 1999, p.262.
7. Frank Lewis, *Simon Pietersz Verelst, 1644–1721,* F. Lewis, Publishers, Limited, Leigh-on-Sea, England, 1979, p. 24, no. 9
8. Collier was christened Evart Calier. His first name is sometimes spelled 'Edward', 'Edwaert', 'Eduwaert' or 'Edwart', and his last name is sometimes spelled 'Colyer' or 'Kollier'.
9. William Smith subsequently practiced in London and for eight years in Gloucester.
10. Testament to their knowledge and appreciation of Dutch art is the volume of engravings and etchings that William, George and John Smith collaborated on over a period of 15 years, some of which were of their own art, but others of which were of works by the Dutch masters that were popular at the time.
11. 'Oh the Roast Beef of Old England' was quoted by William Hogarth as the title for his 1748 painting *The Calais Gate*, which satirised the French.
12. Katharine Baetjer, *French Paintings in The Metropolitan Museum of Art from the Early Eighteenth Century Through the Revolution* (exh. cat.), Metropolitan Museum of Art, New York, 2019, p.15.
13. Charles Stirling records that the first use of the term 'nature morte' was in 1756. Stirling 1959, p.41.
14. Sir Joshua Reynolds, 'Discourse III' (1770), printed in *Sir Joshua Reynolds' Discourses*, Edward Gilpin Johnson (ed.), A.C. McClurg & Company, Chicago, 1891, pp.95–6
15. Germaine Greer, *The Obstacle Race: The Fortune of Women Painters and their Work*, Barbara Ward & Associates, London, 2001, pp.247–9. Moser was also a noted portraitist and painter of historical scenes, see Paris A. Spies-Gans, 'Mary Moser: Portraitist', *Journal 18: A journal of eighteenth-century art and culture*, no.8, Self/Portrait, Fall 2009, www.journal18.org/issue8/mary-moser-portraitist/.
16. John Collier, *A Manual of Oil Painting*, Cassell & Co. Ltd, London, 1886, p.6.
17. Following the exhibition Cezanne at Tate Modern, London (5 October 2022 – 23 March 2023), and a campaign by Philippe Cezanne, the artist's great-grandson and honorary president of the Société Paul Cezanne, we are using throughout the original Provençal spelling of Paul Cezanne's name, without the accent.
18. Wendy Baron, 'British Art in the Time of William Nicholson', *William Nicholson: Catalogue Raisonné of the Oil Paintings*, ed. Patricia Read, Modern Art Press and Yale University Press, London and New Haven, 2011, p.17.
19. William Feaver, Patrick Caulfield Obituary, *The Guardian*, 3 October 2005.
20. Neil MacGregor, quoted in Richard Morphet, *Encounters: New Art from Old* (exh. cat.), National Gallery, London, 2000, p.7.
21. Marco Livingstone, *Patrick Caulfield Paintings,* Lund Humphries, Aldershot, 2005, p.95.
22. Mat Collishaw, interview with Maisie Skidmore, *Another Magazine,* 29 September 2015.
23. Gareth Grundy, 'Peter Saville on his Artwork', *The Observer*, 29 May 2011.
24. Gordon Cheung , 'New Order' on www.seditionart.com
25. Toby Ziegler, email correspondence, 23 January 2024.
26. Balduccini, Francesco Saverio, Firenze, Bibl. Naz. Centr., ms. *Palat.* 565: F. S. Baldinucci, *Vite dei pittori,* II (This *Life* is from 1729);., ms.
27. Michael Bracewell, 'Concerning the art of Glenn Brown', *Glenn Brown: Three Exhibitions* (exh. cat.), Rizzoli and Gagosian Gallery, New York and London, 2009, p.58.
28. E.H. Gombrich, 'Tradition and Expression in Western Still Life', *The Burlington Magazine,* Vol 103, No.698, May 1961, pp.174

## 2. 'Unbroken Quiet': How British Still Life was Stimulated by Post-Impressionism
LYDIA MILLER

1. Richard Shone, 'The Friday Club', *The Burlington Magazine*, vol.117, no.866, May 1975, p.279.
2. The term a 'crisis of brilliance' was coined by Henry Tonks and recorded in Joseph Hone, *The Life of Henry Tonks*, William Heinemann, London, 1939, p.258.
3. *Manet and the Post-Impressionists* (exh. cat.), Grafton Galleries and Ballantyne Press, London, 1910, p.8.
4. G.R.H., 'The Father of Post-Impressionism', *Pall Mall Gazette*, 4 October 1912, p.10.
5. Unknown author, 'Art: The Post Impressionists', *Truth*, 23 November 1910, p.1304.
6. C.J. Holmes, *Notes on the Post-Impressionist Painters, Grafton Galleries, 1910–11*, Philip Lee Warner, London, 1910, p.7.
7. J.D. Fergusson, 'Chapter for an Autobiography', *Saltire Review*, vol.6, no.21, 1960, quoted in Margaret Morris, *The Art of J.D. Fergusson*, J.D. Fergusson Art Foundation, Perth, p.45.
8. Examples of Fergusson's still lifes that include both a blue lamp and a pink box

include *La Bete Violette* (1910, private collection), *Still Life with Blue Lamp* (1912, City Art Centre Collection, Edinburgh) and *Flowers and Pink Box* (1911, The Fergusson Gallery, Perth).
9. Alicia Foster, *Nina Hamnett*, Eiderdown Books, Bath, 2021, p.6.
10. 'The Grafton Group. Vanessa Bell, Roger Fry, Duncan Grant. Second Exhibition,' (exh. cat.), Database of Modern Exhibitions (DoME). https://exhibitions.univie.ac.at/exhibition/626.
11. Jennifer Grindley, 'The Omega Workshops: The Artists', Charleston, 15 September 2020. https://www.charleston.org.uk/stories/the-omega-workshops-the-artists.
12. Unknown author, 'Exhibition of Modern Paintings and Drawings at the Omega Workshops', *The Burlington Magazine*, vol.33, no.189, December 1918, p.233.
13. 'The Life and Opinions of an English "Modern": Ben Nicholson in Conversation with Vera and John Russell', *Sunday Times*, 28 April 1963, p.28.
14. Nina Hamnett, *Laughing Torso*, Ray Long & Richard R. Smith, New York, 1932, p.21.
15. Patricia Reed, *William Nicholson: Catalogue Raisonné of the Oil Paintings*, Yale University Press, New Haven, 2011, p.22.
16. Ibid., p.35.
17. Foster 2021, p.6.
18. Walter Sickert, *A Plate of Mushrooms with Knife and Glass*, sold at Bonhams, Knightsbridge, 24 March 1999, lot 3.
19. Hamnett 1932, p.97.
20. Nicola Moorby, 'Walter Richard Sickert, *The Little Tea Party: Nina Hamnett and Roald Kristian*, 1915–16', *The Camden Town Group in Context*, eds. Helena Bonett, Ysanne Holt and Jennifer Mundy, Tate Research Publication, 2012. https://www.tate.org.uk/art/research-publications/camden-town-group/walter-richard-sickert-the-little-tea-party-nina-hamnett-and-roald-kristian-r1136456.
21. Walter Sickert, 'Little Pictures for Little Patrons', *New Age*, 11 August 1910, republished in Anna Gruetzner Robins (ed.), *Walter Sickert: The Complete Writings on Art*, Oxford University Press, Oxford, 2000, p.271.

## 3. 'Reality and the other thing': Still Life in Interwar Britain

CHLOE NAHUM AND EMMA SHARPLES

1. Paul Nash, 'Giorgio de Chirico', *The Listener*, 29 April 1931, pp.720–1.
2. Most notably in his *Still-life with Apples* (1877–8), which was purchased by John Maynard Keynes in 1918 and caused Virginia Woolf to reflect: 'What can 6 apples *not* be?'. For a detailed consideration of Cezanne's influence on modern writers, see Claudia Tobin, '"The Humbleness of all his Objects": Cezanne, Still Life, and Modern Writers', *The Humble in 19th- to 21st-Century British Literature and Arts*, Presses Universitaires de la Méditerranée, Montpellier, 2017, pp.51–61.
3. Nash 1931, pp.720–1.
4. Paul Nash, 'Unit One: A New Group of Artists', *The Times*, 10 June 1933, p.10.
5. Claudia Tobin has spoken of 'an aesthetic battleground in which the major artistic and ethical debates of modern art were played out'; Tobin, *Modernism and Still Life: Artists, Writers, Dancers*, Edinburgh University Press, Edinburgh, 2020, p.11.
6. For a discussion of women artists, queerness and intimacy in relation to the genre, see Rebecca Birrell, *This Dark Country: Women Artists, Still Life and Intimacy in the Early Twentieth Century*, Bloomsbury, London, 2021.
7. St. John G. Ervine, 'The War and Literature', *The North American Review*, vol.202, no.716, 1915, p.98.
8. Jay Winter has examined the artistic and literary response to the war through classical forms in *Sites of Memory, Sites of Mourning*, Cambridge University Press, Cambridge, 1995, while Ana Carden-Coyne has considered the interaction of classicism with representations of the body in *Reconstructing the Body: Classicism, Modernism and the First World War*, Oxford University Press, Oxford, 2009. For a detailed study of classicism's role in the visual arts in Britain, see Simon Martin, *The Mythic Method: Classicism in British Art 1920–1950*, Pallant House Gallery, Chichester, 2016.
9. André Lhote would himself exhibit with the Seven & Five in 1922. For a complete history of members and exhibitors, see Charles Harrison, *English Art and Modernism 1900–1939*, Allen Lane, London, 1981, pp.345–7.
10. Quoted in Harrison 1981, p.164.
11. Ibid.
12. David Jones, 'Preface', *In Parenthesis* [1937], Faber and Faber, London, 2018, p.xi.
13. H.S. Ede, 'David Jones', *Horizon*, vol.8, no.44, August 1943.
14. Jones 2018, p.183.
15. Paul Hills, *The Art of David Jones*, Tate Gallery, London, 1981, p.36.
16. Ariane Bankes and Paul Hills, *The Art of David Jones*, Lund Humphries, London, 2015, pp.72–3; Paul Hills, *The Art of David Jones*, Tate Gallery, London, 1981, p.35.
17. Quoted in *Ben Nicholson: From the Studio*, Pallant House Gallery, Chichester, 2021, p.36.
18. Jeremy Lewison, *Ben Nicholson*, Rizzoli, New York, 1991, p.10.
19. R.H. Wilenski, 'The Modern Movement in Art', *The Spectator* [12 April 1935], quoted in Hugh St Clair, *A Lesson in Art & Life: The Colourful World of Cedric Morris and Arthur Lett-Haines*, Pimpernel Press, London, 2023, p.82.
20. *Homes and Gardens* [August 1933], quoted in Diana Souhami, *Gluck: Her Biography*, Pandora Press, London, 1988, p. 92.
21. 'Art Exhibitions', *The Times*, 30 March 1930, quoted in St Clair 2023, p.74. St Clair's text gives a detailed account of the critical reception of Morris's works and the design contexts into which they were received.
22. See Simon Martin, *Glyn Philpot: Flesh and Spirit*, Pallant House Gallery, Chichester, 2022, p.137.
23. There is debate around Gluck's pronouns given the artist's request that 'no prefix, suffix or quotes' be used in relation to the chosen name Gluck. We have used she/her pronouns in this instance given their historical usage in Gluck's lifetime, but acknowledge the inadequacies of their selection. For a detailed discussion and thoughtful reflection on this subject see Rebecca Birrell, 'A Note on Pronouns', *This Dark Country: Women Artists, Still Life and Intimacy in the Early Twentieth Century*, Bloomsbury, London, 2021, pp.135–8.
24. Quoted in Louise Campbell, *Studio Lives: Architect, Art and Artist in 20th-Century Britain*, Lund Humphries, London, 2019, p.183.
25. Souhami dedicates a chapter of her biography of the artist to discussing 'The Gluck Frame'; see Souhami 1988, pp.103–11.
26. Nash 1933, p.10.
27. Writing in *Unit 1: The Modern Movement in English Architecture, Painting and Sculpture* in 1934, published to accompany the group's first and only exhibition, Tristram Hillier advocated for 'some form of State intervention' in architecture and decoration, through which 'every sculptor, architect and painter of genuine talent in this country could gain a living … training people's minds to the rhythm of aesthetically satisfying shapes and colour combinations'; Tristram Hillier, *Unit 1: The Modern Movement in English Architecture, Painting and Sculpture*, ed. Herbert Read, Cassell and Company, London, 1934, p.70.
28. Edward Wadsworth, ibid., p.99.
29. For an extensive consideration of British artists and interwar realism see Richard

Morphet, 'Realism and English Art 1919–1939', *Les Realismes 1919–1939*, Musée d'Art Moderne, Paris, 1981.
30. Quoted in Mark Glazebrook, 'Introduction', *Edward Wadsworth*, Mayor Gallery, London, 1982, n.p.
31. Nash 1933, p.10.
32. Ibid.
33. Paul Nash, *Outline* [1949], ed. David Boyd Haycock, Lund Humphries, London, 2016, p.20.
34. Paul Nash, 'On Dreams', undated manuscript, Tate Gallery Archive TGA 8119-18. Nash's immediate source was the poet David Gascoyne's *A Short Survey of Surrealism* (1935), but his words also evoke the famed statement of André Breton's 1924 'Manifesto of Surrealism': 'I believe in the future resolution of these two states, dream and reality, which are seemingly so contradictory, into a kind of absolute reality, a surreality'; André Breton, 'Manifesto of Surrealism' [1924], *Manifestoes of Surrealism*, University of Michigan Press, Ann Arbor, 2010, p.14.
35. Emma Chambers, 'Introduction', *Paul Nash*, ed. Emma Chambers, Tate Publishing, London, 2017, p.12.
36. For more on this subject see ibid., pp.35–47.
37. For a detailed discussion of Nash's photography see Simon Grant, *Informal Beauty: The Photographs of Paul Nash*, Tate Publishing, London, 2016.
38. Walter Benjamin, 'The Work of Art in the Age of its Technological Reproducibility: Second Version', reproduced in *The Work of Art in the Age of its Technological Reproducibility, and Other Writings on Media* [1935], eds. Michael W. Jennings, Brigid Doherty, and Thomas Y. Levin, Harvard University Press, Cambridge, MA, 2008, p.37.
39. Ibid., p.38.
40. See Claude Cahun, 'Beware Domestic Objects!', reproduced in *Surrealist Women: An International Anthology* [1936], ed. Penelope Rosemont, The Athlone Press, London, 1998, pp.59–61.
41. Claude Cahun quoted in Mary Ann Caws, *The Surrealist Look, An Erotics of Encounter*, MIT Press, Cambridge, MA, 1997, p.99.
42. Katherine Conley, *Surrealist Ghostliness*, University of Nebraska Press, Lincoln, NE, 2013, p.49.
43. Cahun 1998, p.60.
44. Ibid.
45. Alyce Mahon, 'Women Surrealists and the Still Life', *Angels of Anarchy: Women Artists and Surrealism*, ed. Patricia Allmer, Manchester Art Gallery, Manchester, 2009, pp.54–5.
46. Conroy Maddox, 'The Object in Surrealism', *London Bulletin*, no.18–20, June 1940, p.40.
47. Richard Morphet, *Meredith Frampton*, Tate Gallery, London, 1982, p.19.
48. André Breton, 'Crisis of the Object' [1936], quoted in Mahon 2009, p.57.
49. Nash undated manuscript.

### 4. Paths to Abstraction

MICHAEL BIRD

1. Virginia Woolf, 'Thoughts on Peace in an Air Raid', *Selected Essays*, ed. David Bradshaw, Oxford University Press, Oxford, 2008, p.219.
2. George Orwell, 'A Nice Cup of Tea', *Evening Standard*, 12 Jan 1946.
3. W.H. Auden, 'As I walked out one evening', *Selected Poems*, ed. Edward Mendelson, Faber and Faber, London, 1979, pp.60–2.
4. 'Ben Nicholson in Conversation with Vera and John Russell', *Sunday Times*, 28 Apr 1983, quoted in Jeremy Lewison, *Ben Nicholson: The Years of Experiment 1919–39* (exh. cat.), Kettle's Yard, Cambridge, 1983, p.10.
5. Ibid.
6. Barbara Hepworth, 'Contemporary English Sculptors', *The Architectural Association Journal*, vol.45, no.518, April 1930, republished in Sophie Bowness (ed.), *Barbara Hepworth: Writings and Conversations*, Tate Publishing, London, 2015, p.14.
7. Le Corbusier, 'The Quarrel with Realism', *Circle: International Survey of Constructive Art*, eds. J.L. Martin, Ben Nicholson and N. Gabo, Faber and Faber, London, 1937, p.68.
8. Ben Nicholson, 'Quotations', ibid., p.75.
9. Patrick Heron, 'Braque', *The Changing Forms of Art*, Routledge and Kegan Paul, London, 1955, p.89.
10. Ibid., p.83.
11. Ibid., p.82.
12. Ibid.
13. Ibid., p.81.
14. John Berger, *Ways of Seeing*, Penguin, London, 1972, p.31.

### 5. 'The World is Still Dark': Death and Existentialism in British Still Life, 1939 to Now

MELANIE VANDENBROUCK

1. Peter Hennessy, *Never Again: Britain 1945–51*, Random House, London, 1992, p.296.
2. Frances Spalding, *John Minton: Dance Til the Stars Come Down*, Lund Humphries, London, 2005, p.43.
3. Michael Bracewell, 'Something Supernatural This Way Comes: Magic and Modernity in British Art', *Tate Etc*, no.17, Autumn 2009. www.tate.org.uk/tate-etc/issue-17-autumn-2009/something-supernatural-way-comes.
4. Margaret Garlake, *New Art New World: British Art in Postwar Society*, Yale University Press, New Haven and London, 1998; Frances Spalding, *Prunella Clough: Regions Unmapped*, Lund Humphries, London, 2012, p.55.
5. Patrick Heron, 'Miss Clough and Miss McCannell', *New Statesman and Nation*, 5 November 1949, quoted in Spalding 2005 p.89.
6. John Berger, 'Machine-life painting', *New Statesman and Nation*, 18 April 1953, pp.454–5.
7. Keith Vaughan, *Journals 1939–1977*, John Murray, London, 1989, p.80.
8. '14 August 1948', in Keith Vaughan, *Journals and Drawings 1939–1965*, Alan Ross, London, 1966.
9. *Modern Art in the United States*, Tate Gallery, London, 1956; Jackson Pollock retrospective, Whitechapel Gallery, London, 1958; *New American Paintings*, Tate Gallery, London, 1959.
10. Michael Ayrton quoted in Justine Hopkins, *Michael Ayrton: Ideas, Images, Reflections*, Fry Art Gallery, Saffron Walden, 2021, p.47.
11. Rosalind Thuillier, *Graham Sutherland: Inspirations*, Lutterworth Press, Cambridge, 1982, p.72.
12. Though this shift, lightening of key' had started to happen in 1945–6, and 'makes his move to the South of France in the spring of 1947 seem like the logical fulfilment of a spiritual need', Douglas Cooper, *The Work of Graham Sutherland*, Lund Humphries, London, 1961, p.40. [Odd phrasing, rogue apostrophe, and possibly some words missing? Please check.]
13. Chris Stephens, 'Graham Sutherland, *The Scales*, 1961–2, catalogue entry', Tate, November 1998. www.tate.org.uk/art/artworks/sutherland-the-scales-t00536.
14. Vaughan 1989, pp.xi–xii.
15. Terry Dennett, 'Notes on "The Final Project: A Photofantasy and Phototherapeutic Exploration of Life and Death", Jo Spence and Terry Dennett, 1991–2 (unfinished)', in Jo Spence, *Cultural Snipping: The Art of Transgression*, Routledge, London, 1995, pp.222–3.
16. Maggi Hambling and Andrew Lambirth, *Maggi Hambling: The Works, and Conversations with Andrew Lambirth*, Unicorn Press, London, 2014, p.142.
17. Maggi Hambling, in *Sanctuary: Britain's*

Artists and their Studios, ed. Hossein Amirsadeghi, Transglobe Publishing, London, p.498.
18. Interview with Hatoum by Michael Archer, in Michael Archer, Guy Brett and Catherine de Zegher, *Mona Hatoum*, Phaidon, London, 1997, p.17.
19. 'Anthropocene' is a contested term, including for its debated chronological timespan, with some believing it starts in 1800, and others in 1945 with the first atomic bomb. In its definition of modernity and characterisation of human activity largely dominated by the Global North, it may also be seen to perpetuate colonialist narratives. It also lacks recognition of the differential human responsibility in ecological decline, notably with regards to colonialism, empire, capitalism, and indigenous populations sensitive stewardship of their environments.
20. 'Katie Paterson, 9 April – 11 June 2022', Ingleby Gallery. www.inglebygallery.com/exhibitions/7145-katie-paterson-requiem/overview/.
21. Roman Krznaric, *The Good Ancestor: How to Think Long Term in a Short-Term World*, WH Allen, London, 2020; Hannah Ritchie, *Not the End of the World: How We Can Be the First Generation to Build a Sustainable Planet*, Chatto & Windus, London, 2024.

### 6. Accelerated Decay: Consumer Culture and Still Life

MIRIAM O'CONNOR PERKS

1. Alison Smithson and Peter Smithson, 'But Today We Collect Ads', ***Ark***, no. 18, Royal College of Art, 1956.
2. Norman Bryson, 'Abundance', *Looking at the Overlooked: Four Essays on Still Life Painting*, Reaktion, London, 1990, pp.104–35.
3. Kobena Mercer (ed.), *Pop Art and Vernacular Cultures*, MIT Press, London and Cambridge, MA, 2007.
4. Linda Nochlin, 'Running on Empty: Women Pop and the Society of Consumption', *Seductive Subversion: Women Pop Artists, 1958–1968*, eds. Kalliopi Minioudaki and Sid Sachs, Abbeville, New York, 2010, p.14.
5. John Wilmerding, *The Pop Object: The Still Life Tradition in Pop Art*, Rizzoli, New York, 2013.
6. Lisa Tickner, '"Export Britain": Pop Art, Mass Culture and the Export Drive', *British Art in the Cultural Field, 1939–69*, eds. David Corbett and Lisa Tickner, Wiley-Blackwell, Hoboken, 2012, p.208.
7. Gregory Salter, *Art and Masculinity in Post-War Britain: Reconstructing Home*, Routledge, London, 2021, p.10.
8. Michael Bracewell, *Modern World: The Art of Richard Hamilton*, Art/Books, London, 2021, p.63.
9. Daniel F. Herrmann, 'Eduardo Paolozzi: Pop Art Redefined', *Eduardo Paolozzi* (exh. cat.), Whitechapel Gallery, London and Berlinische Galerie, Berlin, 2017, p.13.
10. Jessie Swigger, *'History Is Bunk': Assembling the Past at Henry Ford's Greenfield Village*, University of Massachusetts Press, Amherst, 2014.
11. Erica Battle, 'Nostalgia for Now: British Pop and the New Immediacy of Cultural Memory', *International Pop* (exh. cat.), eds. Darsie Alexander and Bartholomew Ryan, Walker Art Centre, Minneapolis, 2015, p.102.
12. Sid Sachs, 'Beyond the Surface: Women and Pop Art 1958–1968', *Seductive Subversion: Women Pop Artists, 1958–1968*, Abbeville, New York, 2010, p.22.
13. Battle 2015, p.104.
14. Simon Faulkner, 'Painting Like a Fan?', *Peter Blake: A Retrospective* (exh. cat.), ed. Christoph Grunenberg, Tate Publishing, London, 2007, p.33.
15. Lewes Biggs, Fiona Bradley and Jean-Pierre Criqui, *Lisa Milroy* (exh.cat.), Tate Liverpool, London, 2001, p.9; author's emphasis.
16. David Hockney, Henry Geldzahler and Nikos Stangos, *David Hockney: My Early Years*, Thames & Hudson, London, pp.63–4.
17. Fredric Jameson, 'Postmodernism and Consumer Society', *Modernism/Postmodernism*, ed. Peter Brooker, Routledge, London, 1992, p.118.
18. David E. Brauer (ed.), *Pop Art: U.S./U.K. Connections, 1956–1966* (exh. cat.), Menil Collection, Houston, 2001, p.32.
19. Patrick Caulfield, p.13.
20. Alice Rawsthorn, 'Richard Hamilton and Design', *Richard Hamilton* (exh. cat.), Museo Nacional Centro de Arte Reina Sofía, Madrid and Tate Publishing, London, 2014, p.130.
21. Ibid., p.131.
22. Simon Baker, 'Conquest of the Useless', *Rubbish, Dipping sauce, Grass peonie bum*, Trolley Books, London, 2019, p.2.

### 7. 'It doesn't shout – it whispers': On the Quietness of Still Life

MELANIE VANDENBROUCK

1. Amy Sherlock, 'Houses in Faraway Winds', *The Point 0: Mohammed Sami*, (exh. cat.), Camden Art Centre and De la Warr Pavilion, 2023, unpaginated.
2. Email conversation between the author and Charlotte Verity, March 2024.
3. Euan Uglow, *The Complete Paintings*, Yale University Press, New Haven and London, 2007, p. 86.
4. With thanks to Mia Jackson for the identification of pot and content.
5. Alison Watt in *Alison Watt: A Portrait Without Likeness*, ed. Julie Lawson, National Galleries of Scotland, Edinburgh, 2021, p.34.
6. Ibid., p.34.
7. Object catalogue entry, Government Art Collection, artcollection.culture.gov.uk/artwork/18777-1/.
8. Michael McMillan, *The Front Room, Diaspora Migrant Aesthetics in the Home*, Lund Humphries, London, 2023.
9. Louisa Buck, 'Tableaux Vivant', *Jane Simpson: Tableau* (exh. cat.), CAC Malaga, p.37.
10. Jane Simpson in Ulrike Groos, 'Ice Ages', *Jane Simpson: Fresh Fresher*, Other Criteria, 2002, p.39.
11. John Russell, 'Rodrigo Moynihan: Still Life Paintings', *Rodrigo Moynihan: Paintings 1970–1973*, Fisher Fine Art Limited, London, 1973, p.9.
12. Ibid., p.10.
13. Lawrence Gowing, 'Introduction', *Rodrigo Moynihan: A Retrospective Exhibition* (exh. cat.), Royal Academy of Arts, London, 1978, p.15.

### 8. I Hear Myself with My Throat

PHOEBE CUMMINGS

1. Maurice Merleau-Ponty, *The Visible and the Invisible*, Northwestern University Press, Evanston, 1968, p.144.
2. Maurice Merleau-Ponty, *Phenomenology of Perception*, Routledge, London, [1945] 2012, p.211.
3. Vivian Sobchack in Laura U. Marks, *Touch: Sensuous Theory and Multisensory Media*, University of Minnesota Press, Minneapolis, 2002, p.13.
4. Vita Sackville-West, *Some Flowers*, Cobden-Sanderson, London, 1937, p.12.
5. Ursula K. Le Guin, 'The Carrier Bag Theory of Fiction', *Dancing at the Edge of the World: Thoughts on Words, Women, Places*, Grove Atlantic Press, New York, 1989, p.170.

# Bibliography


## General

Darsie Alexander and Bartholomew Ryan (eds.), *International Pop* (exh. cat.), Walker Art Centre, Minneapolis, 2015

Hossein Amirsadeghi (ed.), *Sanctuary: Britain's Artists and their Studios*, Transglobe Publishing, London, 2019

Isabelle Anscombe, *Omega and After: Bloomsbury and the Decorative Arts*, Thames and Hudson, London, 1981

Laurence Bertrand Dorléac (ed.), *Les Choses: une histoire de la nature morte* (ex. cat.), Musée du Louvre, Paris, 2022.

Rebecca Birrell, *This Dark Country: Women Artists, Still Life and Intimacy in the Early Twentieth Century*, Bloomsbury Publishing, London, 2021David E. Brauer (ed.), *Pop Art: U.S./U.K. Connections, 1956–1966* (exh. cat.), Menil Collection, Houston, 2001

Peter Brooker (ed.), *Modernism/ Postmodernism*, Routledge, London, 1992

Norman Bryson, *Looking at the Overlooked: Four Essays on Still Life Painting*, Reaktion, London, 1990

Andrew Churchill, Frances Guy, Simon Martin and Stefan van Raay, *Modern British Art at Pallant House Gallery*, Scala Publishers, London, 2004

David Corbett and Lisa Tickner (eds.), *British Art in the Cultural Field, 1939–69*, Wiley-Blackwell, Hoboken, 2012

Radha Dalal, Sean Roberts and Jochen Sokoly (eds.), *The Seas and the Mobility of Islamic Art*, Yale University Press, New Haven, 2021

David Ekserdjian, *Still Life Before Still Life*, Yale University Press, New Haven and London, 2018

Alicia Foster, *Radical Women: Jessica Dismorr and her Contemporaries*, Lund Humphries, London and Pallant House Gallery, Chichester, 2019

Margaret Garlake, *New Art New World: British Art in Postwar Society*, Yale University Press, New Haven and London, 1998

Alexandra Gerstein, *Beyond Bloomsbury: Bloomsbury and the Omega Workshops, 1913–19,* Fontanka, London, 2008

Ben Highmore, Greg Salter, and Hammad Nassar, *Postwar Modern: New Art in Britain 1945–65* (exh. cat.), Barbican, London, and Prestel, London, 2022

Ian Jeffrey, *The Language of Things* (exh. cat.), Kettle's Yard Gallery, Cambridge, 2003

Isobel Johnstone and Roger Malbert (eds.), *It's a Still Life: Sculpture, Paintings, Drawings and Photographs from the Arts Council Collection*, South Bank Centre, London, 1989

Erika Langmuir, *A Closer Look: Still Life*, National Gallery, London, 2001

Kobena Mercer (ed.), *Pop Art and Vernacular Cultures*, MIT Press, London and Cambridge, MA, 2007

Michael McMillan, *The Front Room, Diaspora Migrant Aesthetics in the Home*, Lund Humphries, London, 2009

Kalliopi Minioudaki and Sid Sachs (eds.), *Seductive Subversion: Women Pop Artists, 1958–1968*, Abbeville, New York, 2010

Michael Petry, *Nature Morte: Contemporary Artists Reinvigorate the Still-Life Tradition*, Thames and Hudson, London, 2013

Margit Rowell, *Objects of Desire: The Modern Still Life* (exh. cat.), Hayward Gallery, London, 1997

Gregory Salter, *Art and Masculinity in Post-war Britain: Reconstructing Home*, Routledge, London, 2021

Frances Spalding, *The Bloomsbury Group*, National Portrait Gallery, London, 2005

Jessie Swigger, *'History Is Bunk': Assembling the Past at Henry Ford's Greenfield Village*, University of Massachusetts Press, Amherst, 2014

Richard Shone, *The Art of Bloomsbury, Roger Fry, Vanessa Bell and Duncan Grant,* Tate Gallery, London, 1999

Charles Sterling, *Still Life Painting from Antiquity to the Present Time*, Universe Books, Inc. and Éditions Pierre Tisné, New York and Paris, 1959

Claudia Tobin, *Modernism and Still Life: Artists, Writers, Dancers*, Edinburgh University Press, Edinburgh, 2021

Chris Townsend, *Art and Death*, I.B. Tauris, London, 2008

John Wilmerding, *The Pop Object: The Still Life Tradition in Pop Art*, New York, Rizzoli, 2013

## Artists

Michael Archer, Guy Brett and Catherine de Zegher, *Mona Hatoum*, Phaidon, London, 1997

Harriet Baker, *Margaret Mellis: Modernist Constructs* (exh. cat.), Redfern Gallery, London and Towner, Eastbourne, 2021

Simon Baker, *Maisie Cousins: Rubbish, Dipping sauce, Grass peonie bum*, Trolley Books, London, 2019

Lee Beard, Louise Campbell, Edmund de Waal, Simon Martin and Louise Weller, *Ben Nicholson: From the Studio* (exh. cat.), Pallant House Gallery, Chichester, 2021

Lewes Biggs, Fiona Bradley and Jean-Pierre Criqui, *Lisa Milroy* (exh.cat.), Tate Publishing, London, 2001

Simon Bill and Andrew Wilson, *Gavin Turk: Collected Works 1989–1993*, Jay Jopling, London, 1994

Michael Bracewell, *Modern World: The Art of Richard Hamilton*, Art/Books, London, 2021

Louisa Buck, *Jane Simpson: Tableau* (exh. cat.), Centro de Arte Contemporáneo de Málaga, Malaga, 2004

A.S. Byatt, Peter Carey, Emma Crichton-Miller, Alexandra Munroe, Deborah Saunt, Colm Tóibín and Edmund de Waal, *Edmund de Waal*, Phaidon, London and New York, 2014

Richard Calvocoressi, *Early Works: Lucian Freud* (exh. cat.), Scottish National Gallery of Modern Art, Edinburgh, 1997

Emma Chambers, *Paul Nash* (exh. cat.), Tate Publishing, London, 2016

David Coke, *Hans Feibusch: The Heat of Vision* (exh. cat.), Lund Humphries in association with Pallant House Gallery Trust, London and Chichester, 1995

Douglas Cooper, *The Work of Graham Sutherland*, Lund Humphries, London, 1961

Michelle Cotton, Anthea Hamilton and Catherine Wood, *Anthea Hamilton: Sorry I'm late* (exh. cat.), Firstsite, Colchester, 2012

Iftikhar Dadi, Shezad Dawood and Rachel Garfield, *Anwar Jalal Shemza*, Ridinghouse, London, 2015

Ian A.C. Dejardin and Sarah Milroy, *Vanessa Bell* (exh. cat.), Philip Wilson Publishers, London, 2017

Wendy Baron, *Sickert: Paintings and Drawings*, Yale University Press, New Haven, 2006

Michael Bracewell, Rebecca Daniels, Jennifer Higgie and Simon Martin (with Foreword by Andrew Marr), *Clare Woods: Strange Meetings*, Art/Books, London, 2016

Alicia Foster, *Nina Hamnett*, Eiderdown Books, Bath, 2021

Clare Freestone, *Yevonde: Life and Colour* (exh. cat.), National Portrait Gallery, London, 2023

Ann Gallagher and Molly Donovan (eds.), *Rachel Whiteread* (exh. cat.), Tate Publishing, London, 2017

Rachel Giles, *Charlotte Verity, Echoing Green: The Printed Year*, Ridinghouse, London, 2021

Mark Godfrey (ed.), *Richard Hamilton* (exh. cat.), Museo Nacional Centro de Arte Reina Sofía and Tate Publishing, Madrid and London, 2014
Mark Godfrey, Ulrike Groos, Norman Rosenthal and Jane Simpson, *Jane Simpson: Fresh Fresher*, Other Criteria, London, 2002
Mel Gooding, *Mary Fedden*, Scolar Press, London, 1995
Lawrence Gowing, *Rodrigo Moynihan: A Retrospective Exhibition* (exh. cat.), Royal Academy of Arts, London, 1978
David Farrier, Jay Griffiths, Richard & Florence Ingleby and Jan Zalasiewicz, *Requiem: Katie Paterson*, Arts Editions North, Sunderland, 2022
Anna Gruetzner Robins (ed.), *Walter Sickert: The Complete Writings on Art*, Oxford University Press, Oxford, 2000
Christoph Grunenberg (ed.), *Peter Blake: A Retrospective* (exh. cat.), Tate Publishing, London, 2007
Maggi Hambling and Andrew Lambirth, *Maggi Hambling: The Works, and Conversations with Andrew Lambirth*, Unicorn Press, London, 2014
Nina Hamnett, *Laughing Torso*, Ray Long and Richard R. Smith, New York, 1932
Gerard Hastings and Philip Vann, *Keith Vaughan*, Lund Humphries, London, 2012
Amy de la Haye and Martin Pel, *Gluck: Art and Identity*, Yale University Press, New Haven, 2017
Daniel F. Herrmann (ed.), *Eduardo Paolozzi* (exh. cat.), Whitechapel Gallery and Berlinische Galerie, London and Berlin, 2017
Paul Hills, Charlotte Verity and Edmund de Waal, *Charlotte Verity*, Ridinghouse, London, 2016
David Hockney, Henry Geldzahler and Nikos Stangos, *David Hockney: My Early Years*, Thames and Hudson, London, 1988
Joseph Hone, *The Life of Henry Tonks*, William Heinemann, London, 1939
Justine Hopkins, *Michael Ayrton: Ideas, Images, Reflections*, Fry Art Gallery, Saffron Walden, 2021
Alison James, *A Singular Vision: Dod Procter 1890–1972*, Sansom, Bristol, 2007
Catherine Lampert (ed.), *Euan Uglow: The Complete Paintings*, Yale University Press, New Haven and London, 2007
Julie Lawson, Tom Norman and Andrew O'Hagan, *Alison Watt: A Portrait Without Likeness* (exh. cat.), National Galleries of Scotland, Edinburgh, 2021
Darian Leader, Amy Sherlock and Mohammed Sami, *The Point 0: Mohammed Sami* (exh. cat.), Camden Art Centre and De la Warr Pavilion, London and Bexhill, 2023
Jeremy Lewison (ed.), *A Genius of Industrial England: Edward Wadsworth 1889–1949* (exh. cat.), Cartwright Hall, Bradford, 1989
Marco Livingstone, *Patrick Caulfield*, Lund Humphries, London, 2007
Marco Livingstone and Simon Martin, *Colin Self: Art in the Nuclear Age* (exh. cat.), Pallant House Gallery, Chichester, 2008
Philip Long, *Elizabeth Blackadder*, Yale University Press, New Haven and London, 2016
Norbert Lynton, *William Scott*, Thames and Hudson, London, 2004
Sarah MacDougall, *Mark Gertler*, John Murray, London, 2002
Roxana Marcoci (ed.), *Wolfgang Tillmans: To look without fear* (exh. cat.), Museum of Modern Art, New York, 2022
Simon Martin, *Eduardo Paolozzi: Collaging Culture* (exh. cat.), Pallant House Gallery, Chichester, 2013
Simon Martin, *Edward Burra*, Lund Humphries, London, 2011
Simon Martin, *Glyn Philpot: Flesh and Spirit*, Pallant House Gallery, Chichester, 2022
Simon Martin, *John Craxton: A Modern Odyssey* (exh. cat.), Pallant House Gallery, Chichester, 2023
Simon Martin and Frances Spalding, *John Minton* (exh. cat.), Pallant House Gallery, Chichester, 2017Margaret Morris, *The Art of J.D. Fergusson*, J.D. Fergusson Art Foundation, Perth, 2010
Charlotte Mullins, *Gordon Cheung: Breaking Tulips*, Cristea Roberts Gallery, London, 2015
Jovan Nicholson, *Winifred Nicholson: Liberation of Colour*, Philip Wilson Publishers Ltd, London, 2016
Jenny Pery, *Painter Pilgrim: The Art and Life of Tristram Hillier* (exh. cat.), Royal Academy of Arts, London, 2008
Michael J. Prokopow, *Hurvin Anderson*, Lund Humphries, London, 2021
Patricia Reed, *William Nicholson: Catalogue Raisonné of the Oil Paintings*, Yale University Press, New Haven, 2011
John Russell, *Rodrigo Moynihan: Paintings 1970–1973* (exh. cat.), Fisher Fine Art Limited, London, 1973
Richard Shone, *Michael Craig-Martin: Prints* (exh. cat.), Alan Cristea Gallery, London, 1997
Frances Spalding, *John Minton: Dance Til the Stars Come Down*, Lund Humphries, London, 2005
Frances Spalding, *Vanessa Bell*, Tempus, Reading, 2006
Frances Spalding, *Duncan Grant*, Random House, London, 2011
Frances Spalding, *Prunella Clough: Regions Unmapped*, Lund Humphries, London, 2012
Jo Spence, *Cultural Snipping: The Art of Transgression*, Routledge, London, 1995
Rosalind Thuillier, *Graham Sutherland: Inspirations*, Lutterworth Press, Cambridge, 1982
Ben Tufnell (ed), *Prunella Clough* (exh. cat.), Tate Publishing, London, 2007
Keith Vaughan, *Journal and Drawings 1939–1965*, Alan Ross Ltd, London, 1966
Keith Vaughan, *Journals 1939–1977*, ed. Alan Ross, John Murray Ltd, London, 1989
Andrew Gibbon Williams, *William Roberts: An English Cubist*, Lund Humphries, Aldershot and Burlington, VT, 2004

## Magazines, Newspapers, Journals

John Berger, 'Machine-life painting', *New Statesman and Nation*, 18 April 1953
Michael Bracewell, 'Something Supernatural This Way Comes: Magic and Modernity in British Art', *Tate Etc*, no.17, Autumn 2009
J.D. Fergusson, 'Chapter for an Autobiography', *Saltire Review*, vol.6, no.21, 1960
G.R.H., 'The Father of Post-Impressionism', *Pall Mall Gazette*, 4 October 1912, p.10
Patrick Heron, 'Miss Clough and Miss McCannell', *New Statesman and Nation*, 5 November 1949
C.J. Holmes, *Notes on the Post-Impressionist Painters, Grafton Galleries, 1910–11*, Philip Lee Warner, London, 1910
Conroy Maddox, 'The Object in Surrealism', *London Bulletin*, nos.18–20, The Surrealist Group in England, 1940
*Manet and the Post-Impressionists* (exh. cat.), Grafton Galleries and Ballantyne Press, London, 1910
Richard Shone, 'The Friday Club', *The Burlington Magazine*, vol.117, no.866, May 1975Walter Sickert, 'Little Pictures for Little Patrons', *New Age*, 11 August 1910
Alison Smithson and Peter Smithson, 'But Today We Collect Ads', *Ark*, no.18, Royal College of Art, 1956
Unknown author, 'Art: The Post Impressionists', *Truth*, 23 November 1910, p.1304
Unknown author, 'Exhibition of Modern Paintings and Drawings at the Omega Workshops', *The Burlington Magazine*, vol.33, no.189, December 1918, p.233'The Life and Opinions of an English "Modern": Ben Nicholson in Conversation with Vera and John Russell', *Sunday Times*, 28 April 1963, p.28

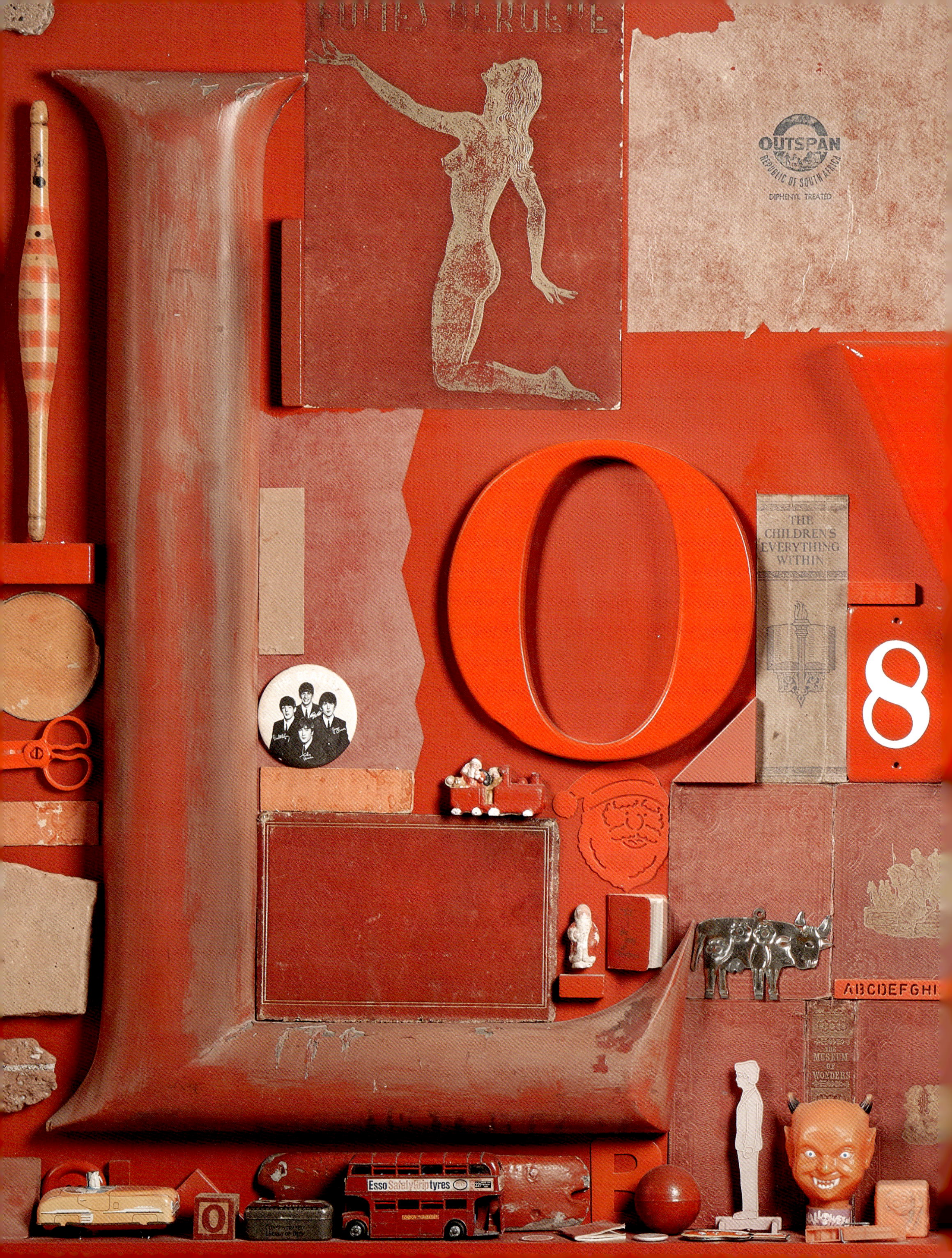
OUTSPAN
REPUBLIC OF SOUTH AFRICA
DIPHENYL TREATED
THE CHILDREN'S EVERYTHING WITHIN
8
ABCDEFGHI
THE MUSEUM OF WONDERS
Esso Safety Grip tyres

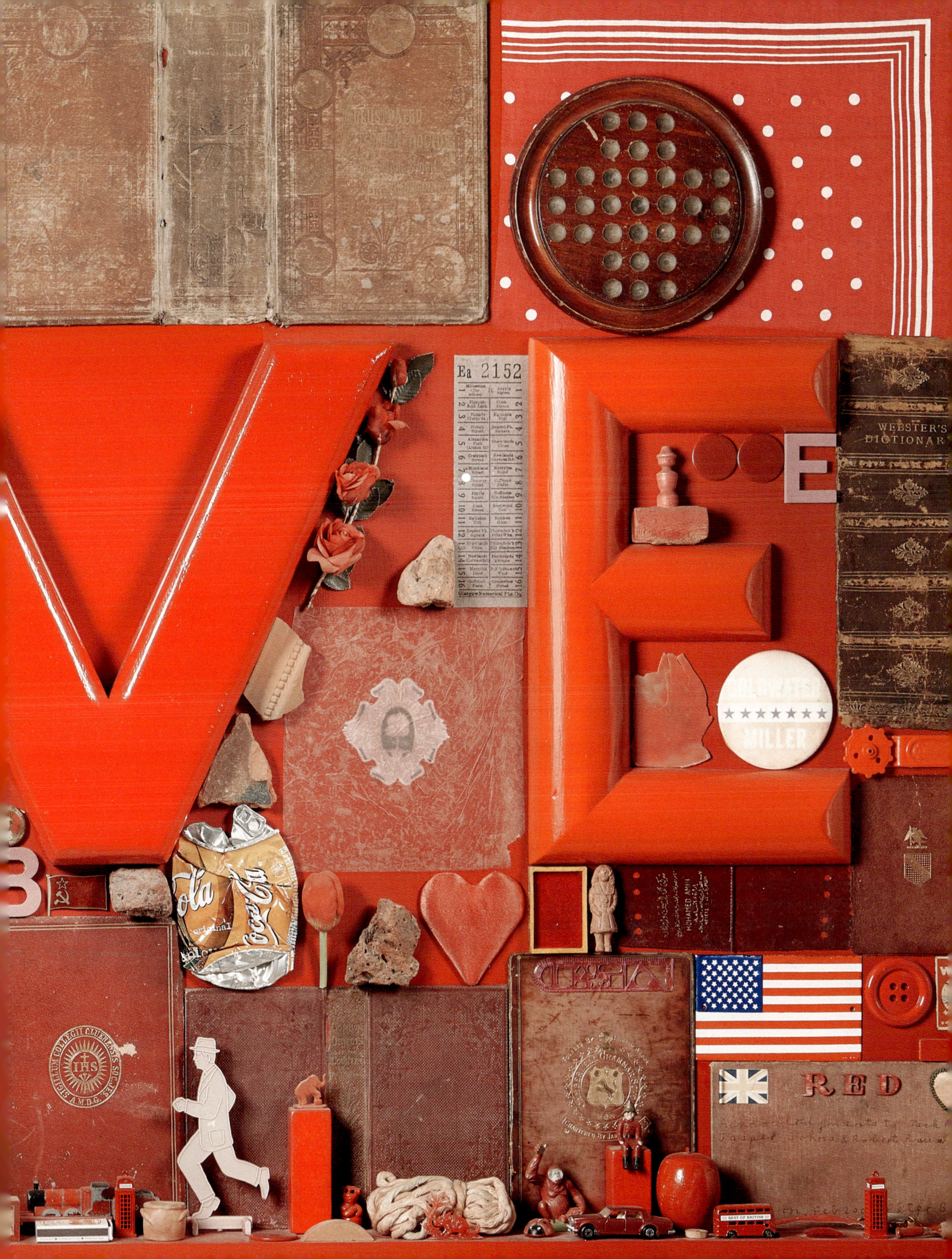
Ea 2152
E
WEBSTER'S
DICTIONAR
GOLDWATER
MILLER
RED

# List of Works

Eileen Agar (1899–1991)
*The Object Lesson*, 1940
Collage & bodycolour on board, 55.8 × 46 cm
Southampton City Art Gallery

Hurvin Anderson (b.1965)
*Still Life with Artificial Flowers*, 2018
Screenprint on paper, 75.2 × 56 cm
Courtesy of the artist and Thomas Dane Gallery

Michael Ayrton (1921–1975)
*Black Still Life, Ram Skull III*, 1959
Oil on board, 101.5 × 76 cm
Private collection

Wilhelmina Barns-Graham (1912–2004)
*Red Table*, 1952
Oil on canvas, 12.3 × 20 cm
Wilhelmina Barns-Graham Trust

Edward Bawden (1903–1989)
*The Boy – Eric Ravilious in his studio at Redcliffe Road*, 1929
Watercolour on paper, 42.8 × 66.5 cm
Towner Eastbourne

Vanessa Bell (1879–1961)
*Design for Omega Bed-end: Vase of Flowers*, 1917
Oil on paper laid on board, 36.8 × 91.4 cm
Private collection, London

Elizabeth Blackadder (1931–2021)
*Cat and Flowers* , 1981
Watercolour on paper, 76.2 × 95.8 cm
Fleming Wyfold Art Foundation

Peter Blake (b.1932)
*Cigarette Pack*, 1959–60
Oil on canvas, 18.5 × 16 cm
Wolverhampton Art Gallery

Peter Blake (b.1932)
*Love*, 2007
Enamel, wood and found objects on panel, 97.8 × 156.8 × 10.1 cm
Pallant House Gallery, Chichester (Accepted under the Cultural Gifts Scheme by HM Government from Lorna Dunphy and allocated to Pallant House Gallery, 2018)

John Bratby (1928–1992)
*Still Life with Chip Frier*, 1954
Oil on canvas, 131.4 × 92.1 cm
Tate: Presented by the Contemporary Art Society 1956

Glenn Brown (b.1966)
*Saint Bimbo*, 2024
India ink and oil paint on panel, 112 × 80 cm
Collection of the artist

Edward Burra (1905–1976)
*Still Life with Teeth*, 1946
Pencil, watercolour and gouache on paper, 56 × 76.5 cm
Private European collection

Claude Cahun (1894–1954)
*Objects in a bell jar (untitled)*, 1936
Photographic print, 23.7 × 17.8 cm
Courtesy Jersey Heritage

Patrick Caulfield (1936–2005)
*Coloured Still Life*, 1967
Acrylic on panel, 56 × 89 cm
Pallant House Gallery, Chichester (Accepted in lieu of Inheritance Tax by HM Government from the estate of MJ Long / Wilson and allocated to Pallant House Gallery, 2021)

Patrick Caulfield (1936–2005)
*Kellerbar*, 1997
Acrylic on canvas, 76.8 × 61.6 cm
Pallant House Gallery (Accepted in lieu of Inheritance Tax by HM Government from the estate of MJ Long / Wilson and allocated to Pallant House Gallery, 2021)

Patrick Caulfield (1936–2005)
*Reserved Table*, 2000
Acrylic on canvas, 183 × 190 cm
Pallant House Gallery, Chichester (Wilson Gift through Art Fund, 2006)

Patrick Caulfield (1936–2005)
*Still Life Ingredients*, 1976
Screenprint on paper, 71.1 × 71.1 cm
Pallant House Gallery, Chichester
Wilson Loan (2006)

Gordon Cheung (b.1975)
*Still Life with Goblet (after Pieter de Ring, 1640–1660)*, 2017
Archival inkjet on 380gsm Hahnemühle Photo Rag paper , 103 × 88 cm
Courtesy the artist and Cristea Roberts Gallery, London

Prunella Clough (1919–1999)
*Bone Drawing*, 1949
Oil on board, 25.5 × 33 cm
Private collection of Amanda Posey & Nick Hornby

Prunella Clough (1919–1999)
*Dead Plants in a Greenhouse*, 1947
Oil on canvas, 48 × 60 cm
Private collection

Peter Coker (1926 – 2004)
*Sunflowers*, 1961
Oil on board, 121.9 × 81.3 cm
Pallant House Gallery, Chichester (Bequest of Mrs Vera Coker in memory of Peter Coker, 2014)

Edwaert Collier (c.1640–c.1707)
*Vanitas Still Life*, 1694
Oil on canvas, 75.3 × 62.9 cm
National Maritime Museum, Greenwich, London; purchased with the assistance of the Society for Nautical Research Macpherson Fund

Mat Collishaw (b.1966)
*Last Meal on Death Row, Texas (Louis Jones Junior)*, 2012
Digital Transfer print on goatskin parchment, 66 × 55 cm
Mat Collishaw

Jean Cooke (1927–2008)
*Through the Looking Glass*, 1960
Oil on canvas, 60.8 × 50.8 cm
Lent by Royal Academy of Arts, London

Maisie Cousins (b.1992)
*Sweet Chilli Sauce*, 2018
Archival pigment print on Hahnemuhle Pearl paper, 118.9 × 79 cm
Courtesy the artist and TJ Boulting

Maisie Cousins (b.1992)
*Wasp*, 2017
Archival pigment print on Hahnemuhle Pearl paper, 29.7 × 42 cm
Courtesy the artist and TJ Boulting

Michael Craig-Martin (b.1941)
*Close Relations*, 1996
Screenprint on paper, 96.5 × 76.3 cm
Pallant House Gallery, Chichester
(Presented by Cristea Roberts Gallery, 2021)

Michael Craig-Martin (b.1941)
*Distant Relations,* 1996
Screenprint on paper, 96.5 × 76.3 cm
Pallant House Gallery, Chichester
(Presented by Cristea Roberts Gallery 2021)

John Craxton (1922–2009)
*Hare on a Table*, 1944–46
Oil on canvas, 51 × 63.4 cm
Pallant House Gallery, Chichester
(on loan from the John Craxton Estate)

Phoebe Cummings (b.1981)
*I Hear Myself with My Throat*, 2024
Unfired clay, site-specific installation, dimensions variable, commissioned by Pallant House Gallery, Chichester, 2024

Bouke de Vries (b.1960)
*Vanitas (Still Life with Globular Teapot)*, 2009/c.1765
Fragmented Bow teapot, butterflies in glass dome, 12.4 cm height × 12 cm diameter
Commissioned by Pallant House Gallery, Chichester (2009) Geoffrey Freeman Collection of Bow Porcelain (2002)

Edmund de Waal (b.1964)
*September Song, II*, 2020
Porcelain, gilded porcelain, alabaster, aluminium and plexiglass, in 5 parts, 70 × 42 × 10 cm
Courtesy the artist and Gagosian

Jessica Dismorr (1885–1939)
*Composition*, c.1935
Oil on card, 46 × 59 cm
Ömer Koç Collection

Valentine Dobrée (1894–1974)
*Composition with Skull and Shells*, n.d.
Oil on board, 55.5 × 44 cm
Reproduced with the permission of Special Collections, Leeds University Library, [University Art Collection], [LEEUA 1993.018]

Mary Fedden (1915–2012)
*Still Life with Artichoke*, 1972
Oil on canvas, 66.4 × 76.5 cm
Pallant House Gallery, Chichester
(Percy Brown Bequest, 1996)

John Duncan Fergusson (1874–1961)
*The Blue Lamp*, 1920s
Oil on board, 45.5 × 40.3 cm
Rugby Art Gallery & Museum, Rugby Borough Council

Anna Fox (b.1961)
*My Mother's Cupboards and My Father's Words* 1999
C-type colour prints, 23 × 31.5 cm
The Hyman Collection, courtesy Centre for British Photography

Meredith Frampton (1894–1984)
*Trial and Error*, 1939
Oil on canvas, 112.7 × 71.4 cm
Tate: Bequeathed by Miss J.B. Dickins 2010, accessioned 2019

Lucian Freud (1922–2011)
*Unripe Tangerine*, 1946–47
Oil on board, 9.3 × 9 cm
Pallant House Gallery, Chichester, UK
(Wilson Loan, 2006)

Roger Fry (1866–1934)
*Still Life with T'ang horse*, c.1919–20
Oil on canvas, 35.6 × 45.7 cm
Tate: Presented by Mrs Pamela Diamand, the artist's daughter 1973

Ori Gersht (b.1967)
*Evertime 05*, 2018
Archival ink on paper, 30 × 68 cm
Courtesy Ori Gersht and Michael Hoppen Gallery

Mark Gertler (1891–1939)
*The Dutch Doll*, 1926
Oil on canvas, 73.6 × 76.2 cm
Brighton & Hove Museums

Winifred Gill (1891–1981)
*Still Life with Glass Jar and Silver Box*, 1914
Oil on cardboard, 48 × 32.8 cm
The Courtauld, London (Samuel Courtauld Trust)

Harold Gilman (1876–1919)
*The Cup and Saucer*, 1915
Oil on canvas, 29 × 27 cm
Private collection, courtesy of Offer Waterman, London

Gluck (1895–1978)
*Lords and Ladies*, 1936
Oil on canvas, 75 × 75 cm
Private collection, London

Spencer Gore (1878–1914)
*Still Life with Apples*, 1912
Oil on canvas, 38.2 × 50.8 cm
Ferens Art Gallery: Hull Museums

Laura Sylvia Gosse (1881–1968)
*Still life with a lobster,* c.1923
Oil on canvas, 26.7 × 35.6 cm
University of Hull Art Collection

Lawrence Gowing (1918–1991)
*Still Life: Vanitas*, 1979
Oil on canvas, 51 × 76 cm
Royal Academy of Arts, London

Duncan Grant (1885–1978)
*The Mantelpiece*, 1914
Oil paint and paper on board, 45.7 × 39.4 cm
Tate: Purchased 1971

Duncan Grant (1885–1978)
*Still Life with Black Coffee Pot*, 1949
Oil on canvas, 58 × 38 cm
Pallant House Gallery, Chichester (Acquired with support from Art Fund, Arts Council England / V&A Purchase Grant Fund, Cate and Nash Olson, and legacies from Margaret Treacher Brown and Lady Heath, 2024)

Maggi Hambling (b.1945)
*Cuddling Skulls*, 1995
Oil on canvas, 40 × 50 cm
Collection of the artist

Anthea Hamilton (b.1978)
*Wild Food*, 2012
Digital print on shantung dupion silk, silk viscose, leather, brushed steel, string, wood, 225 × 225 × 55 cm
Private collection, London

Richard Hamilton (1922–2011)
*The Critic Laughs*, 1968
Laminated screenprint and lithograph with collage and hand additions, 34.2 × 26.4 cm
Pallant House Gallery, Chichester
(Wilson Gift through Art Fund, 2006)

Nina Hamnett (1890–1956)
*Still life (Blue Stove),* c.1915
Oil on canvas, 35 × 25 cm
Private collection

Mona Hatoum (b.1952)
*Natura morta (medical cabinet),* 2012
Murano mirrored glass, steel and glass cabinet, 61.5 × 54 × 17.5 cm
Courtesy Mona Hatoum Foundation

Jann Haworth (b.1942)
*Donuts, Coffee Cups and Comic,* 1962
Fabric, thread and kapok, 65 × 69 × 54 cm
Wolverhampton Art Gallery

Barbara Hepworth (1903–1975)
*Conoid, Sphere and Hollow III*, 1937
Marble 32 × 35.5 × 30.5 cm
UK Government Art Collection

Patrick Heron (1920–1999)
*Round White Table: St Ives: 1953–1954*, 1953–54
Oil on canvas, 91.4 × 45.7 cm
Katharine Heron and Susanna Heron

Patrick Heron (1920–1999)
*Still Life*, c.1948–9
Oil on canvas, 50 × 30 cm
The Courtauld, London (Samuel Courtauld Trust)

Tristram Hillier (1905–1983)
*The Green Bottle*, 1950
Oil on canvas, 61 × 61 cm
Southampton City Art Gallery

Lubaina Himid (b.1954)
*Jug and Two Spoons*, 1989
Acrylic on canvas, 182.8 × 182.8 cm
Courtesy the artist and Hollybush

Damien Hirst (b.1965)
*Bognor Blue*, 2008
Butterflies and household gloss paint on canvas, 91.4 × 91.4 cm
Pallant House Gallery, Chichester (Accepted under the Cultural Gifts Scheme by HM Government from Frank Dunphy and allocated to Pallant House Gallery, 2018)

Ivon Hitchens (1893–1979)
*Flowers*, 1943
Oil on canvas, 61 × 56.3 cm
Pallant House Gallery, Chichester (Mrs Diana King Bequest presented through Art Fund, 2003)

David Hockney (b.1937)
*Postcard of Richard Wagner and a Glass of Water*, 1973
Etching on paper, 21 × 15 cm
The University of Chichester – Special Collections

David Hockney (b.1937)
*Tea Painting in an Illusionistic Style*, 1961
Oil on canvas, 232.5 × 83 × 3.8 cm
Tate: Purchased with assistance from the Art Fund 1996

Howard Hodgkin (1932–2017)
*Still Life,* 1987–90
Oil on wood, 37 cm diameter
Private collection

Frances Hodgkins (1869–1947)
*Still Life: Eggs, Tomatoes and Mushrooms*, c.1929
Oil on canvas, 64 × 53 cm
Brighton & Hove Museums

George Leslie Hunter (1877–1931)
*Still Life with Cut Melon, Glass and Fan*, c.1919/20
Oil on canvas, 48.2 × 44.5 cm
Pallant House Gallery, Chichester (on loan from the Cross Family Collection, 2014)

David Jones (1895–1974)
*July Change*, 1930
Watercolour on paper, 59.5 × 46.7 cm
Pallant House Gallery, Chichester (Kearley Bequest through Art Fund, 1989)

Poppy Jones, b.1985
*Water Glass & Thistle*, 2024
Oil and watercolour on suede, soldered aluminium frame, 30 × 43 cm
Courtesy the artist and Herald St, London

Robert MacBryde (1913–1966)
*Still Life (with Ludo Board and Lemon)*, c.1950
Lithograph in colours, 55 × 39 cm
Pallant House Gallery, Chichester (The Golder-Thompson Gift, 2021)

Margaret Mellis (1914–2009)
*Toy cupboard (thirty),* 1983
Driftwood construction, 54.6 × 59 cm
Estate of Margaret Mellis.
Courtesy The Redfern Gallery

Margaret Mellis (1914–2009)
*Yellow Basket with Bottle*, 1952
Oil on canvas, 51 × 63.5 cm
Estate of Margaret Mellis.
Courtesy The Redfern Gallery

Lindsey Mendick (b.1987)
*The nightmare never ends*, 2024
Glazed ceramic, 69 × 46 cm
Courtesy the artist and Carl Freedman Gallery, Margate

Lindsey Mendick (b.1987)
*Still life with hermit crabs and tooth extraction*, 2024
Glazed ceramic, 68 × 54 cm
Collection credit required

Lee Miller (1907–1977)
*Untitled [Severed Breast, from radical surgery in a place setting 1 & 2], Paris, France*, c.1929
Photograph, 16.3 × 12.0 cm & 16.3 × 11.8 cm
Lee Miller Archives, East Sussex, England

Lisa Milroy (b.1959)
*Plates No. 1*, 2018–23
Oil on canvas, 119.5 × 116.5 cm
Courtesy the artist and Kate MacGarry, London

John Minton (1917–1957)
Cover design for *French Country Cooking* by Elizabeth David, published by John Lehmann, 1951
Private collection

John Minton (1917–1957)
Frontispiece for *A Book of Mediterranean Food* by Elizabeth David, published by John Lehmann, 1950
Private collection

Henry Moore (1898–1989)
*Elephant Skull, Plate XIX (Cramer 132)*, 1969–70
Etching on paper, 23.5 × 31 cm
Pallant House Gallery, Chichester (Hussey Bequest, Chichester District Council, 1985)

Cedric Morris (1889–1982)
*Irises and tulips*, 1935
Oil on canvas, 61 × 50.8 cm
Private collection

Mary Moser (1744–1819)
*Summer flowers on a ledge*, 1768
Bodycolour on paper, 27.9 × 66 cm
The Courtauld, London (Samuel Courtauld Trust)

Rodrigo Moynihan (1910–1990)
*White Plastic Container behind Plywood Board,* 1973
Oil on canvas, 177.8 × 119.4 cm
Private collection

Paul Nash (1889–1946)
*Coronilla,* 1925
Wood engraving on paper, 11.6 × 9 cm
Pallant House Gallery, Chichester (The Clare Neilson Collection Presented by Jeremy Greenwood and Alan Swerdlow through Art Fund 2013)

Paul Nash (1889–1946)
*Dead Spring*, 1929
Oil on canvas, 48.5 × 40 cm
Pallant House Gallery, Chichester
(Kearley Bequest through Art Fund, 1989)

Paul Nash (1889–1946)
*Poisonous Plants, from 'For Urne Buriall and the Garden of Cyrus'*, 1932
Collotype and stencilled watercolour on paper, 31 × 23 cm
Pallant House Gallery, Chichester
(Lucas Bequest, 1995)

Paul Nash (1889–1946)
*Still Life No.1*, 1925
Wood engraving on paper, 11.5 × 11.5 cm
Pallant House Gallery, Chichester
(The Clare Neilson Collection Presented by Jeremy Greenwood and Alan Swerdlow through Art Fund, 2013)

Paul Nash (1889–1946)
*Still Life No.2*, 1927
Wood engraving on paper, 25.5 × 18.2 cm
Pallant House Gallery, Chichester
(The Clare Neilson Collection Presented by Jeremy Greenwood and Alan Swerdlow through Art Fund, 2013)

Paul Nash (1889–1946)
*Untitled*, 1934–35
Photograph, silver gelatin print on paper, 17.2 × 13.9 cm
Pallant House Gallery, Chichester
(The Clare Neilson Collection Presented by Jeremy Greenwood and Alan Swerdlow through Art Fund 2013)

Ben Nicholson (1894–1982)
*1928 (striped jug and flowers)*, 1928
Oil on canvas, 38 × 37 cm
Private collection

Ben Nicholson (1894–1982)
*1934 (Still Life)*, 1934
Oil on canvas, 39.4 × 54.6 cm
Pallant House Gallery, Chichester
(on loan from a private collection, 2015)

Ben Nicholson (1894–1982)
*1943–45 (St Ives, Cornwall)*, 1943–45
Oil and graphite on canvas, 40.6 × 50.2 cm
Tate: Purchased 1945

Ben Nicholson (1894–1982)
*1946 (still life, cerulean)*, 1946
Oil on canvas over board, 63 × 61.5 cm
Pallant House Gallery, Chichester
(Kearley Bequest, through Art Fund, 1989)

Winifred Nicholson (1893–1981)
*Vermillion and Mauve*, c.1928
Oil on board, 66 × 54.5 cm
Private collection

William Nicholson (1872–1949)
*The Silver Casket and Red Leather Box*, 1920
Oil on panel, 33 × 40.5 cm
Private collection, courtesy Hazlitt Holland-Hibbert

Lucy + Jorge Orta (b.1966 & b.1953)
*Aepyornis (Elephant bird egg, Madagascar)*, 2010
Royal Limoges porcelain fossil cast, enamel and platinum drawings, unique piece, Certificate Perpetual Amazonia, 32 × 22 × 15 cm
Courtesy Lucy + Jorge Orta

Lucy + Jorge Orta (b.1966 & b.1953)
*Gallimimus (fossil limb bone, Mongolia)*, 2010
Royal Limoges porcelain fossil cast, enamel and platinum drawings, unique piece, Certificate Perpetual Amazonia, 65 × 11 × 13 cm
Courtesy Lucy + Jorge Orta

Lucy + Jorge Orta (b.1966 & b.1953)
*Palaeomastodon (humerus bone, Egypt)*, 2010
Royal Limoges porcelain fossil cast, enamel and platinum drawings, unique piece, Certificate Perpetual Amazonia, 50 × 20 × 20 cm
Courtesy Lucy + Jorge Orta

Eduardo Paolozzi (1924–2005)
*Meet the People* from *Bunk!*, 1947–72
Lithograph on paper, 34.7 × 25.9 cm
Pallant House Gallery, Chichester
(Wilson Gift through Art Fund, 2006)

Eduardo Paolozzi (1924–2005)
*Real Gold* from *Bunk!*, 1947–72
Lithograph on paper, 31.8 × 24.2 cm
Pallant House Gallery, Chichester
(Wilson Gift through Art Fund, 2006)

Eduardo Paolozzi (1924–2005)
*Refreshing and Delicious* from *Bunk!*, 1947–72
Lithograph on paper, 37.8 × 28 cm
Pallant House Gallery, Chichester
(Wilson Gift through Art Fund, 2006)

Cornelia Parker (b.1956)
*Falling Façade*, 1991
Stretched silver trophies, easel and mirror, 171 × 112.5 × 94 cm
Courtesy the artist and Frith Street Gallery, London

Katie Paterson (b.1981)
*Endling*, 2022
Mixed media in 100 pigments ground from the pre-solar dust of 5 billion years ago to the ginkgo trees of Hibakujumoku, 92 × 92 cm
Courtesy the artist

Samuel John Peploe (1871–1935)
*Still Life of Roses and a Bowl of Apples on a Green Tablecloth*, 1920s
Oil on canvas, 50.8 × 40.6 cm
Pallant House Gallery, Chichester
(on loan from a private collection, 2012)

Grayson Perry (b.1960)
*Let the little children suffer*, c.1986
Ceramic plate, 29.2 cm diameter
Private collection, courtesy England & Co

Glyn Philpot (1884–1937)
*Stachys and Leaves*, 1934–35
Oil on canvas, 89 × 117 cm
Private collection

Dod Procter (1892–1972 )
*Black and White*, c.1932
Oil on canvas, 61 × 50.8 cm
Southampton City Art Gallery

Marc Quinn (b.1964)
*Orchid, The Overwhelming World of Desire (Paphiopedilum Winston Churchill Hybrid)*, 2002
Photographic image on steel, 57 cm
Pallant House Gallery, Chichester (with support from Art Fund and John Ayton MBE and John Booth 2019)

Eric Ravilious (1903–1942)
*Kettle, Teapot, Breadboard, Matches*, 1939
watercolour and pencil design for Dunbar Hay, 39.3 × 51.9 cm
Private collection

Eric Ravilious (1903–1942)
*Ironbridge Interior*, 1941
Watercolour and pencil on paper, 46 × 57.7 cm
Private collection on loan to Towner Eastbourne

William Roberts (1895–1980)
*La nature morte*, c.1948
Watercolour on paper, 49.5 × 31.8 cm
Museum and Art Swindon

Mohammed Sami (b.1984)
*Sunday*, 2019
Acrylic on linen, 90 × 100 cm
Courtesy the artist and private collection

William Scott (1913–1989)
*Cup*, 1974
Gouache and collage on paper, 20.4 × 32.6 cm
Pallant House Gallery, Chichester
(The George and Ann Dannatt Gift, 2011)

William Scott (1913–1989)
*Still life variations 2*, 1969
Oil on canvas, 121.9 × 182.9 cm
Private collection

Colin Self (b.1941)
*The Fishy Tale of the Battered Still Life*, 1987
Multimedia collage, 77.2 × 54 cm
Private collection

Anwar Jalal Shemza (1928–1985)
*Still Life*, 1957
Oil on fibreboard, 64 × 46.4 cm
Estate of Anwar Jalal Shemza

Walter Sickert (1860–1942)
*Mushrooms*, c.1919–20
Oil on canvas, 33 × 40.6 cm
Private collection

Walter Sickert (1860–1942)
*Still Life on a Table*, c.1913
Oil on canvas, 41 × 33.5 cm
Pallant House Gallery, Chichester
(Kearley Bequest, through Art Fund, 1989)

Mike Silva (b.1970)
*Window Light*, 2023
Oil on canvas, 66 × 91.4 cm
Courtesy of the artist and The Approach

Jane Simpson (b.1964)
*Our Distant Relatives,* 2004
Silicone rubber, glass, wood and polyester lacquer, 54.7 × 85.5 × 26 cm
UK Government Art Collection

George Smith (c.1714–1776)
*Still-Life with Joint of Beef on a Pewter Dish*, c.1750–60
Oil on canvas, 61 × 73.7 cm
Chichester City Council

Matthew Smith (1879–1959)
*Flowers and Mixed Fruit*, c.1927
Oil on canvas, 53 × 32 cm
Pallant House Gallery, Chichester (Hussey Bequest, Chichester District Council, 1985)

William Smith (1707–1764)
*Still Life with Grapes, Peaches and Plums*, 1763
Oil on canvas, 30.2 × 36 cm
Pallant House Gallery, Chichester
(Bequest of Mrs Pat Roth, 2016)

Jo Spence (1934–1992)
*The Final Project*, 1991–92
Digital print from medium format negative, 89 × 134 cm
The Estate of Jo Spence, courtesy
Richard Saltoun Gallery, London and Rome

Stanley Spencer (1891–1959)
*Amaryllis*, 1951
Oil on canvas, 76.4 × 50.8 cm
Private collection, courtesy
Daniel Katz Gallery, London

Wolfgang Tillmans (b.1968)
*Hampstead still life*, 2020
Inkjet print, 206 × 138 cm
Maureen Paley, London

Gavin Turk (b.1967)
*Dump*, 2004
Painted bronze, 43 × 47 × 61 cm
Pallant House Gallery, Chichester (Accepted under the Cultural Gifts Scheme by HM Government from Frank Dunphy and allocated to Pallant House Gallery, 2018)

Ursula Tyrwhitt (1872–1966)
*Flowers,* 1912
Watercolour on paper, 40.6 × 38.4 cm
Tate: presented by Mrs Mary McEvoy 1935

Euan Uglow (1932–2000)
*Duck*, 1965
Oil on panel, 75 × 48.8 cm
Private collection

Keith Vaughan (1912–1977)
*Still Life with Skull*, 1952–3
Oil on canvas, 35.5 × 43.5 cm
Collection of Antony Wright, London

Simon Verelst (1644–1721)
*Roses, columbine, and poppies in a glass vase on a marble ledge with some grapes*, n.d
Oil on canvas, 45.7 × 35.6 cm
Private collection

Charlotte Verity (b.1954)
*Spent Stems*, 2014
Oil on canvas, 30.5 × 40.5 cm
Courtesy of the artist Charlotte Verity

Edward Wadsworth (1889–1949)
*Bright Intervals*, 1928
Tempera on canvas laid on panel, 63 × 88 cm
Museum and Art Swindon

Caroline Walker (b.1982)
*My Bottles and Pumps*, 2024
Oil on board, 41 × 33 cm
Courtesy the artist; Stephen Friedman Gallery, London and New York; GRIMM Gallery and Ingleby Gallery, Edinburgh

Ethel Walker (1861–1951)
*Flower Piece No. 4*, c.1930
Oil on canvas, 76.7 × 64 cm
The Courtauld, London (Samuel Courtauld Trust)

Alison Watt (b.1965)
*Wemyss*, 2020
Oil on canvas, 75.5 × 62 cm
Private collection

Rachel Whiteread (b.1963)
*Untitled (For Frank),* 1999
Plaster, polystyrene and steel in three parts, 26 × 90 × 26 cm
Pallant House Gallery, Chichester (Accepted under the Cultural Gifts Scheme by HM Government from Frank Dunphy and allocated to Pallant House Gallery, 2018)

Rachel Whiteread (b.1963)
*Untitled (Pink Torso)*, 1991
Pink dental plaster and wax
9.5 × 17 × 23.5 cm
Private collection

Clare Woods (b.1972)
*Motionless*, 2022
Oil on aluminium, 50 × 50 cm
Courtesy the artist and Cristea Roberts Gallery, London

Yevonde (1893–1975)
*Crisis (A.R.P.)*, 1939
Photographic print, 38.1 × 30.5 cm
National Portrait Gallery, London

Toby Ziegler (b.1972)
*Purple Prose*, 2023
Oil paint and gesso on aluminium, 100 × 80 cm
Courtesy the artist

# Image Credits

Numbers refer to page numbers

© Alison Watt/photo John McKenzie: 150
© Angela Verren-Taunt. All rights reserved, DACS 2024: 64, 86, 87
© Anna Fox, Courtesy Centre for British Photography, London: 117
© Anthea Hamilton. Courtesy the artist, kaufmann repetto, Milan/New York and Thomas Dane Gallery: 26
© Bonhams, London, UK: 112
© Brighton & Hove Museums: 47, 67, 98
© By Permission of The Werthwhile Foundation: 102
© Caroline Walker. Courtesy Stephen Friedman Gallery, London and New York GRIMM Gallery and Ingleby Gallery, Edinburgh/ photo Peter Mallet: 142
© Charlotte Verity: 148
© Chichester City Council: 20
© Clare Woods, courtesy artist and Cristea Roberts Gallery, London: 15
© Colin Self. All Rights reserved, DACS 2024: 138
© Cornelia Parker, Courtesy of the artist and Frith Street Gallery, London/photo Ben Westoby: 35
© The Courtauld/Bridgeman Images: 23, 38, 46, 57, 90
© Courtesy of the Jersey Heritage Collections: 77
© Courtesy Lucy + Jorge Orta / ADAGP Paris, 2024: 123
© Crown Copyright: UK Government Art Collection: 89, 152
© Culture Perth and Kinross/photo Art UK: 43
© David Hockney: 135
© Edmund de Waal. Courtesy of Gagosian/ photo © Prudence Cuming Associates Ltd: 155
© Estate of Anwar Jalal Shemza: 99
© Estate of Duncan Grant. All rights reserved, DACS 2024: 9, 44
© Estate of Eileen Agar. All rights reserved 2024/Bridgeman Images: 79
© Estate of Elizabeth Blackadder. All Rights Reserved 2019/Bridgeman Images. The Fleming Wyfold Art Foundation: 147
© The Estate of Euan Uglow, courtesy of Hazlitt Holland-Hibbert: 148
© Estate of Gluck courtesy of The Fine Art Society: 70
© Estate of Ivon Hitchens: 85
© The Estate of Jo Spence: 118
© The Estate of John Bratby/Bridgeman Images: 128
© Estate of John Craxton: 105
© Estate of Keith Vaughan. All rights reserved, DACS 2024/ photo Justin Piperger: 111
© Estate of Margaret Mellis. Courtesy of the Redfern Gallery: 93
© The Estate of Patrick Caulfield. All rights reserved, DACS 2021: 136, 137
© Estate of Peter Coker: 115
© Estate of Prunella Clough. All rights reserved, DACS 2024/photo Justin Piperger: 106
© Estate of Richard Hamilton: 139
© The Estate of Robert MacBryde: 94 and 95
© Estate of Rodrigo Moynihan, courtesy David Nolan Gallery: 154
© Estate of Ursula Tyrwhitt/photo Tate: 40
© Estate of Vanessa Bell. All rights reserved, DACS 2024: 45
© Estate of William Scott 2024/photo Justin Piperger: 96, 97
© Ferens Art Gallery /Bridgeman Images: 55
© Gavin Turk/Live Stock Market/photo Stephen White: 140
© Glenn Brown/photo Edgar Laguinia: 32
© Gordon Cheung: 30
© Reproduced by permission of The Henry Moore Foundation: 112
© Hurvin Anderson. Courtesy of Thomas Dane Gallery/photo Ricard Ivey: 151
© Jann Haworth: 132
© Katie Paterson, courtesy Ingleby Gallery/ photo John Mackenzie: 125
© Lisa Milroy. Courtesy of Kate MacGarry, London/photo Thierry Bal: 133
© Lubaina Himid, courtesy the artist and Hollybush Gardens, London: 11
© The Lucian Freud archive/Bridgeman Images: 104 and 105
© Maggi Hambling: 119
© Maisie Cousins. Courtesy of TJ Boulting: 141
© Mat Collishaw: 27
© Mike Silva/Documentation by Michal Brzezinski. Courtesy of The Approach, London: 144
© Mohammed Sami, Courtesy Private collection/photo Robert Glowacki: 146
© Mona Hatoum. Courtesy ARTER, Istanbul/ photo Hadiye Cangökçe: 122
© Museum and Art Swindon: 81, 107
© National Maritime Museum, Greenwich, London: 19
© National Portrait Gallery, London: 100
© The Nina Hamnett Estate, courtesy of Bridgeman Images: 49
© Ömer Koç Collection/photo Hadiye Cangökçe: 82, 88
© Ori Gersht: 29
© Courtesy of Pallant House Gallery: 6, 10, 13, 21, 25, 29, 34, 42, 43, 52, 57, 62, 63, 72, 73, 74, 85, 86, 94, 95, 97, 102, 104, 105, 112, 115, 121, 126, 130, 131, 134, 136, 137, 139, 140
© Patrick Heron Trust. All rights reserved, DACS 2024: 90 and 91
© Peter Blake. All rights reserved, DACS 2024: 134, 174–175
© Philip Mould & Company: 58
© Poppy Jones. Courtesy the artist and Herald St, London: 157
© Private collection/photo: 69, 108, 112
Private collection/photo © Christie's, London, 2014: 10
Private collection/photo © Christie's, London, 2020: 17
Private collection/photo © Christie's, London, 2017: 114
Private collection/photo © Courtesy of Hazlitt Holland-Hibbert: 50
Private collection/photo © Grayson Perry, Courtesy England & Co.: 12
© Public domain: 24, 26
© Rachel Whiteread: 121
© Royal Academy of Arts, London/photo John Hammond: 110, 116
© Royal College of Art: 113
© Sally Marriott: 61
© Southampton City Art Gallery/Bridgeman Images: 68, 71
© Special Collections, Leeds University Library, [University Art Collection], [LEEUA 1993.018]: 109
© Tate: 48, 80, 135
© Toby Ziegler/photo Justin Piperger: 31
© Towner Eastbourne: 66, 67
© Trustees of the David Jones Estate: 62
© Trustees of the Paolozzi Foundation: 127, 130, 131
© Trustees of Winifred Nicholson: 65
© University of Hull Art Collection: 53
© Wilhelmina Barns-Graham Trust: 92
© Wolfgang Tillmans. Courtesy of Maureen Paley: 144

# Acknowledgements


### Supporters Circle

Judy Addison Smith
George and Jane Blunden
Edward and Victoria Bonham Carter
Vanessa Branson
Mark Burch
Centre for British Photography
Keith and Helen Clark
Christine and Jolyon Drury
Christine and Derek Dunton
Marion Gibbs CBE
Jamie and Julia Korner
Emma Lochhead
Jac and Roger Mavity
Philip Mould & Company
Gareth Neame OBE
David and Deborah Stileman
Paul and Sandy Thornton
Clare and Hugh Twiss
Tania Slowe and Paddy Walker
John and Susie Wells
Emma and Mark Wippell
Angela and John Wormald

---

We are very grateful to the many individuals and organisations that have provided assistance and support in the realisation of the exhibition and this accompanying book. In addition to those mentioned below there are numerous private collectors who shall remain anonymous

The following individuals have facilitated loans from public collections (plus many others behind the scenes):
Lucy Faithful and Hedley Swain at Brighton and Hove Museums; James Hyman and Saray García Álvarez at the Centre for British Photography; Andrew Watson at Chichester City Council; Ketty Gottardo, Hannah Kauffman, Chloe Le Tissier, Ernst Vegelin von Claerbergen and Barnaby Wright at the Courtauld Gallery; Kerri Offord at Ferens Art Gallery, Hull; Theodore Albano and James Knox at the Fleming-Wyfold Art Foundation Philip Neale at Fry Art Gallery; Eliza Gluckman and Livy Christophers at the Government Art Collection; Ami Bouhassane and Tracy Leeming at Lee Miller Archives; Martha Graves, Hannah Higham, Rebecca Lyons and Joanna Weston at the Royal Academy of Arts; Allison Goudie and Molly Tillet at Royal Museums Greenwich; Katie Boyce at Rugby Art Gallery and Museum; Jemma Craig, Ben Hall and Rebecca Moisan at Southampton City Art Gallery; Katie Ackrill at Museum and Art Swindon; Maria Balshaw, Hilary Floe, Alyson Rolington, Daryl Tappin and Hannah Williams at Tate; Joe Hill and Karen Taylor at Towner Eastbourne; Janet Carter at University of Chichester Special Collections; John Bernasconi at University of Hull Art Collection; Layla Bloom at University of Leeds Art Collection; Rob Airey and Cassia Pennington at Wilhelmina-Barns-Graham Trust; Carol Thompson and Clare Marlow at Wolverhampton Art Gallery

In addition, the following individuals, studio managers and commercial art galleries have assisted in relation to artists and artworks in the exhibition:
Claudia Black at Beaumont Nathan; Robert Diament at Carl Freedman Gallery; Charlie Campbell-Gray and Olivia Ghosh at Christie's; Helen Waters, Tilly Dunne and Algie Mitchell at Cristea Roberts; Daniel Moynihan and Valentina Branchini at David Nolan Gallery; Tom Davies at Daniel Katz Gallery; Ali MacGlip and Courtney King at Frith Street Gallery; Cristina Colomar, Chloe Convey, Adele Minardi, Zoë Santa-Olalla, and Jess Topping at Gagosian; James Holland Hibbert and Olivia Patteson-Knight at Hazlitt Holland-Hibbert; Vaso Papadopoulou at Hekátē Studios; Harriet Balfour, Helen Barr and Richard Morrissey at Herald Street; Kat Lowe and James Skevington at Kate MacGarry; Siobhàn Maguire, Katie Paterson Studio; Catherine Lampert; Beth Hughes, Lubaina Himid Studio; Jonathon Cresswell, Oliver Evans, Mike Iveson and Maureen Paley at Maureen Paley; Eleanor Crabtree, Stuart Shave and James Southall-Ford at Modern Art; Hugh Monk; Luís Manuel Araújo, Mona Hatoum Foundation; Robin Cawdron-Stewart and Stella Vasileiadou at Offer Waterman; Matthew Bradbury at Osborne Samuel; Louisa Hunt and Ben Tufnell at Parafin; Lawrence Hendra and Laura Edmundson at Philip Mould & Co; Laura Selby and Richard Selby at Redfern Gallery; Costanza Simonini and Leah Saltoun at Richard Saltoun Gallery; Frankie Rossi; Tom Rowland at Tom Rowland Gallery; Jon Horrocks and Vivienne Joncourt at Stephen Freedman Gallery; Cécile Barrault, Studio Orta; Jake Miller and Harriet Eyres at The Approach; Amy Luo, Natalie Oleksy-Piekarski and Hannah Wright at Thomas Dane; Hannah Watson at TJ Boulting; Joe Goody at Charlotte Verity's studio; Robin Vousden; Hannah Gruy at White Cube

There are forty living artists represented in the exhibition. Among them, we are grateful to the following for making new work for the exhibition:
Glenn Brown; Phoebe Cummings; Poppy Jones Lindsey Mendick; Caroline Walker

Artists that are lending directly to the exhibition:
Mat Collishaw; Ori Gersht; Maggi Hambling; Mona Hatoum; Lucy + Jorge Orta; Katie Paterson; Charlotte Verity; Toby Ziegler

Artists' estates/individuals who gave permission and provided images for works to be in the book:
Estate of Rodrigo Moynihan; The Nina Hamnett Estate; Estate of Ursula Tyrwhitt; Estate of Winifred Nicholson; Estate of Anwar Jalal Shemza; Bodleian, Oxford; Julie Green at David Hockney, Inc; Jennifer Carding at Tate; Siobhan Maguire at Katie Paterson Studio Ltd; Ana García Rocha at Mona Hatoum Studio; Josie Shenoy at DACS; Joy Ingle at Leeds University Library; Sian Phillips at Bridgeman; Bryn Sayles at Sotheby's; Jamie Mackinnon at the Fine Art Society; Ingram Reid at Bonhams; Jennifer Camilleri at the Royal Academy; Estate of Patrick Heron

The following private collectors, and all other lenders who wish to remain anonymous:
John Craxton Estate; The Cross Family Collection; Ömer Koç Collection; Amanda Posey and Nick Hornby; The Wilson Estate; Antony Wright

We are also grateful to Sarah Deere, Sharon Hambly, Sally Marriott who have worked on the conservation and framing of works from the Pallant House Gallery collection, and to Clare and Hugh Twiss and the Spencer Wills Trust who have funded this work.

Finally we are grateful to all the staff, volunteers and trustees of Pallant House Gallery who have contributed in so many ways.

# Index

Page numbers in *italics* refer to illustrations.